VARIORUM COLLECTED STUDIES SERIES

Studies in
Gregorian Chant

Ruth Steiner

Studies in
Gregorian Chant

Ashgate
VARIORUM

Aldershot · Brookfield USA · Singapore · Sydney

This edition copyright © 1999 by Ruth Steiner

Published in the Variorum Collected Studies Series by

Ashgate Publishing Limited
Gower House, Croft Road,
Aldershot, Hampshire GU11 3HR
Great Britain

Ashgate Publishing Company
Old Post Road,
Brookfield, Vermont 05036–9704
USA

ISBN 0–86078–791–5

British Library CIP Data
Steiner, Ruth
 Studies in Gregorian Chant. – (Variorum Collected Studies Series: CS651)
 1. Chants (Plain, Gregorian, etc.). I. Title
 782.3'22'2

US Library of Congress CIP Data
Steiner Ruth
 Studies in Gregorian Chant / Ruth Steiner.
  p.   cm. – (Variorum Collected Studies Series: CS651). Includes Indexes.
 1. Chants (Plain, Gregorian, etc.) – History and Criticism. I. Title
 II. Series: Variorum Collected Studies Series: CS651
 ML3082.S76   1999
 782.32'22–dc21   99–11124
                                                          CIP

The paper used in this publication meets the minimum requirements of the American National
 Standard for Information Sciences – Permanence of Paper for Printed Library Materials, /
 Z39.48–1984. ∞   ™

Printed by Galliard (Printers) Ltd, Great Yarmouth, Norfolk, Great Britain

VARIORUM COLLECTED STUDIES SERIES CS651

CONTENTS

This volume consists of xi + 312 pages.

PUBLISHER'S NOTE

The articles in this volume, as in all others in the Collected Studies Series, have not been given a new, continuous pagination. In order to avoid confusion, and to facilitate their use where these same studies have been referred to elsewhere, the original pagination has been maintained wherever possible.

Each article has been given a Roman numeral in order of appearance, as listed in the Contents. This number is repeated on each page and quoted in the index entries.

PREFACE

The research described in these articles began in response to the studies on Gregorian chant that were being published in the United States in the late 1950s and early 1960s, works such as Willi Apel's *Gregorian Chant* (Bloomington, 1958) and articles in the *Journal of the American Musicological Society*. Gregorian chant had been 'discovered' by American musicologists, but the notion of going to primary sources for the readings of chants rather than using the standard editions was still new. Primary sources were not easily accessible—only a few were available in facsimile editions—and a scholar who intended to base his studies of chant on such sources had no choice other than to develop a collection of microfilms.

The need for such a collection became even more evident when articles for *The New Grove Dictionary of Music and Musicians* were in preparation. The articles on chant topics published in *Die Musik in Geschichte und Gegenwart* by Bruno Stäblein and his students drew on the resources of a superb collection of microfilms developed by Stäblein himself; and they set a new standard, one that made any work—even an article for a dictionary—that relied for its evidence on a modern practical edition devoid of critical commentary seem a reversion to an earlier age.

As it happened, The Catholic University of America had a long-standing relationship with the noted chant specialist and benefactress Justine Ward. The Dom Mocquereau Foundation, set up after her death to promote the causes in which she most deeply believed, worked closely with the University in advancing those causes, and in 1973 the Foundation agreed to provide limited funding for the new endeavor. The nucleus for the archive was a small private collection of microfilms that had been assembled in the course of specialized studies of offertories, prosulae, and those other chant categories that are discussed in the earlier studies in this collection. Now it could be expanded; long-term foundation support made it possible for the collection to be developed in a systematic way. The research described in this volume would have been impossible without it.

In recent decades there has been a surge in interest in interdisciplinary work, particularly in the field of medieval studies. This has been encouraged by the establishment and phenomenal success of the series of international congresses on medieval studies sponsored by Western Michigan University at Kalamazoo, Michigan, and a host of smaller conferences. Other cultural institutions have supported this trend. 'Matins Responsories and Cycles of

Illustrations of Saints Lives' was begun in an interdisciplinary seminar on Greek and Latin hagiography offered at Dumbarton Oaks and written for the Kalamazoo conference; it first appeared in a Festschrift for a scholar whose main field was Irish language and literature but who had published on hagiography early in his career. 'Matins at Cluny for the feast of St Benedict' was written for a session in a conference on monasticism and the arts that took place at the National Gallery of Art.

Scholars of eastern and western chant have also sought to develop links between their disciplines. As one example, Miloš Velimirović proposed a session on this general theme for the 1980 meeting of the American Musicological Society. 'Antiphons for the Benedicite at Lauds', presented at that meeting, and 'The Canticle of the Three Children as a Chant of the Roman Mass', presented at the meeting of the International Musicological Society in Strasbourg in 1982 were the twin products of an effort to examine the role in worship of a text that is prominent in the rites of both East and West.

The establishment of a chant study group within the International Musicological Society has had enduring consequences. The announced theme for its first meeting in Hungary in 1984 was 'Medieval Monody and Regional Tradition'; the study of 'Local and Regional Traditions of the Invitatory Chant' presented on that occasion was a contribution to a series of intensive studies of a number of distinctive chant traditions, particularly those of the Divine Office. Careful investigation of entire repertories seemed an important next step, and at that point the computer became a necessary resource.

One of the computer databases set up to record systematically the Office chants in individual sources is CANTUS, founded at The Catholic University of America, and funded in part by the National Endowment for the Humanities. It is now located at the University of Western Ontario, with a website at http://publish.uwo.ca/~cantus. Members of the CANTUS staff contributed to the research described in 'Antiphons for Lauds on the Octave of Christmas' by looking through dozens of microfilmed sources and making note of the chants they provided for that Lauds service.

Festschriften provided the occasion for several of the studies in this collection. One where the connection between the subject of the research and the individual being honored is intentionally close is 'The Parable of the Talents in Liturgy and Chant', which was written for Alvin H. Johnson, who long served the American Musicological Society as Treasurer and Executive Director.

Chant research is an immense field. We study the written tradition of chant by comparing the readings of various manuscripts, we match neumes to readings in staff notation, and we study the manuscripts themselves—their grouping, their histories, their notation—in the most minute detail. We contemplate the theoretical system of the ecclesiastical modes, we meditate over the efforts of medieval music theorists to come to terms with the musical system—or systems—that govern chant melodies. But in all this activity we are studying only the most easily visible evidence—the surface detail, if you will—of a great shadowy presence that is, and must perhaps remain, for the most part unknown: the vast and powerful oral tradition in which chant originated and in which it was for centuries handed down.

Perhaps the chant research of the next thirty years will take us away from the manuscripts a little, and in doing so bring us closer to an understanding of what it meant to a medieval cantor to have a role to play in that tradition.

Thanks are due to the publishers who granted permission for articles to be reproduced in this volume and to the libraries that allowed photographs of manuscripts in their collections to be reproduced here. All photographs of sources in the Bibliothèque nationale, Paris should carry the attribution 'Cliché Bibliothèque nationale de France - Paris'. Other attributions are as follows: for the photo of Rouen A 401, 'Coll. Bibliothèque municipale de Rouen, Photo. Didier Tragin'; for the photos of St Gall 390, 'Stiftsbibliothek St Gallen, Cod. Sang. 390'; for that of Rome, Vallic. C 5, 'Su concessione del Ministero per i Beni culturali e Ambientali. Biblioteca Vallicelliana - Roma Ms.c.5,c.99v. Divieto di riproduzione'; for those of sources in the Biblioteca Casanatense, 'Su concessione del Ministero per i Beni Culturali e Ambientali'; for that of the manuscript in the Biblioteca nazionale in Rome, 'Reproduced by courtesy of the Director of the Biblioteca Nazionale Centrale di Roma'; for sources in the British Library, 'By permission of The British Library'; for the Montpellier manuscript, 'Bibliothèque Interuniversitaire de Montpellier - Médecine'; and for the photographs by Wim Swaan in article I, 'Getty Research Institute, Research Library, Wim Swaan Photograph Collection'.

Thanks also to The Catholic University of America and the Dom Mocquereau Foundation for their support of many years' research; to David Hiley and Dom Jean Claire, who have been most generous in sharing their views on chant with me; to Daniel J. Sheerin and F. A. C. Mantello, who have guided me through the interpretation of countless Latin texts; to Bruce Steiner, who generously supported my work and made it possible for me to visit Solesmes, Erlangen, and a number of European libraries, some of them more than once; and to the many students whose interest, enthusiasm, and love for manuscripts have often helped to rekindle my own. Charles T. Downey, a former member of the CANTUS staff, prepared the index for this book.

RUTH STEINER

The Catholic University of America
Washington, D. C.
August 1998

I

The Music for a Cluny Office of Saint Benedict

The role of Scripture and liturgy in molding the monastic imagination, introduced in Chapter 1 by William Loerke and Chapter 3 by Jean Leclercq, is developed by Professor Ruth Steiner. She discusses the dramatic content of the texts and music used for the Feast of Saint Benedict at the most magnificent and influential monastery of eleventh-century Europe, Cluny. Her chapter documents the richness of the Divine Office as celebrated by monks in the Middle Ages, that unending cycle of chanted "hours" to which the monks of Cluny and of the hundreds of monasteries affiliated with Cluny gave the greatest portion of their time. She evokes the grave beauty of a monastic night service where, in the darkened choir, the monks alternated periods of Psalm-singing (the nocturns) with meditative listening to lessons from Scripture and monastic history—including, here, St. Gregory's account of the emergence of Benedict of Nursia in the troubled age of the Lombard invasions.

Ruth Steiner is Professor of Music at the Catholic University of America and has served as a member of the editorial board of the *Journal of the American Musicological Society.*

For monastic communities of the Middle Ages, music and worship were inseparable: singing was a medium of prayer. Observance of the Divine Office entailed hour after hour of chanting. What was this music like? How was it written down? In what forms has it been preserved? An examination of a Cluny office for St. Benedict will provide answers for these questions, and also cast light on a related subject—how monks thought about music, the kinds of ques-

T.G. Verdon, *Monasticism and the Arts*, 'The Music for a Cluny Office for St. Benedict', (Syracuse: Syracuse University Press, 1984), pp. 81–114. By permission of the publisher.

tions they raised, the ways in which they gave expression to their understanding of it.

"*Fuit vir vitae venerabilis gratia benedictus et nomine* ... " ("He was a man of venerable life, blessed in grace as in name"). Thus begins the biography of St. Benedict written by Gregory the Great less than fifty years after Benedict's death.[1] In medieval antiphonals from Benedictine houses, this line stands out like a headline, for it begins the first of the Matins responsories on the feasts of St. Benedict. There is a large initial letter, and often the first few words are written in capitals.

Matins, or "vigils," as St. Benedict called it, is the first part of the Divine Office, the series of daily worship services which he called *opus Dei* ("the work of God") and over which he said nothing should take precedence in the life of monks: "*Nihil operi Dei praeponatur.*"[2] On major feasts, the Matins service in a monastery consisted of an introductory portion and three large sections, called *nocturns* (see Table 4.1.).[3] The first two nocturns began with six psalms and antiphons, the last with canticles and a single antiphon. All three nocturns continued with four lessons, each of which was followed by a responsory: thus there were twelve lessons and twelve responsories in all. The lessons of the first and second nocturns, and sometimes of all three, were usually drawn from the same source: a continuous long text which the responsories separate into sections.[4] The point at which one lesson was separated from what follows is the point at which those taking part in the service were given an opportunity to reflect on its meaning, consider its implications, and make associations between it and parallel ideas in other texts. Often the text of the responsory that follows a particular lesson seems to have been selected or composed in such a way as to encourage this kind of reflective meditation during its musical performance.[5]

The Matins services for feasts of St. Benedict in medieval manuscripts are quite varied, both in the chants that are given and in their arrangement.[6] If the relationsip between lessons and responsories in a particular Matins service is to be studied, one must have a source in which the lessons are given in full—thus a breviary, rather than an antiphonal. In the pages that follow here, two services will be compared. One is that for the Transitus of St. Benedict (March 21) in a eleventh-century breviary of St. Martial de Limoges (Paris, Bibliothèque Nationale, lat. 743).[7] The other is the service for the Translation of the Relics of St. Benedict (July 11) in a late eleventh-century Cluny breviary now in the same library (lat. 12601).[8] This manuscript was taken from Cluny to another monastery in the twelfth century. There it received some additions and corrections, but these are minor, especially in the section to be considered here.

TABLE 4.1

Matins for the Feast of the
Translation of the Relics of St. Benedict (July 11) in the MS Paris, B. n., lat. 12601
(Cluny, *ca.* 1075), fols. 55ᵛ–58ᵛ

Antiphon and Ps. 94
Hymn: Christe sanctorum decus

(First nocturn)
Ant. Fuit vir, with Ps. 1
Ant. Ab ipso puericie, with Ps. 2
Ant. Dum in hac terra, with Ps. 4
Ant. Liberiori genere, with Ps. 5
Ant. Relicta domo, with Ps. 8
Ant. Recessit igitur, with Ps. 10
        Lesson 1, and Responsory: Fuit vir
        Lesson 2, and Responsory: Santus Benedictus
        Lesson 3, and Responsory: Inito consilio
        Lesson 4, and Responsory: Domine, non aspicias

(Second nocturn)
Ant. Compassus nutrici, with Ps. 14
Ant. Expetitus a fratribus, with Ps. 20
Ant. Cumque sibi conspicerent, with Ps. 23
Ant. Inito consilio, with Ps. 63
Ant. Tunc ad locum, with Ps. 64
Ant. Tantam gratiam, with Ps. 91
        Lesson 5, and Responsory: Cumque sanctus Benedictus
        Lesson 6, and Responsory: Intempesta noctis hora
        Lesson 7, and Responsory: Pater sanctus, dum intentam
        Lesson 8, and Responsory: Sanctissime confessor Christi

(Third nocturn)
Ant. Hic itaque, with canticles
        Lesson 9, and Responsory: Dum beatus vir
        Lesson 10, and Responsory: Beatus vir qui
        Lesson 11, and Responsory: Erat vultu placido
        Lesson 12, and Responsory: O beati viri Benedicti

I

TABLE 4.2

Responsories in the first two nocturns of Matins for the Transitus of St. Benedict (March 21), in a breviary from St. Martial of Limoges, Paris, B. n., lat. 743, fols. 104ʳ–106ʳ

R. 1: Fuit vir, from prologue
R. 2: Sanctus Benedictus, from I
  (How a Broken Cleaning-Vessel Was Repaired)
R. 3: Inito consilio, from III
  (How a Glass Vessel Was Broken by the Sign of the Cross)
R. 4: Domine, non aspicias, from XXXII
  (How Benedict revived a Corpse)
R. 5: Cumque sanctus Benedictus, from XXXIV
  (How Benedict Saw the Departure of His Sister's Soul from Her Body)
R. 6: Pater sanctus, dum intentam, and
R. 7: Intempesta noctis hora, from XXXV
  (About the Way That the World Was Gathered Up Before Benedict's Eyes
  and About the Soul of Germanus, Bishop of Capua)
R. 8: Sanctissime confessor Christi (a prayer not derived from the vita)

The service in the St. Martial manuscript has as lessons in the first two nocturns excerpts from St. Gregory's Life of St. Benedict. The series begins with the prologue and continues without omissions nearly to the end of the first chapter, reached in the seventh lesson. For the eighth lesson, the thirty-seventh chapter of the Life is read, complete except for its final sentence. The responsories that alternate with these lessons have texts drawn from the same source, but the selection is different, as may be seen in Table 4.2, where the roman numeral after the opening words of each text indicates the chapter of the Life from which they are drawn. Thus the texts that are heard in the first two nocturns of this service are all—except for the last—from the very beginning of the Life; most of the responsories come from sections of it that are not read in Matins (see Table 4.2).

The effect of combining these responsories, which evoke later episodes in the Life with the reading of the first two of its sections, is not unlike that of the flashback in films. Juxtaposing events in an order other than that of chronology implies that the order in which they occurred is secondary in importance to the events themselves. In the matins service, St. Benedict's life becomes something to be experienced all at once. This effect is enhanced when one's attention is drawn by the arrangement of things to notice the same motif in different parts of the Life. For instance, the third responsory in this office tells how the sign of the cross caused a vessel that held poisoned wine to shatter. It is preceded by a lesson that describes Benedict's nurse weeping over a vessel that she had borrowed and permitted through innocent negligence to fall and break.

When the responsories are compared with the sections of the Life on which they are based, it is evident that there is more selection and reworking of the text in some than in others. This is done, it appears, to make the sung texts concise and to give them good rhythm and clear phrasing. The indications are that any text that was sung was memorized; if so, the parts of the Life to which these chants correspond would be the ones that were known best.

To turn to the Cluny beviary, the feast of St. Benedict that it contains is that of July 11, the Translation of the Relics. The responsories in the first two nocturns are the same as in the St. Martial Office, though the order of the sixth and seventh is reversed. But the lessons are drawn from a different source: the account of the Translation that was written by a monk of Fleury-sur-Loire, perhaps one Adrevald, in the ninth century.[9] The main events it describes are thought to have taken place in the seventh century. In the first nocturn, the lessons begin by describing the Lombard invasion of Italy and its terrible aftermath. Then they summarize the history of Fleury-sur-Loire from its founding. In the second nocturn, the fifth lesson describes the formation of an expedition consisting of a group of monks from Fleury, led by one Aigulphus (Ayoul), and a group of clerics from Le Mans. They intend to rescue the relics of St. Benedict and St. Scholastica, which they believe—as a result of having read Gregory the Great's Life of St. Benedict—must be somewhere in the ruins of Monte Cassino, which had been laid waste by the Lombards. They reach Rome, and go together to pray in St. Peter's. Those from Le Mans decide to linger in Rome for a while to visit the other holy places; but Aigulphus decides to press on to Monte Cassino. Then there is a pause for a responsory. In the sixth lesson, Aigulphus, alone at Monte Cassino and looking for some sign of what he is seeking, is approached by an old man who urges him to reveal the reason for his journey. Aigulphus hesitates, but after reflecting, he explains, in the seventh lesson, why he has come. The old man counsels him not to sleep that night, but to keep watch; and, he says, "When you see a place of this solitude shining with a brilliant light, like a snowy mountain, zealously note the place; for there is to be found what will put an end to your concern." The climax of the story is thus a vision of a bright light shining to mark the place where the remains of Benedict and Scholastica rest. The pause at the end of the old man's words is marked by the responsory *Pater sanctus*, the last in the series of three that sing of other

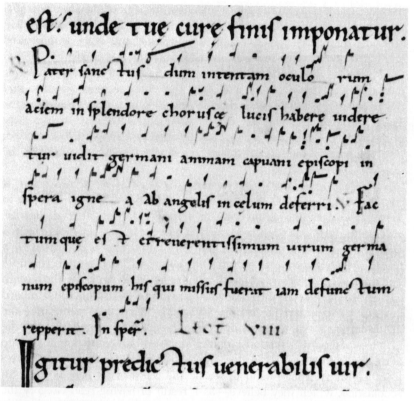

Figure 4.1. Detail from the responsory "Pater sanctus." Lat. 12601, fol. 58ʳ. *Bibliothèque nationale, Paris.*

visions experienced by another monk—St. Benedict himself. The eighth lesson concludes this part of the narrative: Aigulphus sees the miraculous light, finds the relics, and prepares to bring them back to France.[10] Perhaps the rest of the account, describing his return, was read later in the day.[11] The lessons for the Sunday within the octave, and on the octave of the feast, are from the beginning and end of a sermon about St. Benedict by Odo of Cluny, who was the second abbot there, from 927 to 942.[12] In fact, the whole sermon is given; perhaps the rest of it was divided up and read on intervening days.

The responsory *Pater sanctus* thus has a crucial position in the service. If it had been preserved only in this source, there would be no way to transcribe it into staff notation (see Figure 4.1). The musical notation

I

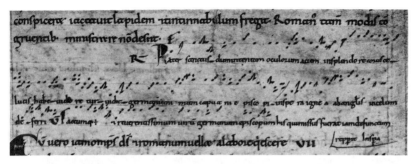

Figure 4.2. Detail from the responsory "Pater sanctus." Lat. 743, fol. 105ᵛ. *Bibliothèque nationale, Paris.*

employed at Cluny consists of neumes—signs that show for each syllable how many different notes there are and whether the melody rises or falls. But the transcriber needs to know how large each interval is, and the relation of the pitch at which one syllable is sung to that of the next. For that one might turn to the St. Martial manuscript (see Figure 4.2). The careful arrangement of the notes there, above and below a dry-point line, makes it possible to know when an interval in the melody is a second, or a third, and so on. But to show more precisely whether each of these is major or minor, a clef is needed. (One is implied by the formula given for the verse of this responsory, but not written.[13]) A twelfth-century antiphonal of St. Maur-des-Fossés (near Paris), lat. 12044, gives the chant in staff notation with clefs (see Figure 4.3). When its reading is matched syllable by syllable with what the Cluny source shows, variants are evident, but not too many of them.[14] A transcription is given in Figure 4.4.

In this melody are heard several turns of phrase that are common among responsories that end, as it does, on the note E, that employ the same musical formulas in their verses, and that have approximately the same range.[15] (Medieval music theorists speak of such responsories as belonging to mode 4; for a fuller discussion of modes see below.) In Figure 4.5, phrases from *Pater sanctus* are compared with some from responsories for St. Stephen; the chants may be said to be as alike and as different as monks who wear the same habit. The melodies are cut from the same cloth, of one design, and then tailored to fit each text. The material that is most likely to be borrowed consists of the groups of notes that set the last few syllables of a phrase. One effect of this is to make the phrasing in these chants clear and graceful, and thus it helps in the effective conveying of the text. But music can do more than this. It can help us to recognize that

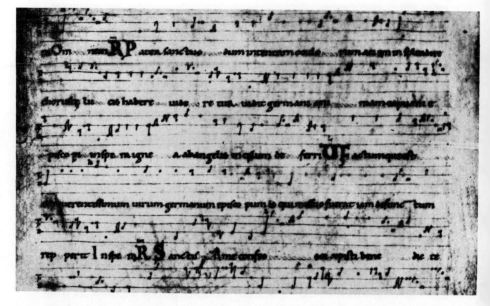

Figure 4.3. Detail from the responsory "Pater sanctus." Lat. 12044, fol. 159ʳ. *Bibliothèque nationale, Paris.*

what is taking place is not an ordinary event, but a celebration. With or without words, music can stir the emotions and give expression to feelings and thoughts in ways that go beyond what words alone can do. This is evident in *Intempesta noctis hora* (see Figures 4.6 and 4.7). At the beginning there is the same kind of relation between text and music as there was in *Pater sanctus*—on each syllable a single note, two or three notes, or (in some cases) a longer series of notes. But on the word *omnem* there is a melisma—a chain of notes. The text here relates that "St. Benedict saw the whole world *(omnem mundum)* gathered up as if in a single ray of the sun."

Gregory the Great follows his account of this miracle with an explanation. His text is set up as a dialogue, and Peter, who has been asking Gregory about St. Benedict, asks, "How can the whole world become visible to a single man?" Gregory replies:

> To a soul that beholds the Creator, all creation is narrow in compass. For when a man views the Creator's light, no matter how little of it, all creation becomes small in his eyes. ... To say that the world was gathered

Figure 4.4. Responsory "Pater sanctus." Lat. 12044, fol. 159ʳ. *Bibliothèque nationale, Paris.*

together before his eyes does not mean that heaven and earth shrank, but that the mind of the beholder was expanded so that he could easily see everything below God since he himself was caught up in God.[16]

What Gregory has described is religious ecstasy, something that for Peter had to be explained in words. Perhaps in the chant the melisma is meant to evoke the same sense of ecstasy, of the excitement of the event itself.[17]

I

Pa - ter   sanc. - tus   dum in. tan.tam o-cu-lo - rum a - ci - em

Vi - de-bant om-nes Ste-pha-num   qui e-rant in   con- -ci-li- -o

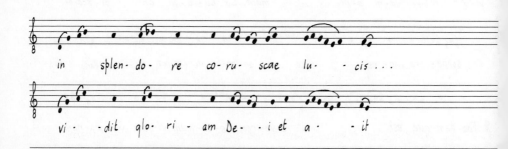

in   splen-do-   re   co-ru-scae   lu - cis ...

vi - dit glo- ri - am De- - i et a- - it

vi-dit Ger-ma-ni a-ni- - mam Ca-pu- a-ni e- - pi-sco-pi

et i-de- o tri-um-phat in coe- lis   co- ro - na- -tus

Figure 4.5. Responsory "Pater sanctus" (for St. Benedict). Lat. 12044, fol. 159^r. *Bibliothèque nationale, Paris.*

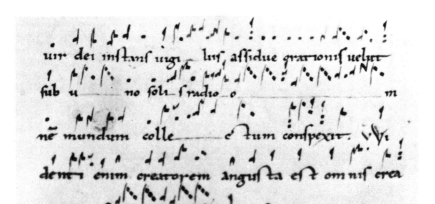

Figure 4.6. Detail, composite, from the responsory "Intempesta noctis hora." Lat. 12601, fols. 57ᵛ–58ʳ. *Bibliothèque nationale, Paris.*

In the third nocturn, both in the Cluny breviary and in that from St. Martial, the lessons are drawn from still another source, the commentary of St. Jerome on the Gospel according to St. Matthew, chapter 19. The first three responsories differ in the two sources, but the last is the same, *O beati viri.* Musically it belongs to the same family of mode IV responsories as *Pater sanctus.* But after the verse the end of the responsory is written out a second time—*"aeterne vite coniunctus est,"*—this time with a long melisma on "coniunctus" (see Figure 4.8). In certain manuscripts the chant appears without this melisma; in the St. Martial breviary, the chant itself is at the top of a page with an ordinary ending, but in the lower margin the melisma is added in a different hand. It appears that the melisma was an afterthought, added later to enrich the music and the service.

Now in certain medieval ecclesiastical centers, the desire to enrich Gregorian chant led to the invention of a dramatically new musical language, that of polyphony. It was this invention that opened the way for those later developments in Western European art music that made it distinctive, utterly unlike the music of other cultures. To be sure, there is no hint of polyphony in the sources under discussion here. But in adding a melisma to this chant, the copyists or compilers are responding to the same impulse as that which prompted the development of polyphony. Hence identifying precisely what music is involved, and how it is handled,

I

Figure 4.7. Responsory "Intempesta noctis hora." Lat. 12044, fols. 158ᵛ–159ʳ. *Bibliothèque nationale, Paris.*

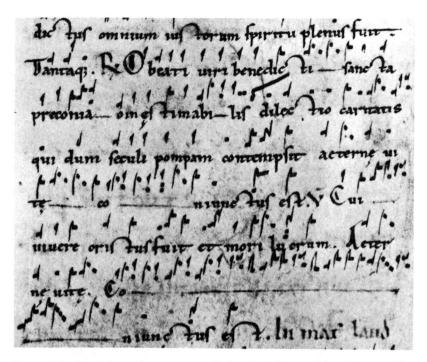

Figure 4.8. Detail from the responsory "O beati viri." Lat. 12601, fol. 58ᵛ. *Bibliothèque nationale, Paris.*

becomes of more than casual interest. At Cluny the melisma is in five sections, of which all but the first and last are repeated: the form might be represented as *a bb cc dd e*. At St. Martial, the melody is about the same, but section *b* is stated only once (see Figure 4.9). At Nonantola (Rome, Bibl. V. E., Sess. 96), the version is similar to that of Cluny, though the notation is quite different; this is a tenth-century source (see Figure 4.10). From San Salvatore del Monte Amiata, near Siena, an early eleventh-century source (Rome, Bibl. Casanatense, 1907), again shows essentially the same reading as Cluny, though here the melisma is incorporated in the respond the first time through (see Figure 4.11). A twelfth-century anti-phonal from the monastery of San Eutizio at Norcia (Rome, Vallic. C 5) gives the melisma with a different *b* section (See Figure 4.12). In all of these sources the repeat of section *d* is not exact; it is varied a little. But in lat. 12044 the second statement of it is exactly like the first. There is also the melisma—which may once have been intended to convey things that

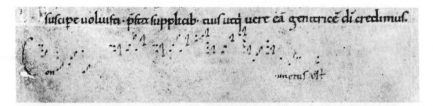

Figure 4.9. Detail from the melisma for the responsory "O beati viri." Lat. 743, fol. 106ᵛ. *Bibliothèque nationale, Paris.*

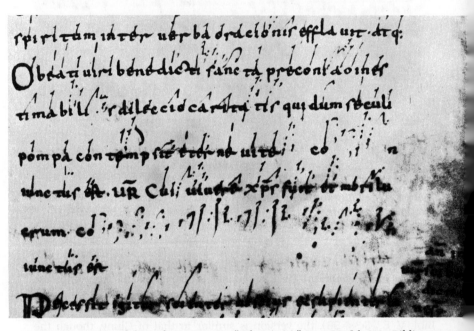

Figure 4.10. Detail from the responsory "O beati viri." Sess. 96, fol. 316ʳ. *Biblioteca nazionale centrale Vittorio Emanuele II, Rome.*

could not be put in words—has been given words, one syllable for each note of the melody (see Figure 4.13). The matter of form in responsory melismas has been exhaustively studied by Thomas Forrest Kelly;[18] for present purposes, it is sufficient to note that the tendency to regularity was stronger in some places than in others, and particularly at St. Maur-des-Fossés. Melismas like this one are added to responsories on major feasts in

I

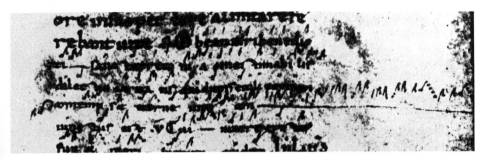

Figure 4.11. Detail from the responsory "O beati viri." *Biblioteca Casanatense, Rome.*

a number of medieval antiphonaries and breviaries, and texts (called *prosulae* or *prosae*) are often supplied for them.[19]

The preceding has been intended as a brief introduction to the music of Cluny and to the context in which it was heard. It seems appropriate next to take up the way in which music was studied there. In the Middle Ages, as now, work in the field of music theory had both a speculative and a practical side. A great deal of attention was given to the *modes* of ecclesiastical chant. It is these modes that are represented on the capitals of two columns in the apse at Cluny, where inscriptions identify the modes symbolized by each of the carved figures.[20] What is the connection between these and the treatment of the modes in the liturgical manuscripts and works on music theory of the time?

It is hard to answer this simply, for we do not know just what the term *mode* meant in the Middle Ages. The definitions provided by the medieval music theorists are in some ways not to the point, and too many exceptions have to be made in their application.[21] According to medieval writers, all chants of one mode end on the same note, have comparable ranges, and use essentially the same scale. These characterizations leave some things unexplained—the very close connections among some chants of the same mode (and sometimes also the different modes), and the use of certain combinations of intervals in one mode and not in another where it seems they would be equally correct. A mode must be, then, something like a family of chants; but precisely what the term meant at different times and places is a central question in current chant research.

In liturgical manuscripts, references to the modes take several forms, but most often they occur in connection with psalmody. In the Matins service for St. Benedict (refer again to Table 4.1) there are twelve

I

96

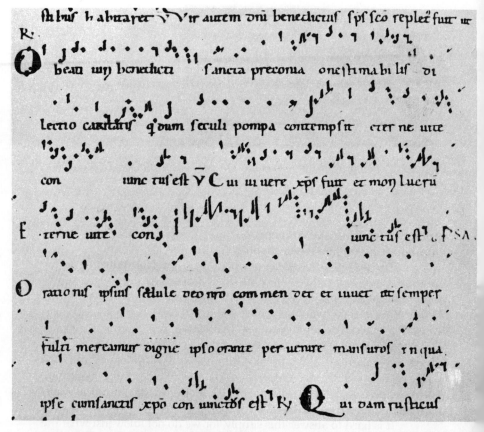

Figure 4.12. Detail from the responsory "O beati viri" with its melisma and prosa. C5, fol. 99ᵛ. *Biblioteca Vallicelliana, Rome.*

psalms. Each is preceded and followed by an antiphon. The psalms themselves are chanted to formulas (called "psalm tones") which give each verse of the psalm the same beginning, the same musical pattern at a division between phrases in the middle, and the same ending. In a psalm, the number of syllables varies from one verse to the next, so the formulas must be flexible; they have certain notes ("reciting tones") that can be repeated as often as necessary to accommodate the text.

How many of these formulas were there? The Cluny manuscript itself does not show, for after each of the antiphons it gives only the *incipit* (opening words) of the psalm to follow, but no musical notation. The

Figure 4.13. Detail from the responsory "O beati viri" with its melisma and prosa. Lat. 12044, fol. 159ᵛ. *Bibliothèque nationale, Paris.*

same is true in other manuscripts—for example, lat. 12584, the earlier of the St. Maur-des-Fossés antiphonals. But most Office manuscripts do contain references to specific psalm tones of one kind or another. One such reference appears in an eleventh-century manuscript that comes from Nonantola (a monastery near Modena) and contains a copy of the old Cluny customary.[22] Among its other contents is a list of incipits of the texts to be sung in the Divine Office, arranged in the order of the liturgical year. Beside the incipits of the antiphons in each service there are the numbers of the tones to be used for the psalm with each antiphon (see Figure 4.14).

It is thus evident that there is a system of psalm tones—as it

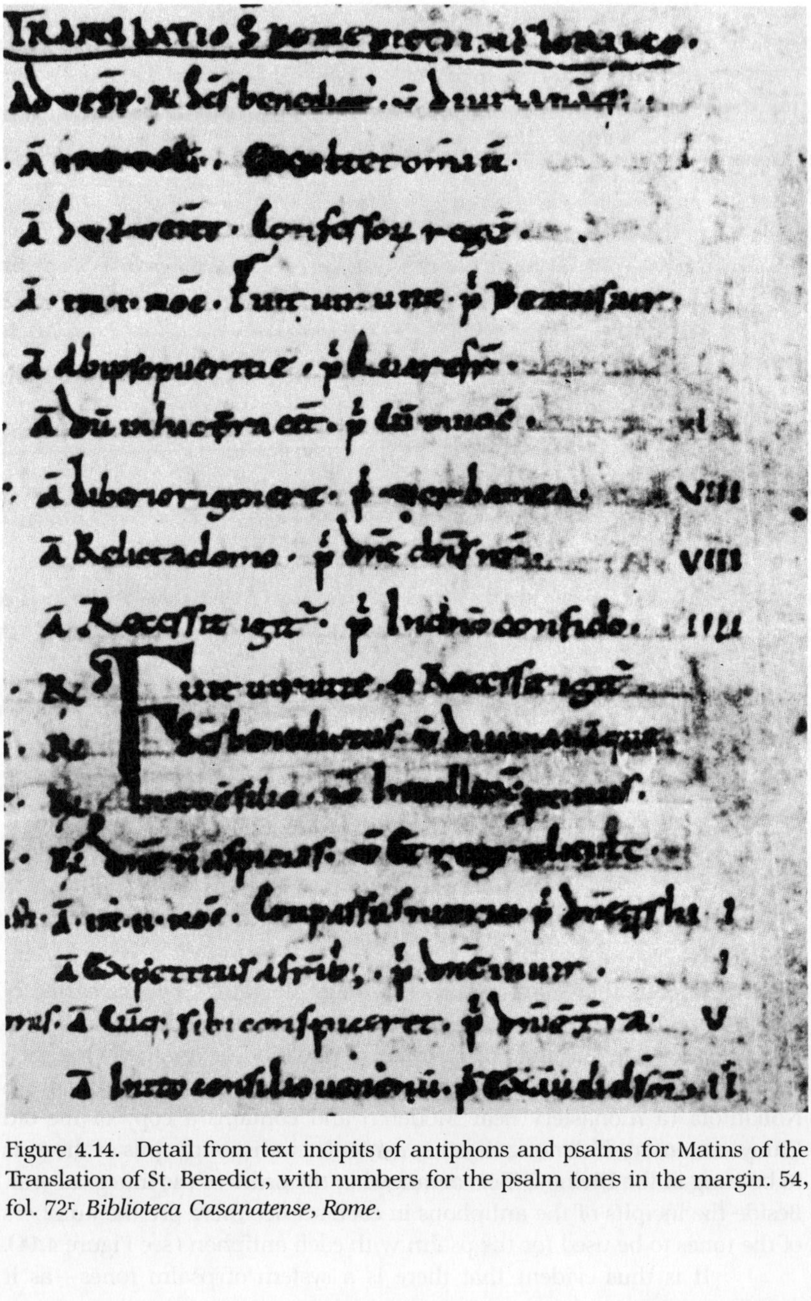

I

Figure 4.14. Detail from text incipits of antiphons and psalms for Matins of the Translation of St. Benedict, with numbers for the psalm tones in the margin. 54, fol. 72ʳ. *Biblioteca Casanatense, Rome.*

happens, eight different musical formulas—worked out in such a way that reference to it can be made with numbers.[23] For the psalm introduced by *Dum in hac terra*, tone 1 is to be employed; for the psalms with *Liberiori genere* and *Relicta domo*, tone 8; for *Recessit igitur*, tone 4. In lat. 12044, the later antiphonal of St. Maur-des-Fossés, a procedure is followed that is standard in later manuscripts: the musical incipits of the psalm tones follow the antiphons, and they are followed in turn by the terminations—the patterns used at the end of each verse of the psalm, which may vary according to how an antiphon begins.

We do not know quite how this system came into being. Its essential features appear fully developed in the earliest sources containing references to it from the eighth and ninth centuries.[24] Medieval music theorists wrote about the system of the psalm tones as part of the larger system of the ecclesiastical modes: the mode of an antiphon determines the choice of psalm tone to be combined with it. These theoretical works drew on three sources: direct observation of the melodies in the repertory, a study of ancient Greek writings on music interpreted and summarized in Latin by Boethius at the beginning of the sixth century, and, if terminology is a good indicator, the modal system of Byzantine chant, though the extent to which this last was known in the West in the ninth century, and how it was understood, is something we cannot know.[25]

All of the manuscripts referred to above present chants in the order in which they occur in the liturgy; but these repertories are sometimes presented in another arrangement. There are in certain sources long lists of antiphons—all of those for which one psalm tone is to be used, then all of those for the next, and so on. These are known as tonaries; they are the result of an immense labor of analyzing and classifying melodies carried out by individuals whom we would now identify as specialists in the theory of music. Occasionally one of them explains his reasons for undertaking such work. Regino of Prum, at the beginning of the tenth century, wrote to his archbishop: "When frequently in the dioceses of your church, the choir singing the melody of the psalms resounded with voices in confusion because of disagreement of tone, and when I had seen your Reverence often disturbed by this sort of thing, I seized the Antiphonary; and, considering it diligently from beginning to end through the order, I distributed the antiphons which I found written in it according, as I think, to their proper tones."[26]

What can he mean by "voices in confusion"? Suppose that one day two singers disagreed on the mode of a certain antiphon, one thinking it mode VI, the other, mode VIII. When they went on to the psalm, they would have chanted two different tones. The result would have been disaster—a series of dissonances so strong that the monks who heard them would probably have stopped singing to try to find out what had gone wrong. The service would have been interrupted, the atmosphere of worship at least partly dispersed. It was clearly desirable to avoid such confusions, and the obvious way was to obtain an authoritative statement of the mode of every antiphon in the repertory—precisely what Regino supplied.

But tonaries have a value beyond the practical aid they offer. Their compilers have had to come to grips with basic issues concerning the materials of medieval liturgical music, and how these are organized and drawn on in the chant repertory. Thus tonaries are of great interest, and Michel Huglo's 1971 study of them is a major contribution.[27] As he points out, some tonaries list every antiphon for a particular psalm tone, organizing them into subgroups if the psalm tone has more than one possible ending. Others give only a sampling. Among these, some do not limit themselves to Office antiphons, but also include responsories, and those Mass chants for which there are verses sung to formulas of their mode. Others even include chants for which no modal formulas are required. These seem to have been drawn up by a teacher (a music theorist) who wanted to present a general picture of a mode through a series of examples of it.[28] (Is there perhaps a parallel between this and a grammar book in which sample phrases are used to demonstrate certain possible constructions?) A student would use such a tonary to become familiar with openings or turns of phrase characteristic of chants in a particular mode, thereby acquiring increasing mastery of the repertory as a whole. (Perhaps a list of the antiphons of one mode is in some ways like a list of the verbs of one conjugation.)

In tonaries and in treatises on music that take the same kind of approach to the repertory, it is hard to avoid the impression that the modes came first, and then all these chants; and yet from certain characteristics in the music itself, we know that this cannot have been the case. Of course, the composition of Gregorian chants continued into the eleventh century, and indeed until much later, and the composers of the later chants knew quite well what they could and could not do in the system. Sometimes they even stressed its features in their works—as, for example, when they wrote the chants for new Offices in such a way that the first of them was in mode I, the second in mode II, and so on.[29] (Much later both Bach and Chopin would produce masterpieces working from a similar point of departure.) But the earlier repertory of Gregorian chant, that in

I

Figure 4.15. Tonary, mode 3. Harley 4951, fol. 298ᵛ. *British Library, London*.

Figure 4.16. Cluny, capital depicting mode 3. *Photo Wim Swaan.*

use up to the ninth century, was the work of men who approached the composing of music in a different way. The theoretical system devised after the fact to interpret it and to put it in order was not entirely success-ful. Rules that are generally valid fail to explain what happens in certain melodies. For such melodies, the manuscripts give an unusual range of

I

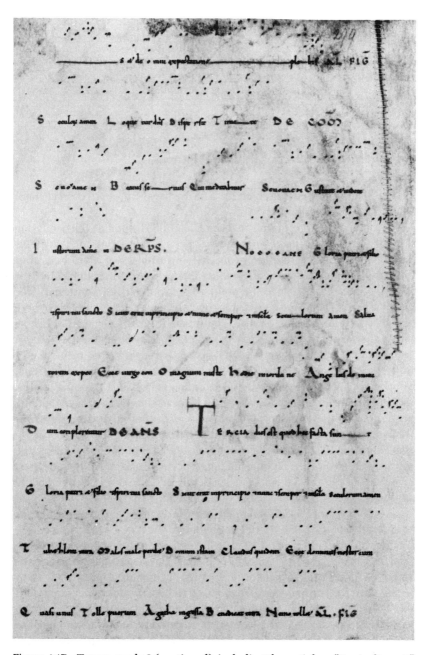

Figure 4.17. Tonary, mode 3 (continued), including the antiphon "Tercia dies est." Harley 4951, fol. 299ʳ. *British Library, London.*

I

104

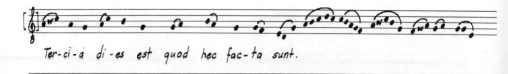

Figure 4.18. Model antiphon for mode 3. Harley 4951, fol. 299ʳ. *British Museum, London.*

variant readings, reflecting the efforts of medieval editors to correct them and bring them into line.[30]

It is quite rare to find in a tonary an illustration at the beginning of the presentation of each of the modes. Yet a whole series of illustrations occurs in the tonary (now unfortunately incomplete) of a gradual from Toulouse (British Library, Harley 4951) that dates from around 1000.[31] It has a picture of a juggler at the point where mode III is introduced. (See Figure 4.15; on the Cluny capital for mode III, shown in Figure 4.16, there is a seated figure holding a lyre.) The music it gives for mode III begins with a characteristic formula that is sung to nonsense syllables, *Noeoeane.* Next comes the melody to be used for the verses and the catalogue of introits of that mode. There follow incipits of selected mode III introits, grouped according to the cadence formulas (some of them quite elaborate) to be employed in their verses, and a version of the introit for the feast of SS Peter and Paul, *Nunc scio vere*, that includes melismas (melismatic tropes) not ordinarily found in that chant.[32] On the next page (see Figure 4.17), selected communions are presented, grouped as the introits were. *Noeoeane* is repeated and followed by the melody to be used for verses of Office responsories of mode III; this is followed in turn by the incipits of several responsories of that mode.

The rubric "DE ANS" then introduces the chant *Tertia dies est quod haec facta sunt*, the model antiphon for the mode. (It is transcribed in Figure 4.18.) This is not a liturgical chant, though it has a New Testament text (Luke 24:21: "It is now the third day since these things happened"). It is one of a series of antiphons, each of which has a text that begins with the ordinal number of its mode—*"Primum quaerite regnum Dei," "Secundum autem simile est hoc,"* and so on—and is intended to demonstrate musically some features of that mode. In this tonary each of the model antiphons is followed by its neumes and a melisma that might be added to any antiphon of the mode.[33] Apparently these melismas were

Figure 4.19. Tonary, end of the mode-3 chants and beginning of those of mode 4. Lat. 1118, fol. 107ᵛ. *Bibliothèque nationale, Paris.*

popular at Cluny—perhaps too popular, for in his *Statutes* Peter the Venerable finds it advisable to limit their use.[34]

The Cluny capitals are dated at around 1090 by Professor Kenneth Conant. In a study of them and their relation to music, Kathi Meyer demonstrated that the inscription for mode III alluded to the text of the antiphon *Tertia dies est* as it stands in its biblical context.[35] The same procedure is followed in the inscriptions for all but one of the other modes. In the inscriptions, the numeral is always retained and made to refer directly to the mode. Thus the mode is linked through the model antiphon to the biblical context or the event from which the text of the antiphon is drawn. *Tertia dies est* is reflected in the Cluny capital in *"Tertius impingit Christumque resurgere fingit"* ("The third mode encroaches; it depicts Christ rising again").

Such characterizations of the modes are examples in the field of music theory of that borrowing of images and ideas from pagan antiquity and infusing them with Christian meaning that is so common in medieval thought. They form a counterpart to the characterizations of the Greek *harmoniai* (modes) found in Plato, where some are said to be "dirge-like," and others to suggest "the utterances of a brave man ... who, when he has failed ... confronts fortune with steadfast endurance."[36] It is often tempting to attribute a mood to each of the ecclesiastical modes. But from the fact that in the chant repertory texts of very different characters are set to melodies of the same mode, and from the way in which a single text in different liturgical roles may have melodies in different modes, it is evident that this would not be valid.

What then are the illustrations in a tonary intended to depict? The only complete illustrated tonary is that of the Bibliothèque Nationale Manuscript lat. 1118, the subject of an excellent study published by Tilman Seebass in 1973.[37] The images there do not illustrate the modes one by one—how could they?[38] Some of them derive from the tradition of Psalter illustrations, a tradition in which the instruments of music referred to in the Psalms, especially Psalm 150, appear time and again, in forms that change according to the understanding of the Latin names: *"Laudate eum in sono tubae ... in psalterio et cithara ... in tympano et choro ... in chordis et organo ... in cymbalis benesonantibus ... in cymbalis iubilationis.*[39] The figure of King David appears at mode I. For modes II, III, V, and VII there are four other musicians, David's companions, who often appear with him in Psalters. But the pictures for modes IV and VIII show jongleurs, the popular entertainers of the Middle Ages. (See Figure 4.19 for the mode IV picture.) The Cluny capital for mode IV shows bells (*cymbala*; see Figure 4.20). Bells are also carried by the figure that stands at the beginning of

Figure 4.20. Cluny, capital depicting mode 4. *Photo Wim Swaan.*

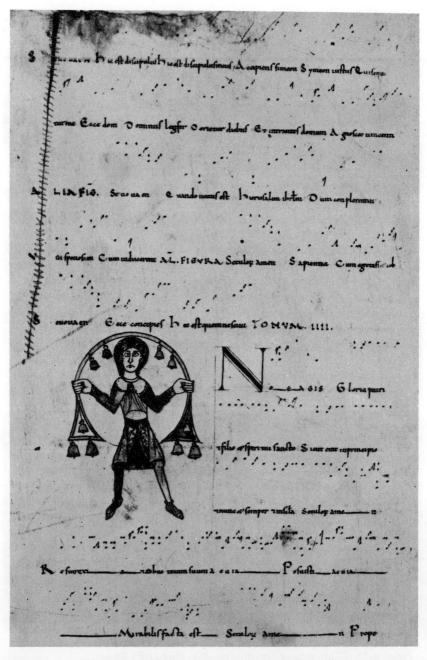

Figure 4.21. Tonary, end of mode-3 chants and beginning of those of mode 4. Harley 4951, fol. 299ᵛ. *British Library, London.*

mode IV in the only other tonary with illustrations of this kind, that from Toulouse (see Figure 4.21).

The representations of the modes on the Cluny capitals make up, as has often been said, a tonary in stone. All the parts of a tonary that can be represented in the medium are present, and the result is a monument both to the ecclesiastical chant of that abbey and to the scholarly analysis of it carried on there. The theory of music must have been studied at Cluny both for what it could help to clarify or correct in everyday musical practice and for its own sake. Indeed, a long tradition attributes unusual diligence in the cultivation of the art and the science of music to that monastery. Unfortunately, this is based, at least in part, on a mistake—the misattribution of a series of treatises about music to Odo of Cluny.[40] It seems now that Odo did not contribute directly to the development of medieval music theory. He did compose a series of chants for the feast of St. Martin, three hymns and twelve antiphons. But his main contributions to music seem to have been those of the enlightened patron—encouraging the effort of others, recognizing the importance of their work, providing a roof under which it could be carried out.[41] There is no questioning Odo's gifts and his achievements in other fields. He was the first great abbot of Cluny and saw in the life and work of St. Benedict a model for his own—"a man of venerable life, blessed in grace as in name." In a sermon about St. Benedict that was read at Cluny in the days following the feast, Odo wrote: "*Ubicunque sancta Ecclesia diffunditur, per tribus, per nationes, per linguas, laus Benedicti frequentatur.*"[42] ("Wheresoever the holy Church is spread, by peoples, by nations, by languages, the praise of Benedict is repeated.") It might have been a motto for the monks of Cluny as they sang.

NOTES

1. The Latin text will be cited in this study as it is given in the edition by Umberto Moricca, *Gregorii Magni Dialogi* (Rome: Tip. del Senato, 1924), the English in the translation by Myra L. Uhlfelder *The Dialogues of Gregory the Great. Book Two: Saint Benedict* (Indianapolis: Bobbs-Merrill, 1967).

2. *Regula monachorum*, edited by D. Philibert Schmitz (Maredsous: Éditions de Maredsous, 1946), XLIII, 7.

3. The services given for the feasts of St. Benedict in six different medieval monastic sources are outlined by R.-J. Hesbert in *Corpus Antiphonalium Officii*, 6 vols. (Rome: Herder, 1963–79), 2: 210–15, 243–45, 493–95. The chant texts referred to by incipit there are edited in full in volumes 3 and 4 of the same work; these texts will be given in the present study as in that edition.

4. The lack of consistency in the division of the lessons from one source to another is striking, but no more so than the diversity in the chants themselves. In many breviaries the lessons are very short, only a few lines each; V. Leroquais points out many examples of this in *Les Bréviaires manuscrits des bibliothèques publiques de France*, 6 vols. (Macon: Protat Fréres, 1934). Some breviaries were made for use by monks who were traveling, who needed relatively small (portable) books from which they could carry out their observance of the Divine Office while they were away from the monastery. In such books some abbreviation of the lessons could be expected. But the Cluny breviary to be discussed below is not a small book; it measures 355 by 237 mm. It seems likely that it gives the lessons in the form in which they were read in the monastery itself.

5. To Mario Righetti, it seems that the responsories placed after each of the lessons of Matins may have either an esthetic role—that of providing articulation for the lessons, which if uninterrupted might become monotonous—or a dramatic one, enabling the congregation to express through prayer the emotions experienced during the reading, in *Manuale di storia liturgica*, 3rd ed., vol. 2 (Milan: Àncora, 1969), p. 769.

6. This variety is clearly demonstrated in the six monastic antiphonals surveyed by Hesbert. A study of the Matins services for feasts of St. Benedict has been undertaken by Linus Ellis, a graduate student in music at Catholic University. He has surveyed these offices as they appear in several dozen sources, working with Hesbert's book and with microfilms in the collection of medieval liturgical manuscripts containing musical notation in the School of Music at Catholic University. The choice of manuscripts to be considered here was made partly on the basis of some of his preliminary work; I thank him for sharing it with me.

7. Hesbert, *Corpus Antiphonalium Officii*, V: 13; Leroquais, II: 418–19. References after this one to manuscripts in the Bibliothèque Nationale, Paris, will omit the name of the library.

8. J. Hourlier, "Le Bréviaire de Saint-Taurin. Un livre liturgique clunisien à l'usage de l'échelle Saint-Aurin," *Études grégoriennes* 3 (1959): 163–73. Solange Corbin identifies this and the gradual lat. 1087 as the only early manuscripts from Cluny containing neumes; as she says, it is surprising that there are so few, yet the matter has been thoroughly studied. (*Die Neumen* [Köln: Arno Volk-Verlag, 1977], p. 130.) The origin of this manuscript had not been determined at the time that Léopold Délisle drew up his *Inventaire des manuscrits de la Bibliothèque nationale, Fonds de Cluny* (Paris: H. Champion, 1884), and thus it is not included there. Leroquais determined its place and date of origin (III, 226–28). Hourlier's first study of it was in "Remarques sur la notation clunisienne," *Revue grégorienne* 30 (1951): 231–40. The modifications in the manuscript, and the additions made after it left Cluny, are all relatively minor; in its 271 large folios it gives lessons, prayers, and chants for the second half of the liturgical year, beginning with Trinity. Except for a few places, detailed by Hourlier, "tout le bréviaire a été neumé par les moines de Cluny," "Le Bréviaire," p. 165.

9. Alexandre Vidier, *L'historiographie à Saint-Benoît sur Loire et les Miracles de Saint Benoît* (Ouvrage posthume revu et annoté par les soins des moines de l'Abbaye de Saint-Benoît de Fleury) (Paris: A. et J. Picard, 1965), 141–49, 153–57. The text is published in *Acta Sanctorum*, Mart. III, 3rd ed., 300–303. Concerning the accuracy of this account by Adrevald, the editors of the Vidier book comment, "Cette double question fort difficile des origines de Fleury et de l'authenticité de la translation est actuellement à l'étude. Elle est plus complexe que l'auteur ne le laisse entendre," p. 145, n. 21. See also P. Meyvaert, "Peter the Deacon and the Tomb of St. Benedict. A reexamination of the Cassinese Tradition," *Revue bénédictine* 65 (1955): 3–70. In his article on "Benedetto di Norcia" in *Bibliotheca sanctorum*, II (Rome: Istituto Giovanni XXIII della Pontificia Università Lateranensis, 1962), Anselmo Lentini speaks of the narratives of the translation as "così favolosi che, se fossero venuti alla luce oggi,

nessun serio studioso li avrebbe accettati," p. 1151. Other recent thought on the subject is summarized by J. Laporte in his article on Fleury in the *Dictionnaire d'histoire et de géographie ecclésiastiques*, Vol. XVII (Paris, Letouzey et Ané, 1971), cols. 441–76.

10. My thanks to Professor Frank Mantello for his guidance in the interpretation of this text and several others.

11. Even though they tell only part of the story, the lessons here are quite long. Hourlier calls attention to the length of the lessons in this breviary, seeing in it a reminder of "les grandes dévotions clunisiennes," "Le Bréviaire," p. 165.

12. In lat. 12601, the sermon extends from fol. to 59ᵛ to 64ᵛ; it is edited in J. P. Migne, ed., *Patroligiae Cursus Completus, Series Latina*, 221 vols. (Paris: Migne, 1844–65), 133: cols. 721–29.

13. This is not to deny that there is a large letter *F* at the beginning of the notation of just this chant. Its role is unclear; but if it is in the original hand, and if it is intended as a clef, then it is an anomaly.

14. It would obviously be extremely interesting to find the Office manuscript with staff notation that gives melodies in forms most closely resembling those rendered in neumes in the Cluny breviary. Doing this would require making lengthy and detailed comparisons of the readings of many melodies, something that could not be accomplished within the time limit set for the completion of this study. But the decision to refer here to lat. 12044 was not entirely arbitrary. In volume II of *Corpus Antiphonalium Officii*, Hesbert explained his decision to survey the contents of an earlier antiphonal of St.-Maur-des-Fossés, lat. 12584, by saying that it could be taken to represent, "avec une précision suffisante, toute la famille clunisienne," p. vi. There is a list of antiphonals and breviaries of the Cluniac type in the same work, Vol. V, p. 411, but it is not complete since Hesbert has included there only books that contain services for the Sundays of Advent. Thus lat. 12601 is absent, as is the fragmentary Cluny breviary described in *Revue bénédictine* 57 (1947): 201–209. For a comparison of the two antiphonals of St. Maur-des-Fossés, see A. Renaudin, "Deux antiphonaires de Saint-Maur," *Etudes grégoriennes* 13 (1972): 53–150. Urbanus Bomm dates lat. 12584 in the 10th or 11th century; see *Archiv für Liturgiewissenschaft* 19 (1978): 286. Michel Huglo has observed, "The adoption of the usages of Cluny in a monastery did not always result in the complete disappearance of earlier liturgical practices, particularly in centers as powerful as Corbie, St.-Denis, or St. Martial: the comparison of the manuscripts of these abbeys with those of Cluny is quite instructive on that point. But it should be recognized that in Paris, St. Maur-des-Fossés, and especially St. Martin-des-Champs were much 'closer' to Cluny than the other abbeys mentioned here," *Les Tonaires: Inventaire, Analyse, Comparaison* (Paris: Heugel, 1971), p. 115.

15. W. H. Frere pointed out many such turns of phrase, of frequent recurrence among Office responsories; see the introduction to his *Antiphonale sarisburiense* (London: Plainsong and Medieval Music Society, 1901–24). Understanding of the compositional procedures that led to such similarities is probably not helped by the use of the term *centonization*, as Leo Treitler has pointed out; see his articles, "Homer and Gregory: The Transmission of Epic Poetry and Plainchant," *The Musical Quarterly* 60 (1974): 333–72, and "'Centonate' Chant: *Übles Flickwerk* or *E pluribus unus?*" *Journal of the American Musicological Society* 28 (1975): 1–23.

16. Uhlfelder, *Dialogues of Gregory*, pp. 45–46.

17. This is not to imply that every melisma that appears near the end of a Matins responsory has this role. Such melismas are a commonplace in a later chant style; in certain Matins services every responsory has a melisma. These add to the solemnity of the celebration in a general way, by adding musically to its richness; but they seem not to be intended to

enhance the expression of the individual words or phrases on which they are heard.

18. In his doctoral dissertation, "Responsory Tropes" (Harvard, 1973), and in two articles, "Melodic Elaboration in Responsory Melismas," *Journal of the American Musicological Society* 27 (1974): 461–74, and "New Music from Old: The Structuring of Responsory Prosas," *ibid.* 30 (1977): 366–90.

19. Helma Hofmann-Brandt surveys the whole subject in her dissertation, "Die Tropen zu den Responsorien des Officiums," 2 vols. (University of Erlangen, 1971). See also my articles, "Some Melismas for Office Responsories," *Journal of the American Musicological Society* 26 (1973): 108–31, and "The Gregorian Chant Melismas for Christmas Matins," *Essays on Music in Honor of Charles Warren Fox*, ed. J. Graue (Rochester, N.Y.: Eastman School of Music, 1979), 241–53.

20. Kathi Meyer, "The Eight Gregorian Modes on the Cluny Capitals," *Art Bulletin* 34 (1952): 75–94; Kenneth Conant, *Cluny. Les Eglises et la maison du chef d'ordre* (Macon: Protat Freres, 1968), 89–91.

21. The matter is admirably dealt with by David Hughes in a work intended to serve as a music history textbook for undergraduates, *A History of European Music* (New York: McGraw-Hill, 1974), pp. 8–19; see also his review of Paul Evans' *The Early Trope Repertory of St. Martial de Limoges*, in *Speculum* 48 (1973): 353–55.

22. The source is MS Rome, Biblioteca Casanatense 54. See B. Albers, "Le plus ancien coutumier de Cluny," *Revue bénédictine* 20 (1903): 174–84; *Consuetudines monasticae*, II (Monte Cassino, 1905); M. Huglo, *Les Tonaires*, p. 41.

23. There is one additional formula, called the *tonus peregrinus*, that is limited in use to a certain group of antiphons, and thus in a certain sense stands outside the system under discussion here. Concerning the treatment of it in some early sources, see Carlton Russell, "The Southern French Tonary in the Tenth and Eleventh Centuries" (Ph.D. dissertation, Princeton University, 1966), pp. 76–80.

24. Huglo discusses these in his first chapter, *Les Tonaires*, pp. 25–45.

25. J. Ponte, "*Aureliani Reomensis Musica Disciplina*" (Ph.D. dissertation, Brandeis University, 1961), Vol. III, pp. 42–49, goes over one area in which Byzantine modal practice seems to have influenced that of the West. See also the text on which this is a commentary, Vol. II, pp. 67–70.

26. Sister Mary Protase LeRoux, "The '*De Harmonica Institutione*' and '*Tonarius*' of Regino of Prüm" (Ph.D. dissertation, Catholic University, 1965), p. 23.

27. Huglo, *Les Tonaires*

28. On p. 29, Huglo introduces the notion of "a special category which we call 'tonaries for teaching' or didactic tonaries, in contrast to practical tonaries, intended for the use of singers, in which all antiphons of the repertory are classified."

29. Huglo, *Les Tonaires*, pp. 122–28.

30. U. Bomm, *Der Wechsel der Modalitätsbestimmung in der Tradition der Messgesänge im IX. bis XIII. Jahrhundert* (Einsiedeln: Benziger & C., 1929); D. Dealande, *Le Graduel des Prêcheurs* (Paris: Editions du Cerf, 1949); K. Fleming, "The Editing of Some Communion Melodies in Medieval Chant Manuscripts" (Ph.D. dissertation, Catholic University, 1979).

31. This is the dating of the illustrations in it given by Tilman Seebass in *Musikdarstellung und Psalterillustration im früheren Mittelalter: Studien ausgehend von einer Ikonologie der Handschrift Paris, Bibliothèque Nationale, fonds latin 1118* (Bern: Francke Verlag 1973), Textband, p. 84. That there were parallels between the illustrations for the modes on the Cluny capitals and those in this manuscript was pointed out long ago; see *Speculum* 7 (1932): 31, where K. Conant thanks Charles Niver for calling his attention to the

drawings in lat. 1118 and Harley 4951, and (opposite p. 33) gives a facsimile of one of the drawings in each manuscript.

    32. G. Weiss, *Monumenta monodica medii aevi, III: Introitus-Tropen I* (Kassel: Baerenreiter-Verlag, 1970), supplementary vol., p. 22, gives this introit as it appears in lat. 909, where the melismatic tropes are similar, though not identical, to those of Harley 4951. See also Russell, "The Southern French Tonary," pp. 83, 88.

    33. For these see Huglo, *Les Tonaires*, pp. 383–90.

    34. "Statuta Petri Venerabilis," edited by G. Constable, *Corpus consuetudinarium monasticarum*, VI (Siegburg: Apud Franciscum Schmitt Success, 1975), 98.

    35. See the works referred to in footnote 20. Even after thirty years, Kathi Meyer's catching these allusions still seems absolutely brilliant. See also Huglo, *Les Tonaires*, pp. 386–87.

    36. O. Strunk, *Source Readings in Music History* (New York: Norton, 1950), pp. 4–5; from *The Republic*, I, 10.

    37. See note 31. Seebass includes first-rate color reproductions of these illustrations.

    38. In his review of Seebass' book, J. McKinnon observes, "As the earliest illustrated tonary, [lat. 1118] leaves us with no precedents to aid in its interpretation; even more basic, the illustrations, unlike most early medieval miniatures, do not function as illustrations in the narrow sense. Thus the first illustration has no specific relationship to the first church mode, in spite of the fact that the first eight illustrations are carefully aligned with the beginning of the eight sections of the tonary. ... Presumably, then, the illustrations relate to the tonary as a whole, perhaps to its general character as a liturgical music book; in this case, they might be borrowed from some well-established genre of medieval illustration having to do with liturgical music," *Journal of the American Musicological Society* 28 (1975): 362.

    39. See the "vergleichende Tabelle" at the end of Seebass' Bildband, and Chapter V of the Textband, "Musik als Thema der bildenden Kunst im früheren Mittelalter," pp. 83–164.

    40. Dom Pierre Thomas, "Saint Odon de Cluny et son oeuvre musicale," *A Cluny: Congrès scientifique; fêtes et cérémonies liturgiques ... 1949* (Dijon: Bernigaud & Privat, 1950), pp. 171–180. For Dom Thomas, "The hypothesis according to which works concerning the theory of music can be attributed to St. Odo has been proven false for all the treatises published under his name except for one—the tonary of the manuscript Monte Cassino 318—and even that is doubtful" (p. 179). Huglo, however, is able to demonstrate conclusively that of all the tonaries attributed to an Abbot Odo, not the smallest fragment can be ascribed to Odo of Cluny (*Les Tonaires*, p. 185).

    41. Dom Thomas puts it as follows: "But the hymns and antiphons written by St. Odo are not his only reason for being remembered by friends of sacred music. If he himself composed verses and melodies, would he not also have encouraged, in the famous Aquitanian monasteries, the developing talents of younger composers and poets? ... The art of musical composition made significant progress beginning at the end of the tenth century; perhaps some credit for that should be given to St. Odo, to the extent that he, as the superior of so many in religious life, had the wisdom to help along those works of artistic creation and transcription that are so effective in combating spiritual sloth and, even more, in maintaining and refining that attraction to the beautiful that is one of the ways in which God reveals Himself to His creatures," *Saint Odon de Cluny*," p. 180.

    42. J. P. Migne, *Patr. lat.* 133, col. 728 D; in lat. 12601, this passage appears on fol. 64ᵛ as part of the fourth lesson on the octave of the feast of the Translation of the Relics of St. Benedict.

II

Tones for the Palm Sunday Invitatory

In the middle ages, the music of the Divine Office began each day with the chanting of Psalm 94, *Venite exsultemus Domino*, known as the invitatory psalm. The text is given below; for chanting it is divided into five sections, with the Gloria Patri as a sixth. The opening phrase of the psalm, a concise expression of the sense of the whole, is shown here returning as a refrain.

1. Venite, exsultemus Domino, jubilemus Deo salutari nostro: praeoccupemus faciem eius in confessione, et in psalmis jubilemus ei.

   (O come, let us sing unto the Lord: let us heartily rejoice in the strength of our salvation. Let us come before his presence with thanksgiving, and show ourselves glad in him with psalms.)

   Venite, exsultemus Domino.

2. Quoniam Deus magnus Dominus, et Rex magnus super omnes deos: quoniam non repellet Dominus plebem suam, quia in manu eius sunt omnes fines terrae, et altitudines montium ipse conspicit.

   (For the Lord is a great God, and a great King above all gods. In his hand are all the corners of the earth: the strength of the hills is his also.)

   Venite, exsultemus Domino.

3. Quoniam ipsius est mare, et ipse fecit illud, et aridam fundaverunt manus eius: venite, adoremus, et procidamus ante Deum: ploremus coram Domino, qui fecit nos, quia ipse est Dominus Deus noster: nos autem populus eius, et oves pascuae eius.

   (The sea is his, and he made it: and his hands prepared the dry land. O come, let us worship and fall down: and kneel before the Lord our maker. For he is the Lord our God; and we are the people of his pasture, and the sheep of his hand.)

   Venite, exsultemus Domino.

4. Hodie, si vocem eius audieritis, nolite obdurare corda vestra, sicut in exacerbatione secundum diem temptationis in deserto: ubi temptaverunt me patres vestri, probaverunt et viderunt opera mea.

   (Today if ye will hear his voice, harden not your hearts, as in the provocation, and as in the day of temptation in the wilderness: when your fathers tempted me, proved me, and saw my works.)

   Venite, exsultemus Domino.

5. Quadraginta annis proximus fui generationi huic, et dixi: semper hi errant corde: ipsi vero non cognoverunt vias meas, quibus juravi in ira mea, si introibunt in requiem meam.

   (Forty years long was I grieved with this generation, and said, It

is a people that do err in their hearts, for they have not known my ways: unto whom I sware in my wrath that they should not enter into my rest.)
Venite, exsultemus Domino.

6. Gloria patri et filio et spiritui sancto: sicut erat in principio, et nunc et semper, et in saecula saeculorum. Amen.
(Glory be to the Father and to the Son and to the Holy Ghost: as it was in the beginning, is now and ever shall be, world without end. Amen.)
Venite, exsultemus Domino.

An invitatory antiphon with the text *Venite, exsultemus Domino* appears in practically every one of the sources consulted for this study: it must have been among the first works of this type. It has a distinctive tone (a formula employed for chanting the psalm with it) and is assigned to Monday in the ferial office.[1] But in the sources at hand it is only one in a large repertory of antiphons for the invitatory, a repertory that has a number of complex and even baffling aspects.

The extent to which certain of its elements are preserved in the sources suggests that the repertory came into being in stages, rather than all at once. There are only a few invitatory antiphons that were sung everywhere on a certain feast, which would mark them as relatively old. In the twelve medieval antiphonals surveyed in *Corpus antiphonalium officii* there are 186 different invitatory antiphon texts[2]; there were another 85 in the first dozen or so manuscripts consulted in the course of the present study. For perhaps 25 of these texts there is more than one melody.[3] Of all of these, the invitatory antiphons for only a handful of feasts can be relied upon not to change from one place to another: Christmas, Epiphany, Palm Sunday, Easter Monday, Ascension, Pentecost, Purification, and Trinity—though this last is a late feast, and represents a different set of circumstances than the rest. Also, among the invitatories in the ferial office there are only minor rearrangements.

More invitatory antiphons are in mode IV than in any other; of these it is the ones for Christmas and Palm Sunday that are the most securely established. The antiphon for Christmas, *Christus natus est nobis*, is thematically connected with one of the tones the manuscripts provide for the

---

[1] How far back can the history of this antiphon and tone be traced? Are they perhaps older than any of the rest? Paolo Ferretti, *Esthétique grégorienne* (Solesmes, 1938), pp. 221-22, expresses the belief that "il y eut un temps, à l'origine, où l'Antienne pour le Psaume Invitatoire des Dimanches ordinaires se composait de deux ou trois Alleluia." In his view, that single Sunday antiphon was later replaced by several that were settings of texts from Ps. 94; *Venite, exsultemus Domino* was among them. The persuasiveness of the arguments Ferretti employs to support this position is diminished by the fact that they do not take into account the distinctive tone to which the psalm is always chanted when this antiphon is sung. This tone has been the object of a good deal of attention: as Peter Wagner wrote (*Einführung in die gregorianischen Melodien, III: Gregorianische Formenlehre* [Leipzig, 1921; reprinted Hildesheim, 1962], p. 182), "Man ist versucht, diese Formel wegen ihrer Regellosigkeit in eine ganz alte Zeit zurückzuversetzen."

[2] Ed. R.-J. Hesbert (6 vols.; Rome, 1963-79).

[3] For the antiphon *Alleluia, alleluia*, there are at least two different melodies; for *Alleluia, alleluia, alleluia*, there are four or more.

invitatory psalm; the cadence at its midpoint matches the termination of the tone. No source connects it with any other tone; and the tone is not joined to any other antiphon except that for Epiphany, which uses the same melody and only slightly different words.

On Palm Sunday, the situation is different. The antiphon is given below, in Example 1.

Example 1. Ant. *Ipsi vero*. Florence, Arcivescovado, manuscript without number, f. 99ʳ

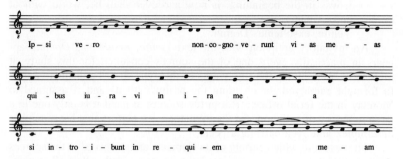

The text is in three clauses, each of them ending in a different form of the same Latin word—"vias meas," "ira mea," "requiem meam." The cadences are on unstressed syllables; though they are in the source quoted here all on the final of the mode, the second and third of them are weakened by a delaying of the last pitch; it does not coincide with the beginning of a syllable. As a result, the movement from one phrase into the next is smooth, and the final cadence is played down. The fourth D-G provides the range for the first two phrases (A is used once as an upper auxiliary); the third phrase begins with C (heard once), and touches on A and B above near the end. The text is the ending of the invitatory psalm.[4]

Given the liturgical stability of *Ipsi vero*, one would expect its melody to be preserved without change in basic outline from one manuscript to another, and in general it is. One would also expect the tone with which the antiphon is combined to remain the same—and such is not the case. In the manuscripts to be reported on here, five different tones are prescribed for the chanting of the psalm with *Ipsi vero*. Two of them are nearly identical, others are more individual, and one is quite different from all the rest.

In Example 2, the third large section of the psalm, beginning "Quoniam ipsius est mare," is shown set to each of these tones.[5] Features that

---

[4]Ferretti, pp. 219-21, identifies 29 antiphons that appear in virtually every source; these, he says, form the nucleus of the repertory. More than half of them are on texts taken from Ps. 94. It should be observed that among later additions to the repertory, chants that appear in a smaller number of sources, are other antiphons similarly based on excerpts from this psalm.

[5]For each of the manuscripts referred to in Example 2, bibliographical information is provided in an appendix to this article.

distinguish them include the intonation, the mediants, the termination, and—perhaps most important—the reciting notes (tenors). For the purpose of the present discussion, these invitatory tones have been assigned the identifying letters P, Q, R, S, and T.[6] (This is to avoid the unintended connotations that other letters or numbers might carry.)

In the third section of the psalm, the first period falls into two musical phrases separated by the flex; these are marked 1a and 1b. The second period is in three phrases, marked 2a, 2b, and 2b′.

Example 2. Five Invitatory Tones: First Period

Example 2, ctd. Five Invitatory Tones: Second Period (beginning)

[6]All but one of these tones have been published previously. Tone P is like the one Ferretti calls 4.c (p. 228). Tone Q is Ferretti's 4.d (p. 228). See also Wagner, p. 178; he gives it as the fourth mode-IV formula of a 13th-century Franciscan antiphonal. Tone Q also appears in W. H. Frere, *The Use of Sarum, II: The Ordinal and Tonal* (Cambridge, 1901), p. x; and the *Liber Responsorialis* (Solesmes, 1895), pp. 16-18. For tone R, see the first of the tones Frere gives under mode IV (p. xxx); tone S follows it.

II

Example 2, ctd. Five Invitatory Tones: Second Period (conclusion) and Third Period

Sources for the five invitatory tones:
Tone P, Verdun, Bibl. mun., 128, fols. 249v-250r
Tone Q, Florence, Arcivescovado, MS without number
Tone R, Paris, Bibl. de l'Arsenal, 279, fol. 560v
Tone S, Worcester, Cathedral Library, F 160, p. 193
Tone T, Toledo, Bibl. capitular, 44.2, fol. 217v

In tone P, the reciting note for 1a is A; for 1b and all of 2, G; for 3, F. The second mediant is like the first, but ends a step higher. The total range of the tone is a seventh, with recitation on the second-highest or third-highest note. (Incidentally, the intonation varies somewhat from one manuscript to another.) Tone Q is like tone P in many ways: their mediants and their terminations are virtually identical. The most important difference is in the intonation, which again is not the same in every manuscript, and in the fact that all through the first period (in tone Q) the tenor is G.

In studying the use of these tones, one finds tone P sung with *Ipsi vero* in the East Frankish regions—Germany and Switzerland—and tone Q in the West, in Aquitaine, and in southern Italy. Manuscripts usually contain one or the other of them, but not both. (However, a 12th-century antiphonal in the Curia Arcivescovile in Florence contains both of them fully notated; it asks for tone Q with *Ipsi vero*, and never calls for tone P.) The Hartker Antiphonal—St. Gall 390-391—has both; it calls for tone P with *Ipsi vero* and reserves tone Q (which it provides with an incipit that is slightly more elaborate than usual) for just one antiphon, *Adoremus Deum quia ipse fecit nos*. Among the other manuscripts that have both tones is an 11th-century Aquitanian antiphonal, Toledo, Biblioteca capitular, 44.1: it conserves space by writing them over a single statement of the complete psalm in alternation—with each other, and with a second form of tone Q that extends the melisma in its incipit. The cues for this tone following antiphons in the manuscript cite only this last version of it.

Tone R employs the same reciting notes and range as tone Q, and in 2b it employs a procedure found also in tones Q and P: accented syllables are raised a step, as are the syllables that precede them. The first and second mediants are identical, featuring a rather conspicuous downward leap of a fourth; and the intonations of the first and second periods are also the same. Tone S has different mediants and different intonations for the first and second periods. The tenor for 1a and all of 2 is G; but for 1b, E is the tenor.

The distinctive flavor of each of these tones is provided by the different intonations, and especially by the mediants, because they are so long, taking up nearly all of the text in some of the sections of the psalm. And yet the notes on which recitation occurs are also quite important structurally; in respect to them, tones R and Q are basically the same, with tones S and P offering only a small departure from the pattern.

The Worcester antiphonal writes out both tones S and Q, specifying tone S for *Ipsi vero* and, like St. Gall 390-391, reserving tone Q exclusively for *Adoremus Deum*.[7] The Verdun antiphonal contains tones P, R, and S; in it *Ipsi vero* is combined with tone P. At Sarum, where tones Q, R, and S were known, tone R was used with *Ipsi vero*. Most manuscripts, however, call for tone Q with *Ipsi vero*; the combination was a popular one.

In examining its musical effect, one finds that in it G, which serves as the reciting tone for the first and second periods of the tone, receives a good deal of emphasis, as does A, the note for accented syllables; and together they play a dominant role in the musical line. F is also employed for reciting, in the third period, and D serves as its complement in certain figures. E is the point of origin for several of the intonations, but otherwise its role is rather understated. Since there is so little stress on the final in the melody, what there is of preparation for the terminal cadence is achieved in part through omission, and this diminishes the force of that cadence. When the antiphon has been sung in full for the last time, the music seems to float away, rather than coming decisively to its conclusion.

It has been observed that chants of modes III and IV have a special quality, one that invites analysis but often eludes objective description. Dom Joseph Gajard has observed that Deuterus is a world of its own, as different from the other ecclesiastical modes as it is from the music of the present. He made this observation in the leading article of the first issue of *Études*

---

[7]The singling-out of this antiphon is striking, epecially since at St. Gall it was sung only on the second Sunday of Lent. At Worcester it was sung on all of the Sundays following Epiphany and Pentecost, which suggests that it may at one time have been in general use as the antiphon for any Sunday in the year, in combination with tone Q.

grégoriennes, of which he was the editor.[8] In it Gajard begins by examining and then rejecting the notion that there might be different, equally valid dialects of chant; and then he focuses on what he calls modal recitation in chants of modes III and IV. From the examples he gives, which are limited in the article to chants of the Mass, it is evident that by modal recitation he means a passage where one note, either B or E, perhaps ornamented, is used for several syllables in succession. (In the same passage, other manuscripts—originating perhaps in northern France or England—have C or F.) The examples show, first, that in such passages the Beneventan manuscripts and many of those from Aquitaine agree, showing B or E; and, second, that their reading agrees with that expressed less precisely in the neumes "in campo aperto" or imperfectly heightened in earlier manuscripts from other regions, such as St. Gall, Laon, and Brittany. Gajard's conclusion is that the readings with B or with E show the chant *in its original form* and that those with C or F—such as are found in the Vatican Edition and the *Liber Usualis*, and in hundreds of medieval manuscripts—are corrupt.[9] Although this article was published only in 1954, the conclusions it states had been reached decades earlier—"certainly before 1920," according to Dom Gajard—and they formed part of the theoretical basis for such editing projects as the *Antiphonale monasticum* of 1934, where the tenor in the psalm tone for mode III is B-natural, rather than C.[10]

A study of the manuscript tradition for various invitatory tones, as well as certain mode-IV antiphons, including *Ipsi vero*, is revealing in this connection. Beneventan sources and some of those from Aquitaine treat *Ipsi vero*, tones P and Q, and other important mode-IV formulas (such as the tone for responsory verses) in a distinctive way: in the final phrase or period, E is written where most other manuscripts have F.[11] Thus in the 12th-century antiphonal Monte Cassino 542 one finds *Ipsi vero* as in Example 3. (See p. 149.)

---

[8]"Les Récitations modales des 3e et 4e modes et les manuscrits bénéventains et aquitans," *Études grégoriennes* I (1954), 44.
[9]"Il ne faut pas avoir peur des mots, il s'agit bien de corruption mélodique," p. 30.
[10]Gajard, p. 15, fn. 1.
[11]Ferretti gives his tones 4.g2, 4.d, 4.c, and 4.E with E rather than F in the final phrase; other modern editors give F.

The fact that the note E is heard more frequently in this reading of both tone and antiphon, and plays a more significant part in their structure, changes the character of the final cadence. Preparation for it takes place less through omission than before; the ending becomes more definite.

The reason for the change from E to F and B to C remains to be understood. It occurred in all genres of chant: was it because of factors unrelated to the original nature and role of the melodies—the development of polyphony, perhaps, as some have suggested? Or did it result from a systematic revision that had as its purpose a change in the basic ground plan for chants of the Deuterus, one that would fundamentally alter their aesthetic effect?

Example 3. *Ipsi vero* and Tone Q. Montecassino 542, pp. 45 and 169.

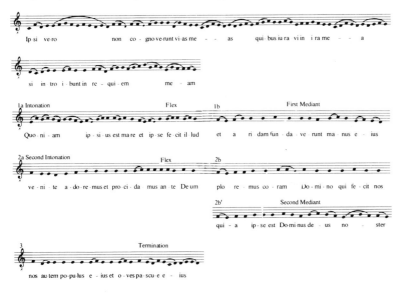

It is important to remember that the versions of the mode-IV chants that have F where in Benevento (for example) E would have been sung are very widely known. They were sung all over Europe throughout the middle ages except in a few areas: this is what was heard at Paris in the 12th and 13th centuries, at Sarum, and almost everywhere else. It is entirely appropriate and necessary for us to be as familiar with the F readings as those with E; even if they are corruptions of the original, they formed part of the basic music vocabulary of their own times.

Not every Aquitanian manuscript of the 11th and 12th centuries has the readings with E: two notated breviaries, Paris, B. n., lat. 743 (11th century, St. Martial), and lat. 742 (12th or 13th century, Ripoll) both have F's at the critical places in their readings. One very important source for the archaic readings of office chants (those with E's) is an antiphonal in the Biblioteca capitular in Toledo, which has the call number 44.2. It contains an overabundance of chants of every kind, including 22 invitatory tones of which the last is incomplete, suggesting that the following page— now lost—which included the end of that tone, may have included still other tones. (A typical collection of invitatory tones may include from nine to thirteen of them; St. Gall 390-391 originally had 15 tones, to which three were later added.) Several of the Toledo tones are unica. They are all written out in a separate section at the end of the manuscript.

Plate 1 shows part of the page where the tone for *Ipsi vero* is given. After the incipits of the antiphons with which the tone is to be combined the tone itself is written out; except for the first few words, the text of the psalm is represented only by its vowels, a procedure employed to save space. Not every one of the antiphons listed on this page is to be found in the manuscript; some are missing now because pages have been lost. However, all of them that are present in the source are chants of mode IV; where the notation of this manuscript does not make this clear, other manuscripts in staff notation provide corroboration.

Between the incipits of the antiphons and the written-out tone come incipits of four other tones. Among them are tones P and Q. What is implied is that antiphons assigned earlier in the manuscript to any of these four tones may, if desired, be sung with this tone. The comment in the manuscript, "Ut supra omnes qui de primo tono," indicates that all antiphons of mode I may be sung "as above," that is, with this tone. Some of the antiphons of which the incipits are given here are assigned to one of the other tones when they are written out in their correct liturgical place earlier in the manuscript. This, along with other features, conveys the impression that the compiler of the manuscript is striving to work extra, newly-invented chants into an already complete liturgical repertory. Or perhaps he is combining chants from several traditions into a single series.

The tone written out here has been given in Example 2 as tone T. The reciting in its first period is on A, in the second on G, and in the third on F. There are two conspicuous downward leaps—a fourth in the flex of the first period, a fifth in the second mediant—and there is a sweeping movement stepwise down a seventh beginning near the end of the first mediant and carrying through the second intonation. It's a more lively and colorful kind of music than one expects to hear in a tone; when tone and antiphon are combined, the tone is more interesting musically than the antiphon.

Although each of the tones under discussion here is combined with *Ipsi vero* in one source or another, whether they should be called "mode-IV invitatory tones" is open to question. It has been the practice to treat invitatory tones as modal formulae; every published explanation of them has done so. But this style of reference is misleading, for several of these

II

TONES FOR THE PALM SUNDAY INVITATORY 151

Plate I. Toledo, Biblioteca capitular, 44.2, fol. 217v

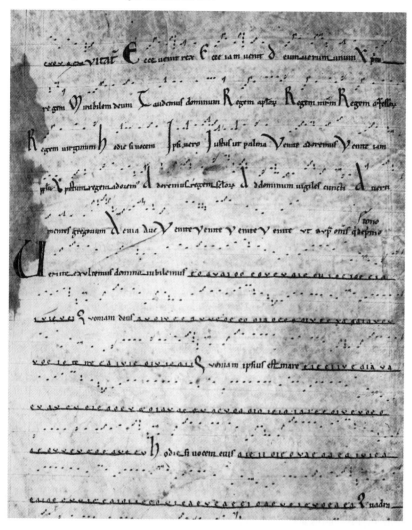

tones are joined—in one manuscript or another—both to antiphons of mode
IV and to antiphons that end on D.

One such manuscript is a 12th-century antiphonal from Vallombrosa,
Florence, Bibl. Laur., Conv. soppr. 560. It is conservative in a number of
ways: for example, it has a very limited repertory of invitatory antiphons;
even for St. Stephen and for St. John the Evangelist, antiphons from the
Common are employed. Only two of its invitatory antiphons end on D:
Surgite vigilemus, for the second Sunday of Advent, and *Regem regum
Dominum*, for All Saints. These antiphon melodies are very similar; with

both of them tone Q is employed; it is also sung with many mode-IV antiphons in this source. How can this use of a single tone with antiphons of two different modes be explained? Either, by some arbitrary decision, it has been declared to belong both to mode IV and mode II, or the grounds for joining a particular antiphon and tone may not be primarily musical—for example, this tone may be associated with liturgical observances of a certain type, such as Sundays and feasts.

A breviary written at Cluny ca. 1075, Paris, B. n., lat. 12601, includes a few additional invitatory antiphons that (in sources in staff notation) end on D. Two of them are set to the same melody, one that much resembles *Regem regum Dominum*; the others are three different, more extended antiphons, for the feast of St. Martin, the Translation of St. Martin, and for St. Benedict.[12] These practices are to be compared with those of a somewhat later source, Paris, B. n., lat. 12044, a 12th-century antiphonal for St. Maur-des-Fossés, near Paris, an abbey that was reformed by Cluny at the end of the 10th century. Here several of the antiphons to which reference has just been made appear again with tone Q, as do antiphons for St. Michael and St. Vincent—rather extended works both of which end on D. But this manuscript also calls for another tone, one that in many later sources is identified as the tone for mode-II antiphons; and ten of its antiphons that end on D are to be combined with it.

How is this to be explained? Perhaps at Vallombrosa archaic customs were being followed in the 12th century. Perhaps what one finds in that source is practices that were current in other places before (1) the enriching of the invitatory repertory with new antiphons that took as their point of departure the mode and even the melody of *Surgite vigilemus*, (2) a loss of innocence—a growing dependence on authority, in the form of theorists of music and their expositions of the ecclesiastical modes, according to which it was improper to follow the older practice of combining antiphons of different modes with the same tone—and, finally, the subsequent invention of one or more invitatory tones to serve in place of tone Q with antiphons ending on D.

None of the sources just referred to is explicit about modal classification, but in those manuscripts that do specify the mode to which each of the invitatory tones belongs, the treatment of tones P and Q bears examination. These sources include antiphonals and breviaries in which invitatory tones are arranged by mode, and also tonaries that include invitatory tones among the chants and formulas of each mode. One solution to the theoretical problems raised by the use of a single tone with chants of two different modes is to restrict tone Q (for example) to antiphons of mode IV, and then provide a mode-II tone for *Surgite vigilemus* and other Protus antiphons. This is done quite often; it's the procedure followed in the *Liber*

---

[12]See my "Reconstructing the Repertory of Invitatory Tones in Use at Cluny in the late 11th Century," *Actes du Colloque de Musicologie* (Orléans, September 1982), (Paris, forthcoming).

Responsorialis.[13] But there are other solutions: in the Sarum tonary and antiphonal, tone Q is declared to be of mode I, and reserved for a few antiphons that end on D.[14] Whether these differ consistently—in range, tessitura, formulas—from the antiphons in that repertory that are combined with the mode-II tone would bear investigation.

Tone Q seems to have sounded to some as if it was "in" mode I— perhaps because some of the terminations employed with it came out on D (though of course the ending of the tone is irrelevant when modality is being determined; it's the ending of the antiphon that matters), perhaps because of the traditional connection with *Surgite vigilemus*, perhaps because of the musical figures incorporated in it: the distinctive opening figure of tone Q is like the intonation of the tone for verses of responsories of mode I.

By way of summary, it may be said that whatever the reason may have been for the distinction made between tone P and tone Q, the use of one rather than the other is related to whether a manuscript follows in general the tradition of the East or the West (though there are some exceptions to this). They are so similar that they may be regarded as two versions of a single tone. Tone T is a late creation, like many of the other chants in the manuscript that preserves it. Tones R and S are assigned to *Ipsi vero* in repertories where the use of tone Q has been curtailed, probably because of the theoretical problems that could not be resolved as long as tone Q continued to be sung with antiphons of both Deuterus and Protus. Tones R and S are both substitutes for tone Q; it's no accident that both of them end on E.

New tones were composed for the invitatory as enrichments of worship; composing one of them was like preparing a new design for a vestment, sketching a plan for a capital, working with color, light, and symbols to create a stained glass window. But if a musical composition is to endure as a work of art it must constantly be re-created in performance. Every new liturgical chant, every new melody for an established text had to have a place made for it in a repertory.

As long as the tradition of office chants was maintained orally, its size had to be limited (obviously) to what could be remembered. The development of the liturgical book (in the 10th century) profoundly affected not only the manner of transmission and preservation of the repertory, but also the repertory itself. For when a written tradition could be relied upon to aid the singers' recollections, their repertory could be significantly enlarged.

---

[13]In *Revue du chant grégorien* IV (1895-96), 146, J. Pothier observed that the *Directorium chori* published by Pustet in 1889 had adopted the mode-I classification for tone Q, and called this "une confusion . . . grave. Elle consiste à donner le chant du psaume *Venite* finissant en d (ré), comme étant du premier mode, tandis qu'en réalité il est du quatrième."

[14]"The Sarum Use reckoned as belonging to the First Mode a Tone and a group of Invitatories, which elsewhere, and more properly, were ascribed to the Fourth. Following the classification given in the Sarum Tonal, we have eight invitatories assigned to the First Mode; and there is an extra one for S. Augustine included in this MS. None of these figure in the older collections; they seem to be an English group: but even so, the English books are not uniform. The Hereford Tonal gives the Tone under the First Mode, with a warning that *quidam imperiti* ascribe it to the Fourth." (W. H. Frere, Introduction to *Antiphonale Sarisburiense* [London, 1901-24], I, 62.)

Writing down the repertory required a close examination of the melodies, an understanding of their character. If analysis and, especially, organization of material aids in its memorization, it is even more necessary when a large body of works is committed to writing for the first time ever. In some of the early office antiphonals one finds such an abundance of chants that it seems the editors and scribes have been caught up in a euphoria of collecting. The large collections of invitatory tones in Toledo 44.2 and St. Gall 390-391 are examples of such lush, even overgrown repertories. How many of these invitatory tones were really in active use? How many of them were known well by the monks or clerics of the institutions whose uses these manuscripts are supposed to represent? Though definite answers to such questions are scarcely to be hoped for, the questions are nonetheless worth asking; for from the time of invention of the liturgical book to the time when printing made it possible for every monk or cleric to have a notated book of his own in his hands whenever he took part in the service of Matins, the chant tradition continued to depend on the ability (and the willingness) of such individuals to memorize whatever they would be expected to sing in that service on a particular day. The tradition was not exclusively written, but oral as well.

Many of the invitatory tones that seem to have been later additions to the basic repertory did not survive for very long in the combined oral-written tradition; they appear in only a few manuscripts, and there are few sources of the 13th century and later that contain any tones other than the most familiar ones. But the existence of such tones, even for a relatively short time, gives us an insight into the character of worship in the 11th century, and the role of music in it.

In some early accounts of Christian psalmody what one finds emphasized is the length of time occupied in psalmody, and the number of psalms that are said. It is not the words of the psalms, or the thoughts to which these give rise, to which attention is given; the emphasis is on endurance, almost as it might be in accounts of physical feats. As long as this emphasis persisted, any artistic development of melodies for the psalms is hard to imagine. But when it began, it marked a significant change. It is an important milestone in the development of religious art, the moment at which music begins to be employed in enhancing worship.

As recent experiments have shown, Christian worship can take place accompanied by almost any kind of music imaginable. What is really exceptional is for there to be no music at all. For centuries, composers have found it challenging to take texts well established in the liturgy and write new music for them that would enrich their functioning. The tones for the Palm Sunday invitatory are a part of that history.

Catholic University of America

APPENDIX

Arras, Bibliothèque muncipale, 465.
Breviary of Saint-Vaast (Arras), 13th century.
See V. Leroquais, *Les Bréviaires manuscrits des bibliothèques publiques de France* (Paris, 1934), I, 53-54.

Florence, Arcivescovado, s. c.
Antiphonal, Florence cathedral, 12th century.
See M. Huglo, *Les Tonaires* (Paris, 1971), p. 186 (where further bibliographical references are given).

Karlsruhe, Badische Landesbibliothek, Aug. LX.
Antiphonal, perhaps from Reichenau; most of its original 12th-century notation has been replaced by German Gothic notation of the 13th or 14th century.
For a description, further bibliography, and a color facsimile of one opening, see Bruno Stäblein, *Schriftbild der einstimmigen Musik* (Musikgeschichte in Bildern, III, Lfg. 4; Leipzig, 1975), pp. 194-95.

London, British Library, add. 52359.
Breviary from Penwortham Priory, Evesham, early 14th century.
See D. H. Turner, "The Penwortham Breviary," *British Museum Quarterly* XXVIII (1964), 85-88.

Paris, Bibliothèque de l'Arsenal, 279.
Breviary of Bayeux, second half or end of the 13th century.
See Leroquais, Vol. II, pp. 334-38.

Paris, Bibliothèque nationale, lat. 1030.
Breviary of Beauvais (summer only), 13th century.
See Leroquais, Vol. III, pp. 14-16.

Piacenza, Biblioteca capitolare, 65.
Liber Officiorum (a full set of notated liturgical books copied into a single volume) begun in 1142.
See Fr. Bussi, *L'Antifonario-graduale della Basilica di S. Antonino in Piacenza, sec. XII: saggio storico critico* (Piacenza, 1977); and Huglo, p. 174, where further bibliography is given.

St. Gall, Stiftsbibliothek, 390-391.
Antiphonal of St. Gall, copied ca. 1000.
Facsimile edition in *Paléographie musicale*, ser. 2, I (rev. ed.; Berne, 1970). Contents are surveyed in *Corpus antiphonalium officii*, II; texts are edited in III and IV of the same work.

Toledo, Biblioteca capitular, 44.1.
Antiphonal from Aquitaine, 11th century.
See D. Raymond Le Roux, "Les Répons 'De Psalmis' pour les Matines de l'Épiphanie à la Septuagésime," *Études grégoriennes* VI (1963), 46.

Toledo, Biblioteca capitular, 44.2.
Antiphonal from Aquitaine, 11th century.
See Le Roux, p. 46; M. Huglo, "Les Livres liturgiques de la Chaise-Dieu. II: Analyse des livres liturgiques casadéens," *Revue bénédictine* LXXXVII (1977), 338, 343 note bb. In *Corpus antiphonalium officii* V,

p. 346, Hesbert refers to it as "un antiphonaire du XIIe siècle, conservé au Chapitre de la Cathédrale de Tolède, . . . qui vraisemblablement est de Tolède même." If the judgement is to be made on the basis of its musical notation, the manuscript should be dated in the 11th century rather than the 12th; the St. Geraldus whose feast is observed on 13 October is not—as a note in the manuscript says—a 12th-century chaplain of Toledo, but rather Gerald of Aurillac, who died in 909, and whose biography, written by Odo of Cluny, is the source of texts for chants in his office.

Verdun, Bibliothèque municipale, 128.

Antiphonal from Saint-Vanne (Verdun), 13th century.

See *Catalogue générale des manuscrits des bibliothèques publiques des départements* V (1879), 497-98.

Worcester, Cathedral Library, F. 160.

Antiphonal, processional, hymnal, gradual, etc., of Worcester Cathedral, ca. 1230.

Facsimile edition of the antiphonal in *Paléographie musicale*, XII (Solesmes, 1922).

III

Local and Regional Traditions of the Invitatory Chant

Any study of the Divine Office is a study of local and regional traditions. Nothing could have made this clearer than *Corpus Antiphonalium Officii*, a work of the late Dom René-Jean Hesbert in which the contents of twelve medieval antiphonals are compared, six of them of the Roman cursus and six of the monastic.[1] Dom Hesbert intended this work to provide the basis for a reconstruction of the archetype; and he devised a way of calculating on a computer what the oldest chants were, and their original arrangement.

But the tool that he invented has other uses. It is indispensable as a reference in identifying, in any Office manuscript, those chants that may be of local origin, and those that may belong to a regional tradition. With it as a starting point one can extend comparisons to additional sources. In beginning work on the tones and antiphons of the invitatory, I took each of the antiphon texts edited by Hesbert and put it on a separate card, and then added the melody from a source with staff notation. The plan was to draw up a list of concordances for invitatory antiphons comparable to that prepared by Prof. Schlager for Alleluias of the Mass.[2] The work is still in its early stages; microfilms of additional sources continue to be added to the collection at the Catholic University of America, and it will be some years before all of the analysis is complete.[3]

[1] *Corpus Antiphonalium Officii* is a work in six volumes; of these, the first two outline the contents of the twelve manuscripts in parallel columns; the next two contain an edition of all the chant texts (Rome: Herder, 1963—79). Among the twelve manuscripts are several of the oldest antiphonals; others were chosen to represent the practice of various regions.

[2] Karlheinz Schlager, *Thematischer Katalog der ältesten Alleluia-Melodien* (Munich: Walter Ricke, 1965). Schlager made complete inventories of the Alleluias in 120 sources and consulted a number of others. His thematic catalogue is an outstanding contribution to chant research, one that has stood up very well under the test of time.

[3] The financial support of the Dom Mocquereau Foundation, which has furthered the development of the microfilm collection over the past decade, facilitated the acquisition of a computer terminal and related equipment, and made possible my travel to this meeting, is hereby acknowledged with gratitude. For the first published results of this

III

Local and Regional Traditions

As one glances through the comparative tables in volumes I and II of *Corpus Antiphonalium Officii*, it is immediately apparent that there are only a few invitatory antiphons that were sung everywhere on a certain feast. (In this respect, the situation is almost entirely different from what we find, for example, in connection with the Introits of the Mass.)[4] In the twelve antiphonals surveyed in that work, there are 186 different invitatory antiphon texts; in the first dozen or so manuscripts consulted in the course of the present study approximately 85 additional antiphons were found. For perhaps 25 of these antiphon texts there is more than one melody.[5] On only a very few feasts is the choice of antiphon fixed. Those for which all the manuscripts agree include Christmas, Palm Sunday, Easter Monday, Ascension, Pentecost, Purification, and Trinity — though this last is a late feast, and represents a different set of circumstances than the rest. The invitatory antiphons in the Ferial Office are relatively stable, undergoing only minor rearrangements.[6]

The manuscripts differ not only in their selection of antiphons but also in the assigning of those antiphons to specific days. For the Sundays beginning with Septuagesima and continuing through Lent, antiphons on texts from the invitatory psalm itself are preferred; but they appear in a different order from one source to another. There is so little consistency that reconstruction of any "original" series seems out of the question. For Advent the picture is even more complicated, for here there is a wider choice of antiphons. For the four Sundays of Advent, only four antiphons are needed, of course; but in the twelve sources surveyed in *Corpus Antiphonalium Officii* there are twelve different antiphons. It is difficult to imagine any way in which an "original series" could have undergone so much "corruption": what seems more likely is that there was once a common antiphon for Advent Sundays, and that the introduction of individual proper antiphons did not take place until a relatively late date, and on a more or less local initiative. There are no

---

research, see "Tones for the Palm Sunday Invitatory," *The Journal of Musicology*, III (1984), 142—56, and "Reconstructing the Repertory of Invitatory Tones and Their Uses at Cluny in the Late 11th Century," *Musicologie médiévale: Notations-Séquences. Actes de la Table Ronde du CNRS à l'IRHT, Orléans-La Source, 6—7 septembre 1982* (Paris: Éditions du CNRS, forthcoming).

[4] The high degree of uniformity in contents among Mass manuscripts, including even the very earliest of them, was demonstrated by Hesbert in *Antiphonale Missarum Sextuplex* (Brussels, 1935; reprinted Rome: Herder, 1967).

[5] In *Corpus Antiphonalium Officii* (hereinafter abbreviated *CAO*) no distinction is made between chants with different melodies, only those with different texts.

[6] The invitatory antiphon assigned to Thursday in some manuscripts is set on Friday in others, and vice versa; see *CAO*, vols. I and II. There are further differences in the ferial antiphon series of the Beneventan sources.

proper invitatory antiphons for Advent in the 11th-century antiphonal of Lyon (Lyon, Bibl. mun., 537); and Saint-Denis never participated fully in this development: even as late as the 12th century it had not acquired a complete series of Advent antiphons.[7]

Invaluable as Hesbert's work is, it offers only indirect assistance to the musicologist who undertakes comparative studies of the tones to which the invitatory psalm was chanted in connection with the various antiphons. Here the models must be the analyses by Wagner, of the tones of a 13th-century antiphonal "secundum consuetudinem curiae romanae" in the Munich Franziskanerbibliothek, and by Frere, of the antiphons and tones of the Sarum rite.[8] Stenzl's overview of the invitatory tones in the manuscripts of Sitten is instructive, and helps to demonstrate that one may find in each ecclesiastical center a distinctive tradition of invitatory tones;[9] one can never anticipate quite what it will be.

The distinctive roles assigned to certain chants in some manuscripts are differently assigned in others. The tone that at Cluny was sung on Sundays and many feast days with a variety of mode-4 antiphons (and even with some of mode 2) was at Worcester restricted to a single antiphon and with it sung on many Sundays through the year — those after Epiphany and after Pentecost — with no alternative being offered. This may be a hint that they once formed part of a Common for Sundays in institutions other than Worcester.

There is no question of the tone for Christmas; it is the same in every source. A thematic link connects it and the single antiphon melody with which it is combined. On Christmas the antiphon text begins, "Christus natus est nobis", on Epiphany, "Christus apparuit nobis". Use of this tone in any other season of the year is quite rare. In a few sources that preserve the old tradition of bidding farewell to the Alleluia on Septuagesima — among them the Antiphonal of St. Éloi of Noyon and the Saint-Denis Antiphonal — the fourfold Alleluia that serves as text for the invitatory antiphon on that day is sung

---

[7] The antiphonal of that period (Paris, B. n., lat. 17296) makes no change in the scheme outlined in the list of incipits in the 11th-century source Paris, Bibl. Mazarine, 384, in which the antiphon of the first Sunday is repeated on the second, and a similar procedure is followed on Sundays III and IV.

[8] Peter Wagner, *Einführung in die gregorianischen Melodien, III: Gregorianische Formenlehre* (Leipzig, 1921; reprinted Hildesheim: Olms, 1962), pp. 176—187; W. H. Frere, *Antiphonale Sarisburiense* (London: Plainsong & Mediaeval Music Society, 1901—24). Frere's comments in the introduction (pp. 62—4) to the facsimile edition (principally of the late 13th-century Barnwell Antiphonal, Cambridge, University Library, MM ii 9) take into account indications given in the Sarum Tonal, which he edited in *The Use of Sarum*, II (Cambridge: At the University Press, 1901), pp. i-lxxvi.

[9] Jürg Stenzl, *Repertorium der liturgischen Musikhandschriften . . ., Band I: Diözese Sitten* (Freiburg, Schweiz: Universitätsverlag, 1972), p. 187.

to the melody of "Christus natus est nobis".[10] Presumably, the Christmas tone joined it on that day. And in a comparably small group of sources, the antiphon for the feast of the Invention of St. Stephen, on August 3, is "In inventione corporis protomartyris Stephani", an adaptation of "Christus natus est nobis" with which, one assumes, the Christmas tone was combined.[11]

As the way in which the tones are employed varies from one source to another, so does the number of tones. Certain tones that one might have thought of as standard are absent from some sources — the tone for antiphons of mode 2, and one for antiphons of mode 4 on which Wagner focused his attention, using it in a musical example intended to demonstrate the characteristics of invitatory tones in general.[12] What tones were included in the earliest repertory; at what date did the various additions to it take place? The number of invitatory tones in manuscripts of the 11th and 12th centuries varies widely, in such a way as to invite attempts at a chronological ordering of them. But apart from Wagner's observation that the tone for Mondays, for which the antiphon consists of the first three words of the psalm, is one for which attempts at establishing an early date had been made,[13] published estimates of the relative dates of composition of the invitatory tones have not come to my attention. The smallest repertory I have encountered is that of a manuscript from Vallombrosa, Florence, Bibl. Laur., Conv. soppr. 560, in which no tones are written out. The musical incipits over the word "Venite" following the antiphons refer to only seven different tones: the ferial tone, the tone for Mondays, a tone for antiphons of modes 2 and 4 on Sundays and feast days, the Christmas tone, and tones for antiphons of modes 3, 5, and 7.

The largest collections known to me are those of Hartker (15 tones, to which 3 were later added)[14] and of an 11th-century Aquitanian antiphonal,

---

[10] See *Paléographie musicale*, XVI (Solesmes: Abbaye Saint-Pierre, 1955), facsimile, fol. 71ʳ; and Paris, Bibl. nat., lat. 17296, fol. 85ʳ.
[11] Among the sources that include this antiphon are Bamberg, Staatsbibliothek, lit. 25, fol. 81ᵛ; Stuttgart, Landesbibliothek, HB I 55, fol. 119; and Graz, Universitätsbibliothek, 211, fol. 107 (facsimile in *Codex Albensis: Ein Antiphonar aus dem 12. Jahrhundert*, ed. Z. Falvy and L. Mezey [Budapest: Akadémiai Kiadó, 1963]).
[12] Wagner, p. 185.
[13] Wagner writes, "Man ist versucht, diese Formel wegen ihrer Regellosigkeit in eine ganz alte Zeit zurückzuversetzen. Vergebens wird man aber auch bei den anderen Psalmformeln nach einer Regel suchen, welche die Auswahl der Tenores bestimmt hätte" (p. 182).
[14] There is a facsimile edition of this manuscript, Sankt Gallen, Stiftsbibliothek, 390−391, in *Paléographie musicale* 2, II (Solesmes: Imprimerie Saint-Pierre, 1900). A leaf is missing from the section devoted to invitatory tones, but the series can be completed on the basis of a later copy, Sankt Gallen, Stiftsbibliothek, 388. See the introduction by Jacques Froger to the reprint of the facsimile (Berne: Herbert Lang, 1970), p. 14*.

Toledo, Bibl. cap., 44.2 (22 tones, of which the last is incomplete, suggesting that others may have followed it in the series).[15] Some of the tones in the Toledo manuscript are clearly intended as substitutes, as novelties for the enhancement of worship on major feasts. But there are also some with distinctive liturgical roles.

Such is the case with one of the tones provided by Hartker, for which a concordance in staff notation exists in the antiphonal Karlsruhe, Badische Landesbibliothek, Aug. LX. This tone is for use on the Monday, Tuesday, and Wednesday of Holy Week, with three antiphons on texts from the invitatory psalm which are all sung to the same simple melody. The presence of these antiphons in other sources implies use of the tone as well, even when its incipit does not accompany the antiphons.[16] The association of this tone with one particular liturgical season is striking, as is the fact that it was unknown in many regions. A manuscript that includes it seems likely to adhere in other respects to a broad tradition shared by manuscripts from what was at one time the East Frankish Empire. What are the other characteristics of such manuscripts? Certainly their notation; also their repertories of antiphons, and in a few instances the readings they give for specific antiphons.

Let me give a single example of the last. One of the antiphons that is very commonly sung on one or another of the Sundays of Lent is "Populus Domini et oves pascuae eius, venite adoremus eum".[17] It resembles other antiphons for Lent in that its text is based on that of the invitatory psalm, and its melody is in mode 7. Indeed one form in which the melody of this antiphon is given is an adaptation of the melody employed for two other Lenten antiphons, "Quoniam Deus magnus Dominus", and "Praeoccupemus faciem Domini". It appears in several sources from Italy.[18] A second version of the melody goes one note higher on the words "et oves", and leaps up a fifth at the beginning of the word "adoremus". This is the reading found at

---

[15] An edition of these tones with commentary is currently in preparation.

[16] The tone is written out in the following sources: Karlsruhe, Badische Landesbibliothek, Aug. LX, fol. 258ᵛ; Graz, Universitätsbibliothek, 29, fols 375ᵛ−376; Munich, Bayerische Staatsbibliothek, Clm. 5539, fols. 22−22ᵛ; Bamberg, Staatsbibliothek, lit. 22; Monza, Bibl. cap., 12/75, fol 93ᵛ. The Codex Albensis is among those in which its use is implied.

[17] The text is edited by Hesbert in *CAO*, vol. III, 1113, where variant readings are cited.

[18] Some examples are Piacenza, Bibl. cap., 65; Lucca, Bibl. cap., 601; Lucca, Bibl. cap., 603; Florence, Bibl. Laur., Conv. soppr. 560 (from Vallombrosa). Other manuscripts that contain this reading of the melody are Worcester, Cathedral Library, F. 160; Arras, Bibl. mun., 465 (from Saint-Vaast); Paris, Bibl. nat., 17296 (from Saint-Denis); the antiphonal of Saint-Éloi of Noyon *(Paléographie musicale,* XVI), and Vienna, Oesterreichische Nationalbibliothek, 1799**.

Bamberg and Klosterneuburg, in Hartker's antiphonal, and — for another example — in the Codex Albensis.[19] In the third version of the antiphon the text ends, "venite adoremus": this is found at Monte Cassino and in several sources from France.[20]

[19] Other sources include Karlsruhe, Badische Landesbibliothek, Aug. LX, and several from northern France: Cambrai, Bibl. mun., C38 (40), Rouen, Bibl. mun., A 261 (244) (from Fécamp). It also appears in a manuscript of the Sarum rite (London, B. L., Add. 52359), in one from Saint-Maur-des-Fossés (Paris, Bibl. nat., lat 12044) and one from Troyes (Troyes, Bibl. mun., 571; from Saint-Loup).

[20] Among them are a later manuscript of Saint-Loup, Troyes, Bibl. mun., 720; also Paris, Bibl. nat., 15181 (from Paris); and Valenciennes, Bibl. mun., 114 (from Saint-Amand).

That there were regional (rather than purely local) traditions in the repertory of antiphons and tones for the invitatory chant is evident in the choice of antiphons for certain feasts. For the feast of St. Stephen, most manuscripts from France and Italy give the antiphon, "Christum natum, qui beatum hodie coronavit Stephanum, venite adoremus". It is a mode-4 chant of which the melody was employed in at least one adaptation. Some East Frankish sources give a different antiphon, "Regem protomartyris Stephani venite adoremus Dominum Jesum Christum", on a melody derived in part from "Hodie si vocem eius", an antiphon for Lent or Passion Sunday.[21] Other chants for this feast are unica, or given in a very small number of sources. It is remarkable that the compilers of certain sources seem to wish to identify with both of the main traditions, giving both "Christum natum" and "Regem protomartyris", one after the other; that practice is followed in Udine, Bibl. Arcivescovile, 84, and in the Codex Albensis. On the feast of St. Lawrence, Udine again gives a choice, "Venite adoremus Regem regum", preferred by the East Frankish sources, and "Beatus Laurentius Christi martyr", found in Worcester, Cambrai, Arras, and Cluny. A third antiphon for this day, "Regem sempiternum", was chosen by Sarum, Paris, and various other sources; still other antiphons had a more limited circulation. In this instance, the Codex Albensis unites in its choice with the East Frankish manuscripts.

It might be possible one day to draw up a list of those antiphons that are characteristic of one region, and those of another, along with their liturgical roles, in such a way that it could be used as an aid in determining the region of which the tradition was most clearly reflected in a source at hand. The feasibility of this remains to be determined. What is truly striking about the repertories of antiphons for the invitatory is the extent to which, and the ways in which, manuscripts of the same general region differ. A comparison of the 12th-century antiphonals of Saint-Denis and Saint-Maur-des-Fossés shows that although they agree in the antiphons they give for the feast of St. Stephen, they differ in many other ways — in the way in which they present the notation for the invitatory tone, in the choice of tone on one day after another, as in the choice of antiphon. There are comparable differences between Sarum and Worcester: once again, it is not simply repertory, but the principles governing the association of tones, antiphons, and feasts that are involved. Thus the tone which at Worcester was combined with a single mode-4 antiphon for Sundays through the year was at Sarum used only with antiphons classified in mode 1 — a miscellaneous group of relatively late chants.[22]

---

[21] For a partial list of concordances, see *CAO* III.

[22] See Frere's comments concerning this group of antiphons in his Introduction to *Antiphonale Sarisburiense*, I, 62.

III

On Advent Sundays, different antiphons were sung at Worcester and Sarum, and with them, different tones. A lacuna prevents us from knowing the Worcester series in full; the two sources may have two antiphons in common for Advent Sundays, but in any case their use is different. For the Fourth Sunday of Advent, Sarum gives "Praestolantes Redemptorem", an antiphon in mode 7 which I thought an unicum, a chant sung exclusively at Sarum, until I realized that it is in that remarkable series of invitatory antiphons that the Codex Albensis provides for week days following that same Sunday.[23]

Identifying a chant as an unicum requires knowing accurately the sources from which it is absent. Precision and patience are prime requisites for such work; and hence incorporating the resources of the computer into the project will add significantly to the possibility of its completion. Yet the study of local and regional chant traditions, like that of the broader tradition, is not without its own rewards. As Leroquais wrote, "Gardez-vous de plaindre ceux qui dressent des catalogues de manuscrits: ce sont les plus fortunés des mortels" — "Don't let yourself feel sorry for those who catalogue manuscripts: they are the happiest of mortals".[24] All of us who work on chant are, in the nice Latin phrase of Father Radó, and in one way or another, "vestigia Leroquais sequentes"[25] — following Leroquais' footsteps, enjoying the rewards he described so vividly even as we struggle to perpetuate in our own work the principles and the rigor of his scholarship.

We have an advantage over many others who work in manuscript studies: the possibility of turning away from the data to the music itself, in its renewed existence, and experiencing that in the context of our own artistic and religious life. We thank our hosts for their extending to us this opportunity to share in their intellectual, cultural, and religious heritage.

[23] In his study of the "Text- und Schriftgeschichte" of the Codex Albensis, p. 36, L. Mezey called attention to these invitatory antiphons. "Praestolantes Redemptorem" is sung on Monday; the others are as follows: Tuesday, [CAO 1165] "Surgite vigilemus venite"; Wednesday, "Emanuel iam prope"; Thursday, [CAO 1164]; "Surgite vigilemus quia"; Friday, [CAO 1182] "Vigilate animo." Among the manuscripts that contain comparable series of invitatory antiphons in the fourth week of Advent are Klosterneuburg, Chorherrenstift, 1013; Lucca, Bibl. capitolare, 603; and Rome, Bibl. Vallicelliana, C 5.

[24] Victor Leroquais, Les Bréviaires manuscrits des bibliothèques publiques de France (Paris: [Mâcon: Protat frères, imprimeurs] 1934), Vol. I, p. i.

[25] D. Polycarpus Radó, O. S. B., Libri liturgici manuscripti bibliothecarum Hungariae et limitropharum regionum (Budapest: Akadémiai Kiadó, 1973), 13.

IV

RECONSTRUCTING THE REPERTORY OF INVITATORY TONES AND THEIR USES AT CLUNY IN THE LATE 11TH CENTURY[1]

The invitatory chant presented in manuscripts of the eleventh century consists of a musical setting of psalm 94, in which the text is divided into five sections, each of which is chanted to the same formula — the invitatory tone. The doxology, chanted to the invitatory tone, makes up the sixth section. There is also an invitatory antiphon, a chant constructed in such a way that its last section can be used independently as a refrain. The antiphon is sung at the beginning, and then in full or in part after each of the sections of the psalm and the Gloria patri. A complete performance of the invitatory psalm in this fashion requires from six to ten minutes[2].

What is the relationship of the invitatory tones to the other tones to which psalm verses are chanted — the psalm tones, tones for the verses of introits, of responsories, and so on ? Is the choice of an invitatory tone, in a particular instance, determined by the mode of the antiphon (as is the case with the psalm tone and the introit tone), or is there some other basis for the choice ? I wish to show how in certain manuscripts, including the one under consideration here today, it is the character of the feast that determines which invitatory tone is to be employed ; and the antiphons are in many cases little more than accessories to the tones. This is of course not a new discovery — we have always known, for example, that there was a ferial tone for the invitatory. But the details of the system deserve our attention.

Though invitatory tones are written out in some manuscripts, this is not the case in lat. 12601 ; they are indicated through incipits that follow the antiphons when those are given in their place in the Office. These incipits then serve as the signs by which the system can be reconstructed. Because signs are involved (in the form of the musical notation of the incipits) and the study of the signs is carried out for the purpose of understanding the system conveyed by them, this work is a kind of semiological research, though not in the sense in which Dom Cardine employed the term.

Reconstructing the system of tones requires going through the manuscript page by page noting down every invitatory antiphon and the musical incipit for the tone to be sung with it, in effect compiling a tonary. There are seven tones in all sup-

IV

plied in the principal hand(s) of the manuscript. (See table I). There is one for Monday, and one for all the other week days. There are three for use on Sundays through the summer : of these, one appears only in this role, another has only one additional use – on the Dedication of a Church – but the third recurs again and again, on many saints' days through the summer, in various commons, and on Trinity.

The other invitatory tones that are called for have a very limited use : one is sung on the feasts of St. Michael the Archangel and St. John the Baptist ; the other is sung only on the feast of SS Peter and Paul. (The same antiphon is sung on the feast of St. Andrew, but there the tone is different). Thus if at Cluny during the summer one heard the words of the invitatory psalm sung to the tone represented here, one would know what day it was, whether or not one could distinguish the words of the antiphon – a remarkable instance of music itself serving as a sign.

There is at least one medieval source that speaks of invitatory tones in these terms, associating each with the day or days on which it is to be sung, without bringing in antiphons except in passing. It is the Sarum tonary ; but there the primary organization is by mode – every invitatory tone is assigned to a mode[3] – while in our list of the Cluny tones, mode has not been mentioned. There is a reason for this : invitatory tones and antiphons are governed by their own systems of organization, which vary from one ms. to another. Some of these are worked out so that they complement the system of the ecclesiastical modes ; others are at odds with it. For example, for several of the invitatory tones there is only one antiphon melody : antiphon combines with tone not because they are of the same mode but because they were composed as parts of single whole[4]. There are still other invitatory tones – and one in particular – with which, in some monasteries and cathedrals, antiphons of different modes were combined.

How does the system of invitatory tones at Cluny compare with those of other institutions ? The Worcester antiphonal[5] is one of those manuscripts that write out invitatory tones in full : we find there a tone whose incipit matches that of the one used again and again on summer feasts at Cluny[6]. But in the Worcester antiphonal, its use is limited to a single antiphon, for Sundays through the year, for which no other tone is given : there are just two references to the tone, one on the Sunday « Domine ne in ira », the other on the Sunday « Deus omnium »[7]. On summer Sundays at Worcester, then, one sang always the same antiphon and tone ; at Cluny there was a choice – three different tones, and for two of them a choice of antiphons. In both music and text these antiphons are suitable for any one of these Sundays ; their texts are all excerpts from or adaptations of the invitatory psalm itself. Certain of the antiphons go with certain tones for musical reasons. Evidently the reason for providing a group of antiphons here is a desire for variety, a kind of richness.

The antiphonals of St. Maur-des-Fossés give the antiphons for Sundays through the year in a manner similar to that of the Cluny ms. : the list is similar, though lat. 12584 has a slightly different selection and omits the incipit for the tone. Lat. 12044 has an additional antiphon, and includes notation of the tone for the first

Table 1

Fer. II	
Fer. III, etc.	
(et in Dedicatione ecclesiae)	
Dom. p. Pent	
(et De Trinitate, in Comm. sanctorum etc.) →	
S. Michaelis, S. Joannis Bapt.	
SS Petri et Pauli	

section of the invitatory psalm[8]. However, for the tone with Adoremus Dominum qui fecit nos it provides only an incipit — presumably that tone has been written out earlier in the book ; since I haven't been able to find it, I presume it was on one of the pages that are now lost[9]. Its use in the earlier antiphonal of St. Maur-des-Fossés parallels its use at Cluny ; the most striking aspect of this is that when the antiphons with which this tone is combined are identified in sources in staff notation, some have the range and ending of chants of mode 4, but others end on D[10]. One example of this can be seen in the choice of antiphons offered for All Saints' Day, both of which in lat. 12584 are sung to the same tone. Regem regum Dominum ends on D in later sources, and In sanctorum sollemnitate, given on the octave in lat. 12044, ends on E.

Further comparison of lat. 12601 and lat. 12584 is hindered by the fact that the latter manuscript often omits the incipit for the tone ; but indications are that the tone that was used so much for saints' days at Cluny was used in a similar way at St. Maur-des-Fossés in the 11th century. The 12th-century antiphonal shows a number of changes[11]. It has several additional tones, one of which is quite distinctive. It is written out on the feast of St. Maur, after the antiphon Regem coelestis gloriae, but a good part of the page has been torn away[12]. Enough remains of the tone to establish that it is the same as one of the invitatory tones of the St. Denis antiphonal, lat. 17296, of which one section is given below in Musical ex. 1. The incipit of this tone appears after a number of antiphons in lat. 12044, indicating that it was sung on many feasts of the sanctorale[13].

An invitatory tone from Paris, B.N., lat. 17296, f. 346v, which resembles the tone given incompletely in lat. 12044, f. 39r

The desire to enrich the repertory is surely one reason for the adoption of new invitatory tones in lat. 12044. But there appears also to have been another : a move to organize the system of invitatory tones and antiphons so that it was more like the system of the ecclesiastical modes. Attempts were made in this direction at St. Maur-des-Fossés (though they were not fully carried out). Thus antiphons that are given with the same tone in the Cluny manuscript and in the earlier antiphonal of St. Maur-des-Fossés are found in the later source with different tones. One of the new tones — associated in other sources with mode 2 — is joined in lat. 12044 only to antiphons ending on D, as in the case of the antiphon Laudemus Deum nostrum, for the Commemoration of St. Paul. Another, said elsewhere to be of mode 4, is used in lat. 12044 for antiphons ending on E, such as Adoremus Regem magnum, for the Invention of St. Stephen. These changes may have been made partly in the interest of musical variety, but they were even more, I suspect, for the sake of modal correctness.

The collections of invitatory tones that one finds in the manuscripts often include the antiphons for each of the tones. Some of these are (or could be) included without any difficult in a tonary of which the basic organization is by mode. Hartker, for example, never mentions mode in connection with invitatory tones, but never mixes antiphons of two different endings for a single tone [14]. By contrast, there is a question concerning mode in the mind of the compiler of the tonary of invitatories of Karlsruhe, Aug. LX ; he observes, « Quod hec invitatoria quarti toni iunguntur huic psalmo primi // usui potius asscribendum est quam rationi » : « The fact that these invitatories of the 4th mode are joined to this psalm [formula] of the first // is to be attributed to custom rather than to reason » [15].

The tonary of lat. 776 deals with the problem of mode in another way [16] : the tone we have discussed so much is given under mode 4 (along with the Christmas and the Monday invitatory tones), but the list of antiphons that precedes it reveals its true nature — along with the mode-4 antiphons are antiphons that end on D in sources with clefs or staff notation. They include Surgite vigilemus and Adoremus Christum. This brings the present discussion back almost to where it began — with a list of antiphons with which one particular tone is to be sung, not a list of antiphons of one mode or another.

How much, and in what ways, does an invitatory tone serve as a sign of the day — the liturgical day — on which it is sung ? How much does the invitatory have in common with those Ordinary chants for which the melodies change according to the character of the feast ? How much, and in what ways, does the antiphon contribute to the meaning of the invitatory as a whole ? Can we, in short, think of the music of the invitatory tones as a semiological system ? Can semiology help us to understand invitatory tones, why systems of invitatory tones differ as they do ? Certainly there are examples in other semiological systems of elaborations like the ones that have been observed here, and also of applications of ideology to limit them. Standing quite near the beginning of the service of Matins, the invitatory tone is in a position to set the tone — the mood — for the day. Is this a part of what it does ?

NOTES

1. For eight weeks during the summer of 1982, a group of twelve college teachers from all across the United States met at the Catholic University of America to study the manuscript Paris, Bibliothèque nationale, lat. 12601, a summer breviary of Cluny of the late 11th century. Funding for this study was provided by the National Endowment for the Humanities under its Summer Seminars program. The group included specialists in various disciplines outside music – philosophy, theology and liturgy, art history, early English, and anthropology – as well as six musicologists. The purpose of the study was to bring to the participants a better understanding of the medieval liturgy in one of its most fully developed forms, an understanding to be drawn on not only in future research but in teaching as well. The directors of the seminar were Daniel Sheerin and me ; additional guidance was provided by three guest lecturers – John Benton, Giles Constable, and Dom Jean Leclercq.

   Each member of the seminar had two research projects to occupy him – one directly connected to the manuscript itself, the other more or less independent of it. My own work on the manuscript was a continuation of a long-term study of the invitatory chant, a study based on sources available in microfilm in a collection at Catholic University that has been developed with the funding of the Dom Mocquereau Foundation.

2. The fundamental studies of this chant are the following. Dom André Mocquereau, *Le Cursus velox et le cursus planus dans la psalmodie du* Venite exsultemus, in *Paléographie musicale*, IV, Solesmes, Imprimerie Saint-Pierre, 1894, pp. 165-170. Dom P. Ferretti, *L'Esthétique grégorienne*, Paris, Desclée, 1938, pp. 215-243. Peter Wagner, *Einführung in die gregorianischen Melodien*, III : *Gregorianische Formenlehre*, Leipzig, 1921 ; reprinted Hildesheim, Olms, 1962, pp. 176-187, 313-315. W.H. Frere, Introduction to *Antiphonale sarisburiense*, London, Plainsong and Mediaeval Music Society, 1901-1924 ; reprinted in 6 vols., Farnborough, Hants. : Gregg Press, Ltd., 1966, vol. I, pp. 62-64. This essay is based on Frere's knowledge of the Sarum Tonary, which he published in *The Use of Sarum*, II, Cambridge, University Press, 1901, pp. i-lxxxvi, and on his analysis of the antiphons in the Sarum Antiphonal.

3. In its presentation of chants and formulas of mode 4, the Sarum Tonary includes five invitatory tones. Concerning the second of these, it says, « Iste Venite dicitur in festo sancti iohannis apostoli » ; concerning the third, « Istud Venite dicitur in die natalis domini et per octavas epyphanie ». (See *The Use of Sarum*, vol. II, p. xxx).

4. One instance is the invitatory tone generally thought to be of mode 3, and its antiphons. Concerning this, see Dom J. Pothier, *Remarques sur le chant des Invitatoires*, in *Revue du chant grégorien*, IV, 1895-1896, pp. 145-151.

5. Worcester, Cathedral Library, F 160 ; facsimile edition in *Paléographie musicale*, XII, Tournay, Desclée, 1922.

6. *Paléographie musicale*, XII, facsimile, p. 195.

IV

7. *Paléographie musicale*, XII, facsimile, pp. 60, 165.

8. The invitatory antiphons for Sundays through the year in the three manuscripts are as follows : Lat. 12601, f. 207v, [1115] Praeoccupemus faciem Domini, [1124] Quoniam Deus magnus, [1009] Adoremus Dominum, [1066] Dominum qui fecit nos, [1007] Adoremus Deum ; lat. 12584, f. 241r, [1115] Praeoccupemus faciem Domini, [1087] In manu tua, [1009] Adoremus Dominum, [1066] Dominum qui fecit nos, [1007] Adoremus Deum ; lat. 12044, f. 29r, [1115] Praeoccupemus faciem Domini, [1124] Quoniam Deus magnus, [1087] In manu tua, [1066] Dominum qui fecit nos, [1009] Adoremus Dominum, Ploremus coram Domino. (The identifying numbers in this list are taken from *Corpus Antiphonalium Officii*, ed. Dom R.-J. Hesbert, vol. III, Rome, Herder, 1968, as is the normalized spelling of the Latin texts ; but the last of the antiphons is not included there). In lat. 12044, the first two antiphons end on G, and the tone given for them matches what the *Liber Responsorialis*, Solesmes, Imprimerie Saint-Pierre, 1895, p. 24 calls « Tonus 7 ». The next two end on F ; for them « Tonus 5 » is given (*Liber Responsorialis*, p. 19). The melodies for the antiphons written in staff notation in lat. 12044 correspond to those conveyed by the neumes of the other sources, as do the incipits for the invitatory tones.

9. The manuscript now begins part way through the responsory [6408] Descendet Dominus sicut pluvia, which comes at the end of the second nocturne of Matins for the Third Sunday of Advent. Its first three words are lacking.

10. There are correspondences in the incipit and in the use of this tone in other sources, where it is written out, that make possible an identification of it as « Tonus 4 d » of the *Liber Responsorialis* (p. 16).

The following antiphons with which this tone is combined in lat. 12601 end on D in sources with staff notation : [1098] Laudemus Deum nostrum (S. Pauli), [1006] Adoremus Christum Regem (Transl. S. Martini), [1056] Confessorum Regem (Transl. S. Benedicti), [1146] Regem regum Dominum (S. Mauritii, Omnium sanctorum), [1103] Martinus ecce migrat (S. Martini), [1080] Gaudete et exsultate (Octava Apostolorum, Comm. Apostolorum) ; the other antiphons with which this same tone is called for, and which end on E, include [1061] Deum verum unum (De Trinitate), [1015] Adoremus Regem magnum (Inventio S. Stephani), [1177] Venite adoremus Regem (Assumptio S. Mariae), [1137] Regem martyrum (SS Corneli et Cypriani, Comm. plur. Mart., Comm. unius Mart.), [1101] Laudemus Dominum (S. Dionysii), [1096] Justus florebit (S. Clementis), [1051] Christum Regem regum (S. Andreae), [1151] Regem virginum (Comm. Virginum), [1009] Adoremus Dominum (Dom. per annum), [1007] Adoremus Deum (Dom. per annum). (For some of these texts more than one medieval melody exists ; in such cases, the final identified in the preceding list is that of the melody to which the neumes of lat. 12601 correspond).

11. For a fuller comparison of the two sources, see André Renaudin, *Deux antiphonaires de Saint-Maur*, in *Études grégoriennes*, XIII, 1972, pp. 53-[150].

12. Lat. 12044, f. 39r. Regem coelestis gloriae [CAO 1127] is evidently not the original antiphon for this feast, for in lat. 12584 it is written in over an erasure. The original antiphon may have been [1006] Adoremus Christum regem, which is given for St. Maur in the manuscript Chartres, Bibl. mun. 89, f. 182v, shown in facsimile in *Paléographie musicale*, 17, Solesmes, Abbaye Saint-Pierre, 1958. There the tone is the same as that of lat. 12584 – the one in frequent use at Cluny.

13. One of these antiphons ends on D – [1078] Exsultemus Domino (In Dedicatione ecclesiae). The others end on E ; they include [1013] Adoremus Regem (S. Joannis Ev.), [1151] Regem virginum (S. Agathae), [1051] Christum Regem (S. Petri), [1177] Venite adoremus (Assumptio S. Mariae), [1057] Corde et voce (Nativitas S. Mariae), [1051] Christum Regem (S. Andreae), [1017] Adoremus Regem saeculorum (S. Nicolai), and Ut Christo celebri (S. Baboleni).

182

14. St. Gall, Stiftsbibliothek, 390-1 ; facsimile in *Paléographie musicale*, Ser. 2, I, Solesmes, Abbaye Saint-Pierre, 1900, where the invitatory tones begin on pp. 439-245. The order of the modes is not followed in this collection ; the first of the tones is for use with antiphons of mode 4.

15. Fol. 255r. Concerning the date and place of origin of this manuscript, see M. Huglo, *Les Tonaires*, Paris, Heugel, 1971, pp. 243, 255 and B. Stäblein, *Schriftbild der einstimmigen Musik*, Musikgeschichte in Bildern, III, 4, Leipzig, VEB Deutscher Verlag für Musik, 1975, pp. 194-195.

16. Fol. 153v. For a description of this tonary as a whole, see Huglo, pp. 140-144.

V

THE TWENTY-TWO INVITATORY TONES OF THE
MANUSCRIPT TOLEDO, BIBLIOTECA CAPITULAR, 44.2

This preliminary editon of the invitatory tones in a single manuscript is intended as a small but significant element in a large work in progress: CANTUS, a database made up of indices of the chants in manuscript and early printed sources of the Divine Office.[1] The database is distributed primarily in electronic form over the Internet via the Gopher server of the Catholic University of America (vmsgopher.cua.edu), but at present the technology available at that site does not allow musical notation to be included. Thus an opportunity to publish the tones in print is most welcome.

The repertory of invitatory tones in the manuscript Toledo, Biblioteca Capitular, 44.2, dating from the late eleventh or early twelfth century, is quite unusual, and a number of the tones are *unica*.[2] The tones, which come after the chants of the antiphoner at the very end of the manuscript, are written in diastematic Aquitanian notation. After the first few words of each of the sections of the psalm and the Gloria Patri, only the vowels of the text are written, with the alignment of neume and vowel usually exact enough to indicate text underlay clearly.[3] For invitatory tones that can be matched with tones appearing in sources in staff notation, determining the value of the dry-point line presents no problem; but for those that are *unica* it is more difficult. A tone may be associated with antiphons of which the mode is known,[4] and

---

[1] Support for the project has been received from the National Endowment for the Humanities, the Dom Mocquereau Foundation, and the Catholic University of America.

[2] The CANTUS index of this manuscript is available both via the Internet and as a book: Ronald T. Olexy et al., *An Aquitanian Antiphoner: Toledo, Biblioteca capitular, 44.2* (Ottawa: Institute of Mediaeval Music, 1992). Evidence relating to the date and provenance of the source is presented in the introduction.

[3] For a facsimile of part of one page of the manuscript, see my "Tone for the Palm Sunday Invitatory," *Journal of Musicology* 3 (1984): 151.

[4] A primitive database, consisting of several hundred 5x8 cards on each of which is written the text and melody of one invitatory antiphon along with indications of manuscripts in which it appears, was an important resource in the preparation of this study.

V

this removes much—though not always all—of the uncertainty about the value of the dry-point line. For this reason, clefs are absent from the transcriptions presented below. In general, a transposing treble clef may be assumed; but it has seemed preferable not to make the clef explicit.

For some tones that appear in many sources, variants are numerous; and there are also many different procedures in the linking of invitatory tones and antiphons that could be commented upon at great length.[5] Because of limitations of space in the present publication, for tones in the Toledo antiphoner that are available in modern editions there will be no attempt to provide a detailed report of variants. The reader can make his own comparisons of the readings in other editions with those presented here. Some instances of differences in melodic readings reflect the idiom of a chant dialect, to which eleventh- and twelfth-century Aquitanian and Beneventan sources often bear witness, in which reciting occurs on E rather than F, the preferred note in other sources. (This forms a parallel with the use of B for reciting in the psalm tone of mode 3 in a few sources, rather than the C that is generally favored.) For the tones that are *unica* or are found very rarely, brief commentaries will be provided.

Editions of Invitatory Tones

There are very few editions of invitatory tones that specify the sources from which the transcriptions were made. One of the oldest, and still fundamental, is that offered by Peter Wagner in 1921.[6] Both the edition and the commentary that accompanies it are models of presentation, and both remain fundamental to work in this field. Following closely on Wagner (in approach, though not in time) is the doctoral dissertation by Willibrord Heckenbach,[7] which presents the twelve invitatory tones of Codex 2 a/b of the Pfarrarchiv of Ahrweiler, dating from around 1400, on pp. 70-104.[8] The invitatory tones of the antiphoner of Piacenza, Biblioteca capitolare, 65 were published together with the CANTUS index of that source.[9] Those of the antiphoner contained in Worcester, Cathedral Library, F. 160 have not been published in a modern edition but are easily available in facsimile in *Paléographie musicale*.[10]

Editions made for practical use include those of the *Liber usualis*[11] and the *Liber hymnarius*,[12] though the lack of critical commentary for either of these is a serious drawback.

[5] For a graphic representation of the lack of agreement concerning the tones for a small group of antiphons, see *New Grove* (1980), s.v. "Invitatory," 9:287, fig. 1.

[6] Wagner, *Einführung in die gregorianische Melodien*, vol. 3 (Leipzig: O. R. Reisland, 1921), 177-80.

[7] Heckenbach, *Das Antiphonar von Ahrweiler* (Köln: Arno Volk-Verlag, 1971).

[8] I thank Susan Hellauer for a letter about a completely different matter in which she mentioned Father Heckenbach's study. A review of his comments on invitatory tones and antiphons led directly to the preparation of this essay.

[9] Keith Glaeske et al., *Piacenza, Biblioteca capitolare, 65* (A CANTUS Index: Ottawa: Institute of Mediaeval Music, 1993), xiii-xvii. The sigla assigned to the invitatory tones in that publication are employed in the CANTUS database for all sources but Toledo, Biblioteca capitular, 44.2.

[10] (Solesmes: Abbaye Saint-Pierre, 1922), 12:192-99.

[11] *Liber usualis*, with introduction and rubrics in English (citations are to the printing called "No. 801"—Tournai: Desclée, 1950).

[12] *Liber hymnarius cum invitatoriis et aliquibus responsoriis* (Solesmes: Abbaye Saint-Pierre, 1983).

The presentation and discussion of invitatory tones by Paolo Ferretti in *Esthétique grégorienne*[13] is highly stimulating, but seems inappropriate to draw upon in this discussion because of the author's failure to identify the edition he cited and the sources from which it was made.

The Structure of an Invitatory Tone

When it is chanted near the beginning of the service of Matins, the invitatory psalm is divided into five sections, rather than the eleven verses that one finds in the Vulgate. (In similar fashion, the text itself is not exactly that of the Vulgate but — like the texts of many chants — seems to preserve a translation that antedates Jerome's Gallican psalter.) The Doxology follows as a sixth section. Normally each section of the psalm is chanted to a musical formula, or tone, that consists of three periods. Each of the periods, in turn, has a structure like that of a psalm tone.[14] The first period begins with an intonation leading to a reciting tone, which may or may not be ornamented, and then — if the length of the text makes it desirable — to a cadence known as a flex. Reciting resumes, and the end of the first period is marked by a mediant cadence. The procedure is repeated for the second period — that is, there is an initium, reciting, perhaps a flex, and a mediant cadence; and the first and second periods may be identical, quite similar, or (in rare instances) quite different. The third period follows the same general outline, though it has no flex, and it ends in a termination that may be different for odd- and even-numbered sections of the psalm.

One feature of invitatory tones that has always attracted attention is the variety in reciting tones, even within a period. Another is the similarity of musical motives and even general contour between certain invitatory tones and other modal formulas. The most detailed investigation of this aspect of the subject is that of Heckenbach, who shows the similarity between the invitatory tones employed with antiphons of mode 5, 7, and 3 with the tones employed for the verses of responsories of the corresponding modes.[15] Although Ferretti also demonstrated essentially the same similarities, the musical examples from a specific source make Heckenbach's presentation highly persuasive. He also finds a similarity between the tone that comes second in his source (it is also second in the Toledo series, and is known as GR in the CANTUS database) and the formula for reciting in verses of responsories of mode 4.

In contrast to these are certain invitatory tones that resemble psalm tones in their relatively subdued style: prevailingly syllabic text setting even in the initia, no ornamentation of the reciting tone, recurring rather than varied initia, close or even exact repetition of the outline of the first period in the second, occasionally the same reciting tone in all three periods. Examples of these "psalm-tone-like" invitatory tones include the one that is no. 21 in the Toledo series (known as PA in the CANTUS database, which appears as no. 7 in Heckenbach's source); and no. 10 in the Toledo series (2 in the CANTUS database, no. 8 in Heckenbach's source).

---

[13] (Solesmes: Abbaye Saint-Pierre, 1938), 215-43.

[14] Exceptions to this rule will be described below.

[15] Heckenbach, 72, 79, 82.

V

62

In light of the general agreement among scholars about the form of the invitatory tone and the principles according to which texts were set to it, the discovery in the Toledo series of tones that do not follow the established practice was unexpected.[16] For some of them the traditional methods of analysis are clearly inappropriate. All examples of unusual text setting occur in the tones that are either unique to the Toledo manuscript or appear in only one other source, Paris, Bibliothèque Nationale, lat. 1121; and they will be discussed in detail below.

The Invitatory Tones of the Toledo Antiphoner
That Are Rarely Found, or Unica:
Concerning Tones 8, 7, and 1

Tone no. 8 in the Toledo manuscript is preceded by one antiphon fully written out, "Venite omnes christicole," and the rubric "De Sancti Jacobi Vit[atorium]." The antiphon is also found in the office of St. James in the Codex Calixtinus, where it ends on D and is assigned the standard mode-2 tone.[17] The tone given as no. 8 is remarkable in a number of ways: first of all, it is not one tone but two, of which one is used for sections 1, 3, and 5 of the psalm and the other for sections 2, 4, and 6. In section 3, the accommodation of extra text syllables is made in an unusual way: both the first mediant cadence and the intonation of the second period are employed twice. Recitation in this tone is on G and D in the first period, and on D and G in the second.

EXAMPLE 3.1. Tone No. 8.

---

[16] In *Western Plainchant* (Oxford: Clarendon Press, 1993), 67, David Hiley calls attention to the recurrence of a figure in the Saint-Denis version of the invitatory tone for antiphons of mode 3. Because it appears not only at the points where the first and second periods are usually said to end but also early in the first and third periods, "it cannot be regarded as a cadential figure." If it is not a cadential figure, it is not the mediant, and the tone has no mediant cadences. The impact of this on one's understanding of the structure of the tone is considerable. Even though versions in other sources of this tone clearly distinguish the cadential figure from the one that appears earlier in the period, the question posed by Hiley's observation recurs when the tones of the Toledo manuscript are considered.

[17] *Liber Sancti Jacobi: Codex Calixtinus*, vol. 2: *Musica*, ed. Dom German Prado (Santiago de Compostela: n.p., 1944), Lám. V (= f. 105v), p. 14. There is not a full office for St. James in the Toledo antiphoner.

V

EXAMPLE 3.1. — *Continued*

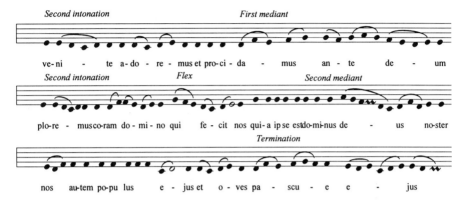

The tone that is employed for alternate sections is also written out by itself as tone no. 7, though with a different intonation. It is characterized by reciting on A in the first and second periods, and in its general line it resembles tone no. 3. Tone no. 7 is also quoted in tone no. 1, in which the six sections of the psalm are set to four different tones. One tone is employed for the even-numbered sections; each of the odd-numbered sections has a tone of its own, with tone no. 7 in the fifth section, once again with a different intonation.

The formula employed in the even-numbered sections of tone no. 1 evidently also existed as an independent tone. Its opening figure is notated over the word "Venite" as the cue for the invitatory tone after three antiphons in the manuscript, all of which end on D: "Nativitatem virginis," "Martinus ecce migrat," and "Adoremus christum regem." The last of these occurs twice in the manuscript — on f. 183r, in the Common of One Confessor, with this tone, and on f. 37r, on the feast of St. Hilarius, with the incipit of tone no. 7.

An unusual matching of text and tone also occurs in the formula employed for the first section of tone no. 1. There the two flexes are identical, as are the two mediant cadences, of which the first occurs early, on "jubilemus deo." This leaves "salutari nostro" without a phrase parallel to it. The ranges of the first and second periods (a ninth, an octave) are remarkable.

The melody employed for the third section of tone no. 1 is unusual. Each of the three periods is arch-shaped, and there is some musical rhyme at the ends of the first two. The flex of the first period resembles that of tone no. 8; but in most ways this melody seems more like a tune than a formula. To summarize: as its first musical setting of the invitatory psalm the Toledo antiphoner offers a medley in which the tone changes from one section to the next.[18] There seems to be no particular uniformity in style among the melodies for the various sections, though it is perhaps not irrelevant that none of them has been found written out in any source.

---

[18] The manuscript Paris, Bibliothèque Nationale, lat. 1030, a thirteenth-century summer breviary from Beauvais, telescopes the presentation of its invitatory tones, which begin on f. 276r. Each time the text of the psalm is written in full, two invitatory tones are given with it — either alternating from section to section, or with one tone in the first three sections replaced by a different one in the remaining three. Because the tones appear in other sources, there is no question about what is intended.

Tones 5, 9, and 6

The tone that comes fifth in the series is employed on three occasions in the liturgical year—the feasts of St. Benedict, All Saints, and the Dedication of a Church, and always with antiphons that end on D. It is not unlike other tones in the formulas it contains, but it is distinctive in the way it matches the formulas to the text. If section 1 is taken as the norm and section 3 is compared to it, it is evident that the figure that should come early in the second period, labelled "B" in the example, has been moved to the first period; and the figure that should mark the beginning of the second half of the first period, "A" in the example, is now at the start of the second period.

EXAMPLE 3.2. Tone No. 5.

In this respect, section 2 follows section 1; section 4, section 3. Section 5 and the Doxology omit figure "B" entirely, but follow section 1 otherwise, though freely. For example, section 5 returns to the opening figure of the tone in the second half of its second period. The flexes, and especially the mediant cadences, are not as fixed as they are in some other tones, and all have the same general contour. In this setting, then, the structure of the psalm has been given a new interpretation. It is still a work in six sections—this is evident in the consistency in the settings of the last part of each section—but the first and second periods of each section are not defined in the traditional way. This tone displays a flexible way of adapting musical formulas to the text that may have characterized other invitatory tones in the period before the oral tradition was codified, regularized, and written down.

The eleventh-century St. Martial troper Paris, Bibliothèque Nationale, lat. 1121 contains another version of the same tone. On f. 175r-v, under the rubric "Vitatorium de Pascha," it has the complete text of the invitatory psalm accompanied by two sets of fairly diastematic neumes, one in brown ink, the other in red. The melody of tone no. 5 is the one written in brown. The incipit is different, but otherwise the formulas are quite similar. However, figure "A" always comes at the beginning of the second half of the first period, except in the Doxology: not only on "jubilemus ei" and "et rex," but also on "et aridam," "nolite," and "generationi." Figure "B" always appears near the beginning of the second period.

EXAMPLE 3.3. Tone No. 5 in Paris, Bibliothèque Nationale, lat. 1121.

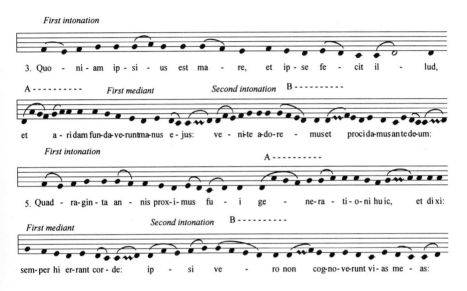

The second of the invitatory antiphons for St. Vincent, "Vincentem mundum," is followed by the incipit of tone no. 1'in the main part of the antiphoner, but at the end of the book it is given as one of the antiphons with which tone no. 9 may be sung. The tone is characterized by reciting on G in the first and second periods, and on D in the third. The mediant cadences are the same; both are on D, the note on which the tone also begins and ends. There are some similarities between this tone and the one that is notated in red on f. 175r-v of lat. 1121; but the similarities do not extend much beyond the first part of the first period. After that point, only a favoring of stepwise movement and generally syllabic style are common traits.

In what now remains of the Toledo manuscript, none of the antiphons is followed by the incipit of tone no. 6, and that tone has no antiphon incipits accompanying it. However, the incipits of tones no. 6 and 7 differ in only one note: an ordinary virga in no. 6, and a symbol for a double note one step higher in no. 7. Hence a transcription of tone no. 6 at the same pitch level as tone no. 7 seems justified. The most striking aspect of tone no. 6 is the way in which it interprets the structure of section 3 of the psalm. "Nos autem populus ejus" is moved to the end of the second period, which is already very long, and "et oves" begins the third. All recitation is on A. The mediants are on similar lines—the first descends a sixth, from B to D; the second, in a greater sweep and with more decoration, from C to C, before returning to D. After the incipit the first period begins like the second, with an outlining of the triad C-E-G.

V

EXAMPLE 3.4. Tone No. 6.

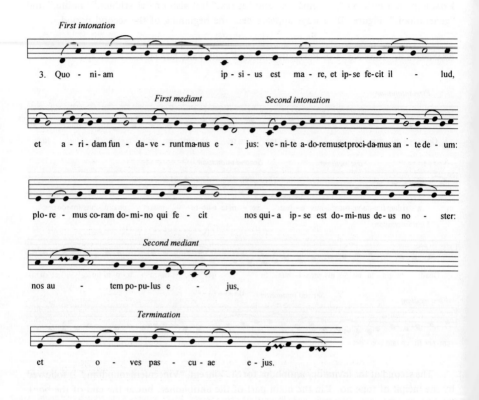

Tone 12

This tone is specified for use with the well-known mode-5 antiphons for Ascension and Pentecost, "Alleluia Christum dominum" and "Alleluia spiritus domini." Its form is unusual: it treats each section of the psalm as if it were in two periods rather than three, and the materials in the formula are applied to the text in such a way that the form of most sections approximates a b a' c. In sections 4 and 5, however, "b" is omitted and the form becomes a a' c. In "b," reciting is on A; in "c," as elsewhere in the tone, on C; otherwise, "b" and "c" are similar. The termination, which quite remarkably echoes the initium, is on F in the odd-numbered sections, otherwise on A.

The contour of the tone is striking: after the opening figure, the line moves from the lower tonic to the upper through a combination of skips, steps, and backtracking. There is a leap down from the fifth above to the tonic at the beginning of "b." Between "b" and "a'" there is a leap up a fifth, then a return to the lower tonic, and then the rise through the octave again in "a'." It seems likely that the B's are to be flatted, though the manuscript does not of course indicate this explicitly.

EXAMPLE 3.5. Tone No. 12.

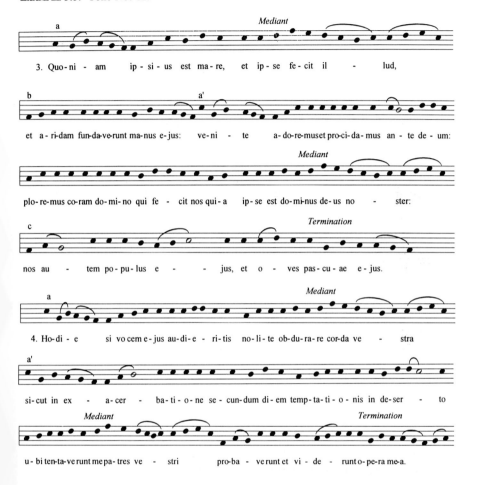

Tone 13

This is among the "tones for the Palm Sunday invitatory" discussed some years ago in an article in the *Journal of Musicology*, [19] and there is little of significance that can be added here to what was said about it then, except perhaps that in more than a decade of exploration of manuscripts of the Divine Office no new source for it has come to light.

But the search continues.

---

[19] See n. 3, above.

EXAMPLE 3.6. Tone Nos. 1-22.

Tone No. 1 **f. 213r-v**

4. is sung to the same formula as 2.

V

Tone No. 1—*Continued*

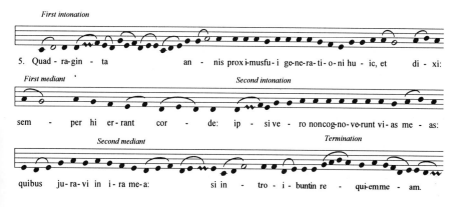

First intonation

5. Quad - ra-gin - ta   an - nis prox i-musfu- i ge-ne-ra-ti- o-ni hu - ic, et   di - xi:

First mediant   *Second intonation*

sem - per hi er-rant   cor - de: ip - si ve - ro noncog-no-ve-runt vi- as me - as:

Second mediant   *Termination*

quibus   ju-ra-vi in i- ra me-a: si in - tro- i- buntin re - qui-emme - am.

6. is sung to the same formula as 2 and 4.

Tone No. 2   f. 213v

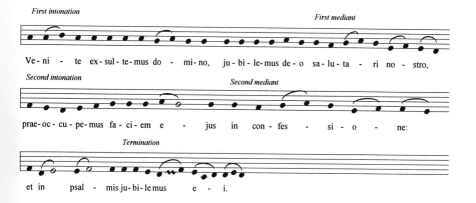

First intonation   *First mediant*

Ve - ni - te ex- sul- te-mus do - mi- no, ju- bi- le-mus de - o sa-lu- ta - ri no - stro,

Second intonation   *Second mediant*

prae-oc- cu- pe-mus fa- ci- em e - jus in con-fes - si - o - ne:

Termination

et in   psal - mis ju- bi- le mus   e - i.

Liber usualis—not included
Liber hymnarius IV*, p. 141 (except for initium)
Wagner (not an exact match, but compare with IV.4, p. 178)
Heckenbach no. 2, p. 75 (except for initium and terminatio)
Ferretti, 4.d, p. 228 (except for initium)
Worcester, p. 195 (except for initium)
CANTUS siglum   GR

Tone No. 3   f. 214r

First intonation   *First mediant*

Ve - ni - te ex - sul - te - mus do - mi - no,   ju - bi- lemus   de - o sa- lu - ta- ri no - stro,

Second intonation   *Second mediant*

prae - oc - cu - pe- mus fa - ci - em e - jus   in con - fes - si - o - ne:

Termination

et in psal - mis ju - bi - le- mus   e - i.

Liber usualis, p. 918
Liber hymnarius IV, p. 138
Wagner IV.3, p. 178
Heckenbach no. 3, p. 77
Ferretti 4.E^2, p. 229
Worcester, p. 194, upper
CANTUS siglum (similar but not identical to the tone called NE)

Tone No. 4   f. 214r

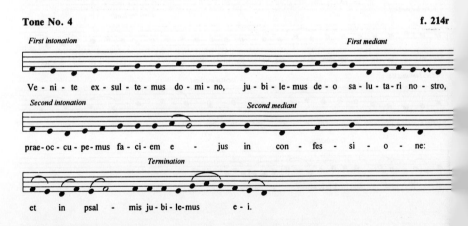

First intonation   *First mediant*

Ve - ni - te   ex - sul - te - mus do - mi - no,   ju - bi - le- mus de - o   sa - lu - ta- ri no - stro,

Second intonation   *Second mediant*

prae- oc - cu - pe- mus fa - ci - em e   -   jus   in   con - fes - si - o - ne:

Termination

et   in   psal - mis ju - bi - le- mus   e - i.

Liber usualis — not included
Liber hymnarius — not an exact match (but compare IV* ad lib., p. 144)
Wagner — not included
Heckenbach — not included
Ferretti — not an exact match (but compare 4.E, p. 229)
Worcester — not included
CANTUS siglum (similar but not identical to the tone called RE)

Tone No. 5

Tone No. 6 f. 215r

Tone No. 7 f. 215r

V

Tone No. 8

First intonation   *First mediant*

Veni - te   ex sul-te-mus do - mi - no, ju - bi - le - mus de - o sa - lu - ta - ri no - stro,

Second intonation   *Second mediant*

prae - oc - cu - pe - mus fa-ci - em e - jus in con - fes - si - o - ne:

Termination

et   in psal - - mis ju - bi - le - mus e - - i.

First intonation   *First mediant*

2. Quo - - - - ni am de-us mag-nus do-mi-nus, et rex mag-nus su-per om-nes de - os:

Second intonation

quo - ni - am non re-pel - let do - mi - nus ple - bem su - am:

Second mediant

qui - a in ma - nu e - jus sunt om - nes fi - nes ter - rae

Termination

et al - - ti - tu - di-nes mon - ti-um ip - se con - spi - cit.

Tone No. 9

First intonation   *First mediant*

Ve - ni - te ex - sul - te - mus do - mi - no, ju - bi - le-mus de - o sa - lu - ta - ri no - stro,

Second intonation   *Second mediant*

prae - oc - cu - pe - mus fa - ci - em e - jus in con - fes - si - o - ne:

Termination

et in psal - mis ju-bi - le-mus e - i.

Tone No. 10   **f. 216r**

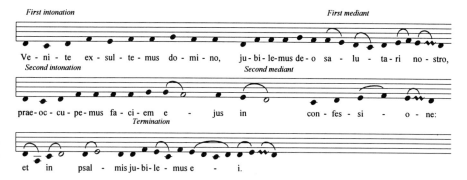

Liber usualis — not included
Liber hymnarius II, p. 133
Wagner II, p. 180
Heckenbach no. 8, p. 87 (but different terminatio)
Ferretti 2.D, p. 227
Worcester, p. 192, upper
CANTUS siglum   2

Tone No. 11   **f. 216v**

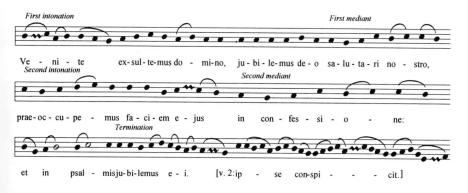

Liber usualis — not included
Liber hymnarius III, p. 135 (but simpler terminatio for odd-numbered verses)
Wagner III, p. 177 (but different terminatio)
Heckenbach no. 1, p. 72 (but simpler terminatio)
Ferretti 3.f, p. 227 (but simpler terminatio)
Worcester, p. 194, lower
CANTUS siglum   3

V

Tone No. 12

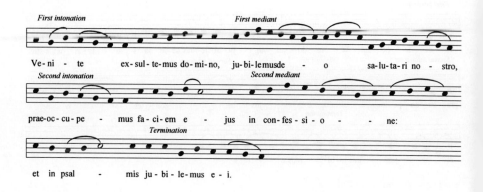

Ve - ni - te   ex - sul - te - mus do - mi - no, ju - bi - le mus de - o   sa - lu - ta - ri no - stro,

prae - oc - cu - pe - mus fa - ci - em e - jus in con - fes - si - o - ne:

et in psal - mis ju - bi - le - mus e - i.

Tone No. 13

Ve - ni - te ex - sul - te - mus do - mi - no, ju - bi - le - mus de - o sa - lu - ta - ri no - stro,

prae - oc - cu - pe - mus fa - ci - em e - jus in con - fes - si - o - ne:

et in psal - mis ju - bi - lemus e - i.

Tone No. 14

Ve - ni - te   ex - sul - te - mus do - mi - no, ju - bi - le - mus de - o sa - lu - ta - ri   no - stro,

Tone No. 14 – *Continued*

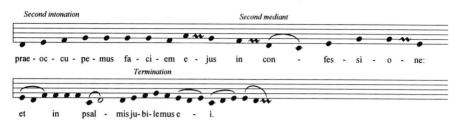

Second intonation   *Second mediant*

prae - oc - cu - pe - mus fa - ci - em e - jus   in   con - fes - si - o - ne:

Termination

et   in   psal - mis ju- bi- lemus e - i.

Liber usualis – not included
Liber hymnarius – not included
Wagner – not included
Heckenbach – not included
Ferretti – not included
Worcester, p. 193, upper
CANTUS siglum   WR

Tone No. 15   **f. 218r**

First intonation   *First mediant*

Ve - ni - te ex - sul - te - mus do - mi - no,   ju - bi - le- mus de - o sa- lu - ta - ri no - stro,

Second intonation   *Second mediant*

prae - oc - cu - pe - mus fa - ci- em e - jus in con - fes - si - o - ne:

Termination

et   in   psal - mis ju- bi - le - mus e - i.

Liber usualis, p. 368
Liber hymnarius – not included
Wagner IV.2, p. 178
Heckenbach no. 5, p. 81 (different initium and terminatio)
Ferretti 4.g, p. 227
Worcester, p. 193, lower
CANTUS siglum   CH

Tone No. 16

Liber usualis—not included
Liber hymnarius—not included
Wagner IV.1, p. 178 (different terminatio)
Heckenbach no. 10, p. 89
Ferretti 4.c^2, p. 228
Worcester—not included
CANTUS siglum   MO

Tone No. 17

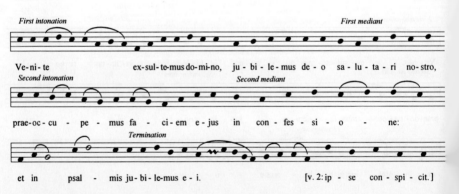

Liber usualis, p. 864
Liber hymnarius V, p. 146
Wagner V, p. 179 (but different terminatio)
Heckenbach no. 6, p. 82 (but different terminatio)
Ferretti 5.g, p. 229 (but simpler terminatio)
Worcester, p. 196, upper
CANTUS siglum   5

Tone No. 18   **f. 219r**

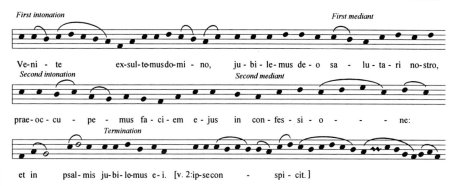

Ve-ni - te   ex-sul-te-mus do-mi - no,   ju - bi - le- mus de - o   sa - lu - ta - ri no-stro,

prae- oc - cu - pe - mus fa - ci - em e - jus   in   con - fes - si - o - - - ne:

et in   psal- mis ju- bi- le-mus e- i.   [v. 2:ip-se con - spi - cit.]

See comments for tone no. 17, which this resembles greatly

Tone No. 19   **f. 219v**

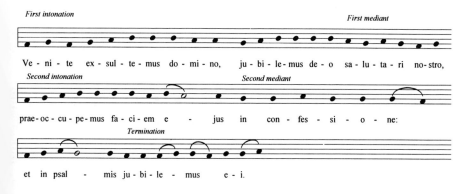

Ve - ni - te   ex - sul - te - mus   do - mi - no,   ju - bi - le- mus de - o   sa - lu - ta - ri   no-stro,

prae- oc - cu - pe- mus fa - ci - em e   -   jus   in   con - fes - si - o - ne:

et   in psal - mis ju - bi - le - mus   e - i.

Liber usualis, p. 1779
Liber hymnarius—compare with Tonus VI, p. 149
Wagner VI.2, p. 179
Heckenbach no. 11, p. 91
Ferretti 6.a férial récent, p. 230
Worcester, p. 192, lower
CANTUS siglum   FE

V

78

Tone No. 20   f. 220r

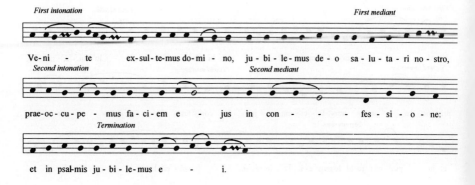

First intonation   *First mediant*

Ve - ni - te   ex - sul - te - mus do - mi - no,   ju - bi - le - mus de - o   sa - lu - ta - ri no - stro,

Second intonation   *Second mediant*

prae - oc - cu - pe - mus fa - ci - em e - jus   in   con - - - fes - si - o - ne:

Termination

et in psal - mis ju - bi - le - mus e - i.

Liber usualis — not included
Liber hymnarius — not included
Wagner — not included
Heckenbach — not included
Ferretti — not included
Worcester, p. 197, lower
Cantus siglum   IN

Tone No. 21   f. 220v

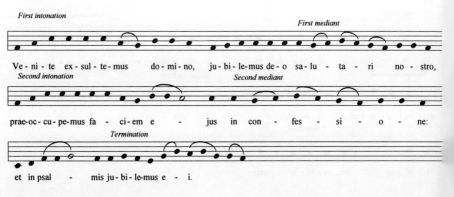

First intonation   *First mediant*

Ve - ni - te ex - sul - te - mus   do - mi - no,   ju - bi - le - mus de - o sa - lu - ta - ri   no - stro,

Second intonation   *Second mediant*

prae - oc - cu - pe - mus fa - ci - em e - jus   in   con - fes - si - o - ne:

Termination

et in psal - mis ju - bi - le - mus e - i.

Liber usualis, p. 768; compare also 765
Liber hymnarius Tonus VI*, p. 154
Wagner VI.1, p. 179
Heckenbach no. 7, p. 85
Ferretti 6.F pascal récent, p. 229 (compare also 6.F pascal ancien)
Worcester, p. 198, upper and lower (two versions of essentially the same tone)
Cantus siglum   PA

V

Tone No. 22   **f. 220v**

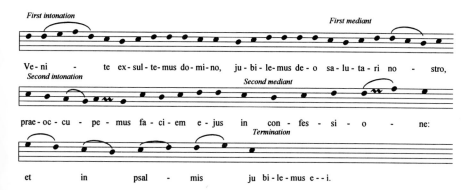

First intonation

First mediant

Ve - ni - te ex - sul - te - mus do - mi - no, ju - bi - le - mus de - o sa - lu - ta - ri no - stro,

Second intonation

Second mediant

prae - oc - cu - pe - mus fa - ci - em e - jus in con - fes - si - o - ne:

Termination

et in psal - mis ju bi - le - mus e - - i.

Liber usualis — not included
Liber hymnarius VII, p. 160
Wagner VII, p. 179
Heckenbach no. 4, p. 79
Ferretti 7.G, p. 230
Worcester, p. 196, lower
CANTUS siglum   7

VI

ANTIPHONS FOR LAUDS ON THE OCTAVE OF CHRISTMAS

The antiphon *Germinavit radix Jesse*, for Lauds on the Octave of Christmas (in earlier times a feast of the Blessed Virgin, later the Feast of the Circumcision),[1] appears in medieval sources in a number of different readings. In the antiphoner Utrecht, Bibliotheek der Rijksuniversiteit, 406 (3 J 7) (12th century, from St. Mary's, Utrecht)[2] it is given as shown in Example 1a. (See examples 1a and 1b overleaf.)

Evidently the melody has been 'transposed' — written so that it ends on *a* rather than one of the finals more customary for plainsong — so that its second degree may be notated as either *b*♮ (a whole step above the final, as on "Ger*mi*navit" and "*ra*dix") or *b*♭ (a half-step above the final, as on "lau*da*mus"). The chant thus sounds at the beginning as if it belongs to the protus maneria (mode 1 or 2), but at the end reveals itself as deuterus (mode 3 or 4). The Utrecht manuscript specifies the mode of a chant through its choice of differentia; and the differentia it gives for *Germinavit* rather surprisingly indicates mode 1, the mode of the beginning rather than the ending of the chant.

Medieval theorists of music stress that one should look to the ending of a chant to determine its mode; yet they make no secret of the fact that singers often look instead to the beginning. The late 11th-century theorist now known simply as 'John' deplores this practice, and gives several instances of it.[3] But it is rarely to be observed in manuscripts, and thus this example is of special interest. The differentia, though notated in neumes, seems clearly to be the mode-1 formula *a-a-aG-GF-Ga-GG*. It also seems likely to be the one that Aurelian (or one of his editors) described as making a

1   For the history of the feast see M. Righetti, *Manuale di storia liturgica*, II: *L'anno liturgico* (3rd edn., Milan 1969), 93-102; *Octave de Noël: Fête du saint nom de Jésus*, Assemblées du Seigneur, 12 (Bruges 1962), 7-11; 'Circoncision (Fête de la)', *Dictionnaire d'archéologie chrétienne et de liturgie*, ed. F. Cabrol and H. Leclercq, III, 2 (Paris 1948), 1717-1728. See also W. Arlt, *Ein Festoffizium des Mittelalters aus Beauvais* (Cologne 1970), Darstellungsband, 38-51, 139.

2   Concerning this manuscript, see *Handschriften en Oude Drukken van de Utrechtse Universiteitsbibliotheek* (Utrecht 1984), 143-4; and I. De Loos, 'Der Neumenbuchstabe S als chromatisches Zeichen im Antiphonale Utrecht, Universitätsbibliothek 406, aus dem 12. Jahrhundert', *Tijdschrift van de Vereniging voor Nederlandse Muziekgeschiedenis* 39 (1989), 5-27.

3   C. Palisca, ed., *Hucbald, Guido, and John on Music*, translated by W. Babb (New Haven 1978), 131.

Example 1a: The antiphon *Germinavit* as it appears in Utrecht, Bibliotheek der Rijksuniversiteit, 406, 36v

Ger- mi - na- vit ra- dix Jes - se, or - ta est stel- la ex Ja-cob: Vir-go pe- pe- rit sal- va - to - rem; te lau - da - mus de- us no-ster. e u o u a e

Example 1b: The antiphon *Innuebant patri ejus* as it appears in Utrecht, Bibliotheek der Rijksuniversiteit, 406, 126r

In- nu - e- bant pa - tri e- jus quem vel- let vo - ca - ri e - um; et scrip- sit, di - cens: Jo- an- nes est no-men e- jus. e u o u a e

very flexible end to the verse ("finem versus oppido flexibillem reddit") in a reference to the antiphon *Germinavit* that begins a long interpolation into chapter XIII (a survey of mode-4 chants) of Aurelian's treatise in the manuscript Oxford, Bodleian Library, Canonici misc. 212. The writer is aware of the irregularity in modal classification caused by the use of this differentia; as he says, "inordinate alterius toni aiunt versiculum eiusdem retinere sonoritatis reciprocationem, cum potissimum sit iuxta initium antiphone versuum modullationem concinere."[4] The reference to *Germinavit* is added after a mention of the antiphon *Innuebant*, which begins with the same stepwise ascending figure as *Germinavit*, but ends on *E* and has one of the standard mode-4 differentiae. (It is shown in Example 1b above.) If there is a source in which both antiphons — *Germinavit* and *Innuebant* — have the "very flexible" mode-1 differentia assigned to them, it has not yet come to my attention.

Chants of mixed mode are mentioned by the music theorists who deal with problems of modal classification, and they often see such problems as evidence of

---

4   The passage is difficult to translate, but it seems to mean, "some say it is contrary to rule for an antiphon of one mode to have the verse [formula] of another." The next clause, "cum potissimum sit iuxta initium antiphone versuum modullationem concinere," refers to the desirablity of having a differentia agree with the beginning of an antiphon. *Aureliani Reomensis Musica Disciplina*, ed. L. Gushee, Corpus scriptorum de musica 21 (1975), 147; for Gushee's discussion of the date and provenance of this version of the treatise, see pp. 30-34. I thank T. Mathiesen for retrieving for me from his immensely valuable database, Thesaurus Musicarum Latinarum, the passages relevant to this discussion.

Antiphons for Lauds on the Octave of Christmas

corruption. John, who may have worked in southern Germany or Switzerland,[5] mentions *Germinavit* in a group of "defective" chants, saying that it "demands a whole tone not only below parhypate hypaton but also below parhypate meson", and as a result requires the notator to "migrate to the higher notes".[6] Evidently John has in mind a version of the chant that in transposition would include both $F\natural$ (the whole step below transposed parhypate hypaton) and $b\flat$ (the whole step below transposed parhypate meson); he does not mention the pitch a half step below transposed parhypate meson, which is represented in the Utrecht reading by $b\natural$.

There are many antiphons in which $b\natural$ is heard in the earlier part, and $b\flat$ at the end; nearly all of them are sung to the melody known as Gevaert's thème 29.[7] The reason given for the failure of thème 29 to conform to one of the scales normally available in the theoretical system is that the melody dates from a time before that system was applied to chant. But the melody of *Germinavit* is not thème 29, nor is it a copy of *Innuebant*, and to understand it fully we must take into account the cycle of chants in which it appears.

Germinavit is one in a series of antiphons that stand out among the chants of the Divine Office for a number of reasons, perhaps first of all for their quality[8] but also because of the extent to which they focus on Mary.[9] There are seven in all: five for Lauds, *O admirabile commercium, Quando natus es[t],*[10] *Rubum quem viderat, Germinavit,* and *Ecce Maria genuit nobis,* plus one for the Benedictus of Lauds, *Mirabile mysterium,* and one for the Magnificat of Second Vespers, *Magnum haereditatis mysterium.*

An explanation for the distinctive character of these antiphon texts was given by J. Parisot in 1896: they are translations of Byzantine hymns "dont le texte grec ne se trouve plus dans les livres actuels."[11] In 1900, in a review of the edition in *Paléographie*

---

5   In determining the most likely place for John to have worked, Claude Palisca took into consideration the manuscript tradition for his treatise (*De musica*), the sources in which chants appear in readings like those John seems to have known, the method he uses for indicating mode and differentia, and the treatises that he cites. Palisca's conclusion is that John probably wrote his treatise "in the area between St. Gall and Bamberg." Palisca, 95.

6   Palisca, 128.

7   Concerning this melody, see W. Frere, Introduction to *Antiphonale Sarisburiense* (London 1901-1924), 70; F. Gevaert, *La Mélopée antique dans le chant de l'église latine* (Gand 1895), 322-30; and D. Hughes, 'Variants in Antiphon Families: Notation and Tradition', *La Musique et le rite sacré et profane,* ed. M. Honegger and P. Prevost (Strasbourg 1986), II, 29-47.

8   "Quis sacerdos, divinum officium persolvens, non miratus est seriem pulcherrimam antiphonarum ad Laudes in Octava Nativitatis Domini, quarum prima sic incipit: "O admirabile commercium..."? Propter suavitatem cantus, lenitatem cursus, splendorem imaginum et altam doctrinam, praestant inter pulchriores totius officii partes." A. Hodüm, 'O admirabile commercium', *Collationes Brugenses* 32 (1932), 394.

9   "Esse . . . si distinguono dal tipo consueto per una forma prolissa, a contenuto biblioco-teologico, e soprattutto per un marcato carattere mariano." Righetti, II, 85.

10 Some sources read "Quando natus es," others "est." See R.-J. Hesbert, *Corpus Antiphonalium Officii* 3 (Rome 1968), 422, where "est" is the preferred reading.

11 J. Parisot, 'Les Rites Orientaux', *Revue des sciences ecclésiastiques,* 8. sér., 3 (1896), 104. Parisot says this in such an offhand way that he seems to be treating it a matter of general knowledge; he does not claim to have discovered it.

VI

musicale of the Ambrosian antiphoner, L. Petit spoke of the "couleur grecque très prononcée" of the chants in the offices of the Purification and the Circumcision, and then observed that the series of antiphons beginning *O admirabile commercium* "n'est qu'une série de tropaires grecs."[12] Neither author presents evidence to support his assertion. The author of an article published in the mid-twenties accepts this attribution of origin so firmly that he writes that the Greek originals for the five antiphons are "sans doute, comme une foule d'autres tropaires, encore enfouies dans les manuscrits."[13]

In volume 3 of Hesbert's *Corpus Antiphonalium Officii* there are references in the editions of three antiphons from the series to a 1936 article by Anton Baumstark — one in which the word "Byzantine" forms part of the title.[14] Seeing these references might lead the unwary reader to assume that the antiphons for which such references occur are translations of Greek chants, or at least have some parallel in Greek hymnody. However, the point that Baumstark makes about one of them, *Ecce Maria genuit*, is that the combining in it of references to the birth and baptism of Christ implies a simultaneous celebration of the two events that is quite uncharacteristic of Byzantine hymns for Christmas, though he is able to cite parallels in Syrian hymnody and in the Latin responsory *Ecce agnus dei* (*CAO* 6575, usually assigned to Christmas).[15] One of the other antiphons (*Quando natus est*, *CAO* 4441) for which Hesbert gives no reference to Baumstark's article, should include one, for he does indeed mention it.[16] The remaining antiphon is *O admirabile commercium*, which Baumstark does not mention. This omission is significant, for what it implies is that after a search through Byzantine hymns for phrases and expressions that occur in these antiphons — a search that was successful for three of them — Baumstark found himself unable to cite a Greek parallel for the opening antiphon of the series.[17]

A reader of Baumstark's article is struck by the diversity that he observes in the five antiphons; if those for the Benedictus and Magnificat are included in consideration the diversity is greater still. The Benedictus antiphon, *Mirabile mysterium*, is unquestionably a translation of a Greek chant, a chant based on a passage in a sermon of Gregory the Theologian (Gregory Nazianzus, Bishop of Constantinople, ca.330-ca.390) — a borrowing that did not escape the eye of Amalarius of Metz (active ca.830), though he knew the antiphon only in its Latin form and the sermon in a rather free

---

12 L. Petit, 'Euchologie latine et euchologie grecque', *Echos d'Orient* 4 (1900), 4.
13 D. Rousseau, 'Les antiennes de la Circoncision', *Revue liturgique et monastique* 10 (1924-25), 57. I thank Brother Thomas Sullivan of Conception Abbey, Missouri, for locating what is apparently the only copy of this periodical in the United States and photocopying the article for me.
14 A. Baumstark, 'Byzantinisches in den Weihnachtstexten des römischen Antiphonarius Officii', *Oriens Christianus*, 3. ser., 11 (1936), 163-87.
15 Baumstark, 185.
16 Baumstark, 176-8.
17 In the article to which reference is made in fn. 8, A. Hodüm cites parallels to the line of thought of *O admirabile commercium* in several different sermons of Leo the Great (reg. 440-461). He finds the Greek equivalent for "commercium" used in the sense that it has in the antiphon in the Oratione de laudibus s. Mariae by St. Proclus (d. 446), whom he identifies as "primus et acerrimus Nestorii adversarius" (p. 399).

Latin translation by Rufinus.[18] Dependence on Greek models is less evident in the other antiphons, and not at all demonstrable for one. It is striking that the evidence assembled by Baumstark did not deter H. Frank from asserting in the same journal only a few years later that "eine und dieselbe Hand die Antiphonen zu den 5 Laudespsalmen, zum Benedictus und zum Magnificat zusammengestellt, d. h. aus byzantinischer Liturgie ausgewählt und übersetzt hat."[19] Including the Benedictus antiphon as an integral part of the series is crucial to the argument Frank presents for a dating of the Latin antiphons, for *Mirabile mysterium* includes a concise statement of the Catholic doctrine of the Incarnation, that enunciated by Leo the Great in a letter of 449 and affirmed by the Council of Chalcedon in 451 — that Christ has two natures in a single person, and that Mary can thus indeed be referred to as the Mother of God — in Greek, Theotocos.

Baumstark calls attention to the appearance at the end of *Germinavit*, the fourth of the Lauds antiphons (thus the antiphon for the Benedicite, the Canticle of the Three Children in the Fiery Furnace) of the phrase "te laudamus deus noster" that also ends the second antiphon in the series, the mode-3 chant *Quando natus est*. Refrains such as this are often found linking the strophes in the various odes of a Byzantine Kanon, as Baumstark observes. They also appear in series of Latin antiphons intended for use with the Benedicite.[20]

Does the fact that *Germinavit* has the same text at its ending as *Quando natus est* have any relevance to the problem of the melody for to which these words are set? In a study of the five Lauds antiphons underlying a motet cycle by Josquin des Pres in which all of them are quoted, Richard Sherr observed that in the manuscript Tours, Bibliothèque municipale, 149, the ending of *Quando natus est* has been modified so as to match that of *Germinavit*.[21] The readings given in seven sources for the endings of the two chants are shown in Example 2 (see overleaf).

The first four sources treat the antiphons as belonging to two different modes, and make the small alterations in "te laudamus deus noster" at the end of *Germinavit* that cause it to "belong to" (to use the characteristic intervals of) mode 1. (Small distinctions of this kind are relatively easy to make and to preserve in notated versions; but can we really believe that they were faithfully preserved in the practice of those who had learned the chants by hearing them sung?) In the other three readings of the two chants, "te laudamus deus noster" is sung at the end of *Germinavit* just as it is in *Quando natus est*. But three different strategies are employed to achieve this identity:

18 *Amalarii Episcopi Liber Officialis*, ed. J. Hanssens, Studi e Testi 139 (1948), IV, 32 (p. 508). See also H. Frank, 'Das Alter der römischen Laudes- und Vesperantiphonen der Weihnachtsoktav und ihrer griechischen Originale', *Oriens Christianus*, 3. ser., 14 (1941), 16.

19 Frank, 15.

20 See 'Antiphons for the Benedicite at Lauds', *Journal of the Plainsong & Mediaeval Music Society* 7 (1984), 15.

21 Professor Sherr presented his paper 'Conflicting Levels of Meaning and Understanding in Josquin's *O admirabile commercium* Motet Cycle' on February 14, 1994, at the conference "Hearing the Motet" at Washington University in St. Louis. I thank him for proposing the antiphon series as a topic for joint investigation, and for giving me a copy of his paper.

Antiphons for Lauds on the Octave of Christmas

Example 2:   The phrase "te laudamus deus noster" as it appears at the end of the antiphons *Quando natus est* (on the left) and *Germinavit* (on the right) in the sources Worcester, Cathedral Library, F 160, fol. 25r; Florence, Biblioteca Laurenziana, Conv. sopp. 560, fol. 36r; Paris, Bibliothèque nationale, lat. 12044, fols. 23v-24r; Arras, Bibliothèque municipale, 465, fol. 65r; Tours, Bibliothèque municipale, 149, fols. 93r v; Metz, Bibliothèque municipale, 461, 137v-138r; and Utrecht, Bibliotheek der Rijksuniversiteit, 406, 36v.

Antiphons for Lauds on the Octave of Christmas

Tours 149 puts both chants into mode 1, leading to some awkwardness in *Quando natus est* because it begins with a figure that is characteristic of mode-3 chants;[22] Metz 461 classifies *Quando natus est* as mode 3 and *Germinavit* as mode 4, enabling them to end identically but making it necessary for the psalm tones employed with them to be different; and Utrecht 406 calls *Quando natus est* mode 3 and *Germinavit* mode 1, once again causing the psalmody for the two antiphons to be chanted to two different tones.

The manuscript readings for the other four Lauds antiphons are largely in agreement,[23] with one exception: for *Ecce Maria genuit nobis* there are two melodies that seem at first glance quite different, being in different modes and having different opening figures. The Utrecht manuscript contains both of them, one on the Sunday within the octave of Christmas, the other on the octave day itself. They are shown in Example 3.

Example 3: The antiphon *Ecce Maria genuit* as it appears on the Sunday during the Octave of Christmas (fol. 35v) and the Octave of Christmas (fol. 36v) in Utrecht, Bibliotheek der Rijksuniversiteit, 406.

Ec-ce Ma- ri- a ge-nu-it no-bis sal- va-torem, quem Jo-annes vi- dens, excla-ma - bat dicens:

Ec-ce ag-nus de- i, ec- ce qui tol-lit pec-ca- ta mundi, al - le - lu- ia.

Ec-ce Ma- ri- a ge-nu - it no-bis sal - va- torem, quem Jo-annes videns, ex cla-ma- bat dicens:

Ec-ce agnus de- i, ec-ce qui tol- lit pec-ca - ta mun-di, al - le - lu - ia.

22 Jacobus of Liège uses *Quando natus est* as one of just two antiphons exemplifying the opening figure with which differentia 1 of mode 3 is associated (*Jacobi Leodiensis Speculum musicae*, VI, ed. R. Bragard, Corpus scriptorum de musica, 3, 1973, p. 264). In the introduction to *Antiphonale Sarisburiense*, W. Frere places *Quando natus est* among the thirty antiphons that use the mode-3 melody he designates as "a" (see p. 69).

23 The first chant in the series, *O admirabile commercium*, is the antiphon selected by Frere as the prototype for a common mode-6 theme; but he says, "the antiphons formed exactly on this model seem to be all of later date" (p. 71). Variations in manuscript readings for it are mostly matters of detail; however, a number of sources write this chant, and indeed every instance of this melody, so that it ends on *c*, thereby avoiding having to write *b♭*.

A closer examination reveals that the two melodies are similar in many respects. The contours of the melodies (especially on "exclamabat dicens", but also in several other places) are so similar that one has almost the impression that a single melody, poorly remembered, has been made to fit into two different modes, with the choice of mode proclaimed by the opening figure and confirmed by the ending. It is difficult to imagine how the singer at Utrecht who sang these two melodies on days that came in close succession was able to remember exactly how they differed. Metz 83 also contains both melodies, on fols. 45r (where the mode-2 melody is written in transposition, with *b*♭ throughout and ending on *G*) and 47v (the mode-5 version).[24] But most sources contain the melody in only one form. French and Italian sources tend to have the mode-5 version, German sources the mode-2 one; but there are exceptions.[25] An antiphoner of the Sistine Chapel copied during the reign of Julius II (probably in 1510), Rome, Biblioteca Vaticana, MS Cappella Sistina 27,[26] has the mode-2 version shown in Musical Example 4a (opposite). However, there is a small variant in the opening of this version: the first four syllables of *Ecce Maria* are usually not set syllabically.[27] Since the syllabic setting of these syllables is a striking feature of the beginning of the section of the motet that Josquin based on this chant, the variant seems worth mentioning. In other respects, however, the form in which the tenor sings the chant melody in each of the points of imitation in Josquin's motet, shown in Musical Example 4b, matches the Sistine Chapel reading (apart from transpositions), and one can imagine that Josquin might have deliberately simplified the opening figure.

This study was undertaken in response to an inquiry from Richard Sherr, who asked whether a chant source, manuscript or printed, could be identified as the one most likely to contain the melodies in the form in which Josquin knew them.[28] The inquiry was made more difficult by the fact that Josquin is known to have traveled a great deal, and his whereabouts for long periods in his life remain unknown. Furthermore, at least one scholar has reversed the procedure that is usually followed — that of looking for a chant source from a place where the composer is known to have been active — and instead used the fact that in one work Josquin quotes a chant in the form it was sung at the Abbey of St. Martin in Tours to argue that Josquin must have composed the work for that house, even though no other evidence exists to prove

---

24 The two readings for the antiphon were evidently both known to the theorist now known as "pseudo-Odo." In order to demonstrate the sound of the descending major third, he quotes the beginning of the mode-5 version; later he mentions *Ecce Maria* among chants of mode 2. (See M. Gerbert, *Scriptores ecclesiastici de musica sacra potissimum* I, St. Blasien 1784; reprint edn., Hildesheim 1963, pp. 256, 260.)

25 I thank C. Downey and K. Glaeske, staff members in the CANTUS project, who searched through the microfilms of 120 manuscripts to find *Ecce Maria genuit nobis*, to match the melody given for it to one of three models, and identify the mode to which it was assigned.

26 I thank R. Sherr for calling this manuscript to my attention.

27 But see Toledo, Biblioteca capitular 44.1, fol. 21r. This is an Aquitanian antiphoner of the 11th century.

28 Josquin's motet appears in several sources; the most recent edition is that of E. Lowinsky in *The Medici Codex*, Monuments of Renaissance Music 3-5 (1968), 4, pp. 28-47. Lowinsky's commentary appears in vol. 3, pp. 129-34, the facsimile in vol. 5, fols. 14v-22r.

314

Antiphons for Lauds on the Octave of Christmas

Example 4a: The antiphon *Ecce Maria genuit* as it appears in the Vatican Library manuscript Capp. Sist., 27.

Example 4b: The pitches in the tenor part at the openings of points of imitation in the section "Ecce Maria genuit" of the motet cycle *O admirabile commercium* by Josquin des Pres.

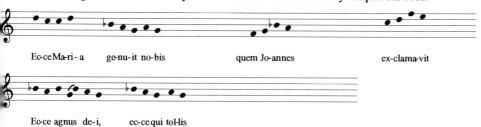

he ever visited there.[29]

Yet another complicating factor lies in the fact that Josquin may have received his earliest musical training in an area there was a confluence of two distinct liturgical and musical traditions. In his article 'Antiphoner' in *The New Grove Dictionary of Music and Musicians*,[30] Michel Huglo characterizes groups of manuscripts as eastern, western, and transitional; the transitional sources include those from Liège, Metz, and Utrecht. Nothing could demonstrate the 'transitional' nature of Utrecht 406 more clearly than the two readings it provides for *Ecce Maria*. One suspects that Josquin knew both of them, and that he had encountered others as he moved from place to place. When he transformed the five antiphons for the Octave of Christmas into a polyphonic motet cycle, he needed a version of *Ecce Maria* to use. In making this decision, how much importance did he attach to the practice of the place in which the motet was to be sung? One cannot know for certain. In any case, it seems likely to have been a matter of choice, of highly informed choice.

29 J. Noble, 'The Genealogies of Christ and their Musical Settings', paper read at the Fifty-first Annual Meeting of the American Musicological Society, Vancouver, British Columbia, November 9, 1985. I thank Professor Noble for giving me a copy of his paper.
30 London 1980, 1, 482-490.

VII

The Parable of the Talents
in Liturgy and Chant

THE ENGLISH WORD "TALENT" IS BORROWED from a Greek word that in New Testament times designated a very large sum of money. (According to one estimate, the wages of a day laborer over a period of twenty years would be roughly equivalent to one talent.)[1] The Scripture passage through which the borrowing occurred is Matthew 25:14–30, where Jesus presents the following parable.[2]

> For even as a man going into a far country, called his servants, and delivered to them his goods; and to one he gave five talents, and to another two, and to another one, to every one according to his proper ability: and immediately he took his journey.
> And he that had received the five talents, went his way, and traded with the same, and gained other five. And in like manner he that had received the two gained other two. But he that had received the one, going his way digged into the earth, and hid his lord's money.
> But after a long time the lord of those servants came, and reckoned with them. And he that had received the five talents coming, brought other five talents, saying: Lord, thou didst deliver to me five talents, behold I have gained other five over and above. His lord said to him: Well done, good and faithful servant, because thou hast been faithful over a few things, I will place thee over many things: enter thou into the joy of thy lord.
> And he also that had received the two talents came and said: Lord, thou deliveredst two talents to me: behold I have gained other two. His lord said to him: Well done, good and faithful servant: because thou hast been faithful over a few things, I will place thee over many things: enter thou into the joy of thy lord.

[1]Carson 1984, 516, gives this estimate and observes that a talent was originally a measure of weight; later it acquired the meaning of the value of that weight of precious metal (gold, silver, or copper).

[2]For an overview of the meanings of "talent" in English, see the *Oxford English Dictionary* (1933), 11:53–54. One of the principal meanings given there is "power or ability of mind or body viewed as something divinely entrusted to a person for use and improvement." The dependence of this definition on interpretations of the parable is evident.

But he that had received the one talent, came and said: Lord I know that thou art a hard man; thou reapest where thou hast not sown, and gatherest where thou hast not strewed. And being afraid I went and hid thy talent in the earth: behold here thou hast that which is thine.

And his lord answering, said to him: Wicked and slothful servant, thou knewest that I reap where I sow not, and gather where I have not strewed: Thou oughtest therefore to have committed my money to the bankers, and at my coming I should have received my own with usury.

Take ye away therefore the talent from him, and give it to him that hath ten talents. For to every one that hath shall be given, and he shall abound: but from him that hath not, that also which he seemeth to have shall be taken away. And the unprofitable servant cast ye out into the exterior darkness. There shall be weeping and gnashing of teeth.[3]

Much of Jesus' teaching was presented in parables, and over the centuries an immense literature has grown up around them. The Fathers of the Church interpreted the parables allegorically in great detail, and this established a tradition that continued through the nineteenth century. A new approach to interpretation, established just before the turn of the twentieth century, led to important developments that were summarized by Joachim Jeremias, who also made valuable contributions of his own. According to Jeremias,

The parables of Jesus are not—at any rate primarily—literary productions, nor is it their object to lay down general maxims ("no one would crucify a teacher who told pleasant stories to enforce prudential morality"), but each of them was uttered in an actual situation of the life of Jesus, at a particular and often unforeseen point. Moreover, as we shall see, they were preponderantly concerned with a situation of conflict. They correct, reprove, attack. For the greater part, though not exclusively, the parables are weapons of warfare.[4]

In studying a parable, Jeremias searches for evidence of, first, the original setting, the actual situation in which Jesus used it; and, second, evidence of the reworking (interpretation) of the story in the primitive Church during the period before the collecting and arranging of the parables in written form in the Gospels (Jeremias 1962, 23). He sees the Parable of the Talents as

the story of a rich man, feared by his servants as an inconsiderate and rapacious employer, who, before setting out on a long journey, entrusts to each of his three servants [a sum of money] to be traded with, either merely not to leave his capital unemployed, during his absence, or with the intention of testing the servants and requiring an account from them on his return. The faithful servants are rewarded with increased responsibility. The emphasis lies on the reckoning with the third servant, who makes the unconvincing excuse that from an excess of caution he has made no use of the money entrusted to him (Jeremias 1962, 61–62).

In his summary, Jeremias assigns equal amounts of money to the three servants. In this he is following what many scholars regard as another redaction of the same original—one that may include elements drawn from a second narrative—the Parable

---

[3]This is the translation of the Douay version, given here because it corresponds more closely than do other translations to the Latin employed in the chants to be discussed below.
[4]Jeremias 1962, 21. The passage in quotation marks is from Smith 1948, 17.

of the Pounds in Luke 19:12–27. (Some commentators lay great stress on the difference in the number of talents.)[5] The servants who have done well with what was entrusted to them are given more to work with: that is their reward, along with a word of
praise from the master and, perhaps, a closer association with him. The audience toward which this parable was first directed would, Jeremias believes, have been familiar with the Old Testament practice of referring to spiritual leaders as "servants of
God." Its target was the scribes, to whom the Word of God had been entrusted; and it
was meant as a warning of a reckoning to come. They would be judged on the basis of
what they have done with God's gift: whether they have used it in accordance with
his will, or carelessly neglected it. Hence it originally functioned as a "crisis parable"
(Jeremias 1962, 62).[6]

For Matthew, and for the early Church, the meaning shifts. The return of the master, the central event in the story, becomes the *Parousia*, the second coming of Christ
as judge; and Matthew treats the Parable of the Talents as eschatological discourse,
setting it in a series of seven "parables of judgment." Now the reward of the faithful
servants is for them to be ushered into "the Messianic banquet"; the unprofitable servant is cast "into outer darkness" (Jeremias 1962, 63). But there are certain details in
the story that cannot be accommodated easily in this interpretation, particularly the
characterization of the master as "inconsiderate and rapacious."

Liturgical use of the Parable of the Talents echoes Matthew in its emphasis on judgment. It focuses on the heavenly reward that awaits a "faithful servant," particularly
one who has devoted himself to spreading the Gospel and promoting the work of the
Church. In interpreting the parable as an allegory, Saint Jerome speaks of the Greek
word "argurion," which he has translated as "pecuniam," as having a double significance, meaning both coins and silver; and he goes on to identify the coins as the
preaching of the Gospel and the silver as the Word of God. The third servant should
have given them to the bankers and the moneychangers—that is, either to other
teachers (this would have been like what the apostles accomplished through conse-
crating priests and bishops in each province), or to all the faithful (who could have
made this "money" double, and returned it with interest, by transforming into action
all the teaching that they had received in the form of words) (Jerome 1979, 226).

In the Latin rite, references to the parable can be found in the earliest of the sources
that specify Gospel readings for individual days, the Würzburg *Capitulare evangeliorum*, where it is identified as the Lesson for the Feasts of SS Marcellus (16 January),
Mark (7 October), and Clement (23 November) (Klauser 1935, 188). All three saints
were popes: St. Clement in the last decade of the first century, Marcellus in 308–309,
and Mark in 336. Thus they were religious leaders who might well have thought of

---

[5]George A. Buttrick put it as follows: "This story in the [King James Version] has given a key word to
our language—talents. A doctrinaire assumption that there is complete equality among men, or a demand
for such equality, is folly. Jesus knew and clearly taught that men differ in talents. There are diversities of
gifts. Some men draw plans for a cathedral, some compose music for its organ, some carve the stone, and
some build the road to the door. But every man is talented. No man is without some gift essential to the
building" (1951, 7:558).

[6]David M. Stanley and Raymond E. Brown link the parables with the miracles, seeing both as "part of a
vigorous assault made by God's dominion (Kingdom) as it entered time." Such parables as the Tenants in
the Vineyard and the Talents "were threats of imminent judgment on the Jewish authorities" (1968,
2:789).

4

themselves, and been referred to by others, as "servants of God."[7] The Proper chants for the Masses on those days are in the earliest sources as listed below.

St. Marcellus	St. Mark	St. Clement
Intr. *Statuit ei* (Sir. 45:30)	Intr. *Sacerdotes Dei* (Dan. 3:84, 87)	Intr. *Dicit Dominus* (Is. 59:21, 56:7)
Grad. *Inveni David* (Ps. 88:21, 22, 23)	Grad. *Inveni David*	Grad. *Juravit Dominus* (Ps. 109:4, 1)
All. *Inveni David* (Ps. 88:21)	All. (varies)	All. *Beatus vir* (Ps. 111:1?)
Off. *Veritas mea* (Ps. 88:25, 26)	Off. *Veritas mea*	Off. *Veritas mea*
Comm. *Domine quinque* (Matt. 25:20, 21)	Comm. *Beatus servus* (Matt. 24:46, 47)	Comm. *Beatus servus* or *Domine quinque talenta*[8]

As these lists demonstrate, on the feast of St. Mark the Communion text does not come from the Gospel for the day. Nor does it in two of the three sources that specify a Communion for the feast of St. Clement; only the third offers a choice, between *Domine quinque talenta* and *Beatus servus*.[9] *Domine quinque talenta* evokes the whole parable, but places its stress on the reward given to the faithful servant:

> Domine, quinque talenta tradidisti mihi: ecce alia quinque superlucratus sum. Euge serve fidelis, quia in pauca fuisti fidelis, supra multa te constituam, intra in gaudium Domini tui.

> ("Lord, thou didst deliver to me five talents, behold I have gained other five over and above." "Well done, faithful servant, because thou hast been faithful over a few things, I will place thee over many things: enter thou into the joy of thy Lord.")

Chants based on this parable also appear in the Divine Office. The one with the most prominent and firmly established role is the Matins responsory *Euge serve bone*, which comes first in the series for the Common of a Confessor in virtually every source.[10]

---

[7]Since the time of Gregory the Great (d. 604), in all official correspondence generated by the papal chancery one of the pope's titles is "servus servorum Dei" ("the servant of the servants of God"). See *Lexikon für Theologie und Kirche* 9 (1964): cols. 695–96, s. v. "Servus servorum Dei."

[8]This chart is based on the sources surveyed by René-Jean Hesbert in *Antiphonale missarum sextuplex* (1935), pp. 28–29, 160–61, 166–67. The manuscript of Mont-Blandin (Brussels, Bibl. royale, 10127–10144) is the one that offers a choice between *Domine quinque talenta* and *Beatus servus*.

[9]The sources covered in *Antiphonale missarum sextuplex* assign the Communion *Domine quinque talenta* also to the feasts of St. Stephen, Pope (pp. 144–45); and SS Cornelius and Cyprian (pp. 156–57). For these feasts, the Gospel specified in the Würzburg *Capitulare evangeliorum* is other than the Parable of the Talents. Hence one would look in vain in these early sources for slavish adherence to the principle that a nonpsalmodic Communion draws its text from the Gospel for the day. What underlies the selection of these texts is evidently a wish to evoke several different Biblical passages that touch on a single theme, that of the faithful servant. It would be interesting to study the consistency of matching of Gospel and Communion in later times, after the period represented by the sources of *Antiphonale missarum sextuplex*, at a point when both would presumably have been included with various alternatives in a Common of Confessors. Two Mass antiphoners of the ninth century include Proper chants *In vigilia pontificis* and *In natale pontificis*; Hesbert (1935, XXIV) refers to these as "messes votives" rather than as Commons. The concept of "Commons" seems to be foreign to such manuscripts in this early period.

[10]For the melody of this responsory, see, for example, *Antiphonale sarisburiense*, ed. W. H. Frere (1901–24), p. 651. For its use in representative sources, see René-Jean Hesbert, *Corpus antiphonalium officii* (1963–79), 1:362–63, 2:686–87, 699. In the sources surveyed in this work, *Euge serve bone* generally serves as the

R. Euge, serve bone et fidelis, quia in pauca fuisti fidelis, supra multa te constituam: intra in gaudium Domini tui.
V. Domine, quinque talenta tradidisti mihi: ecce alia quinque superlucratus sum.
[Refrain:] Intra in gaudium Domini tui.

(R. "Well done, good and faithful servant, because thou hast been faithful over a few things, I will place thee over many things: enter thou into the joy of thy Lord."
V. "Lord, thou didst deliver to me five talents, behold I have gained other five over and above."
[Refrain:] "Enter thou into the joy of thy Lord.")

The near identity of the Communion and responsory texts is striking. What is even more striking is that for the refrain and the five or six syllables that precede it, the musical setting in the responsory is virtually the same as that provided for the same text in the Communion. (Since the music for the word "constituam" and for the end of the responsory consists of cadential formulas that occur in many other chants of this type, it appears that the Communion is based on it rather than being the model.)[11] Although this similarity was pointed out long ago, along with several other examples of musical borrowing between Communions and responsories on the same texts, further study of the practice is clearly needed.[12]

---

first responsory in the Common of a Confessor: in manuscript antiphoners the opening of the text is usually highlighted by being written in large letters, the first of which is often illuminated. Other roles in which the responsory is used (for example, on the feast of St. Otmar in Hartker's Antiphoner) clearly derive from this. If in the Divine Office a series of chants for the Common of Confessors was compiled out of various services originally intended for several individual saints, it is impossible to prove this on the basis of existing material: in the earliest surviving sources the Common of Confessors, and other Commons, are already present.

In Hartker's Antiphoner, and in other sources, *Euge serve bone* is the only responsory derived from the Parable of the Talents. Hartker's other responsories for the Common of a Confessor are based on Psalms or other Biblical passages, or they have non-Biblical texts. Responsories based on Psalms include *Juravit Dominus* (Ps. 109:4, 1), *Posui adjutorium* (Ps. 88:20b, 22, 21), and *Inveni David* (Ps. 88:21, 22, 23). Among those on other Biblical texts are *Ecce sacerdos magnus* (a reworking of Eccl. 44:16, 22, 25, with some added material), *Amavit eum Dominus* (Eccl. 45:9, with some added text), *Iste homo perfecit* (Gen. 6:22, 7:1, and added text), and *Elegit te Dominus* (Eccl. 45:20, with added material). *Vere famulus Dei* is apparently on a non-Biblical text, but its verse is adapted from Eccl. 44:16; other non-Biblical texts include *Iste est qui ante Deum, Iste homo ab adolescentia sua,* and *Dominus qui elegit te.* Hartker refers to two additional responsories by incipit. These come eighth and ninth in his series of fourteen; they are *Famulo meo* and *Cibavit illum.* The latter is borrowed from the feast of St. John the Evangelist; the former also has this role in Hartker, but other sources place it differently.

[11]In the tabulation by W. H. Frere of cadences that recur frequently among various different mode 7 responsories, the melody for the second "fidelis" appears at the end of the cadence he calls d 1; that for "constituam" is cadence b 1; and that for the last three syllables of the respond, G 2 (see his introduction to *Antiphonale sarisburiense,* pp. 44, 49–51).

In his dissertation, Hans-Jörgen Holman (1961) corrects and reorganizes Frere's system of identifying the formulae (see 1:63–75); he calls the setting of the first "fidelis" formulaic, that of "intra in gaudium, and that at the end of the Respond" (see 1:283 for his analysis). The setting for "constituam" Holman identifies as "completely free, not having any relationship to standard phrases in other chants." (For the symbol . . .b and the meaning assigned to it by Holman, see 1:83.)

The responsory *Ibat igitur Saulus,* quoted by Peter Wagner (1921, 341) from the Lucca Antiphoner as an example of the mode 7 responsory style, has a number of phrase endings in common with *Euge serve bone.*

[12]Wagner 1921, 327: "Manche Communionen erscheinen zugleich als Matutinresponsorien." In an appendix to this article there is a list of chants that have this dual function.

6

Example 1. Two versions of a phrase from the Communion *Domine quinque talenta*. A: Brussels, Bibliothèque royale, II, 3823, fol. 21ᵛ; B: Paris, Bibliothèque nationale, lat. 776, fol. 23ʳ

The Communion is normally assigned to mode 7 and written to end on G, though several sources write it a fifth lower. For the phrases "quia in pauca fuisti fidelis, supra multa te constituam," sources from St. Denis and from Cluniac houses give a reading (labeled "A" in Example 1) that differs from that found in the majority of the sources ("B" in the example).

A possible reason for the divergence between the two readings is that the A reading results from singers' confusing the Communion with the responsory, in which there is a short melisma on the second syllable of "pauca." But even in manuscripts that include both chants, such as Cambridge, Fitzwilliam Museum, 369 (from Lewes) and Paris, B. n., lat. 12584 (from Saint-Maur des Fossés), the two are not identical at that point.

Perhaps because an editor has interpreted the text incipit of the Communion as a cue for mode,[13] in a manuscript from Udine the ending is modified so as to make F the final for the chant; and in just one of the sources consulted for this study, the chant ends on E.[14] But in general, the manuscript tradition for this Communion melody is as solid as that for many chants that are indisputably part of the oldest layer of the repertory.

Also on texts from the parable are some seven or eight Office antiphons, for which the manuscript tradition is a good deal less firm that it is for either the responsory or the Communion. Those that appear in the sources surveyed in *Corpus antiphonalium officii* are given below as they are presented in the Common of Confessors in the Rheinau manuscript.[15] The first is an alternative antiphon "in evangelio" (i.e., for the Benedictus) in the service of Lauds; the others are arranged into a series that is ostensibly an alternative for the main series of Lauds antiphons.

[13]In tonaries one finds a series of antiphons that begin with the numbers one through eight, in either ordinal or cardinal form, which are used to demonstrate the properties of the modes. See Huglo 1971, 386–87. It is important to remember that these antiphons were not extracted from the liturgical repertory, but were composed for use in the tonaries (Huglo, 386).

[14]The sources in question are Udine, Bibl. arcivescovile, Oct. 2 (13th century, St. Gall, Moggio [in Aquilea]), fol. 20ᵛ and Brussels, Bibliothèque royale, II, 3824 (mid–13th century, from Saint-Bénigne, Dijon), fol. 258ʳ.

[15]For the incipits, see *Corpus antiphonalium officii*, 2:688; for the complete texts, see vol. 3 of the same work, where the edited texts are printed in alphabetical order under the identification numbers included in parentheses here.

MATUTINA LAUS
IN EVANGELIO

[Ant. *Qui dum esset summus*]

Ant. *Euge, serve bone et fidelis; quia in pauca fuisti fidelis, super multa te constituam, dicit Dominus* (2732)

[Ant. *Amavit eum Dominus et ornavit*]
[Ant. *Iste est qui ante Deum*]

MATUTINA LAUS

Ant. [1] *Domine, quinque talenta tradidisti mihi: ecce alia quinque superlucratus sum* (2370)

Ant. [2] *Quinque michi, Domine, talenta tradidisti, lucratus sum insuper alia quinque* (4542)

Ant. [3] *Euge, serve bone, in modico fidelis, intra in gaudium Domini tui* (2734)

Ant. [4] *Serve bone et fidelis, intra in gaudium Domini tui* (4871)

Ant. [5] *In pauca fuisti fidelis; super multa te constituam, dicit Dominus* (3269)

In Ev. Ant. *Serve bone et fidelis, quia in pauca fuisti fidelis, super multa te constituam: intra in gaudium Domini Dei tui* (4872)

It is difficult to believe that these six antiphons were ever used together as they are shown here, in a Lauds service; there is too much repetition in them.[16] The series seems like a showcase for displaying the results of some industrious collecting of antiphons by one of the compilers of the book. Yet all of these antiphons save one are known outside of Rheinau, even though they seem to exist on the fringes of the Office repertory.

For an impression of where they stand in the various sources, one can turn to the first two volumes of *Corpus antiphonalium officii* (Hesbert 1963–65). Out of the twelve sources surveyed there, just four agree in designating *Serve bone et fidelis intra* (4871) as the fifth antiphon of Lauds in the Common of a Confessor. (The other three sources in which it appears cast it in different roles.) *Euge serve bone et fidelis* (2732) is found in more manuscripts (ten in all), but since it is most frequently included as one of several alternative antiphons for use with the Benedictus of Lauds (six sources), it seems less central in the repertory. The remaining chants seem even more peripheral: specific assignments, such as those of *Domine quinque talenta* and *Quinque mihi Domine* as fifth and sixth antiphons in the second Nocturn of Matins (in the Cluniac manuscript Paris, B.n., lat. 12044), are a rarity. An Ivrea manuscript (Biblioteca capitolare, 106) incorporates five of the antiphons into a very miscellaneous series of seventeen that it sets after the service of Lauds.

The relative stability in assignment of *Serve bone et fidelis* might seem to indicate an early date, were it not that three different melodies have been found for this text. They are shown in Example 2.

The preparation of a detailed list of sources for each of these melodies lies beyond the scope of this article; but it should be noted that melody C, which appears in the Malta manuscript, is not commonly found with this text. (Another unusual linking

---

[16]The antiphons have been arranged in such a way that the texts come in the order in which they appear in the Bible. This is also the case in other antiphon collections, such as the series of antiphons for the Magnificat that one finds in certain sources; concerning this, see Udovich 1980.

VII

8

Example 2. Three melodies for *Serve bone et fidelis intra*. A: Worcester, Cathedral Library, F 160, p. 427; B: Paris, Bibliothèque nationale, lat. 12044, fol. 238ᵛ; C: Mdina (Malta), Cathedral Museum, MS B, fol. 139ᵛ

between text and melody in that source will be commented on later.) The involvement of two different modes serves as a reminder that disagreements between tonaries sometimes reflect differences in musical repertory rather than different approaches toward classification.

The text of *Euge serve bone et fidelis* is quite similar to that of *Serve bone et fidelis, quia in pauca* (4872), for which the sources are significantly fewer. The absence of similarity in melody apparently did not prevent confusion between the two chants: although an earlier manuscript of Klosterneuburg (1012, of the 12th century) notates them clearly one after the other (on fol. 114ᵛ), a later source (1018, 14th century, fol. 188ʳ) telescopes the two, notating the melody of *Serve bone et fidelis, quia in pauca* and leaving the first word, "Euge," without any music. Similarly, the *Liber usualis* (1950, 1200) incorporates the full melody and text of *Serve bone et fidelis, quia in pauca* into an antiphon that begins with the word "Euge." The chant that results from this graft does not appear in any of the medieval sources studied in *Corpus antiphonalium officii*. The two versions of *Serve bone et fidelis, quia in pauca* that are shown in Example 3 indicate the range of possible readings for this chant. For comparison, *Euge serve bone et fidelis* is shown as it appears in the earlier Klosterneuburg source.

Two other antiphons based on the parable, *Quinque mihi Domine* (4542) and *Euge serve bone, in modico* (2734), share the same melody, one identified by Frere as "very popular." As he says, "the number of classical Antiphons that follow it, falls little, if at all, short of 100; and in the Silver Age it was in constant use" (Frere, 1924, 1:65). The Malta manuscript gives two melodies for *Euge serve bone, in modico*: first (on fol. 137ᵛ), the mode 1 melody to which reference has just been made, and then, on the very next page, an equally well known melody in the seventh mode. As for the antiphon *Domine quinque talenta* (2370), it is also in the first mode; the form in which it appears in the *Liber usualis* (1950, 1195) is a fair approximation of what one finds in the sources.

The last chant to be considered here is apparently an antiphon, but it is on a text that corresponds almost exactly with that of the Communion discussed earlier. In a

Example 3. Two versions of *Serve bone et fidelis quia*, and *Euge serve bone et fidelis*. A and C: Klosterneuburg, Chorherrenstift, 1012, fol. 114ᵛ; B: Metz, Bibliothèque municipale, 461, fol. 397ʳ

fairly extended search, this chant has been located in only two sources, both of them representatives of the Aquitanian tradition as it was transplanted into Spain—Toledo, Biblioteca Capitular, 44.2 (11th century) and Huesca, Archivo de la Catedral, 9 (13th century). The notation in the Toledo manuscript, particularly the crowding of the neumes in melismatic passages, suggests that notation was neither present nor intended in the source from which this copy was made, perhaps placing this manuscript version toward the beginning of the written transmission of this work. The notation in the Huesca manuscript, though illegible in places, clarifies the text underlay and makes possible a transcription into staff notation (Example 4).

Despite the modest melismatic expansion in "intra in gaudium," the style in general is sober and monochromatic, in many places like ornamented recitation. Particu-

Example 4. The Aquitanian antiphon *Domine quinque talenta*. Toledo, Bibl. cap., 44.2, fol. 186ʳ; Huesca, Archivo de la Catedral, 9, fol. 275ʳ

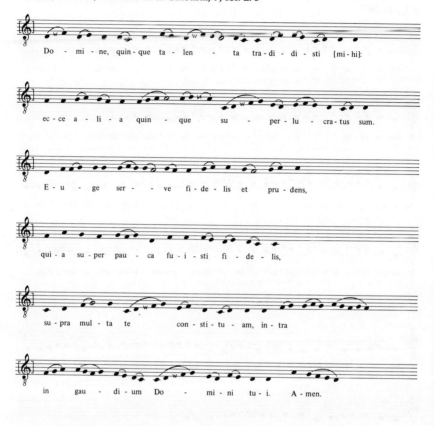

larly striking is the return of the same cadential figure in three places—on "superlucratus sum," "te constituam," and "Domini tui."

The number of different antiphons on texts from the Parable of the Talents goes well beyond what was liturgically necessary. This suggests that the story had a certain appeal that kept composers and liturgists returning to it, just as commentators kept going back to it and working out one interpretation after another. Perhaps it was at least in part because of the incongruities introduced into the story by Matthew. To what extent, and in what ways, did Jesus intend the master to represent God? Some writers say flatly that verse 24b ("Lord, I know that thou art a hard man; thou reapest where thou hast not sown, and gatherest where thou has not strewed") "should not be allegorized" (McKenzie 1968, 2:107). Yet there is evidence that verses 24b–25 of the parable quote a familiar saying about Yahweh, one that reflects a "postexilic sense of

bitterness" (McGaughy 1975, 245). If this is so, Jesus may have constructed the parable around this saying in order to challenge his listeners' understanding of the mission of Judaism. For those in Jesus' audience who believed that mission was to guard
the sacred tradition received from God by Moses and the prophets, the servant whose
whole effort went into preserving his single talent may well have seemed a sympa-
thetic figure. The ending would have shocked them, for it embodies nothing less than
"a new vision of reality" (McGaughy 1975, 243). What are the lessons to be drawn
from this? The range of opinions of writers through history is quite remarkable.

In commenting on the social and economic conditions of his time, Christ mentioned money in many different contexts. In one oft-cited passage, he advised a rich
man who wished to possess everlasting life to sell all he had and give the proceeds to
the poor, "for it is easier for a camel to pass through the eye of a needle, than for a rich
man to enter into the kingdom of God" (Luke 18:25). Whatever their interpretation in
Patristic and medieval times, for Protestant theologians such texts as these assumed a
new significance, partly because of changes in economic life. In discussing pre-
Restoration English Puritans, Christopher Hill writes:

> The preachers, and still more their congregations, might well be genuinely convinced in
> their hearts that industry was a good work, for the "common good," for "the use and
> profit of mankind"; that negligence in business harms the public state. It is a duty to
> God and to the commonwealth to use your talents, said John Preston. Provided you do
> not make gain your godliness, provided you do not seek riches but accept them as the
> blessing of God if they happen to come—then you may lawfully take care to increase
> your estate. . . . It was in fact the labour of generations of God-fearing Puritans that
> made England the leading industrial nation in the world.[17]

In the "Protestant ethic" there is undoubtedly a good deal of prudential morality.
Nevertheless, Max Weber (1958) argued that attitudes and habits promoted by Cal-
vinist theologians were the cause of profound changes in society, in particular the rise
of capitalism. Other economic historians have felt that a causal relationship between
Protestantism and capitalism is not so easy to demonstrate. The consensus today appears to be approximately as set forth in these lines from the article on "Capitalism" in
the 1972 edition of the *Encyclopaedia Britannica*:

> Without in any sense being the "cause" of capitalism, which already existed on a wide
> and expanding horizon, the Protestant ethic proved a bracing stimulant to the new eco-
> nomic order. Doctrinal revision or interpretation seemed not only to exonerate capital-
> ists from the sin of avarice but even to give divine sanction to their way of life. In the
> ordinary conduct of life, a new type of worldly asceticism emerged, one that meant hard
> work, frugality, sobriety and efficiency in one's calling in the marketplace similar to that
> of the monastery. Applied in the environment of expanding trade and industry, the
> Protestant creed taught that accumulated wealth should be used to produce more
> wealth.

Thus certain key elements in the "Protestant ethic," whatever roots they may have
in interpretations of the Bible, are now widely taught through a variety of means,
from graduate schools of business administration to self-help manuals. Many of those
who practice this ethic as part of the way they do business have no idea of how it
developed; perhaps some are unaware that there are cultures in the world in which its

---

[17]Christopher Hill, "Protestantism and the Rise of Capitalism," as quoted in Kitch 1968, 4.

VII

12

basic attitudes are regarded as outlandish. Still, for many individuals even today, stewardship—the responsible use of resources, especially money, time, and talents—is first of all a religious and moral obligation, even though it may also be good business.

And the language of the Bible remains with us. "Talent" was long ago accepted into the common coin of our tongue. A "servant" is now usually a person who does work on the level of cooking or cleaning, but in the phrase "public servant" the word assumes some of the special significance it occasionally had in the Old and New Testaments. And to one who has fulfilled his responsibilities well and managed resources wisely, we still say, "Well done, good and faithful servant!"

Appendix

The list of Communions that serve also as responsories that follows in Table 1 has been compiled from lists drawn up by Peter Wagner (1921, 327–28), Gabriel Beyssac (1908, 13–14), and Joseph Pothier (1912, 138–39). There is a good deal of overlapping among the three. The feasts that are listed are those of the Communions, as assigned in *Antiphonale missarum sextuplex*, and they are followed by the numbers that identify them in that work. (In cases where a Communion appears on more than one feast, I have selected what seems to be its most prominent role; or I have identified the first time in the liturgical year that it is sung.) I have added the identification numbers given for the responsories in volume IV of *Corpus antiphonalium officii* (*CAO*), and sigla for the sources surveyed there in which the responsories occur. (A capital letter indicates that a text is given in full, a small letter that there is only an incipit.) The numbers of the pages in Hartker's Antiphoner (St. Gallen, Stiftsbibliothek, 390–91; reproduced in facsimile in *Paléographie musicale*, Ser. 2, I) on which the chants occur help to demonstrate the extent to which this practice is restricted to one season—Paschal Time, including Ascension and ending in Pentecost. Five chants do not appear in *Corpus antiphonalium officii*; of these, *Dominus dabit* is mentioned by Wagner, *Responsum accepit* by Beyssac, and the others by Pothier.

Hartker supplies musical notation for the full text of only one of the fifteen of these chants that he includes—*Quinque prudentes virgines*. His references to the others are limited to incipits, and of these only six are notated. All are given verses. Four of them come (on p. 270) at the end of a series of responsories, ten in all, that he presents for the one Nocturn of Matins on Pentecost. Three others appear similarly at the end of a series of responsories for the third Nocturn of Ascension (on p. 265).

In the Antiphoner of Monza 12/75 (early 11th century, from Monza), the three Nocturns of Ascension are in standard form, each having three responsories. The borrowed chants are incorporated into these series—one in the second Nocturn, two in the third. On Pentecost, where there is only one Nocturn with six extra responsories, the borrowed chants are relegated to the end. (An exception is made for *Ultimo festivitatis*, which comes fourth in the series of nine.) All are written out in full. A comparison of their notation with that of the counterpart Communions in the gradual of the same manuscript brings to light numerous minor variants—mostly on the order of the substitution of a virga for a punctum—but the melodies

Table 1

Communions as Responsories

Incipit	Feast and Its Number in Antiphonale missarum sextuplex	CAO IV	Sources	Page in Hartker
Dominus dabit	Dom. I Adv.	1		
Magna est	S. Joannis Ev. 1	13	7114 — h r	304
Quinque prudentes virgines	S. Agnetis 1	25	7496 c — H d F	386
Simile est regnum	S. Agnetis 2	28	7669 — D L	
Responsum accepit	Purif. S. Mariae	29		
Qui me dignatus est	S. Agathae	30	7479 g — E MV h D F S L	123
Pascha nostrum	Dom. Paschae	80	7355 — L	
Si conresurrexistis	Fer. III Pasch.	82		
Dum venerit	Dom. IV p. Pasch.	90	6566 c — M h L	270
Gaudete justi	SS Tiburtii et Valeriani	92	6766 B — h R D f L	252
Laetabitur justus	S. Georgii	93	7064 — h r D f	253
Ego sum vitis vera	S. Vitalis	95	6635 C G — E MV h r D f L	253
Tanto tempore	SS Philippi et Jacobi	96	7754 C G — E MV h r D f L	245
Psallite Domino	Ascens. Dni	102	7445 C — MV h r L	265
Pater cum essem	Dom. p. Ascens	103	7360 C — M h r L	265
Ultimo festivitatis	Vig. Pent.	105	7805 C — M h r S L	270
Factus est repente	Dom. Pent.	106	6717 B — M h r L	270
Pacem meam	Fer. IV Pent.	109	7345 c — MV h D L	265
Non vos relinquam	Sab. Pent.	111	7234 c B — M h r D L	270
Tu puer propheta	S. Joannis Bapt. 2	119	7791 C — h R d f s L	276
Benedicite omnes	Dedic. S. Michaelis	157		
Tollite hostias	Dom. XVIII p. Pent.	193		

seem essentially the same. It suggests that the responsory on a given text was copied into the Monza manuscript from a different source from that of the Communion on the same text. (There is one exception, *Ego sum vitis vera;* but here the notation of the responsory melody, which is substantially different from that of the Communion, breaks off after the ninth syllable, suggesting that the notator realized that something was amiss. The responsory *Qui me dignatus est* is not notated.) Table 2, giving folio numbers for these chants, demonstrates again how the chants involved in this borrowing tend to cluster on a few pages of the manuscript, in one part of the liturgical year. (I have not examined all the Communions of the Monza manuscript, and there are perhaps other chants that should be listed here as well.)

Although in the preceding paragraphs I have followed Peter Wagner in speaking of Communions that are used also as responsories, it should be said that in some cases at least—perhaps more than half—the music of these chants seems to be in the style of responsories, with phrases ending in melismatic figures that occur also in other chants in the same mode. This is certainly true in the case of *Tanto tempore*, said by Holman (1961, 1:200, 204) to be "partly centonized." Others in this style include *Qui me dignatus est, Quinque prudentes virgines, Gaudete justi, Laetabitur justus,* and *Non vos relinquam.* This raises the question of whether these chants may originally have been responsories. Since all of them appear as Communions in the sources surveyed in *Antiphonale missarum sextuplex,* the conversion in use would have to have taken place at an early date, well before that of the earliest Office antiphoners; and it may even have caused some of them to lose their original roles, at least in some churches, for they are not so well known as responsories as they are as Communions. But others among the dual-use chants seem by their style definitely to have been composed as Communions—such as *Factus est repente, Pacem meam, Pater cum essem,* and *Ego sum vitis vera;* the last of these is said by Holman (1961, 1·325) to include no standard [responsory] material.

Table 2
Dual-Use Chants in Monza 12/75

Communion (in the Gradual)		Responsory (in the Antiphoner)
18^r	Qui me dignatus est	133^v
56^r	Ego sum vitis	170^r
56^r	Tanto tempore	170^v
60^r	Pacem meam	173^r
58^v	Psallite Domino	173^v
58^r	Pater cum essem	173^v
59^r	Ultimo festivitatis	175^r
54^v	Dum venerit paraclitus	175^v
59^v	Factus est repente	175^v
60^v	Non vos relinquam	175^v

List of Works Cited

A. Manuscripts

Library and Shelf Number	Provenance	Century
Brussels, Bibliothèque royale, II 3824	St-Benigne, Dijon	13
Cambridge, Fitzwilliam Museum, 369	Lewes	13
Huesca, Archivo de la Catedral, 9	Huesca	13
Ivrea, Biblioteca capitolare, 106	Ivrea	11
Klosterneuburg, Chorherrenstift, 1012	Klosterneuburg	12
Klosterneuburg, Chorherrenstift, 1018	Klosterneuburg	14
Mdina (Malta), Cathedral Museum, B	Aquitaine	12
Metz, Bibliothèque municipale, 461	Metz	13
Monza, Biblioteca capitolare, 12/75	Monza	11
Paris, Bibliothèque nationale, lat. 12584	St-Maur des Fossés	11
Paris, Bibliothèque nationale, lat. 12044	St-Maur des Fossés	12
St. Gallen, Stiftsbibliothek, 390-1	St. Gallen	11
Toledo, Biblioteca capitular, 44.2	Aquitaine	11
Udine, Biblioteca arcivescovile, Oct. 2	St. Gall, Moggio	13
Worcester, Cathedral Library, F 160	Worcester	13
Zürich, Zentralbibliothek, Rheinau 28	Rheinau	13

VII

B. Modern Editions and Secondary Literature

Beyssac, Gabriel. "Motets et Tenors." *Rassegna gregoriana* 7 (1908): 9–26.

Buttrick, George A. *The Interpreter's Bible.* 12 vols. New York, 1951–57.

Carson, D. A. "Matthew." In *The Expositor's Bible Commentary,* ed. F. E. Gaebelein, vol. 8, 1–599. Grand Rapids, Mich., 1984.

Frere, Walter Howard, ed. *Antiphonale sarisburiense.* London, 1901–25.

Hesbert, René-Jean, ed. *Antiphonale missarum sextuplex.* Brussels, 1935.

———, ed. *Corpus antiphonalium officii.* 6 vols. Rome, 1963–79.

Kitch, M. J. *Capitalism and the Reformation.* New York, 1968.

Holman, H.-J. "The Responsoria Prolixa of the Codex Worcester F 160." 2 vols. Ph.D. Diss., Indiana University, 1961. Ann Arbor, Mich.: University Microfilms, order no. 61–4447.

Huglo, Michel. *Les Tonaires.* Paris, 1971.

Jerome, Saint. *Commentaire sur S. Matthieu.* Ed. and trans. Emile Bonnard. Paris, 1979.

Jeremias, Joachim. *The Parables of Jesus.* Trans. S. H. Hooke from *Die Gleichnisse Jesu,* 6th ed., 1962. New York, 1963.

Klauser, Theodor. *Das Römische capitulare evangeliorum.* Liturgiegeschichtliche Quellen und Forschungen, 28. Münster in Westf., 1935.

Liber usualis, with Introduction and Rubrics in English. Tournai, 1950.

McGaughy, Lane C. "The Fear of Yahweh and the Mission of Judaism: A Postexilic Maxim and Its Early Christian Expansion in the Parable of the Talents." *Journal of Biblical Literature* 94 (1975): 235–45.

McKenzie, John L. "The Gospel According to Matthew." In *The Jerome Biblical Commentary,* vol. 2, 62–114. Englewood Cliffs, N.J., 1968.

Pothier, Joseph. "Antiennes de Communion 'Ego sum vitis vera' et 'Ego sum pastor bonus.'" *Revue du chant grégorien* 20 (1912): 133–39.

Smith, C. W. F. *The Jesus of the Parables.* Philadelphia, 1948.

Stanley, David M., and Raymond E. Brown. "The Parables of Jesus." In *The Jerome Biblical Commentary,* vol. 2, 788–90. Englewood Cliffs, N.J., 1968.

Udovich, JoAnn. "The Magnificat Antiphons for the Ferial Office." *Journal of the Plainsong and Mediaeval Music Society* 3 (1980): 1–25.

Wagner, Peter. *Gregorianische Formenlehre.* Einführung in die gregorianischen Melodien, vol. 3. Leipzig, 1921.

Weber, Max. *The Protestant Ethic and the Spirit of Capitalism.* Trans. Talcott Parsons from the revised edition (1920) of "Die protestantische Ethik und der Geist des Kapitalismus," first published in 1904–05. New York, 1958.

VIII

Antiphons for the Benedicite at Lauds

The Canticle of the Three Children is the hymn sung by Shadrach, Meshach and Abednego when they were cast into the fiery furnace by order of Nebuchadnezzar. The episode is described in Daniel 3; but the canticle itself is not present in either Hebrew or Aramaic in the canonical form of the Jewish Scriptures. It was, however, present in the form of the Jewish scriptures from which the Septuagint and later the Vulgate were translated.[1]

In liturgical use, it is treated in two sections, of which the first, "Benedictus es Domine Deus patrum nostrorum" (Daniel 3:52-56), was attached in the Byzantine rite to the Prayer of Azariah, which begins with the same words (Daniel 3:26-45). The second section is "Benedicite omnia opera Domini Domino" (Daniel 3:57-88). In Byzantine Lauds these are the seventh and eighth of the nine canticles to which successive odes of a kanon correspond; in each ode a parallel is drawn between the theme of the canticle and the feast of the day.[2]

In the West there are several different liturgical uses for the two parts of the canticle. The second part, "Benedicite", was one of the Mass chants for Saturdays of Ember weeks where, with Daniel 3.56 as its opening (and with some other modifications), it followed directly upon a lesson that was also drawn from Daniel 3. Some sources give a verse paraphrase, "Omnipotentem semper adorant", or other alternatives, as Hesbert has pointed out.[3])

It also appears in the service of Lauds, where on Sundays and feasts it is the fourth in series of five Biblical excerpts each of which is chanted to a psalm tone and preceded and followed by an antiphon.[4] After the Benedicite come Psalms 148-150, treated as a single unit. This juxtaposition is significant because Ps. 148 not only contains many of the same ideas that were incorporated into the Benedicite, but sometimes even its sequence of ideas is preserved [there]", though the Benedicite is more logically structured than is Ps. 148.[5] When the Benedicite is sung in Lauds, the refrain "Laudate et superexaltate eum in secula" is dropped; and the blessings are arranged not in threes, as in the Mass chant, but in pairs, which makes them fit a psalm tone easily. Antiphons are provided; among them there a wide range of musical style, and the texts ry a good deal in character.

On the basis of their texts, the antiphons for the Benedicite at Lauds may be divided into four groups. The first is made up of antiphons that have nothing in them to indicate that they are for the Benedicite, rather than for one or another of the psalms; these may be assigned to the Benedicite in one manuscript and to one of the psalms in another. In reading through the Lauds antiphons in the manuscripts of which the contents are presented in *Corpus Antiphonalium Officii*,[6] one finds a number of feasts for which the antiphons come in one order in one source, another order in another, as in the case of the Lauds antiphons for the feast of St.Maurice presented in Table I, below. This is just one example among many.

TABLE I

Antiphons in Lauds for the feast of St.Maurice in manuscripts surveyed in *Corpus Antiphonalium Officii*, I, 307

Ivrea, Bibl. cap., 106
  1. Sancta legio Agaunensium
  2. Triumphantes sancti martires
  3. Sanctorum corpora sacri
  4. Preciosa sunt Thebeorum
  5. Ecce factus est sacer ille

Monza, Bibl. cap., c.12/75
  1. Sanctus Mauritius legionem
  2. Sancta legio Agonensium
  3. Preciosa sunt Thebeorum
  4. Ecce factus est sacer ille
  5. Sanctorum corpora sacer

Verona, Bibl. cap., XCVIII
  1. Preciosa sunt Thebeorum
  2. Sanctorum corpora sacer
  3. Ecce factus est sacer ille
  4. Sancta legio Aganensium
  5. Triumpharunt sancti martires

The second group includes those antiphons that carry a clear reference to the text of the Benedicite itself, by borrowing words, phrases, or a style of expression from it. There is an

VIII

example of this in the antiphon for Quinquagesima, *Hymnum dicite et superexaltate eum in saecula, benedicite* [3154]. In the third group belong those antiphons that refer to the Biblical context of the canticle: they speak of the fiery furnace, or of the three young men. *Vim virtutis suae oblitus est ignis, ut pueri tui liberarentur illaesi* reads an antiphon for the 3rd Sunday of Lent [5424]. The fourth group of antiphons includes those in which a connection is worked out between the theme of the canticle and that of the day - an interplay of ideas. These are relatively rare in the standard repertories, but in the later sources they become more frequent. Among the rhymed offices of *Analecta Hymnica* a number of such texts appear.[7]

Texts referring to Benedicite or its biblical context

A certain number of texts belonging to the second and third of the groups just described appear in the older antiphonals (those of the 11th and 12th centuries) assigned to Sundays and feasts of the liturgical year. Others appear in series of antiphons for which no specific liturgical assignment is given. These series of antiphons for the Benedicite form a parallel to series of antiphons for the Benedictus of Lauds, and also for the Magnificat of Vespers; and in dealing with them I have drawn on a methodology developed by JoAnn Udovich in studying antiphon series for the Magnificat.[8] There are series of antiphons for the Benedicite in several of the manuscripts surveyed in *Corpus Antiphonalium Officii*; they appear among the chants for the period after Pentecost, before or after the series of responsories from various books of the Old Testament.[9] It is not always easy to know how they were used; perhaps on a given Sunday one could turn to this part of the book and select whatever antiphon one wished.

Among the antiphons in such series there is no particular consistency either in musical style or in text, though the texts do tend to stay fairly close to the Bible, with a few exceptions. Very often the texts take on the character of introductions to the canticle: they set the scene for it. *Tres in fornace ignis deambulabant et collaudabant Dominum Regem; canentes ex uno ore, hymnum dicebant: Benedictus es Deus, alleluia* [5177] is the antiphon that usually begins the series; it reminds the reader vividly of the context in which the canticle appears in the Bible.

Refrain-type texts

Another groups of texts is made up of antiphons that have the quality of refrains. *Laudate et superexaltate eum in saecula,*

benedicite [3587] certainly has this quality, for it begins with the refrain that is used in the Bible for the Benedicite. And yet it does not end there; it goes on to add the "Benedicite". Why? What reason could there be for adding what must be heard, in the context, as a text incipit?

There are parallels for this procedure in other antiphons (see the texts of the antiphons in the series of St.Gall, Stiftsbibliothek, 391 given in Appendix I). They may end in "Benedictus Deus", "Benedictus es Deus", or even "Benedictus es Deus patrum nostrorum" - that is, not with the incipit of the Benedicite but with that of the Benedictus. The texts of these antiphons consist of condensations of the prose narrative that introduces the canticle in the Bible (Daniel 3.46-51); their concluding phrases evoke the Benedictus (Daniel 3.52-56); and thus they prepare the way, concisely and yet fully, for the Benedicite.

Texts similar to these exist in the repertory of Byzantine chant, in hymns of the type known as kanons. The opening stanzas of the various odes of a kanon (called 'hirmoi') often end by quoting the first few words of the canticle to which they correspond. (This may be continued in the following stanzas, and, if so, the quotation becomes a refrain.) A kanon for the Forefeast of the Nativity of Christ has as hirmos in ode 8: "In Babylon of old by the command of God, the fiery furnace worked in contrary ways: burning the Chaldeans, it refreshed the faithful with dew as they sang: O all ye works of the Lord, Bless ye the Lord."[10] On the Meeting of the Lord (the feast of the Purification), the hirmos of the 8th ode reads: "Standing together in the unbearable fire yet not harmed by the flame, the Children, champions of godliness, sang a divine hymn: O all ye works of the Lord, bless ye the Lord and exalt him above all forever."[11] In subsequent stanzas, each of these kanons develops a connection between the canticle and the feast of the day; but the opening stanza is, like the antiphons we have been considering, an evocation of the Biblical context of the canticle. The contrast between the two genres lies in that the Western examples follow the Bible more closely, while the Eastern texts are more fully developed literary works, particularly in their focussing on and highlighting the contrasts in the situation; and for the Western examples there are, of course, no subsequent stanzas. In the Eastern practice, the hymns had greater status: they replaced the canticles. In the West, the antiphon series progressively declined in importance, and they are rarely to be found in manuscripts of the 13th century and later.

TABLE II

Antiphons in Paris, Bibl. nat., lat.1121, fols.230r-231v
(troper, copied before 1031, from St.Martial, Limoges)

Other sources:
Einsiedeln, Stiftsbibliothek, 83 (monastic antiphonal, 12th c., Einsiedeln - 18 antiphons)
Florence, Arcivescovado (secular antiphonal, 12th c., Florence - 13 antiphons)
Lucca, Bibl. cap., 603 (monastic antiphonal, 12th c., Santa Maria di Pontetto, nr. Lucca - 17 antiphons)
Paris, Bibl. nat., lat.909, fols.258r-259r (troper, copied before 1031, St.Martial, Limoges - 20 antiphons)
Paris, Bibl. nat., lat.17296, fols.320v-322r (monastic antiphonal, 12th c., St.Denis - 17 antiphons)
Piacenza, Bibl. cap., 65 (secular antiphonal, later 12th c., Piacenza - 10 antiphons)
St.Gall, Stiftsbibliothek, 391, pp.226-8 (monastic antiphonal, c.1000, St.Gall - 19 antiphons)
Toledo, Bibl. cap., 44.1, fols.160r-v (monastic antiphonal, 11th c., Aquitaine - 26 antiphons)
Toledo, Bibl. cap., 44.2, fols.212v-213r (secular antiphonal, 11th c., Aquitaine - 6 antiphons)
Utrecht, Bibliotheek der Rijksuniversiteit, 406 (3.J.7), fols.123r-v (secular antiphonal, 12th c., St.Marys, Utrecht - 19 antiphons)

* no musical notation
+ form of antiphon longer than that of Paris 1121
v variant form
numbers indicate the order in each source

	Paris 1121	Eins. 83	Flor. Arc.	Lucca 603	Paris 909	Paris 17296	Piac. 65	SGall 391	Tol. 44.1	Tol. 44.2	Utr. 406
[5177] Tres in fornace	1	1	1	1	1	1	1	1	1v	1	1
[5394] Video virum	2	2	2	2	2	2	2	2	*13	2	2
[3595] Laudemus viros	3	5	4		3	5		3			3
[5175] Tres ex uno ore	4		3	3	4	4			*20		
[5180] Tres video viros	5	4	5	4	5	6	3	12	6		*12
[5176] Tres ex uno ore	6	3	6		6	3	10	9	2		9
[3153] Hymnum dicamus	7	6	7	5	7	*7	4	4	12	3	4
[1726] Benedictus Dominus	8	7	8	6	8	8	5	5	*18	6	5
[1361] Ambulabant	9	8		7	9	9		6	*19		7
[3207] In camino ignis	10	10						7	3		6
[1362] Ambulabant	11	9	9	9	10		6	10	*22		10
[3903] Non cessabant	12	11		10	11	10	7	11	5	4	11
[5178] Tres pueri in	13	12			12	*11		13	*21		14
[4945] Sidrac Misac	14		12	+13	+13	*12		15	*14		13
[5179] Tres pueri iussu	15	13		11	14	13	9	16	7		19
[3206] In camino ignis	16	14		14	15	*14		18	4		*17
[3587] Laudate et	17	15		15	16			17	*16		15
[4946] Sidrac Misac	*18	16						14	*24		16
Deus est cui nos	*19		13	12		17			11		
[1392] Ananias Azarias	20	17	10	8	17			19	*15		*18
[1755] Caminus ardebat	21	18	11	16	18	16	8	8	*17	5	8
[3650] Lux erat in flammis	22			17	19	15			*26		
Pueri tres iussu regis					20						
Benedictus es Domine Deus									8		
Benedictum nomen gloriae									9		
Benedictus es in templo									10		
Cantabant sacerdotes									*23		
Omnia opera									*25		

VIII

4

Antiphon series

The series of antiphons in the Western sources vary both in the number of chants that are included, and in their arrangement. Few sources have as many antiphons as does St.Gall 391. But however many antiphons a manuscript may include, it is likely to present them in an order that corresponds at least to a degree with that of the other sources. The longest series of more or less standard antiphons is that found in Paris, Bibl. nat., lat.1121: it has 22 antiphons. In Table II, the repertory of that source is compared with several others; the similarity of ordering is evident, except in the series of antiphons in the manuscript Toledo, Biblioteca capitular, 44.1 - a group that needs to be studied further.[12]

It is not surprising to find the two manuscripts from St.Martial in fairly close agreement. The series in Paris, Bibl.nat., 17296 has a more than casual resemblance to one in an early antiphonal that lacks musical notation - Paris, Bibl. nat., lat.17436. (See Table III.) The same antiphons appear at the beginning and end; and antiphons come in almost the same order, though Paris 17296 omits some of the antiphons of the earlier source and adds two new ones just before the end.

Melodies

When the melodies are transcribed from the different sources and the readings are compared, for some the tradition is unified: the melody is given in essentially the same form everywhere. This is the case with *Tres in fornace*, of which the text was given above. For others, there are disagreements with respect either to text or to modal designation, and sometimes both. The antiphon *Video virum*, a setting of the words uttered by Nebuchadnezzar when he saw the angel in the fire, is a case in point. (See the transcriptions in Example 1.)

A marginal indication in St.Gall 391 identifies *Video virum* as a mode-3 antiphon;[13] but the Utrecht antiphonal (which often gives readings that match up rather well with the neumes in St.Gall) writes it to end on c. A St.Denis antiphonal, Paris, Bibl. nat., lat.17296, ends it on E; the Piacenza manuscript ends it on G. In comparison with other chants in mode 3, the melody is a little unusual: an ascending 4th is outlined on the first three syllables of each phrase of the text - "video", "similem", "confortan-", and "in cami-". All but one of the manuscripts agree in setting the last of these lower than the others, usually a 4th lower. The difficulty may lie in the fact that the melody as orally transmitted failed to conform to any one mode; some manuscripts show it with a b♭ at one point, a b♮ at another (see the reading of

TABLE III

Antiphons "de hymno trium puerorum" in Paris, Bibl. nat., lat.17436 (secular antiphonal, 860-880, for Saint-Médard of Soissons)

* no notation	Paris 17436	Paris 17296
[5177] Tres in fornace	*1	1
[5394] Video virum	*2	2
[5175] Tres ex uno ore	*3	4
[5176] Tres ex uno ore	*4	3
[3595] Laudemus viros	*5	5
[5180] Tres video viros	*6	6
[3153] Hymnum dicamus	*7	*7
[1727] Benedictus es	*8	
[1726] Benedictus Dominus	*9	8
[1361] Ambulabant	*10	9
[4946] Sidrac Misac	*11	
[3206] In camino ignis	*12	
[1362] Ambulabant	*13	
[3903] Non cessabant	*14	10
[5178] Tres pueri	*15	*11
[5179] Tres pueri	*16	13
[1392] Ananias Azarias	*17	
[4945] Sidrac Misac	*18	*12
[3154] Hymnum dicite	*19	
[3587] Laudate et	*20	
[1728] Benedictus es	*21	
[3206] In camino	*22	*14
[2679] Est Deus	*23	17
[3650] Lux erat		15
[1755] Caminus ardebat		16

Other aspects of the two manuscripts are compared by Dom Jacques Froger in 'Le lieu de destination et de provenance du 'Compendiensis'', *Ut Mens Concordet Voci: Festschrift Eugène Cardine zum 75. Geburtstag,* ed. J.B. Göschl (St.Ottilien, EOS-Verlag, 1980) pp.338-353.

the antiphonal of St.Maur-des-Fossés, Paris, Bibl. nat., lat.12044).

Another possibility for the melodic tradition of an antiphon is suggested by the readings of *Caminus ardebat* that are given in Example 2.

When the divergent readings of *Video virum* wer under consideration, it seemed possible to speak of "the melody as orally transmitted" as a single identifiable entity; but in this instance it is evident that more than one melody existed for the text. The melodies from Utrecht and

Example 1

Antiphon *Video virum*

Utrecht 406, f.123r

Vi-de-o vi-rum   si-mi-lem Fi-li-o De - i,   con-for-tan-tem pu-e-ros

Paris 17296, f.320v

Cambrai C.38, f.56r

Piacenza 65

Paris 12044, f.31r

in ca-mi-no ig-nis,   al-le-lu-ia.

Example 2

Versions of the antiphon *Caminus ardebat*

Paris 17296, f.321v

Ca-mi-nus ar-de - bat sep-ti-es quam so-le-bat;

et sanc-ti tu-i, Do-mi-ne, in me-di-o psal-le-bant.

A-na-ni-as di-ce-bat: Sanc-tus De-us;

A-za-ri-as psal-le-bat: Sanc-tus for-tis;

Mi-sa-el u-na vo-ce cla-ma-bat: Sanc-tus et im-mor-ta-lis,

mi-se-re-re no-bis.

Utrecht 406, f.123r

Ca-mi-nus ar-de-bat sep-ti-es quam so-le-bat;

et pu-e-ri tu- -i, Do-mi-ne, in me-di-o psal-le-bant.

A-na-ni-as di-ce-bat: Sanc-tus De-us;

A-za-ri-as psal-le-bat: Sanc-tus for-tis;

Mi-sa - el vo-ce ma-gna cla-ma-bat: Sanc-tus et im-mor-ta-lis,

al-le-lu-ia.

Monte Cassino 542, p.[56]

Ca-mi-nus ar - de - bat sep-ti-es quam so-le-bat;

et sanc-ti tu-i, Do-mi-ne, in me-di-o psal-le-bant.

A-na-ni-as di - ce - bat: Sanc-tus De- -us;

A-za-ri-as psal-le- -bat: Sanc-tus for- -tis;

Mi-sa - el cla-ra vo-ce di-ce - bat: Sanc- -tus

et im-mor-ta-lis, mi-se-re-re no-bis.

St.Denis are similar in range, and even in the outlines of certain phrases ("Ananias dicebat: Sanctus Deus", and so forth); yet their differences are such that they cannot have descended from the same oral original. In each of them both the final of the mode and the note a 5th above have distinctive roles: by the end of the first or second phrase one knows on what note the chant will end; and the frequent cadences on D have something of the quality of half cadences in tonal music. These are features of the style termed 'post-Gregorian' by some writers.[14]

The melody of the Beneventan version of Caminus ardebat moves in a restricted range and is strikingly repetitive. In any setting of this text, one expects to find the parallelism of the phrases "Ananias dicebat ...", "Azarias psallebat ...", "Misael ... clamabat ..." reflected in their musical setting; but when one hears the figure employed in them stated once again on "immortalis", the impression that is conveyed is of an aesthetic that is different from that of the northern melodies. Instead of moving purposefully towards goals (whether final or intermediate), this melody hovers over a relatively small area, stating and then repeating a few basic structural figures.

It should be noted that the text of this antiphon - once again - incorporates a quotation. This time it is the Trisagion.[15] In view of the fact that both the Trisagion and the Benedicite had prominent roles in the Gallican liturgy, it seems possible that at least the text of this antiphon is of Gallican origin.[16]

Benedictus and tonus peregrinus

When the Benedicite is sung in Lauds, it is chanted to a psalm tone, with the choice of tone and differentia determined by the mode and the beginning of the antiphon. (Appendix I includes the mode and differentia indicated in St.Gall 391 for each of the antiphons in the series.) It has been noted by several writers that antiphons with which the tonus peregrinus is combined are very often antiphons for the Benedicite.[17]

There is no question that the antiphon that is mentioned most often in connection with the tonus peregrinus is Nos qui vivimus, a setting of a verse from Ps.113 that is used in connection with that psalm in Sunday Vespers (on Monday in the monastic cursus). Aurelian of Réome, writing in about the year 843, includes three antiphons in the eleventh division of the 7th mode: Nos qui vivimus, Martyres Domini and

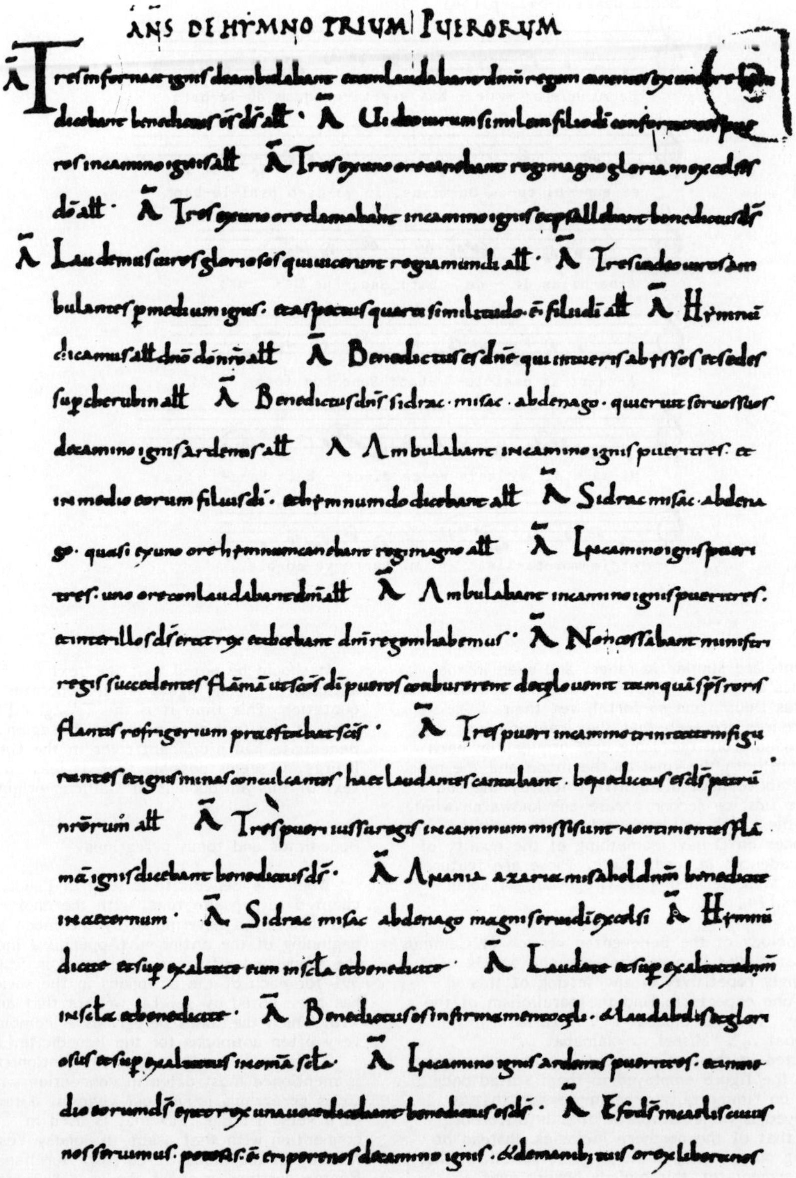

AÑS DE HYMNO TRIVM PVERORVM

Fig. 1   Paris, Bibl. nat., lat.17436, f.96r

Angeli Domini.[18] The latter two are both antiphons for the Benedicite, set to the same melody as *Nos qui vivimus*. His comments concerning the tone to be employed for psalmody with them have been interpreted in various ways.[19] Evidently in his time there was some disagreement concerning this. Aurelian characterizes as "new-fangled" a tone favoured for this use by certain singers, and lends his support to those who continue to sing the verses (of psalmody) with these antiphons "just as they were sung by the ancients".[20] It must be that one of the tones under discussion here is the tonus peregrinus, but which of them is it?

Antiphons associated with the tonus peregrinus in other early tonaries have been enumerated by Russell, in his work concerning the Southern French tonary,[21] and by Atkinson, in his magisterial treatment of the 'Parapteres' in the *Handwörterbuch der musikalischen Terminologie*.[22] In Paris, Bibl. nat., lat.1121, f.205r, the incipits of *Nos qui vivimus* and *Angeli Domini* are given together with the incipit and termination of the special tone. In Paris, Bibl. nat., lat.1118, f.113v, the tone is written out with the incipits of *Nos qui vivimus* and *Martyres Domini* following it. The form of the tone given there is like that in Paris, Bibl. nat., lat.780, f.129v - see Example 3.

The tone as written out in the early sources has the characteristics that set it apart from other psalm tones, in particular the reciting on two different notes: the setting of the second part of the Doxology given in Paris 780 makes it clear that after a second intonation the reciting is indeed on G, a tone lower than that of the first part of the verse. The antiphon incipits accompanying the tone in Paris 780 are *Nos qui vivimus, Martyres Domini, Omnia opera* and *Angeli Domini* - three out of four are for the Benedicite.

The examples just presented are hardly enough to prove the case, but they may suffice to raise the question: can it be that the tonus peregrinus came into being as a tone for the Benedicite (just as there are distinctive tones for the invitatory psalm), and that use of it for other texts (such as Ps.113: *In exitu Israhel*) came as a later development? It is no light matter thus to challenge the significance of the very long association of the antiphon *Nos qui vivimus* with the psalm from which its text derives. Yet in the history of liturgy there are more than a few instances where in the course of 'restoration' an earlier arrangement of chants has been abandoned in favor of one in which the Bible and its ordering controls the sequence of materials. For in the way verses and phrases have been taken out of their contexts and juxtaposed, they have become richly evocative, not only in what they say on the surface but even more in the associations they stir in the listener who remembers the diverse settings in which he first encountered them. The man who connected the antiphon *Nos qui vivimus* with Ps.113 was doing something that was safe, though a little unusual: *Nos qui vivimus* is the beginning of the last verse of the psalm, and usually the antiphons of the Ferial Office have texts that come early in the psalms they accompany.[23] By contrast, the man who connected it with the Benedicite may be said to have been inspired, for he grasped how the worshipper, hearing only a part of the last verse but remembering the whole ending of the psalm, could be stimulated to identify in prayer first with the Psalmist and then with the Three Young Men:

The dead shall not praise thee, O Lord:
nor any of them that go down to hell.
But we that live bless the Lord:
from this time now and for ever.
All ye works of the Lord, bless the Lord.

Example 3

A tone for a special group of antiphons

Paris, Bibl. nat., lat.780, f.129v

Glo-ri-a pa-tri   et fi-li-o   et spi-   -ri-tu-i   sanc-to

Si-cut e-rat in prin-ci-pi-o et nunc et sem-per   et in sae-cu-la sae-cu-lo-rum. A-men.

VIII

If the tonus peregrinus was indeed originally a tone for the Benedicite, then the fact of its having two reciting notes would seem less remarkable. Modal formulas that are not psalm tones often have more than one reciting note - invitatory tones, for example, and formulas for the verses of responsories.[24]

A further study of this question will require more than a little effort, even though most aspects of the tonus peregrinus have already been thoroughly examined by Erbacher.[25] In order to know fully how this tone was used in any individual manuscript - whether in Vespers or in Lauds, and in connection with what antiphons - one must draw up a tonary of the whole source;[26] all of the antiphons and the differentia given with them must be tabulated.

The study of liturgical music thus entails investigating not only the music itself, along with the theoretical systems by which the repertory is ordered, but also its functioning in worship and prayer. The fact that traditional texts are involved - texts from the Bible, along with others with a long history of use in worship - means that each of them comes to the listener or singer enveloped in associations. It is through the interplay of these associations that liturgical texts develop a significant portion of their extraordinary power.

Notes

[1] Carey A. Moore: *Daniel, Esther, and Jeremiah: The Additions*, The Anchor Bible, XLIV (Garden City, N.Y., 1977), pp.39-76.

[2] In *A History of Byzantine Music and Hymnography* (2nd edn., Oxford, 1961), Egon Wellesz demonstrates this through an example that is truly unforgettable: the Resurrection Kanon (the 'Golden Kanon' or 'Queen of Kanons') of John Damascene (pp.206-222).

[3] [R.-J. Hesbert:] 'La tradition bénéventaine dans la tradition manuscrite', *Paléographie Musicale* XIV (Solesmes, 1931), pp.223-4. See also my contribution to *International Musicological Society: Report of the Thirteenth Congress (Strasbourg, 1982)* (forthcoming); and 'The Canticle of the Three Children as a Chant of the Roman Mass', *Schweizer Jahrbuch für Musikwissenschaft*, Neue Folge, 2 (1982), pp.81-90.

[4] For an outline of the service, see 'Lauds', *The New Grove Dictionary of Music and Musicians*, ed. S. Sadie (London, 1980), vol.10, pp.544-5. In an alternative system of terminology for the services of the Divine Office, Matins is called

Vigils (or Nocturns), and Lauds is called Matins. See Robert Taft: 'Quaestiones disputatae in the history of the Liturgy of the Hours: the origins of Nocturns, Matins, Prime', *Worship* 58 (1984), pp.130-158. An important new book on the Divine Office by Father Taft is scheduled for publication in 1986; I thank him for making a copy of the typescript available to me for consultation.

[5] Moore, op.cit. (note 1), pp.42, 75.

[6] René-Jean Hesbert: *Corpus Antiphonalium Officii* (6 vols., Rome, 1963-79). Antiphon texts are printed in full in volume III; in order to determine whether or not an antiphon is meant to introduce the Benedicite one must find where it appears in the various sources by reading through the rubrics and the chant incipits in volumes I and II. In this article, the numbers in square brackets accompanying antiphon incipits are those assigned to them in Hesbert's edition.

[7] Rhymed offices are edited in *Analecta Hymnica*, ed. G.M. Dreves and C. Blume (Leipzig, 1886-1922), vols. 5, 13, 17-18, 24-26, 28 and 45. An office for St.Elizabeth contains the following antiphon for the Benedicite:
    Benedicta vidua,
    Cuius laus assidua
    Laudi confert hominum,
    Benedicit Dominum. (AH 24, 263)
An antiphon in an office for St.Sabina reads:
    Quanta tribus pueris ignes
        tribuere camini,
    Tanta tibi miseri tormenta
        dedere tyranni. (AH 24, 276)
Marcy J. Epstein found that in an office for St.Louis each antiphon in Matins and Lauds was "shaped to fit its particular psalm by the textual devices of paraphrase or thematic continuity"; see her article 'Ludovicus decus regnantium: Perspectives on the rhymed office', *Speculum* 53 (1978), p.289. The antiphon for the Benedicite in that office is:
    Benedixit creatorem
    In suis operibus
    Ludovicus grens morem
    Datum coeli civibus. (AH 13, 187)

[8] *The Medieval Magnificat Antiphons for the Sunday and Ferial Office* (M.A. Thesis, Catholic University of America, 1979; see also her article 'The Magnificat Antiphons for the Ferial Office', *Journal of the Plainsong & Mediaeval Music Society*, 3 (1980), pp.1-25.

[9] Vol.I, pp.238, 376-7; vol.II, pp.727, 744, 748, 756. See also Walther Lipphardt: *Der Karolingische Tonar von Metz*, Liturgiewissenschaftliche Quellen und Forschungen, 43 (Aschendorffsche Verlagsbuchhandlung, Münster Westfalen, 1965),

pp.183-5. Lipphardt suggests that these antiphon series are "possibly relics of the time when it was not yet customary to sing gospel-antiphons to the Cantica".

[10] Mother Mary and Kallistos Ware: *The Festal Menaion* (London, 1969), p.215; the same hirmos also appears in the eighth ode of a kanon for the Synaxis of John the Baptist (p.400).

[11] P.424.

[12] For full identification of each of the manuscripts to which reference is made in this article, see Table II and Appendix II.

[13] In his introduction to the revised edition of *Paléographie Musicale,* sér.2, vol.I (Berne, 1970), Dom Jacques Froger refrains from identifying as that of Hartker the hand that inserted the letters specifying mode and differentia for antiphons. He does say that for all but the last five antiphons of the series, the letters are written "in a small and graceful hand of the 11th century, closely related to that of Hartker" (p.51*).

[14] See for example David Hughes: *A History of European Music* (New York, 1974), p.33.

[15] See Kenneth Levy: 'Trisagion', *The New Grove Dictionary of Music and Musicians,* ed. S. Sadie (London, 1980), vol.19, p.153. The Trisagion is quoted in some antiphons studied by Charlotte Roederer in her doctoral dissertation: *Eleventh-Century Aquitanian Chant: Studies Relating to a Local Repertory of Processional Antiphons* (Yale University, 1971), vol.I, pp.129-139, vol.II, pp.55-6.

[16] See M. Huglo: 'Gallican Rite, Music of the', *The New Grove Dictionary,* vol.7, p.118; and J. Quasten: 'Gallican Rites', *The New Catholic Encyclopedia* (New York, 1967), vol.6, pp.258-262. Lipphardt, op.cit. (see note 9 above), p.185, expresses the view that the series of antiphons for the Benedicite, along with those for the Benedictus Dominus Deus Israhel and the Magnificat, were substantially earlier than the Metz antiphonal of the middle of the 9th century. He continues by offering the suggestion: "Perhaps they belong to a layer common to Milan and the Gallican liturgy."

[17] M. Huglo: 'Antiphon', *The New Grove Dictionary,* vol.I, p.477; Dom Jean Claire: 'The Tonus Peregrinus - a question well put?', *Orbis Musicae: Studies in Musicology 7* (1979-80), pp.3-14.

[18] Joseph P. Ponte III: *The Musica Disciplina of Aurelianus Reomensis* (3 vols., Ph.D. dissertation, Brandeis University, 1961; University Microfilms order no. 62-1207),

vol.II pp.135-6, vol.III p.149. See also Lawrence A. Gushee: *Aureliani Reomensis Musica Disciplina,* Corpus Scriptorum de Musica 21 (American Institute of Musicology, Dallas, texas, 1975), pp.109-110.

[19] Rabanus Erbacher has observed that Aurelian's text "allows of quite contradictory interpretations"; see *Tonus Peregrinus: Aus der Geschichte eines Psalmtons,* Münsterschwarzacher Studien, Bd.12 (Münsterschwarzach, 1971), p.5 Chapter 4 of this work is entitled 'Alter und Herkunft des Tonus Peregrinus': in it Erbacher painstakingly reviews the theories concerning these matters advanced by a number of different scholars.

[20] Aurelian of Réome: *The Discipline of Music,* translated by Joseph Ponte (Colorado Springs, Colorado, 1968), p.41.

[21] Carlton T. Russell: *The Southern French Tonary in the Tenth and Eleventh Centuries* (Ph.D. dissertation, Princeton University, 1966; University Microfilms order no. 67-9182), pp.76-80, 150, 190.

[22] Ed. H.H. Eggebrecht (Wiesbaden, in progress).

[23] Erbacher, op.cit. (see note 19), p.15, n.56) refers to an article by Walther Lipphardt: 'Die Antiphonen der Sonntagsvesper in der altromischen Liturgie', *Der kultische Gesang der abendlandischen Kirche,* ed. Franz Tack (Cologne, 1950), pp.53-63. Lipphardt there identifies *Domus Jacob de populo barbaro* [2427] as the original antiphon for Ps.113: "Here too it is not the antiphon Nos qui vivimus which displays the 'oldest' form, but an antiphon which is frequently encountered in this place in the medieval tradition ... It comes from the second half of v.1 of Ps.113 and has the remarkable text: "Domus Jacob de populo barbaro"." (P.55)

[24] In *Einführung in die gregorianischen Melodien, III: Gregorianische Formenlehre* (Leipzig, 1921), p.112, Peter Wagner pointed out the similarity in structure between the tonus peregrinus and the formula for verses of responsories of mode 1. He held back from expressing a view on the significance of this: "Whether this provides a clue for the explanation of its origin is something I should not care to decide."

[25] Op.cit. (see note 19).

[26] These have been incorporated, in one form or another, into certain facsimiles. In identifying the modal classification of antiphons in the Sarum antiphonal, W.H. Frere found six antiphons with which the tonus peregrinus was to be combined. Three of them are

Nos qui vivimus (to which is joined Ps.113), *Martyres Domini* and *Angeli Domini* (these introduce the Benedicite). The other three antiphons, which are not set to the *Nos qui vivimus* melody, and the canticles they introduce are as follows: *Cum venerit Paraclytus* (for the Benedictus of Lauds), *Da pacem* (for the Magnificat), and *Sapientia clamitat* (also for the Magnificat). (See Frere's index to *Antiphonale Sarisburiense*, London, 1901-24, repr. Farnborough, 1966, vol.I, pp.83-94.) The antiphonal of Worcester, Cathedral Library, F.160 is presented in facsimile in *Paléographie Musicale* vol.XI; I find nothing there to indicate that the tonus peregrinus was known at Worcester. In Lucca, Bibl. cap., 601, of which there is a facsimile in *Paléographie Musicale* vol.IX, two of the antiphons set to the *Nos qui vivimus* melody appear - *Martyres Domini* and *Angeli Domini*. They end on E and are assigned to the second differentia of the 4th tone. Once again, it appears that the tonus peregrinus is simply unknown.

APPENDIX I

Antiphons "ad ymnum trium puerorum" in St.Gall 391

[5177] Tres in fornace ignis deambulabant et collaudabant Dominum Regem; canentes ex uno ore, hymnum dicebant: Benedictus es Deus, alleluia. (Mode 7.5)

[5394] Video virum similem Filio Dei, confortantem pueros in camino ignis, alleluia. (Mode 3.2)

[3595] Laudemus viros gloriosos qui vicerunt regna mundi, alleluia. (Mode 1.3)

[3153] Hymnum dicamus, alleluia, Domino Deo nostro, alleluia. (Mode 8.1)

[1726] Benedictus Dominus Sidrach, Misach, Abdenago, qui eruit servos suos de camino ignis ardentis alleluia. (Mode 7.2)

[1361] Ambulabant in camino ignis pueri tres, et in medio eorum Filius Dei, et hymnum dicebant Deo alleluia. (Mode 8.1)

[3207] In camino ignis pueri tres uno ore collaudabant Deum, alleluia. (Mode 4.8)

[1755] Caminus ardebat septies quam solebat; et pueri tui, Domine, in medio psallebant. Ananias dicebat: Sanctus Deus; Azarias psallebat: Sanctus fortis; Misael voce magna clamabat: Sanctus et immortalis, miserere nobis. (Mode 7..2)

[5176] Tres ex uno ore clamabant in camino ignis et psallebant; Benedictus Deus. (Mode 8.1)

[1362] Ambulabant in camino ignis pueri tres, et inter illos Deus erat Rex, et dicebant: Deum Regem habemus. (Mode 8.1)

[3903] Non cessabant ministri regis succendere flammas, ut sanctos Dei pueros comburerent; e coelo venit tamquam spiritus roris flantis, refrigerium praestabat sanctis, alleluia. (Mode 1.2)

[5180] Tres video viros ambulantes per medium ignis, et aspectus quarti similitudo est Filii Dei, alleluia. (Mode 8.1)

[5178] Tres pueri in camino Trinitatem figurantes, et ignis minas conculcantes, te laudantes canebant: Benedictus es, Deus patrum nostrorum, alleluia. (Mode 8.1)

[4946] Sidrac, Misac, Abdenago, quasi ex uno ore hymnum dicebant Regi magno, alleluia. (Mode 1.1)

[4945] Sidrac, Misac, Abdenago, magni servi Dei excelsi. (Mode 1.1)

[5179] Tres pueri, jussu regis, in caminum missi sunt; non timentes flammam ignis, dicebant: Benedictus Deus. (Mode 8.1)

[3587] Laudate et superexaltate eum in saecula, benedicite. (Mode 8.3)

[3206] In camino ignis ardentis pueri tres, et in medio eorum deambulabat Rex; una voce dicebant: Benedictus es, Deus. (Mode 7.2)

[1392] Ananias, Azarias, Misahel, Domino hymnum dicite in aeternum. (Mode 1.2)

APPENDIX II

Supplementary list of sources

The following sources are mentioned in the article in addition to those listed in Table II:

Cambrai, Bibl. mun., C.38 (40) (secular antiphonal, 13th c., Cambrai)
Monte Cassino, Abbazia, Archivio, 542 (monastic antiphonal, 12th c., Benevento)
Paris, Bibl. nat., lat.780 (gradual, including a tonary, late 11th c., St.Just, Narbonne)
Paris, Bibl. nat., lat.1118 (troper, c.1000, south France [region of Auch?])
Paris, Bibl. nat., lat.12044 (monastic antiphonal, 12th c., St.Maur-des-Fosses, near Paris)

APPENDIX III

Antiphons "DE HYMNO TRIUM PUERORUM" in the St.Denis Antiphonal
(Paris, Bibl. nat., lat.17296, ff.320v-322r)

The transcriptions that follow are intended to demonstrate the musical character of one representative antiphon series. Melodies for the antiphons left without notation in Paris 17296 are supplied from Utrecht 406 and Lucca 603. Orthography and punctuation of the texts are – with minor exceptions – those adopted by Hesbert in *Corpus Antiphonalium Officii* vol.III.

1. Tres in fornace

Tres in for-na - ce ig-nis de-am-bu-la-bant,   et cum lau-da-bant Do-mi-num Re-gem,

ca-nen - tes ex u - no o-re, hym-num di-ce-bant: Be-ne-dic-tus es De-us, al-le-lu-ia.

VIII

14

2. Video virum - see Ex.1

3. Tres ex uno ore clamabant

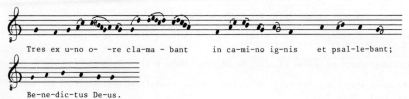

Tres ex u-no o- -re cla-ma - bant   in ca-mi-no ig-nis   et psal-le-bant;

Be-ne-dic-tus De-us.

4. Tres ex uno ore cantabant

Tres ex u-no o-re can-ta-bant Re-gi mag-no: Glo-ri-a in ex-cel-sis De-o, al-le-lu-ia.

5. Laudemus viros gloriosos

Lau-de-mus vi-ros   glo-ri-o-sos   qui vi-ce-runt reg-na mun-di, al-le-lu-i-a.

6. Tres video viros

Tres vi-de-o vi-ros am-bu-lan-tes per me-di-um ig-nis,

et a-spec-tus quar-ti si-mi-li-tu-do est Fi-li-o De-i, al-le-lu-ia.

7. Hymnum dicamus - not notated in Paris 17296. Transcription from Utrecht 406, f.123r

Hym-num di-ca-mus, al-le-lu-ia,   Do-mi-no De-o nos-tro, al-le-lu-ia.

8. Benedictus Dominus

Be-ne-dic-tus Do - mi - -nus   Sid-rach, Mi-sach, Ab-de- -na- -go,

qui e-ru-it ser-vos su-os de ca-mi-no ig-nis ar-den-tis, al-le-lu-ia.

9. Ambulabant in camino ignis

Ambula-bant in ca-mi-no ig-nis pu-e-ri tres,   et in me-di-o e-o-rum Fi-li-us De-i

et hym-num De-o di-ce-bant, al-le-lu-ia.

10. Non cessabant ministri regis

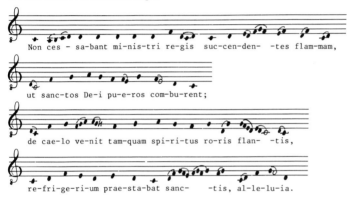

Non ces - sa-bant mi-nis-tri re-gis suc-cen-den- -tes flam-mam,

ut sanc-tos De-i pu-e-ros com-bu-rent;

de cae-lo ve-nit tam-quam spi-ri-tus ro-ris flan- -tis,

re-fri-ge-ri-um prae-sta-bat sanc- -tis, al-le-lu-ia.

11. Tres pueri in camino - not notated in Paris 17296. Transcription from Utrecht 406, f.123v

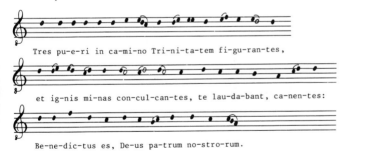

Tres pu-e-ri in ca-mi-no Tri-ni-ta-tem fi-gu-ran-tes,

et ig-nis mi-nas con-cul-can-tes, te lau-da-bant, ca-nen-tes:

Be-ne-dic-tus es, De-us pa-trum no-stro-rum.

12. Sidrac, Misac [4945] - not notated in Paris 17296. Transcription from Utrecht 406, f.123v

Sid-rac, Mi-sac, Ab-de-na-go,   mag-ni ser-vi De-i ex-cel-si.

VIII

13. Tres pueri, visu regis

Tres pu-e-ri, vi-su re-gis,   in for-na-cem mis-si sunt;

non ti-men-tes flam-mam ignis, di-ce-bant: Be-ne-dic-tus De-us.

14. In camino ignis ardentis - not notated in Paris 17296. Transcription from Lucca 603, f.110r

In ca-mi-no ig-nis ar-den-tis pu-e-ri tres,   et in me-di-o e-o-rum de-am-bu-la-bat   Rex;

u-na vo-ce di-ce-bant: Be-ne-dic-tus es, De-us.

15. Lux erat in flammis

Lux e-rat in flam-mis,   ma-jor quam flam-ma u-re-bat;

nam, cum tres pu-e-ros Ba-by-lo-nis   vo-lu-is-set per-de-re rex,

vi-dit junc- -tum qua-si quar- -tum,   in quem cre-de-re dig-num est:

Sal- va -tor e-rat, quem flam-ma ti-me-bat.

16. Caminus ardebat - see Ex.2

17. Est Deus in coelis

Est De-us in coe-lis, cu-i nos ser-vi-mus;   po-tens est e-ri-pe-re nos de ca-mi-no ig-nis

et de ma-ni-bus tu-is o rex, li-be-ra-re.

The close connection between the antiphon series in Paris 17296 and Paris 17436 was
demonstrated in Table III above. Eight antiphons in the earlier manuscript are not included in
the series of the later one; three of them do not appear in any comparable series known to me.
Of these, one is the antiphon for the Benedicite on Quinquagesima, and regularly appears
assigned to that feast, rather than in the series. Another appears to be the respond portion of
the gradual for Trinity: "Benedictus es, Domine, qui intueris abyssos, et sedes super cherubim,
leluia"; perhaps it was included here by oversight. The third begins "Benedictus es in
rmamento coeli"; its text is almost that of the Benedicite antiphon for Sexagesima. It also
esembles closely the opening section of the Mass chant for Ember Saturdays.
Of the five remaining antiphons, the melodies for four can be transcribed from the Utrecht
antiphonal, that for the last perhaps from Lucca 603, though here variants in the text may raise
ubt as to the identity of the work. There is some contrast in both literary and musical style
tween these chants, which were omitted from the series in Paris 17296, and those added to the
ries there: Caminus ardebat and Lux erat in flammis.

drac, Misac - Utrecht 406, f.123v

Sid-rac, Mi-sac, Ab-de-na-go, qua-si ex u-no o-re hym-num di-ce-bant Re-gi mag-no, al-le-lu-ia.

camino ignis - Utrecht 406, f.123v

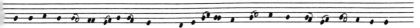

In ca-mi-no ig-nis pu-e-ri tres   u-no o-re col-lau-da-bant De-um, al-le-lu-ia.

ulabant in camino ignis - Utrecht 406, f.123v

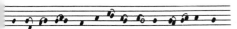

Am-bu-la-bant in ca-mi-no ig-nis pu-e-ri tres,

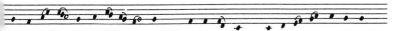

et in-ter il-los De-us e-rat Rex,   et di-ce-bant: De-um Re-gem ha-be-mus.

ia, Azaria - Lucca 603, f.109v

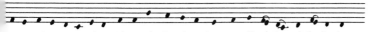

A-na-ni-a, A-za-ri-a, Mi-sa-el, Do-mi-no hym-num di-ci-te, al-le-lu-ia.

late et superexaltate eum - Utrecht 406, f.123v

Lau-da-te et su-per-ex-al-ta-te e-um   in sae-cu-la, be-ne-di-ci-te.

IX

Matins Responsories and Cycles of
Illustrations of Saints' Lives

THE MUSIC OF the medieval Divine Office includes chants of three kinds: hymns, antiphons, and responsories. It is responsories that are to be discussed in this paper—the chants that follow the various lessons of a matins service. I wish to present to the reader one characteristic series of responsories for the feast of St. Benedict, and one for St. Martin, and to compare each with a cycle of illustrations of the saint's life.

In early times the observation of the Divine Office involved almost exclusively texts taken from the Bible, primarily from the book of Psalms. However, even the earliest source in which texts of individual chants of the Divine Office are written out, the antiphonal of the manuscript Paris, Bibl. nat., lat. 17436, dating from the years 860–880, includes several chant series on texts excerpted from or based on saints' lives.[1] To know how this source compares with others, we may consult a work by Dom René-Jean Hesbert, *Corpus Antiphonalium Officii*, in which the contents of six antiphonals of the Roman cursus and six of the monastic are set forth in parallel columns.[2] Even the most cursory glance

---

1. Concerning some of these, see Ritva Jonsson, *Historia: Études sur la genèse des offices versifiés* (Stockholm: Almqvist and Wiksell, 1968), pp. 30–76. Mme Jonsson takes account not only of matins responsories but of all of the chants for the Divine Office. For a survey of the early development of the Office, see Paul F. Bradshaw, *Daily Prayer in the Early Church* (London: Alcuin Club/SPCK, 1981).

2. 6 vols. (Rome: Herder, 1963–1979). In volume 5 of this work, the selection and ordering of matins responsories on the four Sundays of Advent is used as the basis for grouping hundreds of manuscripts of the Divine Office. As Dom Hesbert has pointed out (on p. vi of that volume), the antiphonal—the book containing chants—shows the least change

IX

318

through this work is enough to establish the lack of uniformity in the organization of the services for one day after another; one cannot speak in general of, for example, "the matins service for the feast of St. Benedict"; one must always specify the source in which the service in question appears.

The matins service for a major feast, in the monastic form, consists of an introduction—made up of Psalm 3, the invitatory, and a hymn—and then three large sections, known as nocturns. The first two of these begin with six psalms and antiphons, the last with canticles and a single antiphon. All three nocturns continue with four lessons, each of which is followed by a responsory: thus there are twelve lessons and twelve responsories in all. The lessons are sometimes all from the same source; it may be a continuous text which they separate into sections. Or two texts may be involved, one in the first two nocturns, another in the third. There may be more than two texts. The dividing of the text into lessons may often have been a more or less mechanical process; but there are instances where it seems clearly to reflect thought and judgment.

To turn from lessons to responsories, the most obvious connection among the latter on a particular saint's day is that they all concern the saint; their texts are likely to be excerpts from his *vita*. A case in point is the series of responsories for the feast of St. Benedict in the St. Martial breviary Paris, Bibl. nat., lat. 743, of the eleventh century, which has been discussed in a recent article.[3] A different series of responsories for the same feast is found in a twelfth-century Monte Cassino antiphonal, MS 542 of the Archivio of that monastery. It is nearly identical with the series given in Benevento, Bibl. cap., V, 21, which is one of the sources

___

through time of any of those liturgical books of which the contents were combined to form the breviary. In a particular monastery or cathedral, the lessons of matins on a certain day were far more likely to be changed than were the chants. The notes by Peter Dinter for the new edition of the *Liber Tramitis* (*Corpus Consuetudinum Monasticarum* 10, ed. K. Hallinger [Siegburg: Schmitt, 1980]) show how often this happened in a relatively short period at Cluny, even without taking full account of the lessons in Paris, Bibl. nat., lat. 12601. Given the relative instability of the lessons of matins, and the fact that often within one manuscript a series of responsories may be sung on different days with different series of lessons, correspondence in theme between an individual responsory and the lesson that precedes it may be only the result of happy accident. There is thus a contrast here between the responsory of matins and that of the Mass (that is, the gradual)—a difference not always recognized by medieval commentators on the liturgy, whose writing on this subject was admirably surveyed by Daniel J. Sheerin in a paper delivered at Catholic University on 3 August 1982.

3. "The Music for a Cluny Office of St. Benedict," *Monasticism and the Arts*, ed. T. Verdon (Syracuse, N.Y.: Syracuse University Press, 1983).

surveyed by Dom Hesbert in *Corpus Antiphonalium Officii*, volume 2. The texts are given in Appendix I of this article as they appear in Hesbert's edition (in volume 4), modified only to reflect minor differences, in respect to the designating of verses and refrains, between the Monte Cassino antiphonal and the Beneventan manuscript followed by Hesbert.[4]

Every one of the responsories in the Monte Cassino series is closely connected to the *vita*, not only in content but in phraseology as well. For the first and second of them, the source is the Prologue; for the third and fourth (which are very similar in wording) it is the beginning of chapter 1. Responsories 5 and 6 tell of Benedict's flight to Subiaco and how he made his home there with the help of Romanus (chap. 1). Responsory 7 is a setting of words Benedict addressed to monks who attempted to poison him (chap. 3); Responsory 8 refers to the growing numbers of monks who sought his guidance (chap. 2; the verse is from the end of chap. 1). A story told in chapter 32, of how Benedict raised a child from the dead, is the subject of Responsories 9 and 10. Responsory 11 describes a vision of St. Benedict (chap. 35); Responsory 12 identifies him as the author of a Rule for monks (chap. 36).

What is conveyed through these responsories is thus primarily the broad outline of the saint's life and spiritual growth. There are no references to the miracles at Subiaco described in chapters 5−8, none to the miracles at Monte Cassino (chaps. 9−11), no accounts of how Benedict foretold the future (chaps. 12−22) or of events in daily life at Monte Cassino (chaps. 23−30). Just three miracles are highlighted by being included in this series. The first, which occurred before Benedict went to Subiaco, shows him already able to use miraculous powers to combat the influence of Satan over souls (R. 7). The second is that of raising the boy from the dead, the miracle in which Benedict's power is most evident (Rs. 9 and 10). The third, the vision of the whole world

---

4. Dom R. Andoyer called attention to these responsories in "L'ancienne Liturgie de Bénévent," *Revue du chant grégorien* 23 (1919), 42−44. The musical features that they have in common with other examples of Beneventan chant remain to be identified. (At the Eighteenth International Congress on Medieval Studies at the Medieval Institute of Western Michigan University, Kalamazoo, in May 1983, several papers concerning Beneventan liturgy and chant were presented; but the emphasis there was on tropes, sequences, and chants of the Mass.) An investigation of all of the responsories for St. Benedict in a representative sampling of medieval antiphonaries and breviaries is being carried out by Linus Ellis, a graduate student in the School of Music at Catholic University.

gathered up in a single ray of light, shows Benedict at a climactic moment in his spiritual development—absorbed in God (R. 11).[5]

Since there can be no more than twelve responsories in matins, deciding on the text for each of them requires a high degree of selectivity. The characteristics of the musical genre call for texts that are moderate in length, and consist of two principal parts—the respond and the verse.[6] In order for the musical setting to be successful, the texts must have good rhythm and balanced phrasing; and thus when the wording of responsories is compared with that of the section of the *vita* on which they are based, considerable reworking is often evident.[7]

How much selectivity is involved in the choice of lessons for a matins service? The answer to that question may vary a great deal, depending on how long the lessons are in proportion to the total length of the text from which they are excerpted. An eleventh-century Monte Cassino lectionary—Vatican Library, Vat. lat. 1202—contains the entire text of the life of St. Benedict by Gregory the Great divided into twelve lessons, as follows (references by page and line are to the edition by Umberto Moricca).[8]

> Lesson 1: Prologue—end of chap. 2 (Moricca, 71–80,3)
> Lesson 2: Chap. 3 nearly complete (Moricca, 80,4–84,6)
> Lesson 3: End of chap. 3, chaps. 4–7 (Moricca, 84,7–90,25)
> Lesson 4: First part of chap. 8 (Moricca, 90,26–94,8)
> Lesson 5: End of chap. 8, chaps. 9, 10, and most of 11 (Moricca, 94,9–98,18)
> Lesson 6: End of chap. 11, chaps. 12–14 and beginning of 15 (Moricca, 98,19–102,15)
> Lesson 7: End of chap. 15, chap. 16 (Moricca, 102,15–106,20)
> Lesson 8: Chaps. 17–21 (Moricca, 106,21–112,3)
> Lesson 9: Chaps. 22–24 (Moricca, 112,4–117,3)
> Lesson 10: Chaps. 25–29, beginning of chap. 30 (Moricca, 117, 4–121,9)

5. This outline of the *vita* follows that provided by Odo J. Zimmermann and Benedict R. Avery in the introduction to their translation of the *Life and Miracles of St. Benedict* (St. John's Abbey, Collegeville, Minn.: Liturgical Press, 1949), pp. viii–x.

6. See Helmut Hucke, "Das Responsorium," *Gattungen der Musik in Einzeldarstellungen*, ed. W. Arlt (Bern: Francke Verlag, 1973), 144–191, esp. 166–171 and 182–191.

7. For several examples, see the article referred to in n. 3.

8. *Gregorii Magni Dialogi Libri IV* (Roma: Tipografia del Senato, 1924).

Lesson 11: Continuation of chap. 30, chaps. 31–34 (Moricca, 121,10–128,7)

Lesson 12: Chap. 35–end (Moricca, 128,8–134,18)

If this is to be taken as a serious indication that the whole of this long text is going to be read at matins, and if the responsories of the Monte Cassino antiphonal are inserted after each of the lessons, then in the entire service there are only two responsories that in their texts recall material from the lesson that immediately preceded them. All the rest either return to material that was read somewhat earlier (Rs. 3–8) or anticipate a section of the *vita* that is still to come (Rs. 9–11).

This service can be compared with that of the manuscript Benevento, Bibl. cap., V, 19 (Benevento, twelfth century), which follows the Roman cursus—having only nine lessons and responsories—and in which only selections from the life of St. Benedict are read. The responsories are taken from the series of twelve referred to above; to bring the number down to nine, Responsories 9–11 are omitted. The content of the lessons is as follows:

Lesson 1: Prologue
Lesson 2: First part of chap. 1 (Moricca, 73,6–75,4)
Lesson 3: Continuation of chap. 1 (Moricca, 75,4–77,10)
Lesson 4: Continuation of chap. 1 (Moricca, 77,10–78,8)
Lesson 5: Conclusion of chap. 3 (Moricca, 84,7–86,3)
Lesson 6: Chap. 6 (Moricca, 89,1–19)
Lesson 7: Chap. 7 nearly complete (Moricca, 89,20–90,22)
Lesson 8: Chaps. 9 and 10 (Moricca, 96,21–97,19)
Lesson 9: Chap. 37 and the first part of chap. 38 (Moricca, 132, 4–133,18)

In this service, certain events are recalled only in the lessons: how at Subiaco Benedict recovered the blade of the brush hook from the bottom of the lake (Lesson 6), how Placidus was rescued from the lake (Lesson 7), and how, in the early days at Monte Cassino, Benedict through prayer made it possible for an immovable stone to be lifted and caused a fire in the monastery kitchen to be extinguished (Lesson 8). Through this choice of lessons, emphasis is placed on the power of Benedict as a protector of his monks, an emphasis that appears also in the *Dialogus Miraculorum* of Desiderius, written at Monte Cassino in the mid-eleventh century. Benedicta Ward has seen in this emphasis in the latter

322

work a response to definite needs: "Desiderius . . . was abbot of the monastery of St. Benedict and responsible for many monks and wide possessions; the monks were not only spiritual sons but also tenants of St. Benedict, and for this reason his power was invoked more frequently than his holiness. The miracles recorded by Desiderius illustrate the power of St. Benedict as patron."[9] Another event is recalled only through a responsory—the attempted poisoning (R. 7). There is no reference in the lessons or responsories of this service to the raising of the dead child.

As in the lessons and responsories of matins, so also through series of pictures representing events in the life of a saint, certain emphases can be made. The more limited the number of pictures, the more critical the choice. For the life of St. Benedict, there is a celebrated series of illustrations in the Monte Cassino lectionary.[10] All of the pictures corresponding to events narrated in a single lesson are placed in the manuscript before the beginning of that lesson. Hence the pictures do not stand next to the narrative of the events they represent; they come in groups. Before the first lesson there are two full pages of pictures, showing a number of different episodes. They are accompanied by verses that serve as captions, helping to tell the stories. They are, to be sure, illustrations of the life of St. Benedict, but in this manuscript they are treated not as illustrations of the text they accompany but as a separate narrative—as a life of St. Benedict in pictures with verses that is presented in alternation, section by section, with a life of St. Benedict in words.

There is a direct correspondence between some of these illustrations and the texts of certain responsories. One of them, on fol. 26r, relates to the story of the attempted poisoning. Benedict is shown with hands raised, making the sign of the cross; the vessel of wine, elevated to receive the blessing, is shown at the very moment of its shattering—bits of it are falling through the air. Another group of pictures, on fol. 72r, shows the story of the boy restored to life. The body of the boy lies before the door of the monastery, on the right; on the left, the father meets Benedict returning from work in the fields, in the center, Benedict kneels in prayer. There are other examples; and the illustrations in this

9. Benedicta Ward, *Miracles and the Medieval Mind* (Philadelphia, Pa.: University of Pennsylvania Press, 1982), p. 44.

10. A facsimile edition of this manuscript is currently in press; it will include critical studies of the source, for which the general editor is Paul Meyvaert. The publisher is Johnson Reprints.

series are so abundant that it is difficult to be precise concerning what is stressed in the series and what is omitted from it—apart from the obvious point that there are certain kinds of psychological events, inner states, that are difficult to present in pictures. There is, however, on fol. 79v, a splendid representation of Benedict's vision of the whole world in a single ray of light.

The liturgy and the iconography for St. Benedict have counterparts in works for St. Martin of Tours, and it is with the latter that the remainder of this study will be concerned. For the series of illuminations in the Vatican manuscript there is a parallel in a series of embroidered medallions and panels showing events in the life of St. Martin that date from the first part of the fifteenth century (1430–1435). Their style is that of Franco-Netherlandish art works of the period; and they have been the subject of a distinguished study by Margaret Freeman.[11] Once again, the rather large number of pictures—here, thirty-two roundels, four arched panels, and one oval embroidery—makes it difficult to know what, if any, significance can be attached to the omission of certain events from the series. A further difficulty is that the series is now incomplete, and its original arrangement is unknown. A comparable work in which a more limited number of scenes from the life of St. Martin is shown is a thirteenth-century altar frontal from Iceland now in the Musée de Cluny in Paris.[12]

The work measures about 50 inches in width and $36\frac{1}{2}$ inches in height. There are twelve medallions, each of them about 10 inches across. The order in which they are to be read is that of lines of text on a page; there are four medallions in each horizontal row. Seven of them show events narrated by Sulpicius Severus in his *Life of St. Martin of Tours*, three are connected with stories told in the *Dialogues* (also by Sulpicius Severus), and two with the description of Martin's death given in his *Letter to Bassula*.[13]

In the medallions, Martin is shown first as a soldier, then, after

11. Margaret B. Freeman, *The St. Martin Embroideries* (New York: Metropolitan Museum of Art, 1968).

12. There is a black-and-white reproduction of it in Mrs. Freeman's book (fig. 72, p. 112). The reading of the scenes given here has followed hers, except for that of the first medallion in the lowest line. There are nearly full-size color reproductions of seven of the medallions in Walter Nigg, *Martin von Tours* (Freiburg: Herder, 1977); see plates 4, 12, 18, 19, 36, 39, and 40, and p. 114.

13. For the Latin text of the *Life* and the *Letters*, see Jacques Fontaine, *Sulpice Sévère: Vie de Saint Martin*, 3 vols. (SC 133–135; Paris: Editions du Cerf, 1968–1969). Fontaine's ex-

IX

324

baptism, as a monk, and finally as a bishop. When the sacraments of
baptism and consecration are shown (in the third and sixth of the
medallions), the hand of God appears at the top of the picture, as it does
also in the two scenes (four and five) that show two occasions where the
monk Martin raised a man from the dead. For the two medallions at the
beginning of the series, where the soldier Martin shares his cloak with a
poor man, and then—in a dream—sees Christ holding the portion of
his cloak that he has given away, there is a parallel in the medallions at the
end of the second line. These tell a story from the *Dialogues* (2.1) about
how Martin as bishop of Tours was asked by a poor man for some
clothing, and later gave him his own tunic.

The first medallion in the lowest line shows Martin healing a para-
lyzed girl, an event that took place in the city of Trèves (*Vita*, chap. 16);
the next two show him in the countryside. In one he casts out a demon
from a cow (*Dialogues* 2.9); in the other, he puts a flock of birds to flight
by speaking to them in a commanding voice. If in the first of these we are
reminded of the section of Martin's *Vita* that describes his activity in the
countryside of central Gaul (chaps. 12–15), in the second, it is clear that
the end is at hand. For this episode is told in the *Letter to Bassula*, where it
is immediately followed by a description of the death of Martin.

If this selection is compared with the outline of the whole of the *Vita*
as Fontaine has sketched it out,[14] it is evident that the designer of the
embroidery, wishing to present clearly the broad historical outline of
Martin's life, has done so by limiting severely references to individual
events in his later years. There is thus a parallel between what is shown in
this series of medallions, and the handling of biography in the responsories for Benedict in the Monte Cassino antiphonal.

To what extent can similar procedures be detected in the choice of
lessons and responsories for St. Martin in medieval sources? One manuscript that presents a matins service for St. Martin with fairly extended

tended commentary has been drawn on in a number of places in the present article. For the
text of the *Dialogues*, the Latin is available only in Carolus Halm, *Sulpicii Severi Libri Qui
Supersunt* (*CSEL* 1; Vienna: Apud C. Geroldi Filium Bibliopolam Academiae, 1866),
152–216. There is an English translation by Bernard M. Peebles, "Sulpicius Severus,
Writings," in *FOTC* 7 (New York: Fathers of the Church, Inc., 1949), pp. 79–254. See also
the translation by F. R. Hoare in *The Western Fathers* (New York: Sheed and Ward, 1954),
10–44.
14. Vol. 1, pp. 88–96.

lessons is a Cluny breviary dated ca. 1075—Paris, Bibl. nat., lat. 12601.[15] The lessons are as follows.

Lesson 1: *Vita* 2.1–5
Lesson 2: *Vita* 2.6–8
Lesson 3: *Vita* 3.1–4
Lesson 4: *Vita* 3.5–4.9
Lesson 5: *Vita* 5.1–6
Lesson 6: *Vita* 6.1–7.1
Lesson 7: *Letter to Bassula* 6–13
Lesson 8: *Letter to Bassula* 14–end
Lesson 9: Gregory of Tours, *History of the Franks* 1.9.48
Lesson 10: *Letter to Aurelius* (complete)
Lesson 11: Gregory of Tours, *Liber I de virtutibus S. Martini*, chap. 4 (complete)
Lesson 12: Gregory of Tours, *Liber I de virtutibus S. Martini*, chap. 5 (without last sentence)

In the lessons of the first nocturn, two events of profound significance are narrated: Martin shares his cloak with a beggar (and later has a vision of Christ); and he goes before the emperor to declare that he will no longer serve him, but only Christ. For Martin, the period of military service is transformed into a noviciate; and in the years covered by these lessons, he progresses from passive perfection in the Christian faith to active affirmation of it.[16]

In the lessons of the second nocturn, Martin places himself under the spiritual direction of Hilary of Poitiers. The manifold nature of his vocation becomes evident. Now he undertakes various forms of combat: against pagan error (represented by the brigands he meets in crossing the Alps), against heretics (the Arians), against Satan himself. He feels a call also to asceticism, and to the work of healing, a call to which Hilary gives formal recognition by ordaining Martin as an exorcist. At the very end of Lesson 6, Martin founds the monastery of Ligugé.

With that, the readings from the *Life of Martin* end; the next two

15. Concerning this manuscript, see J. Hourlier, "Le Bréviaire de Saint-Taurin: Un livre liturgique clunisien a l'usage de l'Échelle Saint-Aurin (Paris, Bibl. nat., lat. 12601)," *Études grégoriennes* 3 (1959), 163–173. In the length of the lessons in this breviary, Hourlier sees a reminder of "les grandes dévotions clunisiennes" (p. 165).

16. Fontaine, vol. 1, p. 89.

lessons, comprising most of the *Letter to Bassula*, describe his death. He had a premonition of it; though already ill, he undertook a trip to bring peace among the clergy in a nearby town, and there the end came. Sulpicius gives us the words Martin's disciples used in pleading with him not to die, and also his reply—addressed not to them but to God— "Lord, if I am still necessary to your people, I do not refuse the toil: Thy will be done." [17] The final scene is described in detail (detail faithfully reproduced in the last of the medallions in the Icelandic embroidery), and Martin's last words are reported: "Abrahae me sinus recipit." It is surely, as Bernard Peebles observed, "one of the most eloquent passages in all hagiographical literature." [18]

The lessons of the last nocturn are occupied with burial, with accounts of how news of Martin's death was conveyed to certain individuals, and with mourning. The first of them tells the story of how Martin's body reached its final resting place. The second is the whole of Sulpicius' *Letter to the Deacon Aurelius*. Sulpicius recounts how he learned of the death of Martin, and continues by alternating his laments with praise of the departed. Fontaine has pointed out an exact correspondence between the form of this letter and that proposed by the Greek rhetorician Menander (third century A.D.) for consolatory discourse. He observes that Sulpicius follows the form more strictly than does St. Jerome in his consolatory letters, but modifies the tone of the eulogy in such a way that in the praise of the departed there is more than a hint of cultic veneration. [19] The third and fourth lessons report how Martin's death was revealed to St. Severinus and St. Ambrose in separate visions.

Thus in half the lessons of this service, the central theme is the death of Martin. In the responsories (given here in Appendix II), there is an even greater preoccupation with this subject. No fewer than nine of them incorporate quotations from the *Letter to Bassula*; each of the three passages that follow is drawn on in three different responsories. "Domine, si adhuc populo tuo sum necessarius, non recuso laborem, fiat

---

17. Peebles writes, "The prayer of the dying Martin—and especially his expression of willingness to continue with his earthly work if God so willed, his *Non recuso laborem*— has often been repeated by other saints" (p. 87). Paul Antin cites several examples of this in his study "La Mort de Saint Martin," *Revue des Études Anciennes* 66 (1964), 108–120, pp. 110–111, n. 5.

18. Introduction to the writings of Sulpicius Severus, *FOTC* 7:87.

19. Fontaine, vol. 3, pp. 1180–1182. Concerning the development of the literature of consolation, see Martin R. P. McGuire, "The Early Christian Funeral Oration," in *FOTC* 22 (New York: Fathers of the Church, Inc., 1953), pp. vii–xxi.

Matins Responsories and Cycles of Illustrations   327

voluntas tua," the beginning of the prayer in which Martin responded to his disciples' plea, shows him in inner conflict, his own will opposing that of God, and then yielding. (See Rs. 2, 3, and 9.) "O virum ineffabilem, nec labore victum nec morte vincendum, qui nec mori timuit, nec vivere recusavit," presents Martin as having reached a full monastic *apatheia*, the crowning touch in his sanctity. (See Rs. 3, 4, and 9.) "Oculis ac manibus in coelum semper intentus, invictum ab oratione spiritum non relaxabat," shows Martin steadfast in directing both body and soul heavenward. (See Rs. 2, 5, and 6.)

Still other phrases from the *Letter to Bassula* are found in Responsories 7, 8, 11, and 12. There is also a quotation (in R. 10) from the excerpt from Gregory of Tours that is read in Lesson 12. The only incident in Martin's earlier life referred to directly in these responsories is a vision described at the beginning of the second *Dialogue*: how Martin, having given his tunic to a poor man, entered the church to celebrate Mass, and a globe of fire was seen to spring from his head and rise through the air above him. The two responsories that refer to this event (5 and 6) juxtapose it with a description of Martin's attitude of prayer on his deathbed.

In being chosen to be set to music, these passages have been singled out as themes for meditation; for while they are being sung by some, others will listen. Transformed into the texts of Gregorian chants, they have become part of a cycle: they will be committed to memory, and performed in public year after year. In being incorporated into the liturgy they have had a place assured to them in a body of material that is widely, even popularly, known. The passages in the literature concerning St. Martin to which these chants correspond will become, for many, those that are most familiar.[20]

20. This is not the place for extended comparisons, but the two that follow may be of interest. A breviary from Marmoutier dating from the second half of the thirteenth century, Tours, Bibl. mun., 153, includes eleven of the Cluny responsories in its matins service, in the following order (the numbers here refer to the order in which the same chants occurred in the Cluny MS): 7, 8, 2, 9; 3, 4, 1, 11; 10, Hesbert 6621 *Ecclesia virtute roboratur*, 5, 12. (For several of these the verses are different from those of Cluny.) The lessons are all from a short passage (sections 6–12) of the *Letter to Bassula*; it seems likely that the responsories that accompanied the reading of the longer excerpt from the *Letter to Bassula* in the Cluny breviary appear here at the beginning of the service because of their connection with this text: for example, Cluny R. 7 begins with an echo of the opening of the excerpt, "Beatus Martinus obitum suam longe ante praescivit." An Amiens breviary of about the same date, Amiens, Bibl. mun., 112, which follows the Roman cursus, has the following series of responsories (again indicated by numbers derived from their position in the Cluny matins): 1, 7, 8;

IX

328

Why are the responsories for this matins service for the feast day of St. Martin focused so much on his death? In the early centuries of Christianity, when persecution and martyrdom were facts of everyday life, the story of the Three Children in the Fiery Furnace was often evoked, in various ways, as a model for response to the threat of violent death. After the Peace of the Church, there was a need for models of other kinds; and Martin, as an aged man, rich in years and in achievements, free as only one can be who "neither fears to die nor refuses to live," meeting death with ineffable grace, meets the needs of a time when many Christians could reasonably expect to have a long life and a peaceful death.

It is thus evident that deciding upon texts for lessons and responsories in the medieval Divine Office was far from being a matter of routine. Different choices reveal different attitudes toward the material that was being drawn on, and they reflect the spiritual and even political needs of different times. There are thousands of manuscripts; at present, we can only guess at what a fuller examination of their contents will reveal.[21]

Appendix I

*Responsories in Matina for the Feast of St. Benedict
in the antiphonal Monte Cassino, Archivio, 542 (twelfth century)*

R. 1 (Hesbert 6751): Fuit vir vitae venerabilis, gratia Benedictus et nomine; ab ipso pueritiae suae tempore cor gerens senile, aetatem quippe moribus transiens, nulli animum voluptati dedit.

2, 5, 12; 3, 10, 11. The lessons in the first two nocturns are excerpted from the *Letter to Bassula*; those in the third nocturn are excerpted from the texts read as lessons 9, 11, and 12 in the Cluny service. It is remarkable that in all of these responsories there is no mention of the incident in Martin's life that has been presented most often through the visual arts—the dividing of his cloak with the poor man. In surveying responsories for the feast of St. Martin that appear in a number of different sources, Martha Fickett has found some that do refer to this event. Her doctoral dissertation, soon to be completed at Catholic University, is entitled "Chants for the Feast of St. Martin of Tours." It is primarily concerned with music, and includes transcriptions and analyses of a good sampling of the total musical repertory—antiphons as well as responsories, chants of the Mass as well as those of the Divine Office.

21. An earlier version of this paper was presented at the Seventeenth International Congress on Medieval Studies at Western Michigan University, Kalamazoo, in May 1982, and at the Conference on Medieval and Renaissance Music at the University of Manchester in August of that year. It was begun as a report for a seminar in Greek and Latin hagiography offered at Dumbarton Oaks under the joint direction of Giles Constable and Ihor Ševčenko in the spring of 1981.

V. Relicta domo rebusque patris, soli Deo placere desiderans, sanctae conversationis habitum quaesivit.—Ab.
V. (added later, over the preceding text) Recessit igitur, scienter nescius et sapienter indoctus.—Aetatem.

R. 2 (Hesbert 7252): Nursia provincia ortus, Romae liberalibus litterarum studiis traditus fuerat, sed cum in eis multos per abrupta vitiorum ire cerneret, eum quem quasi in ingressum mundi posuerat pedem retraxit.
V. Ne si de scientia ejus aliquid attingeret, ipse quoque postmodum immane praecipitium totus iret.—Eum.

R. 3 (Hesbert 6836): Hic itaque, cum jam relictis litterarum studiis petere deserta decrevisset, nutrix quae hunc artius amabat sola secuta est.
V. Relicta domo rebusque patris, soli Deo placere desiderans, sanctae conversationis habitum quaesivit.—Nutrix.

R. 4 (Hesbert 7448): Puer Domini Benedictus, cum jam relictis litterarum studiis petere deserta decrevisset, nutrix quae hunc artius amabat sola secuta est.
V. Recessit igitur, scienter nescius et sapienter indoctus.—Aetatem.

R. 5 (Hesbert 6248): Benedictus, Dei famulus, mala mundi plus appetens perpeti quam laudes, pro Deo laboribus fatigari quam vitae hujus favoribus extolli.
V. Nutricem suam occulte fugiens, deserti loci secessus petiit.—Pro.

R. 6 (Hesbert 7890): Vir Dei mundum fugiens, Romanus monachus hunc euntem reperit, quo tenderet requisivit. Cujus cum desiderium cognovisset, et secretum tenuit et adjutorium impendit, eique sanctae conversationis habitum tradidit, et in quantum licuit ministravit.
V. Tribusque annis, excepto Romano monacho, omnibus incognitus mansit.—Cujus.

R. 7 (Hesbert 7158): Misereatur vestri, fratres, omnipotens Deus! quare in me ista facere voluistis? Numquid non dixi vobis quia meis ac vestris moribus non conveniret? Ite, et secundum mores vestros patrem vobis quaerite, quia me post haec habere minime potestis.

330

V. Tunc ad locum dilectae solitudinis rediit, et solus in superni spectatoris oculis habitavit secum dicens.—Ite.

R. 8 (Hesbert 6298): Coeperunt postmodum multi mundum relinquere, et ad almi patris magisterium festinare: liber quippe tentationis vitio, jure jam factus est virtutum magister.

V. Nomen itaque ejus per vicina loca cunctis innotuit, factumque est ut ex illo jam tempore a multis frequentaretur.—Liber.

R. 9 (Hesbert 6532): Dum beatus Benedictus ab agri opere cum fratribus reverteretur, ecce quidam rusticus defuncti filii corpus ante januam monasterii luctu aestuans projecit.

V. Quem, mox ut orbatus rusticus aspexit, clamare coepit: Redde filium meum, redde filium meum.—Ante.

R. 10 (Hesbert 7223): Non aspicias, Domine, peccata, sed fidem hominis hujus qui resuscitari filium suum rogat, et redde in hoc corpusculo animam quam abstulisti.

V. Vix in oratione verba compleverat, coepit reviviscere qui erat mortuus, et jam viventem patri reddidit.—Et redde.

R. 11 (Hesbert 6974): Intempesta noctis hora, cuncta sub silentio, vidit beatus Benedictus fusam lucem desuper cunctas noctis tenebras effugasse.

V. Mira autem valde res in hac speculatione secuta est: nam omnis mundus velut sub uno solis radio collectus ante oculos ejus adductus est.—Vidit.

R. 12 (Hesbert 7894): Vir enim Domini, inter tot miracula quibus in mundo claruit, doctrinae verbo non mediocriter fulsit. Scripsit namque monachorum Regulam, discretione praecipuam, sermone luculentam.

V. Cujus si quis velit subtilius vitam moresque cognoscere, in ipsa institutione Regulae potest invenire.—Scripsit.

Appendix II

Responsories in Matins for the Feast of St. Martin of Tours in the Cluny breviary Paris, Bibl. nat., lat. 12601 (ca. 1075)

R. 1 (Hesbert 6825): Hic est Martinus, electus Dei pontifex, cui Dominus post apostolos tantam gratiam conferre dignatus est, ut in virtute Trinitatis deificae mereretur fieri trium mortuorum suscitator magnificus.

V. Sanctae Trinitatis fidem Martinus confessus est.—Ut in virtute.

R. 2 (Hesbert 6513): Domine, si adhuc populo tuo sum necessarius, non recuso subire propter eos laborem: Fiat voluntas tua.

V. Oculis ac manibus in coelum semper intentus, invictum ab oratione spiritum non relaxabat.—Fiat.

V. Gravis quidem est, Domine, corporeae pugna miliciae; nec deficientem causabor aetatem: munia tua devotus implebo.—Non recuso.

R. 3 (Hesbert 7258): O beatum virum Martinum antistitem, qui nec mori timuit, nec vivere recusavit!

V. Domine, si adhuc populo tuo sum necessarius, non recuso laborem, fiat voluntas tua.

R. 4 (Hesbert 7301): O vere beatum, in cujus ore dolus non fuit, neminem judicans, neminem damnans; numquam in illius ore, nisi Christus, nisi pax, nisi misericordia inerat.

V. O virum ineffabilem, nec labore victum nec morte vincendum, qui nec mori timuit, nec vivere recusavit.—Numquam.

R. 5 (Hesbert 7310): Oculis ac manibus in coelum semper intentus, invictum ab oratione spiritum non relaxabat.

V. Dum sacramenta offerret beatus Martinus, globus igneus apparuit super caput ejus.

R. 6 (Hesbert 6558): Dum sacramenta offeret beatus Martinus, globus igneus apparuit super caput ejus.

V. Oculis ac manibus in coelum semper intentus, invictum ab oratione spiritum non relaxabat.—Globus.

332

R. 7 (Hesbert 6217): Beatus Martinus obitum suum longe ante praescivit, dixitque fratribus dissolutionem sui corporis imminere, quia indicavit se jam resolvi.

V. Viribus corporis coepit repente destitui. Convocatisque discipulis in unum, dixit. —Dissolutionem.

R. 8 (Hesbert 6463): Dixerunt discipuli ad beatum Martinum: Cur nos, pater, deseris? aut cui nos desolatos relinquis? Invadent enim gregem tuum lupi rapaces.

V. Scimus quidem desiderare te Christum, sed salva sunt tibi tua praemia, nostri potius miserere quos deseris. —Invadent.

R. 9 (Hesbert 6377): Cum videret beatus Martinus discipulos suos flentes, motus his fletibus, conversus ad Dominum dixit: Domine, si adhuc populo tuo sum necessarius, non recuso laborem.

V. O virum ineffabilem, nec labore victum nec morte vincendum, qui nec mori timuit nec vivere recusavit; sed conversus ad Dominum dixit. —Domine.

R. 10 (Hesbert 7257): O beatum virum, in cujus transitu sanctorum canit numerus, angelorum exsultat chorus, omniumque coelestium virtutum occurrit psallentium exercitus.

V. Ecclesia virtute roboratur, sacerdotes revelatione glorificantur, quem Michael assumpsit cum angelis. —Virtutum.

R. 11 (Hesbert 7295): O quantus erat luctus omnium, quanta praecipue moerentium lamenta monachorum! Quia et pium est gaudere Martino et pium est flere Martinum.

V. Beati viri corpus usque ad locum sepulcri hymnis canora coelestibus turba prosequitur. —Quia.

R. 12 (Hesbert 7132): Martinus Abrahae sinu laetus excipitur; Martinus, hic pauper et modicus, coelum dives ingreditur, hymnis coelestibus honoratur.

V. Martinus episcopus migravit a saeculo; vivit in Christo gemma sacerdotum. —Martinus.

X

THE GREGORIAN CHANT MELISMAS OF CHRISTMAS MATINS

How Christmas was celebrated in word and song during the Middle Ages is the subject of this paper. Yet, only one small detail of the liturgy for this day can be discussed here, for in the manuscripts of the Middle Ages the lessons, prayers, and chants for Christmas fill page after page. On Christmas, for example, there was not one Mass, but three. The first of these was celebrated while it was still dark, when the first cock crowed, the second at dawn, and the third at the usual hour. Even in addition to these, in the early hours of the morning, a very long service took place, the canonical hour of Matins.[1]

Matins was divided into three sections, or Nocturnes, and each of them began with the chanting of several psalms and antiphons and continued with the reading of lessons. After each lesson a responsory was sung. The number of these varied from place to place, but usually in a cathedral there were three lessons and responsories in each nocturne, and, in a monastery, four.

Though the lessons and responsories vary from one manuscript to another, and a particular responsory may appear in the first Nocturne in one source, in the third Nocturne in another, certain procedures were common. One of these was, on a few important feasts, to give the final responsory of one or more Nocturnes a special character. This was done musically by adding a melisma, a long melody sung to one syllable, near the end of it. Responsories are rather ornate chants, in any case; yet their melodies are usually not unique, being instead based on a group of well-known musical formulas, so the addition of a melisma would add a good deal of musical interest to one of them.

It is impossible to say when this custom of adding melismas began. Amalarius of Metz (who wrote toward the middle of the 9th century) describes it in terms that suggest it was gaining currency at his time. Nonetheless, one theory concerning these melismas is that the few that appear in the earliest notated sources represent a more wide-spread procedure that was almost entirely suppressed in a reform of chant that took place at some time earlier than that when the manuscripts were written.[2]

It is difficult to evaluate this particular idea, but a consideration of two Christmas responsories to which melismas were sometimes added may shed some light on the

---

[1]At Rome, the office of Matins was doubled; see Giuseppe Löw, "Natale," *Enciclopedia cattolica*, VIII (1952), pp. 1671-72. The relationship of the two Matins services has been studied by Dom Raymond Le Roux, "Aux origines de l'Office Festif: Les antiennes et les psaumes de Matines et de Laudes pour Noël et le 1er janvier," *Etudes grégoriennes*, IV (1961), pp. 65-171.

[2]Dom Louis Brou, "Le joyau des antiphonaires latins," *Archivos Leoneses*, VIII (1954), pp. 31-2.

practice. The responsories will be studied here basically as they were in use at the monastery of St. Gall.

Manuscripts 390 and 391 of the St. Gall Stiftsbibliothek together form an antiphonary that was written around the year 1000. The fourth responsory given there for Christmas, the one that ends the first Nocturne, is *Descendit de celis*. It comes at the end of a page. At the beginning of the next page, one finds the last two words of the chant written three times, each time with a different series of neumes over them — "fabricae mundi" (see Plate I).[3]

Though the neumes of this manuscript show some fascinating things about the rhythm of the melismas, they are not precise enough about intervals to enable the melodies to be transcribed. The melodies have to be found in another source. There is no great difficulty in this, for a 13th-century antiphonary from Worcester has the melismas clearly written in staff notation.[4] At least it has the first two of them; but a problem arises with the third, for the St. Gall neumes for the third melisma cannot be made to match the one in Worcester. One must look in manuscripts that are more closely related to the St. Gall one, and thus in two 12th-century antiphonaries from Klosterneuburg (near Vienna) the third melisma does match, and it is also written in such a way that it can be transcribed.[5]

In the Klosterneuburg sources the melody is provided with a text: "Facture plasmator et conditor." The length of the text is determined by the melody, for each note has been given just one syllable. The phrasing of the text also follows the musical phrasing closely; one finds that notes grouped together in a neume in the St. Gall antiphonary are grouped together in the later sources by being given the various syllables of a single word. Such texts as these are called by several different terms: the manuscripts most often call them "prosae" though "prosulae" might be a better term, since it is generally used to refer only to texts, such as these, that are composed to fit pre-existing melismas.

The Klosterneuburg antiphonaries are not the only sources to give a text for the St. Gall version of the third of the "fabricae" melismas. On p. 7 of St. Gall 390 a 13th-century hand has written another text, "Auscultate omnes ubique fideles," that fits this

---

[3]Just at this point, the otherwise excellent facsimile edition fails the reader (*Paléographie musicale*, Series 2, Vol. I, p. 46). The third melisma is made partly illegible by shadows that cover the writing. A look at the manuscript itself removes the difficulty. I am indebted to Dr. Eva Irblich of the Stiftsbibliothek St. Gallen for allowing me to consult this manuscript, and for arranging for me to have a good photograph of this page.

[4]Worcester, Cathedral Library, Codex F. 160; facsimile in *Paléographie musicale*, XII.

[5]The Klosterneuburg antiphonaries 1010 and 1013 are referred to in Bruno Stäblein's article "Tropus," *Die Musik in Geschichte und Gegenwart* (henceforth *MGG*), XIII (1966), Example 9 d, after col. 816. This example shows the text for the melisma that is for use on the feast of St. John the Evangelist, but both manuscripts also give a text for the same melisma that is to be used on Christmas. Two other manuscripts that give this melisma in neumes are the 12th-century antiphonaries Bamberg, Staatsbibliothek, Msc. Lit. 23 (f. 19r) and Msc. Lit. 24 (f. 11r).

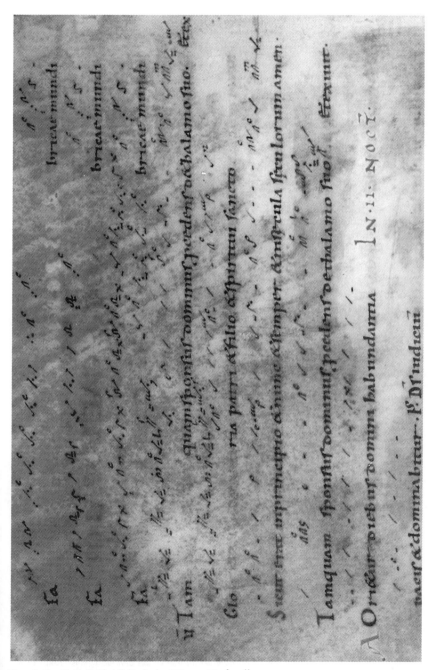

Plate I: St. Gall, Stiftsbibliothek, 390, p. 46, detail.

243

melisma.[6] A third text for it appears in an 11th-century troper-proser from Germany, Oxford, Bodleian Library, Selden supra 27.[7]

The way the text is presented in this manuscript deserves comment. At the beginning of the section of the manuscript devoted to tropes of the conventional type, several pages are given over to prosulae for various sections of the R. *Descendit* and another Christmas responsory. The first of them, "De celis venit," fits one of the melismas that the St. Gall and Worcester antiphonaries had in common. Next comes a text for the long melisma often found in the verse of this responsory (and concerning which it is not possible to go into detail here). This is followed by a text, "Conditor lucis aeterne deus," for the third melisma of St. Gall; and then comes a text for the *Gloria patri*, which has the same melody as the verse. Then follows the text "Celestis aule rex et glorie," which fits the third melisma of Worcester. It is very unusual to find both of these melismas in a single source—the third melisma of St. Gall and the third melisma of Worcester.[8]

The three melismas of Worcester were widely known and sung, with and without texts, through the middle ages and until the 16th century.[9] Their St. Gall counterparts have not been preserved in nearly so many sources, which suggests that they perhaps enjoyed a more local popularity. Since the difference between the two sets lies in their third melismas, can anything be drawn from a comparison of them?

What stands out about the St. Gall third melisma is its very regular form—a a b b c c. Generally speaking, the more regular a form is, the greater the tendency of many scholars to assign a late date to it; hence, despite the archaic appearance of this melisma

[6]The text also appears in St, Gall, Stiftsbibliothek, 380, p. 116. It is published, and another source is referred to, in Léon Gautier, *Histoire de la poésie liturgique au moyen âge, I: Les tropes* (Paris, 1886; reprinted in Ridgewood, N. J.: The Gregg Press Incorporated, 1966), pp. 166-167, fn. XVII. (The manuscript referred to in the second paragraph of fn. XVIII, p. 167, should be Paris, Bibl. nat., nouv. acq. [lat.] 1535, not 1235).

[7]The manuscript may be from Eichstätt, Heidenheim, or Freising-Tegernsee; see H. Husmann, *Tropen- und Sequenzenhandschriften* (Répertoire international des sources musicales, B v [1]; Munich, 1964), pp.163-64.

[8]The texts are as follows:
Oxford, Bodleian Library, Selden supra 27, f. 60r (for the "St. Gall" third melisma):
    Conditor lucis a*et*erne d*eu*s
    fons sapientiae astra creans
    arva regens mari et imperans
    factor matris natus hic de matre
    procedens hodie thalamo patris in gracili nascitur presepio
    angeli psallebant in celis laudes in excelsis domino deo nostro
F. 60v (for the "Worcester" third melisma):
    Celestis aule rex et glorie d*eu*s aeternae
    Cui laus ab angelicis ordinibus sonant iugiter
    Volens pro nobis homo fieri hodie natus est ex virgine
    Quem ovantes celi cives terris predicant
    Quem syderis novi splendor annunciat opificem fabrice

[9]See my article "The Responsories and Prosa for St. Stephen's Day at Salisbury," *The Musical Quarterly*, LVI (1970), pp. 162-182; and Wulf Arlt, *Ein Festoffizium des Mittelalters aus Beauvais* (2 vols.; Köln, 1970), Darstellungsband, pp. 110-115.

in the St. Gall antiphonary, it may be a later substitution for an original melisma that has a less regular form.[10] It is possible that this original melisma was the one given in Worcester; it does appear in a quite early source, the 10th-century gradual and antiphonary of Mont-Renaud.[11] The unusual way in which the melody is notated there (in the margin of the page, vertically, written from bottom to top) constitutes part of the abundant evidence that the manuscript was not originally intended to include musical notation. The editor of the facsimile edition of this source believes, however, that the notation was added rather soon after the completion of the text.

Still another version of this third melisma has been preserved. It begins and ends like the third melisma of Worcester, but a little past half way through it has two additional phrases. The earliest sources to contain this melody are of the 10th and 11th centuries, and they come from Aquitaine. In them the melody is given in texted form. There are three texts, and each of them is given in the three manuscripts Paris, Bibliothèque nationale, lat. 1084, 1118, and 1338. (Two of the texts also appear, without musical notation, in n. a. lat. 1871.)[12] The melody is thus written in these sources a total of nine times. Two of the texts, *Fac domine deus* and *Rex regum*,[13] and their music in 1338 are in great part illegible, which is especially to be regretted since 1338 is set up with more space between the lines of text than the other manuscripts, allowing more exactness in the diastematic musical notation. However, the notation of the remaining text, *Facture tue*, in 1338 is not precise enough to permit reliable transcription from it alone (see Plate II).

[10]Stäblein refers to it as an "Ersatz-Melisma für das dritte Neuma," *op. cit.* If the reasoning above is valid, then the character of this melisma adds to the evidence that, despite the early date of the St. Gall antiphonary relative to other sources, the liturgy it presents is not that of "la plus pure tradition monastique," but has been subjected to a number of revisions. See Dom René-Jean Hesbert, *Corpus antiphonalium officii*, II: *Manuscripti "Cursus monasticus"* (Rome, 1965), pp. VI-IX.

[11]Facsimile in *Paléographie musicale*, XVI, f. 56v.

[12]For the date and place of origin of these manuscripts, see Husmann, *op. cit.*

[13]This is given in part, with a translation, in Richard L. Crocker, *A History of Musical Style* (New York, 1966), p. 33.

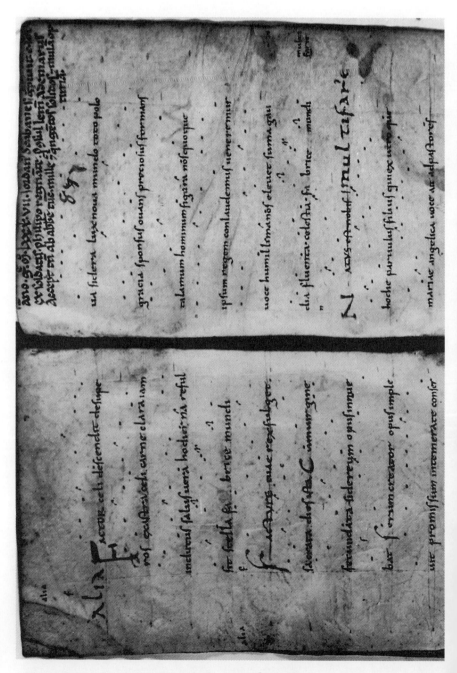

Plate II: Paris, Bibliothèque nationale, lat. 1338, fs. 86v-87r

246

A long search has identified eight manuscripts that have this melody in staff notation or exact diastematic notation.

A. Florence, Curia Arcivescovile, Antiphonary (12th-century antiphonary of Florence)
B. Rome, Biblioteca Vallicelliana, C. 5 (12th-century antiphonary of San Eutizio, near Norcia)
C. Toledo, Biblioteca Capitular, 44.2 (12th-century Aquitanian antiphonary)
D. Amiens, Bibliothèque municipale, MS 112 (13th-century notated summer breviary of Amiens)[14]
E. Lucca, Biblioteca Capitolare, 603 (12th-century antiphonary of Santa Maria di Pontetto, near Lucca)
F. Metz, Bibliothèque municipale, 83 (13th-century antiphonary of Saint Arnould, in Metz)
G. Paris, Bibliothèque nationale, lat 8898 (late12th-century rituale of Soissons)
H. Verdun, Bibliothèque municipale, MS. 128 (13th-century antiphonary from St. Vanne)[15]

When these manuscripts are compared with each other and with the earlier Aquitanian sources it becomes evident that the melody varied a good deal from place to place. This is particularly true with respect to the end of the sixth and the beginning of

[14]It may seem strange to find a summer breviary on this list. Two of the *fabricae* melismas are given in it for a responsory on the feast of Saint Firmin (Sept. 1), *Honestus vero presbiter* (fs. 270r-270v). The same sort of thing happens in the St. Denis antiphonary Paris, B. n., lat. 17296, where the *fabricae* melismas are appended to the R. *Post passionem* on the feast of St. Denis, as Jacques Handschin pointed out (*New Oxford History of Music*, Vol. II [London, 1955], p. 145). In a 13th-century notated breviary of Marmoutier (Tours, Bibliothèque municipale, 153), one of the shorter *fabricae* melismas is incorporated into the last Matins responsory for Saint Martin (*Martinus abrahe sinu*, f. 183r). Similarly, in the antiphonary of San Eutizio the R. *Iste sanctus digne* has one of the shorter *fabricae* melismas supplied for use in the refrain after the verse (Rome, Bibl. Vallicelliana, C. 5, f. 299r). *Iste sanctus digne* is an adaptation of *Descendit de celis*, so this borrowing is not surprising. In St. Gall 390-391, *Iste sanctus* is the last responsory on the feast of St. Gall (p. 325-131 of the facsimile edition), and there it is given the melisma referred to earlier as "the St. Gall version of the third melisma."

[15]Of the manuscripts in this list, C and F are known to me only from a brief examination of photographs of them at Solesmes. I am profoundly indebted to Dom Raymond Le Roux who in the most gracious way imaginable made it possible for me to see these photographs, and made many valuable comments and suggestions regarding this study. F was destroyed in World War II; there is a facsimile of one folio in *Paléographie musicale*, III, Pl. 171. D is described in Victor Leroquais, *Les bréviaires manuscrits des bibliothèques publiques de France* (Paris, 1934), I, pp. 12-14. E is referred to in R. Baralli, "Un frammento inedito di 'Discantus'," *Rassegna gregoriana*, XI (1912), col. 5; and in *Paléographie musicale*, IX, Introduction, p. 12*. There is a facsimile of one page in *Paléographie musicale*, II, Pl. 34. I am grateful to Monsignore Giuseppe Casale of the Biblioteca Capitolare Feliniana in Lucca for allowing me to visit his library during August, when it is ordinarily closed, and for calling this manuscript to my attention. The page in G where the melody appears is reproduced in facsimile in Ernst H. Kantorowicz, *Laudes Regiae: A Study in Liturgical Acclamations and Mediaeval Ruler Worship* (Berkeley and Los Angeles, 1946), p. 256. H is briefly described in *Catalogue général des manuscrits des bibliothèques publiques des départements*, V (Paris, 1879), p. 497. There are prosulae for this melody in the manuscripts as follows: A, "Facinora nostra" (see below, fn. 17); B, "Ante secla deus est;" E, "Concepit Maria."

X

the seventh phrase, where no two sources agree. Musical example 1 shows the various readings of this passage.

Example 1

The transcription that follows as Musical example 2 shows *Facture tue* with the melody that seems to be given for it in lat. 1338.[16]

[16]Professor Daniel J. Sheerin of Catholic University was kind enough to look over this text and suggest some emendations. Lat. 1338 actually has in line 1 *tuae*, line 2 *onus innuebat*, line 3 *Serum*, line 8 *suma*.

248

Example 2

[1] Fac-tu-re tu-e rex ful-get sa-cra-ta di-es is-ta

[2] Cum uir-gi-ne fe-cun-da-ta si-de-re-um hon-nus in-nu-ba

[3] Re-rum cre-a-tor o-pus im-ple-vit

[4] pro-mis-sum in-te-me-ra-te con-ser-ua

[5] si-de-ra lux no-ua mun-do to-to po-lo gra-ci-a

[6] spon-sus o-uans pre-ci-o-sus for-mans ta-la-mum ho-mi-num fi-gu-ra

[7] nos quo-que ip-sum re-gem con-lau-de-mus ue-ne-re-mur uo-ce hu-mil-li-ma

[8] nos e-le-uet sum-ma gau-di-a flu-en-ta ce-les-ti-a fa - bri-ce mun-di

The close relationship between the longer form of the third melisma given above and the shorter form that appears in the Worcester antiphonary is made particularly clear in two other prosulae given to the longer form. One of them is found in two 11th-century manuscripts from northern Italy: a troper from Novalesa (west of Turin, in the mountains close to the French border), and an Ivrea antiphonary.[17] The other appears in a late 13th-century Dijon breviary.[18] Both of these texts begin with the words "Facinora

[17]Respectively Oxford, Bodleian Library, Douce 222, fs. 4r-4v(see Husmann, *op. cit.*, pp.160-161); and Ivrea, Bibl. cap., CVI (described by Dom René-Jean Hesbert in *Corpus antiphonalium officii, Vol. I: Manuscripti "Cursus Romanus"* [Rome, 1963], pp. XX-XXI; Pl. IV shows f. 8v, where part of the prosula occurs). The prosula on fs. 20v-21r of the Florence antiphonary (A in the list given earlier) is like this one, but not quite the same.

[18]Baltimore, Walters Art Gallery, W. 109, fs. 187r-187v.

nostra," the words of the most popular prosula of the Worcester third melisma; at the point in the melody where the added phrases occur, new words are supplied.

In writing about this triple melisma, Amalarius of Metz tells his readers explicitly that it originated in the responsory *In medio* for the feast of St John the Evangelist (27 Dec.) and was only later transferred to *Descendit de celis* and Christmas.[19] It is true that in some manuscripts one or another form of the triple melisma is found with this responsory, but it seems unlikely that such a conspicuous musical elaboration could have been invented for a feast that is in comparison to Christmas of so much less importance. It may be appropriate to re-evaluate Amalarius' testimony, especially in view of the two following observations.

First, Amalarius sees himself both as a historian of the liturgy and as an interpreter of it. His interpretations are imaginative—even fanciful—and exhaustive. In discussing the triple melisma and the feast of St. John the Evangelist he seizes upon the fact that in *In medio* the melisma falls on the word "intellectus," and he expatiates on the relevance of this word to the spiritual state of one who sings a melisma.

In the last responsory, that is the "In medio ecclesiae," contrary to the accustomed manner of the other responsories, a triple *neum* is sung, and its versicle and "gloria" are protracted beyond their usual length by a *neum*. Indeed not without cause has this been done by the men of old. They wished to suggest to us through this some teaching which could, perhaps, have been beyond the minds of the chanters, of whom some part is always changing from the things which pass away to things eternal, and does rejoice rather in things eternal than in things which pass away. For the aforementioned *neum* occurs, among other words, around the word "understanding." So when, o chanter, you come to "understanding," sing the neum, that is, fix your stance in things abiding and permanent. What does this intend? It intends, of course, to teach you that, if ever you come to the "understanding" in which divinity and eternity are beheld, you should pray with the yearning of your mind, tarrying in that "understanding." For if you shall have understood those things, it will delight you to tarry there, in these things which you will joyfully sing, that is you will rejoice without words which pass away.[20]

---

[19]Stäblein, *MGG*, XIII, cols. 811-812.

[20]In novissimo responsorio, id est "In medio ecclesiae," contra consuetudinem ceterorum responsoriorum, cantatur neuma triplex, et versus eius atque gloria extra morem neumate protelantur. Non enim frustra hoc actum est a prioribus. Voluerunt nobis per hoc aliquam doctrinam insinuare, quae forte poterat excedere mentem cantorum, quorum pars aliqua saepe mutatur a transitoriis ad aeterna, et laetatur potius in aeternis quam in transitoriis. Fit enim neuma memoratum, inter cetera verba, circa verbum intellectus. Quando veneris, cantor, ad intellectum, celebra neuma, id est fige gradum in stantibus et manentibus rebus. Quid hoc vult? Vult nempe te docere, se aliquando veneris ad intellectum in quo conspicitur divinitas et aeternitas, ut desiderio mentis preceris, morans in eo. Si enim intellexeris illa, ibi te delectabit morari, in his quae iubilabis, id est laetaberis sine verbis transitoriis. (J. M. Hanssens, *Amalarii episcopi opera liturgica omnia*, Tomus III [Studi e testi, 140; Vatican City, 1950], p. 54. The translation above is by Prof. Sheerin.)

For Amalarius as interpreter, the word "intellectus" is richer in possibilities than the words associated with the melismas in *Descendit de celis*, "fabricae mundi," which mean, approximately, "of the fabric of creation."[21]

Second, it appears that at least one part of the triple melisma did originate elsewhere in the liturgy of the feast of St. John the Evangelist. The first of the three melismas given in St. Gall is found regularly at the end of the second verse of the offertory *Gloria et honore*. This offertory is assigned in modern chant books to the Common of a Martyr not a Bishop; in the early manuscripts it is assigned to the feasts of a number of individual saints, but it is normally written down in full only the first time it appears in the liturgical year—in the first of the two Masses for the feast of St. John the Evangelist.[22]

What follows is, to be sure, only conjecture; but it seems worthwhile to ask whether Amalarius, knowing of the early connection between one part of the triple melisma and the feast of St. John, and familiar with a contemporary practice of singing the triple melisma on the word "intellectus" in *In medio*, let his imagination be over-stimulated by the link that he saw between the meaning of the word and the character of the music, so that he made a false statement about the origin of the practice.

The second of the responsories for which the St. Gall codex gives a long melisma is *Verbum caro*, the twelfth in the series, and the one that might be expected to close this part of the office of Matins. It does in many sources; in this particular manuscript, however, it is followed by six more responsories, which were perhaps for occasional use as substitutes for responsories in the series or as extra chants ad libitum.

The melisma, on "et veritate," is incorporated into the responsory at the end of p. 48. Its phrases are separated by x's (which seem to have served as indications for articulation), and are roughly in the musical form a a b b c a. (C is short, and there is no x separating it from the final a.)

A melisma which matches these neumes rather well can be found, again, in the Worcester antiphonary, on p. 33 of the facsimile edition. The cue indicates that this melisma is to be sung with the R. *Verbum caro* in second vespers of Christmas, though the responsory itself is given a few pages earlier with the Matins chants.[23] The melisma bears the rubric "prosa," though no text for it is given here. However, textings of this

[21]His interpretation of these words is given *ibid.*, p. 56: Eo neumate monstrant difficultatem magnam inesse in scola cantorum verbis explicare quomodo idem qui natus est hodierna die ex Maria virgine, fabricasset mundum et ornasset, et quomodo ipse sit lux et decus universae fabricae mundi.

[22]Dom René-Jean Hesbert, *Antiphonale missarum sextuplex* (Rome, 1967; originally published 1935), No. 13, pp. 18-19, p. 246. The borrowing of this offertory melisma in the responsory was noted by K. Ott in "Die Buchstabenübertragungen des Kodex von Montpellier," *Die Kirchenmusik: Zugleich Mitteilungen des Diöcesan-Cäcilienvereins Paderborn*, XI (1910), pp. 99-100.

[23]This may explain why this melisma is not included in the list of "melismatic tropes" for Matins responsories in the Worcester antiphonary given in the *Journal of the American Musicological Society*, XVI (1963), pp. 42-44. Dom Louis Brou comments about this melisma that it "n'est guère connu en dehors des mss. de l'école de Saint Gall." (*Op. cit.*, p. 28.) In the gradual and antiphonary of St. Éloi de Noyon this melisma is written upside down in the margin, in a hand other than that of most of the musical notation. (*Paléographie musicale*, XVI, commentary, p. 27, fn. 1.)

melisma have been preserved in other sources, and one of them is widely known. It is "Quem [or quam] aethera;" it is given with the "et veritate" melisma following the R. *Verbum caro* in the Klosterneuburg manuscripts 1010 (f. 23v) and 1013 (f. 31v), in St. Gall 380 (pp. 116-117), and (in a 13th-century hand) earlier in St. Gall 390 (pp. 1-8). The text has been published repeatedly.[24]

There is another text that seems also to have been written for the "et veritate" melisma. It begins "Iubilent superni" and is found in the 11th-century manuscript Cambrai, Bibl. mun.,78 (79) on fs. 50r-50v, after a set of texts for the "fabricae" melismas.[25] In Musical example 3 the melody is transcribed primarily as it appears in the Worcester antiphonary, but with modifications to make it correspond more closely with the neumes of the Cambrai manuscript.

Example 3

lu - bi - lent su - per - ni ci - ves al - ma quo - que se - ra - phin col - le - gi - a

na - tus est in ter - ris ho - mo chri - stus ex pro - ge - ni - e da - vi - ti - ca

sol - vens ca - te - nas se - vis - si - mi de - cep - to - ris

qua nos te - ne - bat cru - de - li - tas in - fer - na - lis

gau - de - te gen - tes

po - pu - li re - demp - ti ve - ra e - nim no - bis ho - di - e pax de - scen - dit

[24]See Wolfgang Irtenkauf, "Das Seckauer Cantionarium vom Jahre 1345 (Hs. Graz 756)," *Archiv für Musikwissenschaft*, XIII (1956), pp. 122, 138. In addition to the sources referred to above and those Irtenkauf mentions the following can be named: Bamberg, lit. 23, fs.19v-20r, and lit. 24, 11v-12r; Verdun, Bibl. mun., 128, fs. 38v-39r; Metz, Bibl. mun., 83, f. 29v; Rome, Bibl. Vallicelliana, C. 5, f. 29v; and Udine, Arcivescovado, in fol. 25, f. 3r (12th-century antiphonary of Treviso?).

[25]The manuscript is described by Heinrich Husmann, *op. cit.*, pp. 101-102. Still another text for this melody, beginning "Gloria superno genitori," follows "Quem aethera" in Oxford, Bodleian Library, Selden supra 27, f.61r.

There are references to "Quem aethera" as a prose for *Verbum caro* in breviaries and ordinals of the 13th to 16th centuries.[26] The "et veritate" melisma was still known (and perhaps even sung in the liturgy) in the late 17th century. In his study of Gregorian chant, Guillaume Gabriel Nivers published this melisma in full, disapprovingly, as an example of the sort of excess that the chant reforms of the 16th century should have succeeded in eliminating.[27]

This study of melismas for *Descendit de celis* and *Verbum caro* has involved examining how melismas were interpolated into chants originally composed without them, and how texts were provided for them. It has shown some unexpected connections between widely scattered manuscripts. It has offered additional evidence to show that the chants of the office were subject to frequent modifications of various kinds. And it has sought to demonstrate once again the rich imagination and fascinating ways of the medieval mind.

[26]Among them are the following: a Sarum ordinal of *ca.* 1270 (Walter Howard Frere, *The Use of Sarum, II: The Ordinal and Tonal* [Cambridge, 1901], p. 31); an Exeter ordinal of 1337 (*Ordinale Exon.*, I [Henry Bradshaw Society, XXXVII; London, 1909], p. 66); and a printed York breviary of 1526 (*Breviarium ad usum insigis metrop. ecc. Eboracensis* [Paris, 1526], f. diii).

[27]Guillaume Gabriel Nivers, *Dissertation sur le chant grégorien* (Paris, 1683), p. 74.

XI

Some Melismas for Office Responsories

Sancte Stephane, sydus martyrum Christo preclarus: audi voces nostras.

T HIS SIMPLE PRAYER formed the text of the last Responsory of Matins
on the feast of St. Stephen in the Cathedral of Sens. It was set to the
melody of a Responsory for the feast of SS. Peter and Paul, *Petre amas me*
—a traditional one in mode IV that draws on the typical formulas of that
mode.

This is surely an unpretentious way of ending the last Nocturn of
Matins on the feast day of the patron saint of a major cathedral—too
unpretentious for tastes at Sens, apparently, for various manuscripts of
Sens that have preserved this Responsory give it with various embellish-
ments, that is, different melismas added to it. Among these manuscripts are
the following:

> Paris, B. n., n. a. lat. 1535 (an antiphonary of the end of the 12th cen-
> tury). See Fig. 1.
> Paris, B. n., lat. 1028 (a notated breviary of the second half of the 13th
> century). See Fig. 2.
> Baltimore, Walters Art Gallery, W. 108 (a notated breviary of *ca.*
> 1300).[1]

Like these, other medieval manuscripts occasionally add melismas to
Responsories. The melisma is placed near the end of the Responsory,
in the section that is used as a refrain after the verse (and the Gloria Patri,
if it is sung). In some cases, the melisma is incorporated in the Responsory

[1] For a list of liturgical sources of Sens, see Henri Villetard, *Office de Saint
Savinien et de Saint Potentien,* Bibliothèque musicologique, Vol. V (Paris, 1956),
pp. 91–114. Villetard did not know of the Walters Breviary, but there seems little
reason to doubt that it originated in Sens, as is said by Seymour de Ricci in *Census
of Medieval and Renaissance Manuscripts in the United States and Canada* (New
York, 1935), I, 777, No. 130. The Walters Breviary is small in size and beautifully
executed; it contains only the feasts of the Temporale, except for a few saints' days
after Christmas. I am profoundly indebted to Miss Dorothy Miner of the Walters
Art Gallery for graciously permitting me to examine this manuscript on several
occasions, and to Albert and Mary Ellen Meyer, who first called my attention to it.
The dates given here for the two other manuscripts are taken from Jacques Chailley,
"Un Document nouveau sur la danse ecclésiastique," *Acta musicologica,* XXI (1949),
20, 22; Villetard says they are both of the 13th century. Lat. 1028 is described by
Victor Leroquais in *Les bréviaires manuscrits des bibliothèques publiques de France*
(Paris, 1934), III, 3–5. Leroquais's catalogue has been relied on for dates and places
of origin of other breviaries referred to in this study.

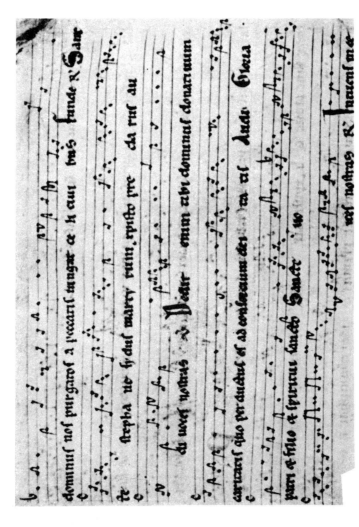

Figure 1. R. *Sancte Stephane sydus*, in Paris, B. n., n. a. lat. 1535, fol. 25 (detail)

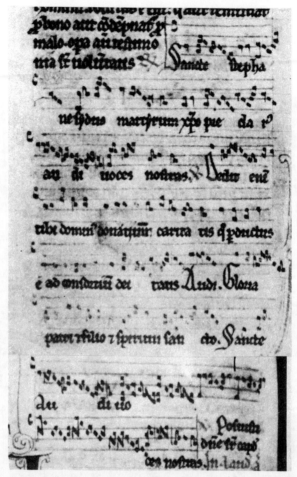

Figure 2. R. *Sancte Stephane sydus*, in Paris, B. n., lat. 1028, fol. 55ᵛ (detail, composite)

and can be identified as added material only if the Responsory (or its melody, with different words) is found elsewhere without the melisma, or if the melisma can be shown to be borrowed from another chant.[2] In other cases the melisma is written after the verse, preceded by a cue for the refrain.

The melisma that n. a. lat. 1535 gives is borrowed from an Offertory; it is the "cor meum" melisma from ℣. 3, "Viam iniquitatis," of the

[2] For another interpretation, that essentially every melisma that occurs in a responsory is a "trope," a later addition, see Hans-Jörgen Holman, "Melismatic Tropes in the Responsories for Matins," this JOURNAL, XVI (1963), 36–46; and Willi Apel, *Gregorian Chant* (Bloomington, Ind., 1958), p. 442.

Quinquagesima Offertory *Benedictus es . . . in labiis.*[3] (The Walters Breviary gives a shortened form of this melisma—about the first half of it.) This melisma occurs again in the manuscript, on fol. 89ʳ–89ᵛ, where it follows *Petre amas me* in both melismatic and texted form. The text, a prosula written to fit this melody, one syllable per note, begins "Psallat in isto die."

The "cor meum" melisma is long and complex, and it stands out in a manuscript of Office chants. It does appear in other such manuscripts; in a 12th-century antiphonary of the Abbey of St. Denis (Paris, B. n., lat. 17296) the last Responsory for St. Stephen is *Patefacte sunt* (fol. 31ʳ–31ᵛ; also a mode IV chant), and the "cor meum" melisma accompanies it.[4] The same melisma also appears in the 12th-century manuscript Laon, Bibl. mun., 263, though not among the chants for St. Stephen.[5] It is given instead in Prime of Epiphany (fol. 113ʳ–13ᵛ) in a quite different role. The psalms for Prime on this day end with the line of Psalm 118 on which the melisma falls in the Offertory; although the rest of the psalm is chanted to the mode VI psalm tone (transposed), this last line, "Viam mandatorum tuorum cucurri cum dilatares cor meum," is sung to the melody given it in the Offertory, including the melisma. Afterwards, there is a prosula, "Cor meum reple tuo lumine."

There are two other antiphonaries in which this prosula appears. Paris, Bibl. Ste. Geneviève, 117, is of the end of the 13th century and of the use of St. Michel de Beauvais.[6] In it the "Cor meum reple" prosula (here, as is more usually the case, beginning "Cor nostrum reple") follows the R. *In columbe specie* in Matins of Epiphany (fol. 44ᵛ), and it is also used in the procession on that day.

The other antiphonary is of the 12th century and from the Premonstratensian abbey of Saint-Marien at Auxerre—Paris, B. n. lat. 9425. The Office for St. Stephen given in this manuscript is said to have been borrowed from the Cathedral of St. Stephen of Auxerre,[7] and indeed the Responsories and prosulae or proses[8] given for St. Stephen are extraordinarily

---

[3] Carolus Ott, *Offertoriale sive versus offertoriorum* (Paris, 1935), pp. 28–30.

[4] This antiphonary is one of twelve studied by Dom René-Jean Hesbert in *Corpus antiphonalium officii* (henceforth CAO), 4 vols. (Rome, 1963–70). I have often relied on the evidence of these manuscripts to determine which of two musically identical chants is the original and which the adaptation: a chant that appears in all or nearly all of the twelve is taken to be better established in the liturgy and hence older than one that appears in only a few of them.

[5] For a discussion of these, see David G. Hughes, "Music for St. Stephen at Laon," *Words and Music: The Scholar's View*, ed. Laurence Berman (Cambridge, Mass., 1972), 137–59.

[6] Solange Corbin, ed., *Répertoire de manuscrits médiévaux contenant des notations musicales*, I: *Bibliothèque Sainte-Geneviève, Paris*, par Madeleine Bernard (Paris, 1965), pp. 61–62.

[7] Pl. F. Lefèvre, *La Liturgie de Prémontré* (Louvain, 1957), pp. XIII, 99 fn. 39.

[8] Perhaps ideally "prosula" should be reserved for situations where a text is written for a melisma that originated in a piece of Gregorian chant, and "prosa" for

interesting. Here (fol. 45^r–45^v) the "Cor nostrum reple" prosula follows the R. *Sancte dei preciose*.[9]

Various things suggest that this use of the "Cor nostrum reple" prosula is rather different from that of the "cor meum" melisma in *Petre amas me* and *Sancte Stephane sydus* at Sens. First, the melody is given only in texted form, not melismatic. Second, the text is a well-established one, known in a number of sources of the 10th to 12th centuries in what appears to be its original role, that of Offertory prosula.[10] Third, the text has no special relevance for the days on which it is used, or the chants that it follows. It seems that the "Cor nostrum reple" prosula was regarded by the compilers of these last two antiphonaries as an independent piece, like a prosa, that could be moved around rather freely, rather than as something that could exist only as an appendage to a larger work.

The "iniusticia" melisma of the Offertory *Gressus meos* had even wider use than "cor meum," as Kenneth Levy has shown; it originated as a sequentia and was taken over into the Offertory.[11] There seem to be significant correspondences in the uses of these two melodies, since "iniusticia" is also used as a melismatic trope for Responsories[12]—at Sens, for example, for the following:

Christmas	R. *In principio*	n. a. lat. 1535, fol. 20
		lat. 1028, fol. 51^r–51^v
		Walters, fol. 131^r–31^v
St. Stephen	R. *Lapides torrentes*	n. a. lat. 1535, fol. 23^v
		lat. 1028, fol. 54
		[Walters, fol. 142^v: no melisma!]
St. John Baptist	R. *Precursor Domini*	n. a. lat. 1535, fol. 85^v
		[lat. 1028, fol. 206^v: no melisma!]

---

independent works in syllabic style intended for specific liturgical functions. But the situation in Matins is so complex it is not always clear which term to use.

[9] Concerning this Responsory, see my article "The Responsories and Prosa for St. Stephen's Day at Salisbury," *The Musical Quarterly*, LVI (1970), 162–82. The typical mode I melisma that ordinarily comes near the end of this rather late Responsory (on "collegio") has been shortened in this manuscript.

[10] Paris, B. n., lat. 776, fol. 33; lat. 903, fol. 32^r–32^v; lat. 1084, fol. 15^r–15^v; lat. 1338, fol. 101; lat. 9449, fol. 27; n. a. lat. 1235, fols. 41^v–42; and Oxford, Bodl. 775, fol. 102^v. (I am indebted to Alejandro Planchart for letting me know of this last source.)

[11] Kenneth Levy, "*Lux de luce*: The Origin of an Italian Sequence," *The Musical Quarterly*, LVII (1971), 40–61.

[12] Henri Villetard, *Office de Pierre de Corbeil* (Paris, 1907), pp. 133–34, reports that in a Sens antiphonary of 1765 this melody was given as the melisma to be added to Responsories of the eighth mode when these occurred in Vespers of "fêtes annuelles." Other writers who have commented on uses of this melisma with various Responsories include Jacques Chailley ("Un Document nouveau sur la danse ecclésiastique," *Acta musicologica*, XXI [1949], 18–23), who found it in a Sens manuscript of the beginning of the 14th century, marked with what he plausibly

The "iniusticia" melisma was also used with Responsories in places other than Sens; for example, it follows *Lapides torrentes* in the St. Denis antiphonary (lat. 17296, fol. 30); but so far no prosulae for it in this role (as Responsory melisma) are known to me.[13]

The "cor meum" melisma is not the only one used in the R. *Petre amas me*. In the summer breviary Amiens, Bibl. mun. 112 (fols. 185ᵛ–86), this Responsory is followed by a different melisma, one that is more commonly found with the R. *O beati viri Benedicti* (Fig. 3). Often it has the prosula "Consors merito."[14] This is one of very few Responsory melismas or prosulae (apart from those that originated in Offertories and those of the R. *Descendit de celis*) to appear in manuscripts of the 10th and 11th centuries. The melisma appears in Nonantolan notation in a section of the manuscript Rome, Bibl. Vittorio Emanuele, Sess. 96, that Bannister thought came from the second half of the 10th century.[15] The prosula is given in Paris, B. n., lat. 1084 (fol. 2ᵛ), which is thought to have been written for Aurillac in the 11th century,[16] and in lat. 1338 (fol. 125).[17]

Another early source for the "Consors merito" melody is the 11th-century breviary of St. Martial de Limoges, Paris, B. n., lat. 743 (fol. 106ᵛ). The melisma was added after the page was completed, though perhaps not very long after; it is written in the lower margin. The melody and its prosula are thus known over a wide geographical area (in Italy, Aquitaine, and Northern France) and a long span of time (from the 10th century to at least the 13th), though they are found in only a small fraction of all the manuscripts that give the R. *O beati viri Benedicti*. The Amiens breviary gives this same melisma again, on the feast of St. Martin (fols. 314ᵛ–15), in the last Responsory, *O quantus erat luctus*.

Still another melody was attached to the R. *Petre amas me*. In his masterly study "Tropus," for *MGG*, Bruno Stäblein published a "verbeta"

referred to as "une véritable séméiographie des pas de danse du préchantre" (p. 23). See also Wulf Arlt, *Ein Festoffizium des Mittelalters aus Beauvais*, 2 vols. (Cologne, 1970), Vol. I (Darstellungsband), p. 223.

[13] For some prosulae for it as an Offertory melisma, see my "The Prosulae of the Manuscript Paris, B. n., f. lat. 1118," this JOURNAL, XXII (1969), 384–87.

[14] Published by Peter Wagner in *Einführung in die gregorianischen Melodien* (Leipzig, 1911–21), III, 509, from the 12th-century antiphonary of St. Maur des Fossés, Paris, B. n., lat. 12044, fol. 159ᵛ.

[15] H. M. Bannister, *Monumenti vaticani di paleografia musicale latina* (Leipzig, 1913), Tav. 54 b, #269; text volume p. 97.

[16] There is not perfect agreement on this; see Heinrich Husmann, *Tropen- und Sequenzenhandschriften*, RISM, B V¹ (Munich, 1964), pp. 120–22.

[17] Lat. 1338 is of the 11th century and from the region of St. Martial de Limoges, if not St. Martial itself. (See Husmann, *op. cit.*, pp. 136–37.) It is unique among the Aquitanian tropers in that it presents a brief series of prosulae for various Responsories, not only *Descendit de celis*. The series includes a prosula for the "inviolata" melisma of the R. *Gaude Maria virgo* (fol. 124ᵛ); one for "quod patrarat" in the R. *Igitur perfecti sunt;* "Consors merito"; "Iam turma celica," a text not for a Responsory but for the "iniusticia" melisma in its role as sequentia for the Alleluia *Confitemini* in the Easter vigil; and then another prosula for "inviolata," ending on fol. 126.

Figure 3. R. *Petre amas me*, in Amiens, Bibl. mun., 112, fols. 185ᵛ–86 (detail, composite)

—a text—for this Responsory, one that up to the time of his writing had been found only in Spain.[18] The verbeta has an unusual melody, as Stäblein shows; it is in three sections, each of them repeated and ending with the same melody as the others. It seems to be essentially the same as the melody that comes toward the end of the last Responsory, *Gloriosus Domini Germanus*, for the feast of St. Germanus of Auxerre in the remarkable Santo Domingo de Silos antiphonary (11th century, in Mozarabic neumes), London, B. M., add. 30850, fol. 224 (229)^v [19] (Fig. 4). It is virtually the same as the melody that ends this Responsory and bears a prosula beginning "Pacis perpetue" in the Sens breviary (lat. 1028, fol. 221^v); just the melisma appears in a 13th-century breviary of Marmoutier (Tours, Bibl. mun., 153, fol. 116), with its second and third sections transposed up a fourth (Ex. 1).

It is a little surprising to find the same melisma used in *Gloriosus Domini Germanus* and *Petre amas me*, since the latter is in mode IV and the former in mode VIII. This particular melisma seems more at home in *Gloriosus Domini Germanus;* the distinctive figure that recurs often in the melisma, c–a–g–$b\flat$–$b\flat$–g–a–f–g, also appears twice in the Responsory. One is tempted to speculate that the melisma went to Spain in the office of St. Germanus and, once in Spain, was transferred to *Petre amas me*.[20]

The texts of the Responsories of the Sens Matins for St. Germanus are rather interesting, for they all come from a life of the saint by a "Constantinus presbyter" that has been published both in the *Acta Sanctorum* and the *Monumenta Germaniae Historica*.[21] At Sens, there were nine proper Responsories for the feast; at Silos, eight; and at St. Denis, three. They are shown in the list below. The numbers in parentheses after the incipits in the Sens column indicate the sections of the *vita* from which the texts are drawn.

Sens	Silos	St. Denis
1. Hic Germanus (1)	1. Hic Germanus	1. O quam preclara
2. Erudiebatur profecto (1)	2. Erudiebatur profecto	2. Germanus plenus
3. O quam preclara (4)	3. Hic vir beatissimus	3. Gloriosus domini
	4. O quam preclara	

[18] *MGG*, Vol. XIII, Notenbeispiel 12, after col. 816; see also col. 815.

[19] This is one of the manuscripts surveyed in CAO; see especially Vol. II.

[20] In CAO, Vol. II, p. XIX, Hesbert comments, "On peut se demander comment le culte de saint Germain d'Auxerre, honoré évidemment en France . . . a pu parvenir en Castille: c'est sans doute par l'intermédiaire des livres liturgiques français—probablement monastiques—qui apportèrent la liturgie romaine en Espagne." A theory counter to that given above could also be proposed: that the melisma and Responsory originated separately and that the presence in the Responsory of a figure that was prominent in the melisma was one reason for the connecting of the two. This seems to have been the case in the R. *Dum beatus Lupus*, discussed below.

[21] *Acta Sanctorum*, Julii Tomus VII (1868), pp. 195–232; *Monumenta Germaniae Historica, Scriptorum Rerum Merovingicarum*, VII (1919), 251–83. The numbers of sections in the list above are taken from the latter edition.

XI

116

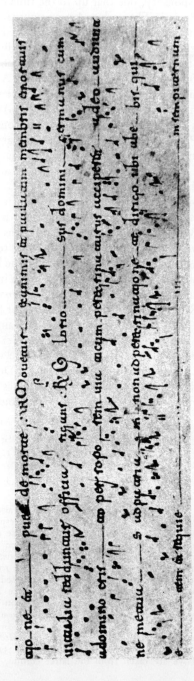

Figure 4. R. *Gloriosus Domini Germanus*, in London, Brit. Mus., Add. 30850, fol. 224 (229)ᵛ (detail)

Example 1

R. *Gloriosus Domini Germanus* and prosula "Pacis perpetue," Paris, B. n., lat. 1028, fol. 221'

118

[Prosula]

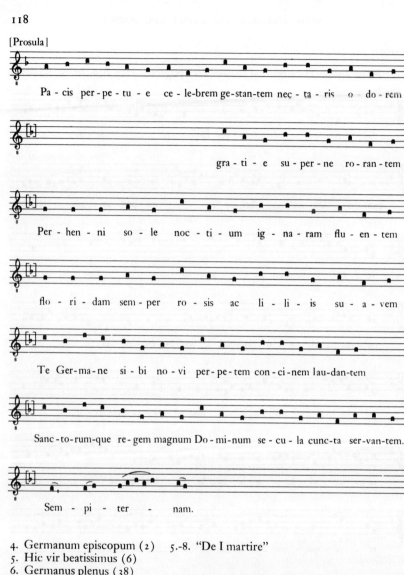

Pa - cis per-pe - tu - e ce - le-brem ge-stan-tem nec - ta - ris o do - rem

gra - ti - e su - per - ne ro - ran - tem

Per - hen - ni so - le noc - ti - um ig - na - ram flu - en - tem

flo - ri - dam sem - per ro - sis ac li - li - is su - a - vem

Te Ger - ma - ne si - bi no - vi per - pe - tem con - ci - nem lau-dan-tem

Sanc -to-rum-que re - gem magnum Do - mi-num se - cu - la cunc-ta ser-van-tem.

Sem - pi - ter - nam.

4. Germanum episcopum (2)   5.-8. "De I martire"
5. Hic vir beatissimus (6)
6. Germanus plenus (38)

7. Presul insignis (13)   9. Germanum episcopum
8. Excubabat diebus (16)   10. Excubabat diebus
9. Gloriosus Domini Germ.   11. Germanus plenus
   (41)   12. Gloriosus Domini
                                 Germanus

It can be seen that the texts come at Sens in the order in which they
do in the *vita*, except for the final responsories of the first and second
Nocturns. These two are particularly dramatic texts; perhaps the displace-

ment was made in order to give a strong ending to these Nocturns. In some cases the text is taken just as it appears in the *vita;* in others modifications have been made. There is an instance of this in the sixth Responsory, which tells of St. Germanus bringing a dead boy back to life. The text of the *vita* follows and then that of the Responsory; words they have in common are in italics.

Vita, section 38

Inhaerent senioris sui manibus sacerdotes, ut pro parentum orbitate et defuncti reditu Domino supplicaret. Diu restitit, sancto pudore confusus; cessit tandem misericordiae et caritatis imperio. Fidei arma concutiens, *turbas eiecit mortuo*que, in oratione *prostratus, adiungitur. Rigat lacrimis* terram, in caelum alti gemitus porriguntur, *vocat planctibus Christum.* Interea movetur exanimis, et paulatim membris emortuis vitalia redduntur officia. Oculi lucem quaerunt, micant digiti, lingua iam resonat; *uterque consurgit, ille de oratione,* iste *de morte.*

Responsory

Germanus plenus Spiritu Sancto, *turbas ejiciens, prostratus adjungitur mortuo, riga*ns *lacrimis* solum, *vocat planctibus Christum; uterque consurgit, ille de oratione,* et puer *de morte.*

The main concern of the arranger of the Responsory text was evidently to tell the important facts of the story concisely, so that the Responsory could make sense independent of the *vita.* The arranger seems to have kept as much as he could of the original language; but he had to sacrifice the moving succession of terse pharses that narrate the boy's gradual return to life.

The Sens Responsories make a satisfactory and complete set, and it would be instructive to learn how many other manuscripts have the nine Responsories in the same order. One is tempted to see Sens as giving the original order, Silos as representing a rather transparent effort to adapt a Roman Office for a place where the monastic use was followed, and St. Denis as representing a place where less was made of the feast, and the three Responsories selected were the most memorable of the series. However, given the small number of sources known to me at the present time, this speculation is probably premature. When the texts of the Responsories at Sens are compared with the Matins lessons of the same manuscript (lat. 1028, fols. 219ᵛ–21ᵛ), one finds that two Responsories (the seventh and eighth) are based on texts not read at all during the lessons; and that Responsory and lesson texts are not matched up: the sixth Responsory gives the conclusion of the story narrated in the seventh and eighth lessons.

The Responsory in this series for which the melisma under discussion is given, *Gloriosus Domini Germanus,* is last in all three sources. The text tells how Germanus was told by God in a dream that his death was near.

Gloriosus Domini Germanus, cum a Domino Christo per soporem viaticum

XI

peregrinaturus acciperet, ab eo audivit: Ne metuas; ad patriam, non ad peregrinationem, te dirigo, ubi habebis quietem et requiem sempiternam.

It is for the climactic word "requiem" that lat. 1028 gives this unusual melisma, and later the text "Pacis perpetue," and Add. 30850 gives the melisma, but lat. 17296 gives neither a melisma nor a prosula—noteworthy because this manuscript does give one or the other on several saints' days. The melisma and prosula melody of lat. 1028 seem to match the melisma of Add. 30850 in principle, though not down to the smallest detail.

Other Responsories in this office have melismas; one of them is *Erudiebatur profecto*, the melody of which is borrowed (except for the first phrase) from the R. *Sancte Paule apostole*. The melisma, however, did not originate here, for it comes from the antiphon of the Offertory *Stetit angelus*, where it is sung to the words "et ascendit."[22]

The "cor meum" melisma and the melody of *Sancte Stephane sydus* are thus connected, together and separately, like strands in a web with many other Responsories and melismas. In lat. 1028, a different melisma is given for *Sancte Stephane sydus*, one that leads to further connections.

This melisma consists of three phrases, each of them repeated, followed by an unpaired phrase. It seems to have a strong mode I character, and its use here in connection with a mode IV chant is noteworthy.[23] The melody would seem familiar to any student of the Sarum antiphonary; there—in somewhat modified form, with a different fourth phrase, followed by a repeat of the opening—it follows the R. *Centum quadraginta* (the last Responsory on the feast of the Holy Innocents), bearing the prosula "Sedentem in superne."[24]

One curious thing about this melody—henceforth "the S melisma"—is that the first part of it is sometimes used in other contexts; and the remainder of it is sometimes found without the first phrase. The first two phrases appear at the opening of the initial melisma of *Ecce iam coram te*, a Responsory for St. Stephen that was used at Sens and in a number of other places, though it seems from the manuscript tradition to have been

[22] It may be more correct to refer to this as the "ascendentem" melisma of the Off. *Viri Galilaei;* for the relationship of these two Offertories, see René-Jean Hesbert, *Antiphonale missarum sextuplex* (Rome, 1967; originally published 1935), pp. LXVI and CVIII. There is a Notre Dame clausula on this melisma, F Nr. 457 (fol. 184ᵛ); see Gordon A. Anderson, "Newly Identified Tenor Chants in the Notre Dame Repertory," *Music and Letters*, L (1969), 167.

[23] Villetard reports (*Office de Pierre de Corbeil*, p. 157) that this melisma was used in the printed Sens antiphonary of 1765 to end Responsories in modes I, II, and IV and that it appears in "tous les documents liturgiques senonais."

[24] *Antiphonale sarisburiense*, ed. W. H. Frere (London, 1901-24; reprinted in 1966 and issued in 6 vols.), II, 71. The prosula also appears in the printed Sarum antiphonary of 1519, fol. lxxxiᵛ. Given the differences between the melody of "Sedentem in superne" and the Sens melisma, it might be misleading to refer to the latter as the "sedentem" melisma, convenient though that would be; I shall call it "the S melisma," a mode of reference that may seem to call up both Sens and "sedentem" without being too explicit.

a rather late chant.[25] The longest of the three melismas for *Descendit de celis* was sometimes added at the end of this chant (as, for example, in lat. 1028, fol. 55, and in *Variae preces*[26]), and the Montpellier motet manuscript has a motet by Petrus de Cruce on the "Ecce" melisma.[27]

The first part of the S melisma is also used in the Alleluia *Posuisti*. Though not in the earliest sources (it is not given in any of the manuscripts surveyed in *Antiphonale missarum sextuplex*), this Alleluia is well represented in sources of the 11th century; according to Schlager it is part of the standard repertoire and one of the most frequently adapted melodies—there are nine different verses for it.[28] The melody is strongly stated in the Alleluia: at the beginning, at the beginning of the verse, and again on the last word of the verse, and it seems to lend its flavor to the whole chant.[29]

Before the use of this melody with other Responsories is taken up, a few words may be said concerning its use in other roles. In the special Offices for the feast of the Circumcision at Sens and Beauvais, "Sedentem in superne" was used as an independent piece: at Sens as the Terce Versicle, at Beauvais as a prosa after the psalms and antiphons in the second Nocturn of Matins.[30]

At Laon, "Sedentem in superne" was inserted into the Gloria that now appears as part of Mass XI in the modern chant editions.[31] It was set between the words "Jesu Christe" and "Cum Sancto Spiritu"—just at the point where one of the so-called "Regnum prosulae" might be found, though of course the "Regnum" melody is different.[32] This use of "Seden-

[25] Of the sources surveyed in CAO, only the St. Denis and St. Maur des Fossés antiphonaries give this chant, and they have it on the Inventio (in August) rather than on December 26. The earliest source I know for *Ecce iam* is the tonary of the 11th-century Gradual of St. Michel de Gaillac, Paris, B. n., lat. 776, fol. 150ᵛ; but here the melisma is given in somewhat different form, and the characteristic intervals of the beginning of the melody are not present.

[26] Solesmes, 1901, pp. 79–80. Willi Apel, *op. cit.*, p. 442, quotes this melisma from the *Processionale monasticum*.

[27] Yvonne Rokseth, *Polyphonies du XIIIᵉ siècle* (Paris, 1935–39). The motet, "S'amours eüst—Au renouveler—Ecce," is No. 253 of the manuscript; it opens the seventh fascicle. It is referred to in the *Speculum musicae* of Jacobus of Liège (E. de Coussemaker, *Scriptorum de musica medii aevi*, II [Paris: Durand, 1867], 401 a), and the ascription to Petrus de Cruce is made there.

[28] Karl-Heinz Schlager, *Thematischer Katalog der ältesten Alleluia-Melodien* (Munich, 1965), pp. 22, 30, and 90–91. This is Schlager's melody No. 46.

[29] There is another parallel here with "cor meum" (as well as "iniusticia"). One segment of that appears in a phrase that, as Manfred Bukofzer pointed out (*Studies in Medieval and Renaissance Music* [New York, 1950], p. 251), occurs both in an Alleluia (*Surrexit Dominus*, S. 74, *Graduale romanum*, p. 248), and a Gradual (*Domine praevenisti, Graduale romanum*, p. [48]).

[30] Villetard, *Office de Pierre de Corbeil*, pp. 106–7, 160–61, 222; Arlt, *op. cit.*, pp. 97, 99–100.

[31] Laon, Bibl. mun., 263, fols. 32ᵛ–33ᵛ.

[32] For this melody, see Klaus Rönnau, "*Regnum tuum solidum*," *Festschrift Bruno Stäblein zum siebzigsten Geburtstag*, ed. Martin Ruhnke (Kassel, 1967), pp. 195–205.

tem in superne" is perhaps the most difficult to understand: how can one justify interrupting a Gloria only once, to interpolate a melody that has such a distinct character of its own and a text that has more relevance to the Sanctus of the Mass than the Gloria?[33] The use of a phrase from "Sedentem in superne" as a Gloria trope at Sens (in the same Mass XI Gloria) makes more sense: here in a full set of tropes—nearly all of which, words and music, have been shown to be borrowed from other sources— the phrase "in superne majestatis arce" follows "Qui sedes" of the Gloria text.[34]

In other sources, *Centum quadraginta* is sometimes followed by different melismas and prosulae. Stäblein has shown that at Laon it was given the triple melisma of *Descendit de celis* and provided with prosulae. (The first two melismas are given in the manuscript; the third, the longest one, is not there, evidently because of the loss of a leaf.)[35] Stäblein has referred to another prosula for this Responsory, "Est praevius dux," given in a Bamberg antiphonary (12th century; Staatsbibliothek, Msc. Lit. 24), for which the melody has not been found in transcribable form.[36] In the St. Denis antiphonary (lat. 17296, fol. 41ᵛ), *Centum quadraginta* is followed by still another melisma, one borrowed from an Offertory: the "orationis meae" melisma of V. 3, "Venite et videte," of the Offertory for the fifth Sunday after Easter, *Benedicite gentes*[37] (Fig. 5). The same melisma was also used at the monastery of St. Vanne in Verdun, in a Responsory for St. Sanctinus, *Sacerdotum gloriosum;* it appears in the 12th-century manuscripts Verdun, Bibl. mun., 108 and 129 (fol. 208ᵛ).

In the Sens breviary (lat. 1028), the full S melisma was used with several chants. Of them, two more can be mentioned here: *Inter natos mulierum*, for the feast of St. John the Baptist, and *Felix Maria unxit*, for the feast of St. Mary Magdalene. *Inter natos mulierum*, like *Centum quadraginta*, is a mode I chant in classic style, and, also like it, appears in various

---

[33] In referring to "Sedentem in superne" as "une prosule de *Regnum*," Villetard (*Office de Pierre de Corbeil*, p. 106) was evidently following the lead of Blume and Bannister in Analecta hymnica, Vol. XLVII. Although they printed "Sedentem in superne" as a Regnum prosula, they did comment that it seemed to have little in common with the other texts except the point at which it was inserted into the Gloria: "Der ursprüngliche Charakter des Regnum-Tropus ist in vorstehender Dichtung stark verwischt; sie hat mit demselben fast nur dieses gemeinsam, dass sie als eine Erweiterung in das Gloria eingeschoben ist und zwar zwischen die Schlussworte 'Iesu Christe' und 'Cum sancto spiritu'" (p. 298). Of the sources for "Sedentem in superne" listed in Analecta hymnica, Vols. X and XLVII, it is not clear which give this text as a responsory prosula, which as a Gloria trope, and which as an independent piece. Arlt (*op. cit.*, pp. 99-100) has found it used with the Responsories *Hic qui advenit* and *In medio;* he refers to Wagner's showing a melisma with a melody similar to this one with the R. *Et valde mane.*

[34] Villetard, *Office de Pierre de Corbeil*, p. 201.

[35] These prosulae are printed by Stäblein in *MGG*, Vol. XIII, Notenbeispiel 9, after col. 816.

[36] *Ibid.*, col. 815.

[37] Ott, *op. cit.*, pp. 71-74.

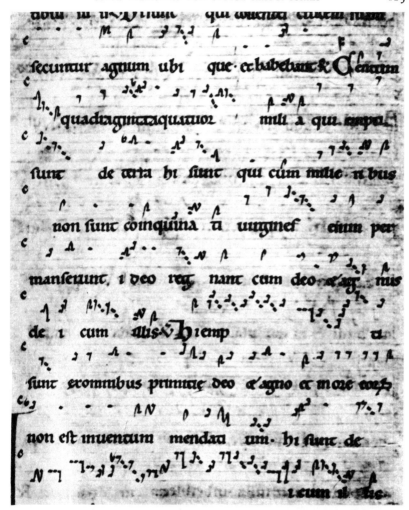

Figure 5. R. *Centum quadraginta*, in Paris, B. n., lat. 17296, fol. 41ᵛ (detail)

sources with several different melismas. Among them are two antiphonaries of St. Maur des Fossés, Paris, B. n., lat. 12584 and lat. 12044. Some
writers say both of them are of the 12th century, but 12584 seems clearly
to be the older;[38] it is notated in staffless neumes, while 12044 has staff
notation. *Inter natos mulierum* appears in both, though in 12044 it is
written in a hand later than that of the rest of the manuscript. Both
manuscripts give a melisma for *Inter natos;* lat. 12044 (fol. 145ᵛ) follows

[38] It is studied in CAO, especially Vol. II.

this with the prosula "Prepara Iohannes baptista." The form of the melody is roughly *x aa' bb y;* it is like (though not entirely the same as) the melisma given for this Responsory in Tours, Bibl. mun., 153, fol. 79 (Ex. 2).

Example 2

Prosula "Prepara Iohannes baptista" for R. *Inter natos mulierum,* Paris, B. n., lat. 12044, fol. 145ᵛ

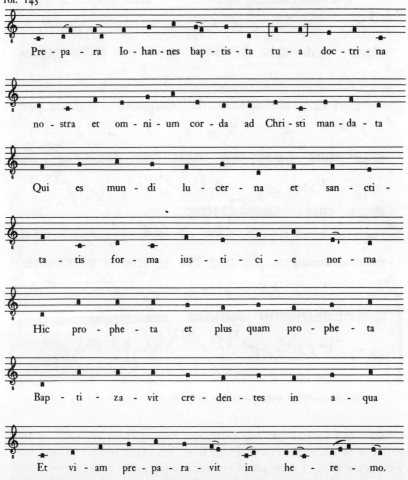

Another melisma is given with *Inter natos* in the Amiens breviary (Amiens, Bibl. mun., 112, fol. 175; Fig. 6). This one is shorter than the other and through composed; lat. 17296 gives it with the first Responsory for St. John the Evangelist, *Valde honorandus est* (fol. 33ᵛ), which is in mode II.

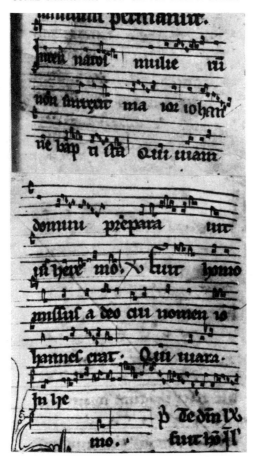

Figure 6. R. *Inter natos mulierum,* in Amiens, Bibl. mun., 112, fol. 175 (detail, composite)

The situation with respect to *Felix Maria* is rather more complicated, for not only the melisma but the melody of the Responsory itself varies from one manuscript to another. The mode II melody given in the Sarum antiphonary agrees in the main with that of lat. 1028, except for the omission from Sarum of the melisma. In the Worcester antiphonary, however, though a few passages are the same as they are in the other sources, the piece has been reworked: it is now in mode I, and new melismas have been placed at the beginning and end.[39] This appears to be related to the fact that *Felix Maria* is a relatively late addition to the chant

[39] Worcester, Cathedral Library, F. 160 (13th century). Facsimile edition in Paléographie musicale, Vol. XII (Tournay, 1922), p. 337.

repertory, part of the liturgy for a feast that was only gradually adopted during the course of the Middle Ages (Ex. 3).[40]

In addition to the uses of the full S melisma with Responsories in the Sens manuscripts (and the list above has not been intended as a complete one), certain instances may be cited where only part of this melody was used—specifically, all but its opening phrase.[41] It was used in the Office for St. Martin and in three Offices distinctive of the use of Sens: the feasts of the Relics of Sens (January 7), of St. Lupus (September 1), and St. Paula (January 27). The Responsories to which it was added are respectively *Martinus Abrahae sinu, Concede nobis, O venerandum antistitem,* and *O admirabilem feminam.*

Martinus Abrahae sinu is a well-known chant that often serves as the last Responsory of Matins for St. Martin. In at least one other manuscript it is given a melisma, one different from that of Sens—the Marmoutier breviary, Tours, Bibl. mun., 153 (fol. 183), where the melisma provided

Example 3

R. *Felix Maria unxit,* Worcester, Cathedral Library, F. 160, p. 337; and Paris, B. n., lat. 1028, fol. 216' (from Sens)

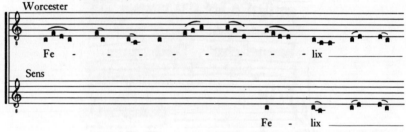

[40] Victor Saxer, *Le culte de Marie Madeleine en occident des origines à la fin du moyen âge,* 2 vols. (Auxerre, 1959); and B. de Gaiffier, "Notes sur le culte de Sainte Marie-Madeleine," *Analecta bollandiana,* LXXVIII (1960), 161–68.

[41] Villetard seems to have regarded as the same what have been referred to here as the entire melody and part of the melody: see *Office de Pierre de Corbeil,* p. 157, note A.

XI

128

is one of those more frequently associated with the Christmas Responsory
Descendit de celis. *Concede nobis* is, on the other hand, a relatively
late chant, one not found in every manuscript, and one of which the
liturgical assignment varies a good deal.[42] In the St. Maur des Fossés
antiphonary (lat. 12044, fol. 200ᵛ), it is followed by a prosula, "Perpetua
mereamur," to a melody different from that of the Sens melisma.[43]

The Offices for St. Lupus and St. Paula are interesting in a number of
respects. The Responsories for St. Lupus have texts that are, for the most
part, freely adapted from the *vita* of the saint published in the *Acta Sanctorum*.[44] Two of them are given particularly long melismas: *O venerandum
antistitem*, the sixth Responsory, at the end of the second Nocturn,
and *Dum beatus Lupus*, the eighth. *O venerandum antistitem* is accompanied in n. a. lat. 1535 by not only the melisma in question but a prosula
for it as well: "Insignis de Christo." (In lat. 1028 the melisma is omitted.)
These have been published by Chailley.[45]

The text of *O venerandum* is based on material read immediately before it in the sixth lesson and tells how while St. Lupus was celebrating
Mass one day a brilliant jewel descended from heaven into the cup in his
hands. The prosula takes up the same ideas—the "insignis de Christo" is
the jewel.

Dum beatus Lupus, on the other hand, is based on a part of the *vita*
that is not read in the Matins lessons as they are recorded in lat. 1028, fols.
242–43ᵛ. The two texts are given below.

Vita, section 18

Revertente igitur Sancto *ad propria*, dum ad Miledunum castrum evenisset
mansio ei oportuna, *repente immane horreum* usque ad summum plenum
[*ignis*] *vallavit incendium*, nec poterat expectantium quisquam praestare
auxilium. Tunc vir Domini in orationem prosternitur, fulmen immissum super
incendium cernitur. Illico flamma extinguitur, illaesa apotheca reservatur,
Christus per Pontificem collaudatur, meritum Sacerdotis agnoscitur.

Responsory

Dum beatus Lupus ab exilio *ad propria* remearet adepta *mansio*ne *repente
horreum immane ignis vallavit* incendium. Sanctisque solutis precibus incolume
mansit ac integrum. ℣. *Christus per Pontificem collaudatur, meritum Sacerdotis
agnoscitur.*

[42] Concerning an apparently invalid attribution of this work to Robert II the
Pious, King of France from 996 to 1031, see Paléographie musicale, X, 25–26, fn. 4;
G. M. Beyssac, "Le Graduel-antiphonaire de Mont-Renaud," *Revue de musicologie*,
XL (1957), 132; and finally Michel Huglo, *Les tonaires* (Paris, 1971), pp. 91–92, fn. 2.
[43] This is published by Apel, *op. cit.*, pp. 436–37. In lat. 12584 the prosula is written
in a later hand on the last page, with a cue for the prosula, also in a later hand,
at the point in the manuscript where the Responsory occurs (fol. 353). Of the
Sens manuscripts only lat. 1028 has the melisma. Because of a lacuna the Office in
n. a. lat. 1535 is fragmentary (fol. 69ʳ–69ᵛ), but *Concede nobis* is there, without
this melisma.
[44] Septembris Tomus I (1868), pp. 248–65.
[45] *Op. cit.*, pp. 22–23.

Dum beatus Lupus has in n. a. lat. 1535 (though not in lat. 1028) a melisma provided for use in the refrain after the verse. It goes without saying that it is unusual for this to be done in the eighth Responsory of a feast, especially when there is no melisma for the ninth. The melisma is borrowed from the Offertory *Super flumina*, where it appears on the word "meminero" in ℣. 2, "Si oblitus fuero."[46]

Various things should be considered in connection with this borrowing. The "meminero" melisma has one particular figure, *c–(e)–f–e–c–d*, that is used repeatedly; this figure also appears in the Responsory and may help to explain why this particular melisma was chosen for it. Another melisma from *Super flumina* was used in a different Responsory—the "Ierusalem" melisma of ℣. 3, "Memento domine," which is used on the word "Ierusalem" in the R. *Qui vicerit* for St. John the Evangelist in the manuscript Laon, Bibl. mun., 263, fol. 100ᵛ. (The same melisma occurs, again on the word "Ierusalem," in the Alleluia *Te decet* [Schlager 360].) On the basis of liturgical tradition, *Super flumina* appears to be a relatively late Offertory,[47] but whether its style differs in important respects from that of other Offertories remains to be determined. Finally, it is possible that the musical borrowing from this particular Offertory for *Dum beatus Lupus* was also intended to remind the listeners of a connection between the themes of the two texts: *Dum beatus Lupus* begins with a reference to the saint's return from exile, and *Super flumina* may have seemed to the singers of Sens even as it does to many persons now, the most poetic of all Biblical reflections on this subject.

The Responsories for the Sens office for St. Paula were organized in a distinctive way. Each of them has a melisma and a text that comes· from the lesson that immediately precedes it. The Vespers Responsory comes from the text read in the first lesson of Matins. Thus the texts for the Office, and in one way the music, seem clearly unified.

The impression of uniformity in musical style is, however, an illusion; for the melodies for most of these Responsories have been borrowed —from at least three different feasts—while others appear to be newly composed, though perhaps not from new material. For example, *O admirabilem feminam*, the Vespers Responsory, is the one that uses the abbreviated form of the S melisma. When it is compared with *O venerandum antistitem*, for St. Lupus, it becomes evident that the two chants must have been composed, if not one in imitation of the other, at least after the same model, for there are numerous close resemblances in their melodies.

It has been possible to identify the models for six of the other Responsories in the Office. These are listed below.

[46] Ott, *op. cit.*, pp. 119–22.
[47] This JOURNAL, XIX (1966), 179–80.

1. Sancta Paula Graccorum	Benedicat nos Deus (Trinity)
2. Inter doloris aculeos	Operibus sanctis (Nicholas)
3. Sicut inter multas	Christi miles preciosus (Vincent)
4. Curiose Christi pauperes	Qui cum audissent (Nicholas)
5. Nesciebat se matrem	Beatus Nicholaus (Nicholas)
6. Ingressa Christi sepulchrum	O beata Trinitas (Trinity)

The melismas in these first six Matins Responsories for St. Paula are shorter than those spoken of earlier in this study—the melismas borrowed from Offertories and the S melisma in both its forms. The Responsories that were the models for these St. Paula chants and others like them were either written for rather late Offices (such as Trinity and St. Nicholas) or else represent individual chants composed as additions to the liturgy or substitutions for earlier works, and they seem to demonstrate a new attitude toward Responsory style. In the manuscript tradition there is every evidence that the melismas formed part of such Responsories from the start.

The seventh Responsory, *Paula ardentior fide*, has a melisma in common with a Responsory for the second Sunday of Lent, *Oravit Iacob*, but the two melodies are otherwise independent. (It is unusual to find a melisma in a Lenten Responsory in a manuscript from France; they are more common in Italian sources. A 12th-century antiphonary in the Curia Arcivescovile in Florence[48] has on fol. 82 a prosa for this Responsory, though it is apparently not related musically to this melisma.)

It is significant that in lat. 1028 this Office for St. Paula appears in the correct place in the Sanctorale, but in the earlier manuscript, n. a. lat. 1535, it comes at the end. This suggests that it was a new Office, put together shortly before or at the time of compiling of n. a. lat. 1535—the end of the 12th century. Numerous efforts on my part to determine a precise occasion for the setting up of this new Office have been unsuccessful.

St. Paula was a Roman widow who enjoyed the spiritual guidance and the companionship of St. Jerome. She went to the Holy Land, visited the holy places, and set up a convent at Bethlehem, where she died on January 26, 404. Her *vita* (from which the Sens lessons and Responsories are taken) is by St. Jerome, and part of it forms a fascinating guide to the Holy Land as it existed in the fourth century. The body of St. Paula was brought to France at an undetermined time, and it was among the many gifts of Charlemagne to the Cathedral of Sens. The relics have been authenticated three times, most recently in 1966.[49]

---

[48] Briefly described by Michel Huglo, *op. cit.*, pp. 186-87.
[49] Giuseppe Del Ton and Maria Chiara Celletti, "Paola di Roma," *Bibliotheca sanctorum*, 13 vols. (Rome, 1961-70), Vol. X (1968), cols. 123-36.

XI

The end of the 12th century was a time of particular glory for Sens. The new cathedral was under construction. Pope Alexander III was at Sens for a year and a half, beginning in 1163, making it temporarily the capital city of Christendom, and in 1164 he consecrated an altar in the choir of the new church. The nave was completed in 1175 or 1180.[50] A formal record of the holy relics of Sens, drawn up at the time of their translation in 1192,[51] provides more than adequate substantiation for the statement one finds repeated often—that this was of all the cathedrals in France the one most rich in relics. Later, in 1234, the Cathedral of Sens was the site of the wedding of St. Louis and Marguerite de Provence.

But this was also the time of a rising interest in the wider world, and particularly Jerusalem and the Holy Land. The relics of St. Paula had, after all, been at Sens for centuries. Perhaps the intensifying of her cult had a double purpose. Reading and singing about St. Paula and her life in the Holy Land might have been meant to foster piety in the usual ways, but it might also have been intended to have a second effect: to incite the faithful to emulate the example of St. Paula, to visit the holy places themselves, to walk the earth where Christ had been, to take up His Cross.

In this article, three types of melismas in Matins Responsories have been described: those borrowed from other chants, particularly Offertories; those that seem to have served primarily as Responsory melismas, being transferred from one chant to another; and those in late Responsories that were composed as part of their chants. These procedures are fascinating to follow, and as additional breviaries and antiphonaries are studied other practices will undoubtedly come to light. The richness and variety of the medieval liturgy makes it an irresistible and inexhaustible subject for study.

[50] Whitney S. Stoddard, *Monastery and Cathedral in France* (Middletown, Conn., 1966), pp. 112-19.
[51] Reproduced in facsimile by René Fourrey in *Sens: Ville d'art et d'histoire* (Lyons, 1953), opposite p. 52; see also p. 81.

XII

THE RESPONSORIES AND PROSA
FOR ST. STEPHEN'S DAY AT SALISBURY

THE study of medieval manuscripts of Gregorian chants for the
Mass leads one very early to the conclusion that the differences
among them are relatively minor. An introit, a gradual, an offertory,
or a communion assigned to a specific Sunday or feast day in one source
is almost always assigned to the same day in another. There are exceptions, of course, and they are often significant and fascinating. The
number of Masses provided for specific saints' days vary, as do the
saints thus honored. Votive and processional antiphons may or may not
be included. There may be additional alleluias on some days and an
occasional alleluia which is an unicum or known in a relatively small number of sources. But the prevailing impression made by the sources is one of
uniformity.

Manuscripts of chants for the Office, on the other hand, are much
more varied. They seem not to have been standardized, but left free to
reflect local preferences and customs, or those of a particular religious
order, to a much greater degree. There is a broad range of difference
in the responsories and antiphons provided for many feasts. The variety
among medieval antiphonaries is quite evident among the twelve manuscripts analyzed in Dom René-Jean Hesbert's *Corpus antiphonalium officii.*[1] These differences depend in part of course on whether a source
conforms to the monastic or the secular Office; but there is at least one
source that seems to follow neither consistently. This is the celebrated
late 10th- or early 11th-century Hartker Codex (St. Gall 390-391); it
has been observed that this source is in perfect conformity neither with
the *cursus monasticus* (in which there are four responsories in each of

[1] Vol. I: *Manuscripti "Cursus Romanus"*; Vol. II: *Manuscripti "Cursus Monasticus"* (*Rerum ecclesiasticarum documenta, Series maior: Fontes*, VII, VIII; Rome,
1963, 1965). Some of the twelve manuscripts were chosen for study by Dom Hesbert
because they are among the oldest antiphonaries extant; the others represent various
geographical areas or particular religious orders.

the Nocturnes of Matins) nor with the *cursus Romanus* (three responsories in each Nocturne), but mixes them, and occasionally also seems
to follow other systems.[2]

Looking at the responsories of Matins, one finds that their number
varies from one source to the next. The differences in the number of
responsories provided for a particular feast among the sources analyzed
by Hesbert often result from the presence or absence of extra responsories at the end of each series. For example, for the three Nocturnes of
St. Stephen's Day (December 26), the Hartker Codex has three, three,
and four responsories; the Antiphonary of San Lupo of Benevento (end
of the 12th century; Benevento, Biblioteca Capitolare, V. 21) four, four,
and five; and the Verona Antiphonary (11th century; Verona, Biblioteca Capitolare, XCVIII) three, three, and seven. Dom Hesbert observes that these extra responsories ("répons surnuméraires") are common in sources representing a variety of traditions. He suggests that they
may have been used during the week, or during the octave of a feast, or
perhaps were simply ad libitum.[3]

Similarly, the responsories for a particular feast may appear in various orders,[4] and — even more interesting — the responsories themselves
may vary. Thus, among the twelve manuscripts analyzed by Dom Hesbert, only two give exactly the same responsories for St. Stephen, and
in the same order (even here one of the manuscripts gives the incipit
of an additional responsory at the end of the series). Seven responsories
appear in all twelve of the manuscripts. Two more appear in all but one
of them. Another seventeen responsories are assigned to this day by the
twelve manuscripts; of these, eleven are named in only one source each.

Walter Howard Frere wrote a study of responsories in the introduction to his facsimile edition of the Sarum Antiphonal which is the most
detailed published work on this subject.[5] Bishop Frere believed that
chants were "ancient" if they appeared in several early manuscripts from

---

[2] Dom Hesbert comments on the Hartker Codex in *op. cit.*, Vol. II, pp. VI-IX.

[3] *Ibid.*, Vol. II, p. VIII.

[4] As Dom Hesbert points out (*op. cit.*, Vol. I, p. XII), the responsories in a
series all serve the same function, and thus are interchangeable, unlike Mass chants,
each of which has a distinctive role.

[5] *Antiphonale Sarisburiense* (London, 1901-1924; reprint by Gregg Press, Farnborough, 1966). The introduction is in Volume I of the 1966 reprint. Hans-Jörgen
Holman, "The *Responsoria Prolixa* of the *Codex Worcester F 160*" (Ph.D. dissertation, Indiana University, 1961; Ann Arbor, Mich.: University Microfilms), takes
Bishop Frere's method of analysis as a point of departure for a more systematic study
of the melodies and provides a detailed survey of the repertory of the Worcester
Antiphonary.

different places with the same or approximately the same liturgical function. The other chants — those that were not in general use — could, he thought, be regarded as later, "or, at any rate, not part of the original nucleus." [6]

In analyzing the music of the responsories, Bishop Frere begins with the "ancient" chants of each group and goes on from them to the more recent ones. The main emphasis in his analysis is on the use of common themes in responsories in the same mode. It appears that Frere's basic criterion for distinguishing "ancient" from later chants is the evidence of the manuscript tradition: "fixity means antiquity." However, along with his analysis of the sources Frere is also making a detailed stylistic analysis, and occasionally he is led to aesthetic judgments such as the following: "The last [responsory] of the group is one from the later office of St. Denys ... it shows its later origin by eccentricities" (p. 47); and "A similar instance, though probably of later date, is R. *Viri Galilei*, ... where the artistic copying of the second phrase by the fifth shows a more developed stage of musical sensibility than that of the early Gregorian period" (p. 45). Bishop Frere apparently felt that there was internal as well as external evidence of a late date for these works. Since even important aspects of musical style are often easier to sense than to define, one can understand why Frere was not more specific as to the ways in which the later melodies differed musically from the earlier ones; but one must regret it. It is evident from Frere's analyses, however, that even among the "ancient" responsories there is considerable variety in the handling of the themes, some being more, and some less, dependent on them.

The typical responsory, as described by Peter Wagner (who wrote before the introduction to *Antiphonale Sarisburiense* was published), has a text either from one of the narrative or prophetic books of the Bible, or from the Vita or Passio of a saint; and it is set to music in three periods, each of which falls into two halves.[7] (Some responsories have Psalm texts; usually these consist of two verses of a Psalm and are in two rather than three periods.) The most common modes for responsories are VIII, VII, I, and II.

Every responsory has a verse, which is ordinarily sung to a formula, or "tone," that is determined by the mode of the responsory. Some verses have original melodies. A particular responsory may be assigned

---

[6] *Op. cit.*, p. 2.

[7] Peter Wagner, *Einführung in die gregorianischen Melodien*, III: *Gregorianische Formenlehre* (Leipzig, 1921), 330-31.

one verse in one source and a different verse in another; or in a single source there may be one verse for the feast itself and another for use during the octave. Some responsory verses are of great interest, but a consideration of the verses of responsories has, wherever possible, been omitted from the pages that follow so that the main findings of this study might be more concisely presented.

Frere, Wagner, and others writing about responsories have tended to focus their attention on those chants that are fairly consistent in their use of melodic formulas. It seems appropriate now to take a different approach: to take a series of liturgically related chants and study them from the textual and the musical point of view, to determine how much consistency or disparity there is in compositional practice among them.

The responsories for the feast of St. Stephen as presented in the Erlyngham Breviary form a group of some interest.[8] There are nine of them: four in mode IV, three in mode VII, and two in mode I. The following table lists them in their liturgical order.[9]

Responsories for St. Stephen (December 26)
in the Erlyngham Breviary

First Nocturne	Mode
*Hesterna die	VII
*Videbant omnes stephanum	IV
*Impetum fecerunt	I
Second Nocturne	
*Impii super iustum	VII
*Lapidabant stephanum	IV
Lapides torrentes	VII
Third Nocturne	
**Intuens in celum	IV
**Patefacte sunt	IV
Sancte dei preciose	I

[8] *Antiphonale Sarisburiense* is identified on its title page as "a reproduction in facsimile of a manuscript of the thirteenth century," but the manuscript in question, Cambridge, University Library, Mm. ii. 9, is incomplete. A number of leaves are missing from the beginning of it. For this part of the facsimile, reproductions were made of the appropriate folios of the Erlyngham Breviary (Salisbury, Chapter Library, MS 152), which is of the second half of the 15th century. Frere describes this manuscript in the introduction, p. 78. The responsories for Dec. 26 are to be found in Vol. II of the 1966 reprint, pp. 57-60.

[9] In medieval Latin, spelling is not consistent, and editors vary in the degree to which they modify the spellings of their texts. For this study the following rule has been applied: texts taken from a specified source are copied as they stand, except that abbreviations are resolved, and v and u are differentiated; texts that are cited without reference to a definite source are given in the form in which they appear in modern liturgical publications such as the *Breviarium monasticum* (Mechelen, 1939).

166

It was pointed out above that there are seven responsories for St. Stephen that are used in all the manuscripts surveyed in *Corpus antiphonalium officii*, I and II. Five of these are included in the Erlyngham Breviary; of them, two (*Videbant omnes stephanum* and *Lapidabant stephanum*) are in mode IV, two in mode VII, and one in mode I. (They are starred in the table.) With the two mode-IV responsories just mentioned can be grouped another two in mode IV, each of which appears in all but one of the manuscripts of the *Corpus antiphonalium officii*, and both of which are used in the Erlyngham Breviary. (They are given double stars in the table.)

The four mode-IV responsories all use the same opening, the one identified as IV* by Bishop Frere; they have a number of internal phrases in common and the same ending, and Frere regards them all as "ancient." [10] The texts of three of them are Biblical. *Lapidabant stephanum* and *Intuens in celum* are taken from the account of the martyrdom of St. Stephen in Acts 7:55-60. *Videbant omnes stephanum* is drawn from Acts 6:15. *Patefacte sunt* is non-Biblical. The mode-VII responsories include two that appear in all of the manuscripts of *Corpus antiphonalium officii, Hesterna die* and *Impii super iustum,* and one that appears in only half of those sources (three in the *cursus Romanus* and three in the *cursus monasticus*), *Lapides torrentes.* None of them is Biblical.

The text of *Hesterna die* is very similar in style to a sermon on St. Stephen by Fulgentius (467-533). [11]

> Hesterna die dominus natus est in terris
> ut stephanus nasceretur in celis
> ingressus est dominus mundum
> ut stephanus ingrederetur in celum.

> (Yesterday the Lord was born on earth,
> that Stephen might be born in heaven;
> The Lord entered the world,
> that Stephen might enter heaven.)

The form of this text is clear: two balanced periods. This balance is

[10] *Op. cit.,* I, 33-34.

[11] The Erlyngham Breviary contains the texts of the lessons for Matins, and part of this sermon is given there. It is published in full in J. Fraipont, *Sancti Fulgentii episcopi ruspensis opera* (*Corpus christianorum,* Series latina, XCI A; Turnhout, Belgium, 1968), pp. 905-909. The sermon begins as follows: "Heri celebravimus temporalem sempiterni regis nostri natalem: hodie celebramus triumphalem militis passionem." ("Yesterday we celebrated the birth in time of our eternal King; today we celebrate the victory through suffering of [His] soldier.") Part of its second sentence is used as the verse of this responsory.

emphasized by the musical setting, for it is made up of two large periods whose second sections (corresponding to those parts of the text that begin "ut stephanus") are identical. The musical form is thus *abcb; a* and *c* have basically the same contours, but *a* is rather ornate and *c* is little more than recitation on a single note. The music for *b* is florid; it ends in a melisma that appears very often in mode-VII responsories. Despite the precise organization of both text and melody, Frere calls this responsory "ancient"; presumably he is guided here by its omnipresence in the early sources, not by its style.[12]

The text for one of the other responsories in mode VII is similar to this in structure:

> Impii super iustum iacturam fecerunt
>   ut eum morti traderent
> At ille gaudens suscepit lapides
>   ut mereretur accipere coronam glorie.
>
> (The ungodly fell upon the just man,
>   that they might put him to death;
> but he received the stones rejoicing,
>   that he might earn a crown of glory.)

The melody for this reflects its structure, but to a lesser extent than was the case in the preceding responsory. The music for "ut eum morti traderent" does return, but not until the words "coronam glorie." The beginning of that section is set to another melody. The climax of the chant comes in the third phrase, "at ille gaudens suscepit lapides," which is ornate and high; it goes up to a'. Frere gives this responsory first among his "typical responds of the seventh mode" and analyzes its melody in full.[13]

The third mode-VII responsory — the one that is less well represented in the sources and hence probably a later addition to the repertory — has a short text that is also used for one of the Lauds antiphons on the same day: "Lapides torrentes illi dulces fuerunt / Ipsum secuntur omnes anime iuste." It is said to be "later" by Frere (Vol. I, p. 48); it begins with the melody used for the words "at ille gaudens suscepit" in *Impii super iustum*. There are two large phrases, the first of which ends on D and the second on G. Hence the musical rhyme found in the other mode-VII responsories is missing here.

One of the two responsories in mode I is *Impetum fecerunt*. It ap-

---

[12] *Op. cit.*, I, 45.
[13] *Ibid.*, I, 43-44.

pears in all of the sources under discussion and has a Biblical text, from Acts 7:57, 58, and 59. The melody matches that of Wagner's typical mode-I responsory rather well, and it is given an analysis by Frere that reveals it to consist entirely of melodic formulas that are standard in mode-I responsories.[14]

The other mode-I responsory is the last of the series. It is *Sancte dei preciose*. It appears in a number of other sources, though not always as the last responsory and not always on December 26. Among the sources studied in *Corpus antiphonalium officii*, none of those in Volume I, representing the *cursus Romanus*, give this responsory. Four of the six sources in Volume II, showing the *cursus monasticus*, do give it; two have it in the same liturgical position as does the Erlyngham Breviary, and the other two have it instead on the feast of the *Inventio Sancti Stephani* on August 3.[15]

The most superficial examination of its text (see Ex. 1, below) reveals that *Sancte dei preciose* differs from the other responsories in an obvious way. It is in rhymed accentual poetry, while all the rest of them are in prose. The meter of *Sancte dei preciose* is the familiar trochaic tetrameter catalectic, a common one among hymns. *Sancte dei preciose* is itself found with a different melody as a hymn; indeed, in this form, it appears on the very next page of the Erlyngham Breviary as well as in a number of other sources.[16]

The text appears in *Analecta hymnica* with the title "Oratio ad sanctum Stephanum," and the editor, Guido Maria Dreves, refers to it as a "lied." He arranges it in three stanzas, and follows it with the comment that in slightly changed form (involving principally the changing of first person references from singular to plural, the rearranging of the poem into two stanzas, and the adding of a paraphrase of the *Gloria patri* as a third stanza) it became widely known as a hymn.[17] To Dreves, then, the original form of the poem was basically that in which it happens to appear as a responsory in the Erlyngham Breviary.

[14] Wagner, *op. cit.*, p. 331; Frere, *op. cit.*, I, 21.

[15] The earliest source known to me to contain the responsory *Sancte dei preciose* is London, British Museum, Add. 30850. This is the 11th-century Silos Antiphonary, a source of distinctive importance in that it contains Gregorian chants written in Mozarabic notation.

[16] Bruno Stäblein, *Monumenta monodica medii aevi*, Band I: Hymnen (I) (Kassel and Basel, 1956), presents the hymn melody on p. 82 and comments on the text and melody on p. 540.

[17] *Analecta hymnica*, XLVIII (Leipzig, 1905), 83-84.

Whether the melody given for it there is the original one remains very much open to question.

The earliest source Dreves knows for the poem is one he dates as 11th-century: Angers, 283 (274). There it appears in the middle of a series of eleven poems. In two other works in the series the poet identifies himself as Bishop of Angers; Dreves concludes this must be Eusebius Bruno (d. 1081), and ascribes all eleven poems to him.[18] *Sancte dei preciose* is also printed by Raby, who calls it a "rhythmical prayer" and

Ex. 1

San- cte   de - - i   pre- ci-o - - se   pro- tho-mar- tir   ste-pha-ne

qui vir- tu - te   ca -ri - ta - tis   cir-cum- ful- -tus   un- di - que

do - mi - num pro in- -i - mi - co   ex - o - ras-ti po - - pu - lo.

Fun -de   pre - - ces pro   de - vo - to ti - bi   nunc

col - - - - - - -   le-gi - o.

V.Ut   tu -o   pro-pi- ci- a - tus   in- ter-ven-tu   do- mi - nus

nos pur-ga- tos   a pec- ca - tis ium -gat   ce - li ci- vi - bus.

Sancte dei preciose: Oh Stephen, holy protomartyr, precious in God's eyes, you who — supported round about on all sides by the power of love — prayed to the Lord for a hostile people, now pour forth prayers for this community devoted to you, that the Lord, made favorable by your intervention, may join us, purged of sin, with the citizens of heaven.

[18] *Ibid.,* p. 79.

repeats Dreves's ascription of the work to Eusebius Bruno.[19] This attribution seems of doubtful validity for at least two reasons: *Sancte dei preciose* is not in the same style as some other poems in the series (it is substantially shorter and simpler than those in which the poet identifies himself), and it is much more widely known than any of them.

The melody of *Sancte dei preciose* (shown with its verse in Ex. 1) makes use only occasionally of the melodic formulas for mode I. It falls into four large phrases, each of which corresponds to one line of the poem. (The last two lines of the text, printed by Dreves as the third stanza, form the verse of the responsory; their musical setting will be described a little later.) The last phrase serves as the refrain, to be sung after the verse, and again after the prosa.

The style is relatively florid. Although there is an occasional syllable for which there is only one note, nowhere are more than two syllables in succession set this way. The melody used for the first two words is substantially like the beginning of the Christmas responsory *Descendit de caelis,* though more ornate, and there are other points where the melodies may be compared. The similarity of the openings and the difference in style between them can be seen in the two brief excerpts given in Ex. 2.[20]

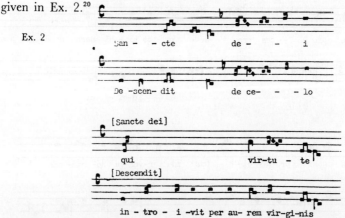

Ex. 2

All four phrases of the responsory end on D. The point of rest in the middle of the phrase (after the first eight syllables of each line) falls on A three times and G once. (One should note that among the typical mode-I responsories analyzed by Frere cadences on A are relatively uncommon.) The cadences on A in this work are all different; but those

[19] F. J. E. Raby, *A History of Christian-Latin Poetry,* 2nd ed. (Oxford, 1953), p. 264.

[20] This reading of *Descendit de caelis* is taken from the Erlyngham Breviary (*Antiphonale Sarisburiense,* II, 47).

on D are much the same, giving almost the effect of musical rhyme. The impression made by this melody is one of four successive arches, three of which begin with a downward dip, and all of which are heavily ornamented. The half-line with the highest tessitura is the one that begins the refrain, "Funde preces." The final half-line is prolonged by an extensive melisma on the word "collegio" in which there is repetition of two successive phrases.

This piece has had an unusual fascination for musicologists because of a remarkable circumstance. Two lines from it — those that serve as the verse when the poem is treated as a responsory — appear with a polyphonic musical setting written in letter notation in a source which, when first published in facsimile, was said to be 10th-century. As such, it was one of the earliest examples of polyphony. More recently the music in this source has been regarded as a later addition to it, possibly of the 11th or even the 12th century.[21] In the polyphonic setting of the verse, the lower of the two voices has a melody that is a somewhat elaborated version of the "tone," or melody formula, for verses of responsories in mode I. This melody is essentially the same as that given in the Erlyngham Breviary for the verse of *Sancte dei preciose.*

After the verse, and before the expected indication for the *Gloria patri,* the Erlyngham Breviary gives an additional text beginning "Te mundi climata." One's first surmise is that this is a prosula for the melisma on "collegio" at the end of the responsory — that is, a text composed to fit the melody, with one syllable for each note in it. This is not the case, however; instead, the melody to which these words are set is one usually associated with the Christmas responsory *Descendit de caelis.*

In some sources this responsory has not one but three melismas pro-

---

[21] The 10th-century dating and a facsimile of the original notation of the piece as it appeared in Oxford, Bodleian Library 572, were given by H. E. Wooldridge in *Early English Harmony* (London, 1897), Vol. I, Pl. 1. Very soon after, in the first edition of *The Oxford History of Music* (Oxford, 1901), I, 91, Woolridge revised his dating by saying that although the manuscript as a whole was 10th-century, the music had been inserted after 1100; yet in style and notation it suggested the 11th century. This correction was incorporated by H. V. Hughes into Vol. II of *Early English Harmony* (London, 1913). Through its inclusion as No. 26b. in Vol. I of the *Historical Anthology of Music,* ed. A. T. Davison and Willi Apel, rev. ed. (Cambridge, Mass., 1949), the piece — that is, just the verse of *Sancte dei preciose* set in two-voiced polyphony — has come to be very widely known. Students of musical palaeography find a facsimile of the original notation in Willi Apel's *The Notation of Polyphonic Music,* 5th ed. (Cambridge, Mass., 1961), p. 205. The verse was also transcribed by Hugo Riemann — in measured rhythm, of course — in his *Handbuch der Musikgeschichte,* 2nd ed. (Leipzig, 1920), Vol. I/2, p. 141.

172

vided for its next-to-last word. This *neuma triplex* is well known in musicological literature; it has been commented on by Wagner, Handschin, Apel, Holman, Stäblein, and others.[22] By way of brief summary of their observations it may be said that *Descendit de caelis* appears in some sources (such as the 12th-century antiphonary Lucca, Biblioteca Capitolare, 601,[23] and the Erlyngham Breviary) with a short and ordinary melody on its penultimate word.[24] In other sources, however, this is not the case. In them the penultimate word (usually "fabricae," sometimes "conditor" if an alternate version of the text is used) is written three times, with three different melismas; this is how it appears in the 13th-century Worcester Antiphonary.[25] Apparently the first melisma is to be used when the responsory is sung by the chorus (perhaps after being sung through by a soloist), the second incorporated into the refrain after the verse, and the third in the refrain after the *Gloria patri*.

That these melismas are later additions to the chant is suggested not only by the evidence of the manuscript tradition but also by an explicit statement of Amalarius (early 9th century). According to him, the *neuma triplex* originated in connection with the responsory *In medio* for the feast of St. John the Evangelist (December 27), and was only later transferred to *Descendit de caelis*.[26] The *neuma triplex* was also used with several other responsories. According to Handschin, Laon 263, a late 12th-century source, gives it with *Centum quadraginta* on the feast of the Holy Innocents (December 28); and a 12th-century manuscript from St. Denys (Paris, Bibliothèque Nationale, lat. 17296) gives it on the feast of St. Denys with the responsory *Post passionem*.[27]

Although the melodies are sometimes written only as melismas (as

[22] Bruno Stäblein provides an overview of the subject in cols. 811-16 of his important article "Tropus" for *Die Musik in Geschichte und Gegenwart* (hereafter *MGG;* Vol. XIII [1966], cols. 797-826.)

[23] *Paléographie musicale*, Vol. IX (Tournai, 1906), facsim., pp. 32-33.

[24] The words of this responsory appear in different versions in the sources; see Dominique Catta, "Le texte du répons 'Descendit' dans les manuscrits," *Etudes grégoriennes*, III (1959), 75-82.

[25] Worcester, Cathedral Library, F. 160; *Paléographie musicale*, Vol. XII (Tournai, 1922), facsim., p. 31.

[26] J. M. Hanssens, *Amalarii episcopi opera liturgica omnia*, Tomus III (*Studi e testi*, 140; Vatican City, 1950), pp. 54, 56. Bruno Stäblein, in *MGG*, XIII, cols. 811-12, makes a careful analysis of the statements to establish precisely the inferences that can be drawn from them. Jacques Handschin publishes the responsory *In medio* with the *neuma triplex* on pp. 143-44 of his article "Trope, Sequence, and Conductus" in the *New Oxford History of Music*, Vol. II, rev. ed. (London, 1955).

[27] *Ibid.*, pp. 143-45.

in St. Gall 390-391, in the 10th-century gradual and antiphonary of Saint-Éloi de Noyon,[28] and in the Worcester Antiphonary), they are found very frequently with texts. Whether these versions with text should be called "prosulae" (as they were above) or "prosae" seems open to question. Each of these terms conveys some of the appropriate connotations, but neither of them is perfectly adequate. What is involved is the provision of text for a melisma which is itself a musical trope, and the sources have no distinctive term for this; they usually use the word "prosae." One of the earliest sources to supply texts with these *fabricae* melismas (the *neuma triplex*) is Paris, Bibliothèque Nationale, f. lat. 1118.[29] For one of the melismas it gives four texts; for the next (which it calls "alia fabrice") it gives three, and for the third (quite appropriately termed "fabrice maior," since it is a great deal longer than the others), three.

There is a substantial amount of variety in the readings of the *neuma triplex,* and especially of the third *neuma,* in the sources. There are apparently at least three basically different forms of the third *neuma,* and each of them is subject to variations. The best-known form of it is that given, for example, in the Worcester Antiphonary; when the phrase "the third *neuma*" is used later in this study it will be to refer to this. The melody given with the texts for the *fabrice maior* of Paris lat. 1118 begins like its counterpart in the Worcester Antiphonary, but it is substantially longer. Still another form of the third *neuma* is given by Wagner; it is transcribed from a 15th-century breviary from Lausanne and seems generally to correspond with the neumes given for the third *neuma* in St. Gall 390-391.[30]

Texts are given with the *neuma triplex* in Paris, Bibliothèque Na-

[28] *Paléographie musicale,* Series II, Vol. I, p. 46; and Series I, Vol. XVI, facsim., fol. 56ᵛ.

[29] There are various opinions about the date of this manuscript. Some scholars believe it can be dated 987-996. Heinrich Husmann, however, believes that it was written in the 11th century but copied, at least in part, from an earlier model. (*Tropen- und Sequenzenhandschriften* [*Répertoire international des sources musicales,* B v¹; Munich, 1964], p. 124.) Its place of origin is unknown, according to Husmann; it came to the Bibliothèque Nationale from the library of St. Martial de Limoges, but it was not written there.

[30] Wagner, *op. cit.,* III, 347-48. Prof. Stäblein transcribes a melody that is essentially similar to Wagner's in *MGG,* XIII, Ex. 9 d., after col. 816. Stäblein calls it not another version of the melody but an "Ersatz-Melisma für das dritte Neuma." For a transcription of the *neuma triplex* as it appears in the Worcester Antiphonary, see Hans-Jörgen Holman, "Melismatic Tropes in the Responsories for Matins," *Journal of the American Musicological Society,* XVI (1963), 37.

tionale, n. a. lat. 1235, a 12th-century source from Nevers; they are transcribed in Ex. 3.[31]

It is these texts for the *neuma triplex* that seem to have been more widely used than any others; this is the group that Dom Martène found to have been used, for example, in the Christmas liturgy at Langres. He quotes from a Langres ordinal as follows: "Responsorium tertiae lectionis, *Descendit de coelis*. Prosa, *Fac Deus munda* inter responsorium & versum cantatur. Versus *Tamquam sponsus*. Prosa *Familiam*. Post *Gloria Patri*

Ex. 3a.

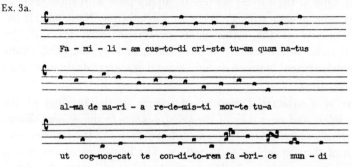

Fa - mi - li - am cus-to-di cri-ste tu-am quam na-tus
al-ma de ma-ri - a re-de-mis-ti mor-te tu-a
ut cog-nos-cat te con-di-to-rem fa -bri- ce mun - di

Familiam: Oh Christ, protect your servants, whom you, born of loving Mary, have redeemed by your death, that they may know you, the maker of the fabric of creation.

Ex. 3b.

Fac de-us mun-da cor-po-ra nos-tra et a-ni-mas di-e is-ta
ut tu-i pro-tec-ti dex-tra con-lau-de-mus auc-to-rem fa -bri- ce mun-di

Fac deus: Make clean, oh Lord, our bodies and souls this day that, protected by your right hand, we may extol the maker of the fabric of creation.

[31] These texts come in the order *Familiam — Facinora — Fac deus* on fol. 243[r]-243[v] of Paris, Bibl. nat., n. a. lat. 1235. The order in which they are given in the example is that in which they are more commonly found. The melody given with the text *Facinora* is the one that has been referred to earlier as "the third *neuma*." In the third line of it, after "regis," n. a. lat. 1235 has the additional word "patris" without music; it is apparently a mistake. I am indebted to Prof. Bernard M. Peebles for help in preparing some of the translations of Latin texts given in this article.

Ex. 3c.

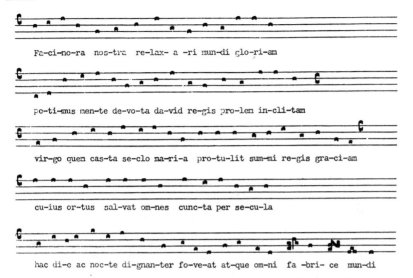

Facinora: That our sins be forgiven is the prayer that we devoutly make to the glory of the universe, the noble offspring of King David, whom the chaste virgin Mary bore to the world, the gracious gift of the highest king, whose birth gives all men salvation through all ages; may he this and every day and night graciously sustain [them]. Of the fabric of creation.

prosa altera *Facinora nostra."* [32] Further investigation suggests how widely known these prosae were. There is evidence of their use at Tours, Laon, Sens, Dijon, and Paris; [33] there are musical sources showing them to have been used not only at Nevers but also at St. Maur-des-Fossés

[32] Edmond Martène, *De antiquis ecclesiae ritibus,* rev. ed. (Venice, 1783), Tomus III, Liber IV, p. 34. The date of the source from which this excerpt is taken is not specified.

[33] Dom Martène, *loc. cit.* The Tours ordinal in which these textings appear is said by him elsewhere to be "300 years old." For Laon the information comes from Ulysse Chevalier, *Ordinaires de l'Église Cathédrale de Laon (Bibliothèque liturgique,* Vol. 6; Paris, 1897), p. 46, in which practices of the 12th and 13th centuries are described. Henri Villetard writes about early 13th-century customs at Sens (which is the seat of an archbishop who until the 17th century had preeminence over the bishops of Chartres, Auxerre, Meaux, Paris, Orléans, Nevers, and Troyes) in his *Office de Pierre de Corbeil* (Paris, 1907), where the prosae are mentioned on pp. 89-90 and 135-36. In his *Histoire de l'Église Saint-Bénigne de Dijon* (Dijon, 1900), L. Chomton is working from what he believes to be a 15th- or 16th-century copy of a 13th-century source; he describes the use of prosae for the responsory *Descendit* on p. 397. The elaborately illuminated *Bréviaire de Philippe le Bon* is said by its editor, V. Leroquais (Brussels, 1929), to reflect the use of the Cathedral of Notre Dame in Paris; the prosae appear on p. 44 of the text volume of this edition.

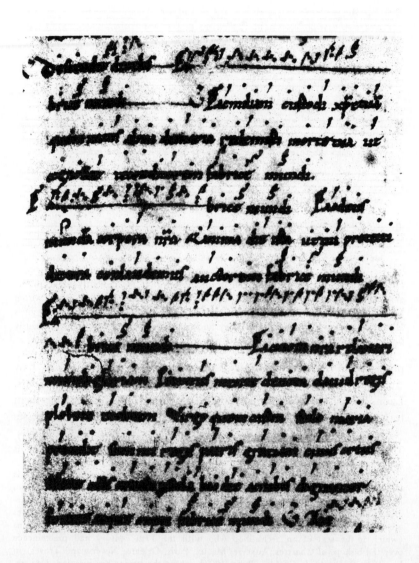

The Fabricae melismas with prosae from Paris,
Bibliothèque Nationale, lat. 9449, fol. 5ʳ
(Nevers, 1059 or 1060).

(Paris, Bibliothèque Nationale, lat. 12044, 12th century).[34] In these different places sometimes only two of the three prosae were used, and they are not always given in the same order. *Facinora nostra* was used also at Novalesa (it appears in Oxford, Bodleian Library, Douce 222)[35] and Bayeux.[36]

It is now time to return to the text *Te mundi climata* which follows the verse of the responsory *Sancte dei preciose* in the Erlyngham Breviary. The melody to which it is set is the third *neuma*. It should be noted that, since *Descendit de caelis* is given without extra melismas in the Erlyngham Breviary, this is the first appearance of this melody in the manuscript. A few pages later it reappears for the feast of St. John the Evangelist, following the responsory *In medio* and provided with the text *Nascitur ex patre*.

Since the *neuma triplex* had long been associated both with the feast of St. John the Evangelist and with Christmas, it is not surprising that someone should have decided to use the third *neuma* on the intervening day as well. Whether this innovation was made first at Salisbury or not is hard to determine, since so few of the sources that might provide proof are available.

There is one closer link between *Te mundi climata* for St. Stephen and the prosae for Christmas. This is a text of the third *neuma* beginning *Te laudant alme rex*, intended for use on Christmas, which *Te mundi climata* resembles very closely in form and in wording.[37] It seems

[34] In Vol. I of his *Einführung in die gregorianischen Melodien*, 3rd ed. (Leipzig, 1911), Peter Wagner prints the texts given in Paris, Bibl. nat., lat. 12044 (with some emendations) on pp. 291-92.

[35] Oxford, Bodleian Library, Douce 222 is a manuscript of the second half of the 11th century from the abbeys of St. Peter, Breme, and La Novalesa, Lombardy (*Latin Liturgical Manuscripts and Printed Books* [Oxford, 1952], p. 21). It is the only source known to me where some textings also found in Paris, Bibl. nat., lat. 1118 and the manuscripts related to it are combined with one of the prosae of the better known group. The texts given in this source for the three melismas are *Conditor mundi* (this is essentially the same as *Fabrice mundi* in Paris, Bibl. nat., lat. 1118), *Felicia angelorum* (in Paris, Bibl. nat., lat. 1118), and *Facinora nostra*. The version of *Facinora nostra* given here is longer by some forty syllables than that of Paris, Bibl. nat., n. a. lat. 1235, but all but the last line of the shorter version is given, with minor variants, before material foreign to it appears.

[36] Ulysse Chevalier, *Ordinaire et Coutumier de l'Église Cathédrale de Bayeux* (*Bibliothèque liturgique*, Vol. 8; Paris, 1902), p. 55.

[37] Ulysse Chevalier lists both these texts, along with useful bibliographical information, in his *Repertorium hymnologicum* (*Subsidia hagiographica*, IV); *Te laudant alme rex* is R. H. 41186 (Vol. IV [Louvain, 1912], p. 335), and *Te mundi climata* is R. H. 20166 (Vol. II [Louvain, 1897], p. 648, with additional comment in Vol. V [Brussels, 1921], p. 384).

to have been the model for *Te mundi climata*. Though it is not given in the Erlyngham Breviary, it is referred to in a Sarum ordinal of ca. 1270.[38] It was also used at Exeter, Hereford, Hyde Abbey (near Winchester), and Rouen; it appears in a 13th-century notated breviary at Hereford as well as in the Hereford Breviary printed in 1505.[39] I have not seen the notated breviary, but the words are easily fitted to the melody, and they appear along with *Te mundi climata* in Ex. 4. In the phrase that begins "ut pelleres," where the texts have differing numbers of syllables, it is the Christmas text that follows the melisma given in the Worcester Antiphonary more closely.

So far attention has been drawn to the character of the music and of the texts associated with *Sancte dei preciose*, but not to the way in which this responsory was performed. There are, however, descriptions given in various sources of the liturgical action that the singing of *Sancte dei preciose* accompanied. This chant was used not only as the last responsory of Matins but also during a procession that took place after Vespers on the eve of St. Stephen's Day.[40] The descriptions of this procession given in the Erlyngham Breviary (facsimile, Vol. II, p. 55) and in the 1519 printed Sarum Antiphonal (fol. lxi^v) are very similar, but not quite so detailed as those given in the New Ordinal of Salisbury:

Let all the deacons gather outside the choir, in front of the altar of St. Nicholas. Then let them, wearing silk copes, and each with a burning candle in his hand,

[38] Walter Howard Frere, *The Use of Sarum*, II: *The Ordinal and Tonal* (Cambridge, 1901), 30. Frere distinguishes between the Old Ordinal (ca. 1270) and the New Ordinal (middle of the 14th century). The references that follow are to the Old Ordinal unless otherwise stated.

[39] Walter Howard Frere and Langton E. G. Brown, *The Hereford Breviary*, I (Henry Bradshaw Society, Vol. XXVI; London, 1904). The text of the prosa is given on p. 145, but the comments on editorial practice in the preface, pp. vii and ix, should also be consulted. Although *Sancte dei preciose* is given with a prosa on St. Stephen's Day, this prosa is not *Te mundi climata* but one beginning *Collectionibus sanctis* that does not fit the familiar melody. In his *Histoire du Bréviaire de Rouen* (Rouen, 1902), pp. 119-120, Amand Collette prints three textings, one for each of the *fabricae* melismas: *Felix Maria, Familiam custodi,* and *Te laudant.* The same three textings were used at Exeter, according to the Exeter ordinal prepared by Bishop John de Grandisson in 1337. They are mentioned in J. N. Dalton, *Ordinale Exon.,* I (Henry Bradshaw Society, Vol. XXXVII; London, 1909), p. 65. They are again given in full in J. B. L. Tolhurst, *The Monastic Breviary of Hyde Abbey, Winchester* (Henry Bradshaw Society, Vol. LXIX; London, 1932), fol. 20.

[40] For a more complete discussion of processions, see Frank Ll. Harrison, *Music in Medieval Britain* (2nd ed.; London, 1963) pp. 88-97; Terence William Bailey, "The Ceremonies and Chants of the Processions of the Western Church; With Special Attention to the Practice of the Cathedral Church of Salisbury" (Ph. D. dissertation, University of Washington, 1968; Ann Arbor, Mich.: University Microfilms).

proceed outside the choir on the south up to the west door of the choir, and then let them pass through the middle of the choir. Let them go out at the north door of the presbytery, and going around the choir let them approach the altar of St. Stephen, with an archdeacon or deacon at the head of the procession beginning the responsory *Sancte dei preciose,* and with a cleric wearing a surplice carrying a staff, a taperer, a thurifer, and a boy carrying the book with a light preceding the priest.[41]

Ex. 4

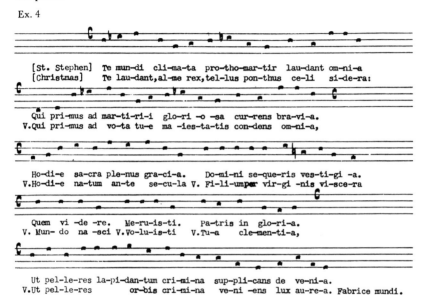

[St. Stephen] Te mun-di cli-ma-ta pro-tho-mar-tir lau-dant om-ni-a
[Christmas] Te lau-dant,al-me rex,tel-lus pon-thus ce-li si-de-ra:

Qui pri-mus ad mar-ti-ri-i glo-ri -o -sa cur-rens bra-vi-a.
V.Qui pri-mus ad vo-ta tu-e ma -ies-ta-tis con-dens om-ni-a,

Ho-di-e sa-cra ple-nus gra-ci-a. Do-mi-ni se-que-ris ves-ti-gi -a.
V.Ho-di-e na-tum an-te se-cu-la V. Fi-li-um per vir-gi -nis vi-sce-ra

Quem vi -de -re. Me-ru-is-ti. Pa-tris in glo-ri-a.
V. Mun- do na -sci V.Vo-lu-is-ti V.Tu-a cle-men-ti-a,

Ut pel-le-res la-pi-dan-tum cri-mi-na sup-pli-cans de ve-ni-a.
V.Ut pel-le-res or-bis cri-mi-na ve-ni -ens lux au-re-a. Fabrice mundi.

Te mundi climata: Oh protomartyr, all the regions of the world praise you, the first to win the glorious rewards of martyrdom. Today, full of sacred grace, you follow the footsteps of the Lord, whom you were deemed worthy to see in the glory of the Father, that, through asking for favor, you might drive away the sins of them that cast the stones.

Te laudant: They praise you, loving king — the earth, the sea, the heavens, the stars; who first created all things according to the desires of your majesty, born today before all ages, the son of a virgin's womb. In your kindness you willed to be born to the world, so that you might drive away the sins of the world, coming as a golden light of the fabric of creation.

[41] Frere, *The Use of Sarum,* Vol. II, p. xxv: "Conveniant omnes diaconi extra chorum, scilicet ante altare S. Nicholai. Deinde processionaliter in capis sericis, singuli singulos cereos ardentes in manibus deferentes, extra chorum ex parte australi usque ad ostium chori occidentale procedant, et sic per medium chori transeant: ad ostium presbiterii septentrionale exeant, et circuendo chorum ad altare S. Stephani accedant, archidiacono vel alio diacono in primo processu incipiente R. *Sancte dei*

The Exeter Ordinal also describes the procession and the singing of this piece:

Let the procession go out in order through the north door of the choir, circle the choir, and enter it on the south near the altar of St. Stephen, singing the responsory. Let one archdeacon or deacon representing St. Stephen begin it alone, standing in the middle, and let the chorus sing it through, the responsory *Sancte dei preciose*. Let all the deacons together solemnly and harmoniously sing the verse *Ut tuo propiciatus* without *Gloria patri*. The chorus [should then sing] *Funde preces*. Then let the deacons sing the prosa in the same place before the altar, and after each verse let the choir respond A or E or O with the melody of the preceding verse.[42]

The printed Sarum Antiphonal of 1519 shows a little more clearly how the alternation is to be made between the performance of the prosa with text and its melismatic performance. In it each phrase is written out twice, first with text, then over the vowel A. According to a rubric, the melismatic repetition of each phrase may be made either by the chorus or by the organ. Some of the phrases thus defined are quite short; "Quem videre" and "Meruisti" are done separately, and consist of only four notes each.

Marginal additions in the Old Ordinal of Salisbury give similar instructions for a procession at the end of Matins on St. Stephen's Day.[43] They indicate, however, that there was a procession at this time only in Salisbury Cathedral, not in parish churches. The more usual time for a procession was after Vespers on the eve of a feast, as at Exeter. In such cases the responsory was sung with its prosa during a procession after second Vespers on Christmas, and without it at the end of Matins.

Sources thus document the use of the prosa *Te mundi climata* at Salisbury as early as ca. 1270 and as late as 1519. It was in use at Exeter in 1337. No Continental sources consulted in the course of this

---

preciose, quodam clerico in superpelliceo virgam gestante, ceroferario, thuribulario, et puero librum cum lumine deferente precedentibus sacerdotem." (There is a plan of Salisbury Cathedral in Harrison, *op. cit.,* p. 89.)

[42] Dalton, *op. cit.,* pp. 68-69: "Et sic eat processio ordinate exeundo per hostium aquilonare chori circuiendo chorum et intrando per partem australem ad altare sancti Stephani, cantando responsorium. Quod unus solus archidiaconus vel diaconus, sanctum Stephanum signans, incipiat, stans in medio, et chorus percantet. R. *Sancte dei.* Omnes simul diaconi solempniter et concorditer dicant V. *Ut tuo propiciatus* absque *Gloria patri.* Chorus *Funde preces.* Diaconi dicant Prosam ibidem coram altari, et post unumquemque versum respondeat chorus A. vel E. vel O. cum cantu versus precedentis."

[43] Frere, *The Use of Sarum,* II, 34-35. Frere comments on the marginal additions, *ibid.,* pp. xii-xiii, and dates them as made probably between 1319 and 1337, p. xx.

The prosa *Te mundi climata*
from the Sarum Antiphonal published in Paris in 1519.

182

study had this prosa, nor have any sources earlier than the 13th century been found to contain it.

This study of the nine responsories associated with the feast of St. Stephen in the Erlyngham Breviary has led to several conclusions. First, the responsories associated with a particular feast in one source may be rearranged in another, and a greater or smaller number of them may be replaced by other responsories. Second, among responsories on even the oldest feasts, the texts may vary a good deal in character, style, and origin: they may be Biblical or non-Biblical, narrative or devotional, prose or poetry. Third, the practice of adding melismas to responsories on certain days was fairly widespread. And, finally, the provision of texts for these melismas is far from rare, with some texts known over a rather large area.

It is particularly the melismas found with responsories in sources of the later Middle Ages that are fascinating to study. With or without their texts, they function as semi-independent entities that may apparently be moved from one chant to another rather freely. The work of unraveling the relationships of these melismas, establishing the course of development of the practices associated with them, and determining their origins is only just beginning.

XIII

Some Questions about the Gregorian
Offertories and Their Verses

THE ATTENTIVE READER of Willi Apel's *Gregorian Chant* (Bloomington,
Indiana, 1958) learns that offertories, and especially their verses, differ in style from other Gregorian chants in their use of repetitions of
text and/or music, of unusually wide ranges, of unusual notes—low F
and E♭—and of unusual melodic intervals and progressions.[1] Professor
Apel believes that the melodies for the offertory verses were composed
during the second half of the ninth century, or at the beginning of the
tenth.[2] This date is considerably later than those proposed by various
writers for the composition of other Mass chants.[3] Does the relatively
late date at which Mr. Apel thinks the melodies for the offertory verses
were composed have any relationship to their style? He thinks it does,
that "certainly they represent a dramatic climax in the development of
the chant which stands in marked contrast to the quiet greatness of the
earlier melodies, a contrast not dissimilar to that between Beethoven
and Bach."[4] This is an important conclusion, and one of considerable

---

[1] The repetitions are discussed by Apel on pages 364-375; the ranges, p. 151; unusual notes, pp. 151 and 165 (fn. 29); intervals and progressions, pp. 252-258.

[2] *Ibid.*, pp. 512-513.

[3] The question of when various types of Gregorian chant were composed is an
extremely difficult one. Since there is considerable agreement among even the earliest
manuscripts containing musical notation, it seems that the liturgy and the chants associated with it must have been standardized in fundamental respects some time before the writing of the earliest manuscripts. However, if one wishes to determine
when in the period antedating musical notation a piece was composed, and takes in
hand the currently available evidence, one is confronted by a rather small number of
relatively unspecific comments about chant—the dating of which may be open to
question—made by persons whose main interest was something else. It is difficult to
work with such testimony, but one must try. Peter Wagner's reasoning for his dating
of the melodies for the graduals, for example, is as follows. It seems clear from some
comments of St. Augustine (354-430) and Pope Leo the Great (reigned 440-461) that
at their time the responsorial chant between the lessons in the Mass included an entire
Psalm. However, the Gregorian sacramentary and subsequent manuscripts offer only
one verse for all but one of the graduals. One possible inference is that the shortening
of the text for this chant was connected with the composition of ornate melodies for
it—that the melodies now known for the graduals were written when they were reduced from full Psalms to just a response and a verse. Further, there is evidence, according to Wagner, that in the Gallican church this shortened text was in use by the
middle of the sixth century. Wagner concludes that the shortening of the gradual text
and the composition of melodies for it—the melodies now known!—must have taken
place between 450 and 550. (Peter Wagner, *Einführung in die gregorianischen
Melodien*, 3d ed. (Leipzig, 1911-1921), I, 82-84.

[4] Apel, *op. cit.*, p. 375.

interest. An inquiry into the sources and interpretations which underlie it seems justified.

The use of repetitions in the offertories has been much discussed, especially by Peter Wagner (*Einführung in die gregorianischen Melodien* III, 421-428) and by Professor Apel (pp. 364-375); nothing significant can be added to their observations here. The ranges and unusual notes Mr. Apel mentions can be dealt with briefly. It is the way in which unusual melodic intervals and progressions seem to be used in offertories and their verses that is of particular interest in this study.

In the section of his book devoted to melodic progressions found in Gregorian chant (pages 252-258), Mr. Apel finds that several of the most unusual progressions appear only in offertories, or else once in an offertory and once in some other type of chant. Among these unusual progressions are the following:

1. The only leap of a seventh in Gregorian chant, in *Domine Deus meus*, verse 2, final melisma (Ott, p. 175); Apel, pp. 253, 364.
2. The only example of a leap of a fifth followed by one of a fourth in the same direction, in *Constitues*, verse 2, on the word "speciosus" (Ott, p. 132); Apel, pp. 257, 364.
3. One of only two examples of two successive downward leaps of a fourth (the other is in an alleluia), in *Posuisti*, verse 2, on the word "eius" (Ott, p. 138); Apel, p. 256.
4. The only example of movement through an octave using only two intermediate pitches, in *Viri Galilaei*, verse, on the word "euntem" (Ott, p. 173); Apel, p. 257.
5. One of only two examples of two successive downward leaps of a third and a fifth (the other is in a gradual), in *Confitebor tibi, Domine*, verse 2, on the word "iucunda" (Ott, p. 46); Apel, p. 255.
6. The only examples in chant of two successive upward leaps of a fourth and a third, in (a) *Afferentur . . . post eam* (S. Agathae), verse 2, on the word "adducentur" (Ott, p. 164); Apel, p. 255; and (b) *Veritas mea*, verse 2, on the word "meo" (Ott, p. 149); Apel, p. 255.

The references to "Ott" in the preceding list are to the only modern edition of chant that contains a complete collection of offertory verses with their antiphons.[5] The verses of the offertories, which are found in many of the early chant manuscripts, gradually disappeared from manuscripts written during the 11th, 12th, and 13th centuries, although they lingered longer in some areas.[6] The verses were officially removed from the offertories by the Council of Trent; only the offertory of the Mass for the Dead retained its verse. Thus, when the Vatican edition of the

[5] C. Ott, *Offertoriale sive versus offertoriorum* (Paris, 1935).
[6] Wagner, *Einführung* I, p. 112.

Gradual was published in 1908, only the offertory antiphons were included, not the verses. There was, however, no objection to the singing of the offertory verses—indeed, many liturgists thought it preferable for the time during which offerings were made to be filled by the singing of these verses rather than by the organ solo which had become the traditional "offertory"—and thus the way was open for a practical edition which gave readings of the offertory verses compatible with those of the offertory antiphons already available in an approved edition.

Ott's edition was, then, for practical use. However, it contains more information about sources and variant readings than do most other practical editions of Gregorian chant. It has a preface, an "epilogus criticus," "notae criticae," and a list of *errata*. The enthusiasm with which its appearance was greeted by various reviewers was somewhat restrained; the anonymous reviewer for *Revue grégorienne* expressed the following reservations:

> It still remains nonetheless that this edition can only be a provisional one. There are too many problems, not only of a melodic nature but especially with regard to modality and the choice of clefs—which frequently change as one passes from the antiphon to the verse—for one not to feel the need of more extended comparative studies.[7]

Dom Lucien David, commenting on Ott's edition in articles in the *Revue du chant grégorien*, went even further:

> Ott informs us in a note that he corrects "when necessary" the strict readings of Montpellier in accordance with studies in modality which he made concerning it in *Die Kirchenmusik* of 1910; but when the reading of Montpellier is clearly confirmed by documents from various schools, it seems to us that one must then bow to the facts and not declare that all the manuscripts are wrong, and with them all the singers of past centuries.[8]

In a review published in 1950, Urbanus Bomm makes specific comments on Ott's readings of various offertories, particularly in cases where Ott transposes only part of a chant; and he makes the general observation that "frequently the editor transposes smaller sections of a melody without referring in his list of variant readings to his sources or giving the original reading." Bomm goes on to say that "many of [Ott's] decisions are to be lamented, such as those cases in which a melodic climax has been transposed down; and—above all—the fact that the virtuoso modulations and displacements of the oldest source (the Montpellier manuscript) are subjected to pedantic corrections."[9]

---

[7] *Revue grégorienne* XXI (1936), Bibliographie liturgique, no. 18.

[8] *Revue du chant grégorien* XXXIX (1935), p. 145. The writer of this article has translated both this and the preceding statement from the French.

[9] *Archiv für Liturgiewissenschaft* I (1950), pp. 398-399: "Häufig wendet Hg. die Teiltransposition bei kleineren Melodieabschnitten an, ohne in seinem Variantenverzeichnis einen Hinweis auf seine etwaige Quelle oder auf die Originallage der

A fourth source in which there is comment on Ott's edition is Hubert Sidler's dissertation *Studien zu den alten Offertorien mit ihren Versen*.[10] In his approach to the subject Sidler shows remarkable impartiality and detachment. He speaks of Ott with respect and gratitude (apparently Ott was gracious and cooperative, and lent Sidler various materials while he was doing his study), and he emphasizes that Ott's was only a practical edition; but at times he criticizes the *Offertoriale* in no uncertain terms.

One's response to this kind of critical comment about an edition is to be very mistrustful of the edition, and—so far as possible—to check every note in it against the sources before using its reading of a chant as the basis for stylistic analysis. Ott says of his sources:

In making my edition I made particular use of the famous bilingual manuscript Montpellier H 159, adding for comparison . . . the manuscripts St. Gall 339, Einsiedeln 121, Laon 239, and the Codex Bohn at Trier. . . . Since this edition is intended for regular use I have made it as similar as possible to the Vatican edition.[11]

Of these manuscripts only two—Montpellier H 159 and the Codex Bohn—notate pitch exactly enough to serve as the basis of editions of the melodies[12] (the others contain valuable and sometimes conflicting indications of rhythm, but Ott's edition does not contain rhythmic markings). In his "notae criticae" Ott refers to additional manuscripts: Paris,

---

Stelle zu bieten. Auch hier muss man manche Entscheidung bedauern, sei es, dass glanzvolle Höhepunkte in tiefere Lage versetzt wurden, sei es vor allem, dass virtuose Modulationen und Verschiebungen, die im ältesten Melodiezeugen, dem Codex von Montpellier, überliefert sind, einer schulmässigen Regulierung weichen mussten."

Bomm's Göttingen dissertation, *Der Wechsel der Modalitätsbestimmung in der Tradition der Messgesänge im IX. bis XIII. Jahrhundert* (Einsiedeln, 1929), touches on some offertories.

[10] Verlag des musikwissenschaftlichen Instituts der Universität Freiburg (Schweiz), 1939. Sidler studies only the first sixteen offertories of Ott's collection.

[11] Ott, *op. cit.*, Prooemium, unnumbered page following the title page.

[12] The Montpellier manuscript is an 11th-century source which records melodies both in French neumes and in letter notation. It is presented in facsimile in *Paléographie musicale*, vol. VIII. Two important studies of this manuscript and its notation have appeared; they are Hubert Sidler, "Zum Messtonale von Montpellier," *Kirchenmusikalisches Jahrbuch* 31-33 (1936-1938), pp. 33-50; and Michel Huglo, "Le tonaire de Saint-Bénigne de Dijon (Montpellier H. 159)," *Annales musicologiques* IV (1956), pp. 7-18. The letter notation of the Montpellier manuscript has separate symbols for $b\natural$ and bb—a vertical i and one which has a distinct slant and cross bars at top and bottom, respectively—which only rarely look similar enough to cause doubt for the transcriber. There are also a small number of special symbols which sometimes replace certain letters; because their meaning is not perfectly clear, these symbols are written over the notes for which they stand in the transcriptions included in this paper.

The Codex Bohn is now manuscript 2254 of the Stadtbibliothek in Trier. It is briefly described in the Solesmes publication *Le graduel romain, II: Les sources* (Solesmes, 1957), p. 144. The other three manuscripts mentioned by Ott are reproduced in *Paléographie musicale*, vols. I, IV, and X.

B. n., f. lat. 903; Graz, Universitätsbibliothek, 807; Paris, B. n., n. acq. lat. 1235; and Leningrad, O v I 6.[13] Wagner lists a number of other manuscripts which have the offertory verses (*Einführung* I, p. 112), and the list could undoubtedly be extended. For the present study, the manuscripts Montpellier, Leningrad, and Paris 903 have been the principal sources used.

What information, then, do the sources provide concerning the unusual traits of the offertories mentioned in the first paragraph of this study? First of all, the unusual notes: are they in the sources?

The E♭ Mr. Apel mentions occurs twice toward the end of the second verse of the offertory *In virtute tua* (Ott, p. 153). The music for the first three syllables of this verse is notated in Ott a fourth lower than in Montpellier.[14] Then Ott takes up the pitch level of Montpellier, dropping again to a fourth below it for the last two words. The two versions are compared in Example 1.

Ott seems to have been moved to transpose the beginning of the verse by similarities in the musical settings for the two statements of the words "magna est gloria eius in salutari tuo." Apparently because in Montpellier the music for the repetition of "gloria eius in salutari tuo" is very similar to the music for the first occurrence of that phrase, Ott made the two identical. Transposing the music for the first statement of "magna est" down a fourth made the beginnings of the two phrases more alike. The version of the beginning given in Example 1 incorporates Ott's later corrections, and is more like that of Montpellier. It is not clear why Ott changed the cadence on "eius" from *f* to *g*.

Ott's reason for transposing the ending of the verse down a fourth is likewise obscure. The transposition may have been suggested to him by the leap up of a fourth between "impones" and "super" and the leap down of a fourth between the end of the verse and the beginning of the refrain, both of which are reduced to unisons if the passage is transposed. However, Ott seems to have made an elementary miscalculation and concluded that the notes indicated as *b♭*'s in the manuscript

[13] *Op. cit.*, p. 192. Ott's notes are in Latin, and in referring to manuscripts he latinizes the names of cities. The manuscript Paris, B. n., f. lat. 903 he calls "S. Aredii," for Saint-Yrieix, the monastery for which it was compiled. A facsimile of a large part of this 11th-century source is found in *Paléographie musicale*, vol. XIII. Graz, Universitätsbibliothek, 807, a 12th-century source, was regarded by Peter Wagner as representing the German tradition; there is a facsimile of one page from it in Wagner's *Einführung*, II, 323. Paris, B. n., n. acq. lat. 1235 is discussed on p. 111 of *Le graduel romain, II;* most of it was written in the 12th century. The source Ott calls the "Codex Rotomagensis" is in Leningrad; a facsimile of this 12th-century manuscript, which was probably written in Rouen, was published by Jean-Baptiste Thibaut in *Monuments de la notation ekphonétique et neumatique*, St. Petersburg (now Leningrad), 1912.
[14] Ott later changed his mind about this, and on p. 195 suggests an emendation which is like the reading in Montepellier, except that it avoids the *b♭*'s in the source.

Ex. 1 *In virtute tua*, v. 2

Montpellier (*Paléographie musicale* VIII, 264)

Ma - gna est glo - ri - a e - - ius in sa - lu - ta -

Ott, *Offertoriale*, pp. 152-153; emendation of the beginning from p. 195 (only passages where Ott's reading diverges from that of Montpellier are included).

Montpellier

ri —————— tu - o ma - - - - - - - - - -

Montpellier

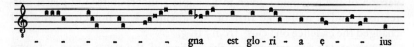

- - - - - - - - - gna est glo - ri - a e - - ius

Ott

Montpellier

in sa - lu - ta - ri tu - o glo - ri - am

Montpellier

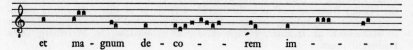

et ma - gnum de - co - - rem im - - - -

Montpellier

- - - - - po - - nes su - per e - -

Ott

Montpellier

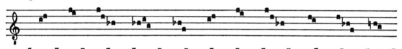

- - - - - - - - - - - - - - - -

Ott

Montpellier

- - - - - - - um De - si - de - ri - um

Ott

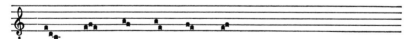

would have to be represented by e♭'s in his edition. Since he was transposing down a fourth rather than a fifth, b♭ would properly have been represented by f, and b♮ by f♯. The presence of e♭'s in Ott's transposition
changes the arrangement of whole and half steps in the melody, something he cannot have intended.[15] (The alternation between b♭ and b♮ in

[15] On p. 195, Ott quotes a different version of the passage in question from the
Graz manuscript. In the Graz reading, there are no e's, flat or natural. It is not clear
whether Ott has transposed the Graz version or not. Ott justifies the e♭ in his edition with this comment on p. 185: "In fine V. 3 sec. H [Ott's *siglum* for the Montpellier manuscript] non semitonium E, sed plenus tonus Es legitur, qua de causa ♭
ponendum erat."

this passage in Montpellier is quite unusual, and Ott's transcription does not give any hint of it. There is room for doubt about whether some of these b's are flat or natural; see footnote 12.)

The presence in the "retransposed" passage of a note which could not be notated in any system acknowledged by medieval theorists—that is, $e\flat$—might have explained to Ott why the passage was not written at its proper level by the notator of the Montpellier manuscript. The theory behind such "retranspositions" as this is that some medieval singers, at least, would recognize that these passages were to be sung at a different pitch than the surrounding music, and that they would somehow know when, for how long, and by what interval to transpose. What the signposts were for such transposition is uncertain. Usually, the only indications modern transcribers find are of the sort mentioned above, which are never clear enough to dispel all doubt.[16] Much clearer evidence would be provided by another manuscript source in which the passage in question was untransposed, and in which the difficulty (in this case, the $e\flat$ which Ott believed was necessary) was handled some other way (perhaps changed to a d.)[17]

At any rate, if Bomm, Sowa, or Jacobsthal—the scholars who have produced particularly important studies on the use of accidentals other than $b\flat$ in the medieval performance of Gregorian chant—if these men had produced editions of chant, Mr. Apel would have found many more $e\flat$'s, and $f\sharp$'s as well. The fact that the only $e\flat$ he found was in an offertory verse tells more about the edition in which that verse was published than it does about the offertory verses in general.

The other unusual note mentioned by Mr. Apel, the low f, is found in the offertory *Tollite portas*, a piece whose very wide range—two octaves—also wins it mention.[18] That Ott was apprehensive about the wide range of the piece in his edition is suggested on p. 192 of his critical notes, where he proposes clef changes which reduce its range to a tenth. The whole of the second verse of this offertory, in which Ott's low f occurs, is written an octave higher in Montpellier than in Ott's edition.

The antiphon of this offertory has a surprising and baffling ending. Sidler's efforts to establish a definitive reading for it ended in a presentation of five alternatives.[19] His preference is very cautiously expressed, and seems to be for a literal transcription of the Montpellier reading,

[16] Jacques Handschin, for example, transposed sections of the final melisma of the responsory "In medio" in transcribing it for his article "Trope, Sequence, and Conductus." (*New Oxford History of Music*, II [London, 1955], 142-143.) Although his reading was supported by at least one other manuscript source, he cautions the reader against regarding it as a critical edition.

[17] This problem is discussed by Gustav Jacobsthal in *Die chromatische Alteration im liturgischen Gesang der abendländischen Kirche* (Berlin, 1897), pp. 218-219.

[18] *Op. cit.*, p. 151.

[19] Sidler, *Studien*, pp. 43-47.

though there are some difficulties in the latter. Such a literal transcription is given in Example 2.

Ex. 2 *Tollite portas*

(a) end of the antiphon

Liber usualis

rex _____ glo - ri - ae

Montpellier (*P. m.* VIII, 275)

rex _____ glo - ri - ae

(b) end of v. 1

Ott, p. 15

qui   ha - bi - tant   in   e - - o

Montpellier

qui   ha - bi - tant   in   e - - o

A comparison of the literal transcription of Montpellier with Ott's version of the same piece shows that the Vatican edition of the Gradual, which Ott used for his reading of the antiphon, gives a simpler and modally clearer ending for the antiphon, and that Ott has transposed the ending of the first verse down a fourth. The second verse, as mentioned above, was transposed down an octave by Ott. The manuscripts Paris 903 and Leningrad agree with Montpellier in general, though they present readings of the ending of the antiphon which differ slightly from that of Montpellier.

In considering other offertories with wide ranges it is good to keep in mind that many scholars agree on the need for some partial transpositions to produce valid transcriptions of Gregorian chants from the Montpellier manuscript. Attractive though the prospect is of simply letting the manuscript speak for itself, the evidence of other manuscripts and even within Montpellier suggests that some "retranspositions" must be made, and that some of those in Ott's edition may be entirely appropriate.[20] Also, when in one of the appendices to the edition Ott has proposed clef changes which result in a major change in the relationship of offertory antiphon and verses, and which dramatically reduce the range of a piece, it seems fitting and fair to take account of them as one uses and evaluates his edition. Ott's notes (p. 193) for the offertory *Laudate Dominum* suggest a clef change which reduces its range from a thirteenth to an octave. The wider range won it mention on Mr. Apel's list of offertories with very wide ranges (p. 151). Undoubtedly, it is Ott's editorial practices and not the composers' intentions which have caused the inclusion of at least some, if not all, of the other chants on this list.

The first of the unusual melodic progressions found in offertories (see the list given above) is a leap of a seventh in the final melisma of the offertory *Domine Deus meus*. When one consults the Montpellier manuscript the seventh is indeed there—the low d at the very end of one line of letter notation, the high c' at the beginning of the next. Could there have been intervening notes, notes written after the d which were lost when the margins of the Montpellier manuscript were trimmed? The Leningrad manuscript provides the answer. In Example 3, the notes forming the seventh in Montpellier and in Ott are starred; the notes between them are provided by Leningrad. The repetitiousness of this melisma and its dwelling on the major third a-g-f and the two minor thirds which frame it, f-d and c'-a, are striking.

There is a leap of a fifth followed by a fourth in the same direction in *Constitues eos*, verse 2, on the word "speciosus." According to Wagner (*Einführung*, III, 419), *Constitues eos* was the model for *Benedictus sit* (the offertory for Trinity Sunday, a feast whose proper may have been written by Alcuin [735-804], and one whose chants utilize pre-existing melodies.)[21] Both offertories are in the Montpellier manuscript, and the similarities and differences between them there are of some interest. Example 4 shows that although the passages in these two offertories in which the critical intervals are found are quite similar, one

[20] Ott published a study dealing with the problems of transcribing from Montpellier, "Die Buchstabenübertragung des Codex von Montpellier," *Die Kirchenmusik* (*Mitteilungen des Diöcesan-Cäcilienvereins Paderborn*) 1910, pp. 97ff. I have not been able to consult this article. According to Ott, it formed only a part of his study; the rest was never published because *Die Kirchenmusik* ceased publication (*Offertoriale*, p. 183). Sidler and David comment on this article; in addition, Sidler had access to the manuscript of the rest of the study and makes comments on it. According to Sidler, Ott does not always in the *Offertoriale* adhere to principles advanced in his article (Sidler, *Studien*, p. 74).

[21] Dom René-Jean Hesbert, *Antiphonale missarum sextuplex* (Brussels, 1935) lxxii, fn. 3.

Ex. 3 *Domine, Deus meus in te:* near the end of v. 2

Montpellier (*P. m.* VIII, 201); the notes between the asterisks are supplied from Leningrad o v I 6, fol. 40ʳ, as seen on Pl. XIX of J. B. Thibaut, *Monuments de la notation ekphoné-tique et neumatique de l'Église latine.*

[altissime]

has two leaps of a fourth where the other does indeed have a fifth followed by a fourth. Whether one reading is more correct than the other is an important question, but one which cannot be answered without the consultation of additional sources.

The two successive downward leaps of a fourth mentioned by Mr. Apel occur in the second verse of the offertory *Posuisti. Posuisti* ap-

Ex. 4 *Constitues eos,* v. 2

Montpellier (*P. m.* VIII, 230)

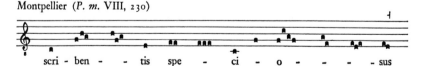

scri - ben - - tis spe - ci - o - - - - sus

Benedictus sit, v. 2

Montpellier (*P. m.* VIII, 233)

su - - - per che - ru - - - - - bim

pears to be an adaptation to a new text of the melody for the offertory *Angelus Domini*. Wagner states the relationship the other way around (*Einführung*, III, 420), but the presence in *Posuisti* of repeated notes to accommodate the words "in salutari" make it appear that *Posuisti* is not the original text (see Example 5). The use of repeated notes to set successive syllables, and of syllabic style in general, is rare among offertories; Wagner counted only eight passages in the antiphons of medieval offertories where four or five successive syllables were given just one note each; see *Einführung*, III, 418. A comparison of the parallel passages in these two related offertories shows a number of differences—again, just at the critical point, so that the two downward leaps of a fourth in one are not found in the other.

The offertory *Viri Galilaei*, in which Apel noted the interval of an octave spanned through only two intervening pitches, is not in the mod-

Ex. 5 *Posuisti*, v. 2

Montpellier (*P. m.* VIII, 282)

[Magna est glo-] - - - - - - - - - ri - a

e - - - - - - - - - - ius ___

Angelus Domini, v. 2 Montpellier (*P. m.* VIII, 280)

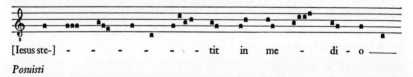

[Iesus ste-] - - - - - - tit in me - di - o ___

Posuisti

in sa - lu - ta - ri tu - - - - - - o

Angelus Domini

e - - o - - - - - rum

ern Roman Gradual; but it seems to have served as the model for at least two early adaptations, *Justorum animae* and *Stetit angelus*.[22] *Viri Galilaei* appears in four of the six early antiphonals of the Mass whose contents are compared by Dom Hesbert in *Antiphonale missarum sextuplex*. Despite his belief that *Viri Galilaei* is not part of the primitive collection of offertories, Hesbert regards it as the model for the other two; he finds no sources for *Stetit angelus* dating before the second half of the 9th century.[23] All three offertories are in Montpellier. The interval which caught Mr. Apel's eye appears in the two offertories related to *Viri Galilaei* in slightly different form. Example 6 reveals it to be a variant of an idiom of mode 1 rather than a radical departure in melodic composition.

Ex. 6 From the verse of *Viri Galilaei*

Montpellier (*P. m.* VIII, 211)

e - un - - - - - - - - - tem

The downward leap of a third followed by one of a fifth is clearly notated in Montpellier for the melisma on "iucunda" in verse 2 of the offertory *Confitebor tibi, Domine, in toto*. Paris 903 and Leningrad have slightly different readings, which change one of the intervals in this passage; they are shown in Example 7. Do these readings represent efforts to tame the native rudeness of the passage, found in its primitive splendor only in Montpellier? Or is one of them the original version of the melody, and Montpellier's reading a mistake?

Mr. Apel's examples of upward leaps of a fourth followed by a third are in the manuscripts. As he points out, they all involve the notes *c*, *f*, and *a*. This brings to mind the fact that two successive ascending leaps of a fourth, found rather often in offertories, usually involve the notes *d*, *g*, and *c'*. Such leaps are found in Example 5, and are particularly likely to occur in offertories in modes 3 and 4.

There are aspects of the offertories' style far more important than the presence or absence of certain intervals singly or in various combinations: use of repetition, both literal and varied; use of melodic rhyme; the presence of long melismas within or at the ends of verses; the sweeping character of some melismas and the hovering quality of others; the contrasting tessituras of antiphon and verses; use of the refrain. The foregoing discussion has contributed nothing but detail to the stylistic

---

[22] In Ott's edition, *Justorum animae* and *Stetit angelus* are very much alike. *Viri Galilaei* seems to have provided a number of melismas for both, but it differs from them at many points, particularly in the verse.

[23] Hesbert, *op. cit.*, lxv-lxvi, cviii.

175

Ex. 7 *Confitebor tibi, Domine in toto*, v. 2: melisma on "iucunda"

Montpellier (*P. m.* VIII, 197)

Leningrad, fol. 58ʳ (Thibaut, Pl. XXVIII)

Paris 903 (*P. m.* XIII, 111)

analyses of the offertories presented by Wagner and Apel. It may, however, be significant that three of the five cases of unusual progressions actually found in the sources occur in offertories which were either models for early adaptations or themselves adaptations. Yet relatively few early offertories are adaptations; the chances are only about one in ten that an offertory found, for example, in the Montpellier manuscript will be a model or an adaptation of another offertory in the same collection.

One other example of adaptation is of such interest that it deserves mention here. There are two offertories beginning with the words "Afferentur regi virgines." One of them, in mode 1, continues with the words "post eam," and is assigned to the feast of St. Agatha. The other is in mode 4, and continues with the words, "proximae eius." Both of these offertories are cited in the Mass antiphonals studied by Hesbert, though frequently without sufficient text to make clear which of the two is intended for a specific feast (in these sources, the first word is spelled "offerentur"). *Afferentur . . . proximae* is unambiguously indicated in one or two of the manuscripts compared by Hesbert as the offertory for the feasts of St. Lucy and the Nativity of the Virgin. There is another offertory that uses the same melody as *Afferentur . . . proximae;* it is *Exsultabunt sancti,* assigned in several of Hesbert's sources to the feasts of St. Basilides and his companions, the octave of the feast of the apostles Peter and Paul, and the vigil of the feast of the apostles Simon and Jude. Mr. Apel refers to *Exsultabunt sancti* as a "later adaptation"; since both of these offertories are present in Hesbert's antiphonals and in Montpellier, they seem to present evidence of a rather early adaptation.

That *Afferentur . . . proximae* is the model is clear from the passage given in Example 8, where the extra syllables in the text of *Exsultabunt sancti* are accommodated by repeated notes, in a manner reminiscent of a reciting tone and quite uncharacteristic for offertories.

Ex. 8 *Exsultabunt sancti*, v.

Montpellier (*P. m.* VIII, 222-223)

Lae - te - tur Is - ra - el in e - o qui fe - cit

Afferentur . . . proximae, v. 1 Montpellier (*P. m.* VIII, 226)

Lin - gua me - a ca - - - la - - -

Exsultabunt

e - - - - - - - um et fi - li - i Si -

Afferentur

- - - - mus scri - bae

Exsultabunt

- on

Afferentur

ve - lo - - - - - - - - - - ci - ter

Exsultabunt

ex - sul - tent in re - ge su - - - - - - o

Afferentur

scri - ben - - - - - - tis

* * * * *

The style of the offertory verses is distinctive, more like that of some alleluias than of any other type of Mass chant. Is Mr. Apel justified in assigning the offertory verses to the second half of the ninth or the early tenth century? His date rests on the evidence of two music theorists, Aurelian of Réomé and Regino of Prüm. In his recent study of Aurelian, Joseph Ponte takes up the subject of Aurelian's statements about the offertory verses, and what sort of interpretation they admit.[24] According to Ponte, when Aurelian says that "no one is a singer who doubts that the verses of the offertories are inserted in them by means of the tones," he may very well be suggesting that there are persons, whom he does not care to dignify by the title "singer," who do in fact doubt it. The "new" melodies for the offertories may already have been in existence; perhaps they can be said to have been composed during the first half of the ninth century. Mr. Apel, on the other hand, believes that Aurelian's reference to a tone for the offertories of each mode means that "we must conclude that at the time of [Aurelian's] *Musica disciplina*, that is about 850, the verses of the Offertories were still sung to a set of eight standard Offertory tones similar in character to those for the Introits and the Responsories."[25]

Mr. Apel draws his *terminus ad quem* from the fact that offertories are not listed in the tonary of Regino of Prüm (d. 912) or in "the later tonaries (all of which, it will be remembered, are catalogues of chants whose verses are sung to a standard melody)."[26] This statement about tonaries seems too strong. Michel Huglo, in reporting the discovery of a very early tonary, has pointed out that they may be either practical or theoretical.[27] If tonaries are practical, they list all the chants in each category for which tones are required for the verses; if theoretical, they list selected chants from all genres (including graduals and alleluias) as examples of each of the modes. Indeed, the very early tonary Huglo discovered (he dates it 800) is one of the theoretical, rather than the practical type. The most famous theoretical tonary of all is the Montpellier manuscript, for in it chants are arranged by mode and by type, and there are marginal comments indicating the ranges of many chants. On its first seven leaves is copied a version of Regino of Prüm's *De harmonica institutione*. However, Mr. Apel's conclusions about Regino seem correct: there is no evidence that he knew anything about tones for the offertory verses.

What sort of tones Aurelian had in mind for the offertory verses is

[24] Joseph P. Ponte, III, "Aureliani Reomensis *Musica disciplina:* A Revised Text, Translation, and Commentary," Ph. D. dissertation (Brandeis University, 1961), I, 4-10.
[25] *Op. cit.*, p. 512.
[26] *Loc. cit.*
[27] Michel Huglo, "Un tonaire du graduel de la fin du VIII⁰ siècle (Paris, B. n., lat. 13159)," *Revue grégorienne* XXXI (1952), pp. 227-228.

not perfectly clear. He makes one comment which may be revealing: the piece *Recordare mei* is considered by some to be an offertory, but he regards it as a responsory.[28] Ponte reasons that if a single piece could be thought of as a responsory by some and as an offertory by others, then the tones for the verses of offertories must be the same as those for responsories. The reason Aurelian does not describe the offertory tones in detail, according to Ponte, is that they are the same as the tones for the verses of the responsories, which Aurelian does discuss thoroughly.[29]

There is, however, one fact that clouds the picture. Dom Pothier noted that the usual melody for the offertory *Recordare mei* was different from that for the responsory beginning with the same words.[30] However, in some manuscripts the responsory melody is given for the offertory. There is nothing unusual about the existence of two chants of different genres beginning with the same words, but it is unusual for there to be confusion about which of the melodies was intended for a particular liturgical function. Aurelian may have been one of those who knew only the responsory melody for this text. In this case, his remark would be quite appropriate to the situation; it would contribute nothing to our knowledge of the offertory tones.

Since Aurelian's comment to the effect that offertory verses are sung on tones is so important in the dating of the melodies preserved in the manuscripts for these verses, it may be worthwhile to give some consideration to the offertories he mentions. Aurelian lists one offertory for each tone. (One additional offertory, *Sanctificavit Moyses*, is referred to in Aurelian's discussion of chants in mode 2, but Aurelian does not assign it explicitly to that mode. He seems rather to have brought it in only to illustrate a point about changes that may be made in the text of a refrain to make it fit better with a verse.) Of these eight offertories, five are from the *temporale* and three from the *sanctorale*. Are these offertories a fair sampling of typical works, or do they give disproportionate emphasis to special types? A comparison of Aurelian's list with the early tonary described by Huglo reveals that Aurelian mentions only one offertory found in the earlier tonary, and that is *Sanctificavit Moyses*.[31] On the other hand, all four of the offertories mentioned in the *Alia musica* are named by Aurelian.[32] An investigation of the liturgical

---

[28] Ponte, *op. cit.*, II, 80; III, 61.

[29] *Ibid.*, I, 5-6.

[30] Dom Joseph Pothier, "Exemples d'offertoires empruntés à d'anciens versets," *Revue du chant grégorien* IV (1895-1896), p. 165.

[31] Huglo, *Revue grégorienne* XXXI (1952), pp. 225-227.

[32] The *Alia musica* is generally thought to have been written by several persons and to have reached its final form *ca.* 900. It is published in Gerbert, *Scriptores* I, 125-147; but the commentary and corrections provided by Wilhelm Mühlmann in *Die Alia musica (Gerbert, Scriptores I): Quellenfrage, Umfang, Inhalt und Stammbaum* (1914) should be utilized. The offertories mentioned in the *Alia musica* appear in Gerbert on pp. 133 b, 136 a, 137 b, and 140 a.

role of Aurelian's offertories produces some surprising results. Three of the four offertories from the *temporale* are assigned to Sundays after Pentecost, as follows:†

Mode 1 *Super flumina* (Ps. 136)	Fer. V Hebd. V Quad.
	Dom. XX p. Pent.
Mode 2 *Ad te Domine levavi* (Ps. 24)	Dom. I Adv.
	Fer. V p. Cin.
	Fer. IV Hebd. II Quad.
	Dom. X p. Pent.
Mode 3 *Deus tu convertens*	Dom. II Adv.
	Fer. VI Q.T. Adv.
Mode 4 *Justus ut palma*	S. Joannis Ev.
	S. Joannis Baptist.
Mode 5 *Immittet angelus* (Ps. 33)	Fer. V Hebd. 1 Quad.
	Dom. XIV p. Pent.
Mode 6 *Stetit angelus*	Dedic. S. Michaelis
Mode 7 *In virtute*	S. Stephani (and nine others)
Mode 8 *Si ambulavero* (Ps. 137)	Fer. V Hebd. III Quad.
	Dom. XIX p. Pent.

It has frequently been noted that many of the offertories for the Sundays after Pentecost take their texts from the book of Psalms, going through the Psalms in order, but not consecutively.[33] In addition, these offertories are generally borrowed from week days in Lent (except Thursdays; the Masses for Thursdays in Lent were not instituted until the pontificate of Gregory II, 715-731).[34] There are notable exceptions to this general rule: the offertories for the seventh, twelfth, fourteenth, and seventeenth and following Sundays after Pentecost. It has been proposed that the original corpus of Masses for Sundays after Pentecost included what the modern Gradual knows as Sundays I-VI and VIII-XVII, and that the formularies for the other Sundays are more recent.[35] This belief is supported by the nature of the offertory texts, especially by the offertory texts for the Sundays following XVII.

A "normal" offertory for a Sunday after Pentecost would have a text taken from a Psalm which had a higher number than that for the offertory of the preceding Sunday and a lower number than that for the

† The offertories are listed with the feasts to which they are assigned by the sources included in Hesbert's *Antiphonale missarum sextuplex*. The Biblical sources are indicated for the texts of those found on Sundays after Pentecost, and those mentioned in the *Alia musica* are starred.

[33] See, for example, Antoine Chavasse, "Les plus anciens types du lectionnaire et de l'antiphonaire romains de la messe," *Revue bénédictine* 62 (1952), pp. 12-13, 61-64.

[34] Antoine Chavasse, "Le carême romain et les scrutins prébaptismaux avant le ix⁰ siècle," *Recherches de science religieuse* 35 (1948), p. 340.

[35] Chavasse, *Revue bénédictine* 62 (1952), pp. 61-64.

following Sunday, and it would also be assigned to a week day (other than Thursday) in Lent—the occasion for which it was, presumably, originally composed. Of the eight offertories Aurelian lists, three of the four assigned to Sundays after Pentecost fail to meet this definition of "normal." *Si ambulavero*, for Sunday XIX, has a text from a Psalm whose number is not in the regular series, and it appears on a Thursday in Lent; the same is true of *Super flumina*, for Sunday XX; *Immittet angelus*, for Sunday XIV, has a text from a Psalm with a number appropriate to its position, but it is found only on a Thursday in Lent.

Thus there may be some reason to believe that the texts of these offertories belong not to the original corpus of offertories but to a somewhat later time. The fact that that all of the Thursdays in Lent borrow their offertories from other days suggests, however, that by 715-731 new offertories were no longer being written. Stylistic analysis of the melodies for the offertories of the original corpus and of those which may be later additions may reveal whether the melodies, too, were composed at different times; but such analysis can be made only when better editions of these melodies than Ott's become available.

Another offertory in Aurelian's group of eight can be assigned a relatively late date; this is *Stetit angelus*, which has been discussed earlier.[36] The remaining four offertories on Aurelian's list may be part of the earliest repertory. What this means, and what effect it should have on one's evaluation of Aurelian's testimony, is far from clear; but it seems to merit consideration.

The modes Aurelian assigns to the offertories he mentions are sometimes different from those assigned to them in most other sources, but there is perfect agreement with the *Alia musica*. Thus, *Immittet angelus* is said by Aurelian and the *Alia musica* to be in the fifth tone; the other sources assign it to the eighth. Bomm's discussion of this piece examines various reasons for this unusual modal assignment without clarifying the matter very much.[37] *Stetit angelus* is assigned to mode 6 by Aurelian and the *Alia musica;* other sources place it in the first or second mode. Bomm believes that range and a melodic relationship to the sixth-mode introit *Omnes gentes* are factors in this classification.[38]

As scholarly interest in medieval music increases, it seems inevitable that some of the ideas and evaluations of writers of even the recent past will be shown to be inaccurate or incomplete, on the basis of a reexamination of the sources. This paper has endeavored to point out some

---

[36] Ott points out (*Offertoriale*, p. 185) that the verses of *Stetit angelus* and *Justorum animae* are like the alleluia verse, *Veni, Domine*. In the verse of this alleluia (for the fourth Sunday in Advent) there are two melismas, one which appears in the offertories in question and another which occurs also in some graduals. See Wagner, *Einführung*, III, 402.

[37] Bomm, *Der Wechsel*, pp. 176-180.

[38] *Ibid.*, pp. 180-181.

of the hazards in using, as the basis for stylistic analysis, chant melodies from editions lacking in critical apparatus. It has also shown some of the problems one may encounter in using a theorist's statement to assign a date to a particular musical genre—in this case, the melodies of the offertory verses. It has sought not so much to advance hypotheses and draw conclusions as to pose questions and suggest modes of approach. It will have served its purpose if it stimulates, as does Professor Apel's monumental and deeply challenging book, new and more comprehensive inquiries.

XIV

Holocausta medullata: An Offertory for St. Saturninus

The early history of Christianity in Gaul is a story of individual communities and of those who first preached the faith there, of those who worked to establish the Church. Those men and women were remembered as saints, and the regular recurrence in the calendar of their feast days helped to keep their memories alive. The cult of a local saint also strengthened the sense of community among Christians in the regions where it was observed. Devotion to a saint could take many forms, and its recorded manifestations provide valuable evidence of regional culture.

Saturninus was the first bishop of Toulouse; he was active during the second quarter of the third century, and martyred around the year 250[1]. There are Masses for his feast day (November 29) in both Mozarabic and Gallican service books, and two complete series of chants for the Proper of the Mass in the 11th-century Aquitanian gradual Paris, B.n., lat. 776[2].

This manuscript has been mentioned repeatedly as a possible repository of chants held over from the Gallican repertory into the Gregorian[3]. It is typical for articles concerning Gallican chant to include in their musical examples chants transcribed from lat. 776[4]. Its contents were surveyed by Sr. Anthony Marie Herzo; the pro-

---

1 Les RR. PP. Bénédictins de Paris, *Vies des Saints*, Paris 1954, XI, pp.973-990; and Anne-Véronique Gilles, *L'Évolution de l'hagiographie de Saint-Saturnin de Toulouse et son influence sur la liturgie*, in: *Cahiers de Fanjeaux*, 17: *Liturgie et musique*, Toulouse 1982, pp.359-79.

2 This manuscript was copied and notated at Ste. Cécile, Albi, for St. Michel de Gaillac: see Michel Huglo, *La Tradition musicale aquitaine: Repertoire et notation*,in: *Cahiers de Fanjeaux*, 17, pp.253-68, especially p.267, note 21, where additional studies are cited.

3 Olivier Cullin writes as follows: "Il est certain qu'un dépouillement systématique de ce manuscrit nous révèlerait d'autres pièces encore inconnues et probablement gallicanes." He identifies the offertory *Salvator mundi*, which appears at the very end of lat. 776 (fol. 146v) as "Une pièce gallicane conservée par la liturgie de Gaillac," in: *Cahiers de Fanjeaux*, 17, pp.287-97. But whether there was anywhere in pre-Carolingian Gaul a repertory of liturgical chant comparable in scope, development, and organization to that of Toledo or Rome remains to be demonstrated. Hence the term "Gallican chant" as currently employed may in some instances be misleading.

4 The most important of these are the articles by Michel Huglo in *The New Grove Dictionary of Music and Musicians*, London 1980, 7, pp.113-25, and by Bruno Stäblein in *Die Musik in Geschichte und Gegenwart*, vol. 4, Kassel 1955, cols. 1299-1325. These incorporate many observations made in a series of studies on "Le chant gallican" by A. Gastoué published in: *Revue du chant grégorien* in 1937-1939, and then separately as a book, Grenoble: Librairie Saint-Grégoire, 1939.

cessional antiphons that it contains have been studied by Charlotte Roederer; its Alleluias were inventoried by Sr. Anthony Marie, and by Karl-Heinz Schlager as well[5]. But it has never been the subject of a comprehensive study.

The first of the two Masses for St. Saturninus begins on fol. 122r, and includes only one chant that is written in full, the introit *Domine praevenisti Saturninum*[6]. The gradual, alleluia, offertory, and communion are represented in incipits of chants to be borrowed from other days, as follows: gradual, *Domine praevenisti* (St. Nicomedes, Martyr, fol. 115r); alleluia, *Hic est vere martir* (St. Menna, Martyr, fol. 120r); offertory, *Posuisti Domine* (St. Gorgonius, Martyr, fol. 113v); communion, *Magna est* (St. John the Evangelist, fol. 16v). The introit *Christe Deus plebem tuam* begins the second series of proper chants. All have non-Biblical texts. The gradual, *Adiuva sancte tuos precibus*, has a verse (mislabeled R.) which begins *"Ut valeant famulis sic ducere"*; both respond and verse are set to formulas characteristic of mode-5 graduals, although no specific chant has been identified as the principal model for this one[7]. For the alleluia, *Saturninus pontifex magnus*, the model is *Dies sanctificatus*, identified by Schlager as the alleluia melody most frequently employed for adaptations (in which new words are set to pre-existing melodies)[8]. The communion, *Proficiat nobis domine*, seems to be a new composition in the Gregorian style: the opening and some other figures may have been copied from the communion *Dicite pusillanimes*, but there are several features that are distinctive.

The offertory, *Holocausta medullata*, is given in transcription in the musical example. The text is a prayer to the Lord in which the memory of His beloved Saturninus is invoked.

---

[5] Sr. Anthony Marie Herzo, *Five Aquitanian Graduals: Their Mass Propers and Alleluia Cycles*, Ph. D. dissertation, University of Southern California, 1967 (Ann Arbor, Mich.: University Microfilms, Order number 67-10,762); Charlotte Roederer, *Can We Identify an Aquitanian Chant Style?* in: *Journal of the American Musicological Society* 27 (1974), pp.75-99; *Eleventh-Century Aquitanian Chant: Studies Relating to a Local Repertory of Processional Antiphons*, Ph. D. Dissertation, Yale University, 1971; see also Clyde Brockett, *Unpublished Antiphons and Antiphon Series Found in the Gradual of St-Yrieix*, in: *Musica Disciplina* 26 (1972), pp.5-35; Karl-Heinz Schlager, *Thematischer Katalog der ältesten Alleluia-Melodien*, München 1965. In *Monumenta Monodica Medii Aevi, VII: Alleluia-Melodien I*, Kassel 1968, Schlager edited a number of melodies from lat. 776.

[6] The Introits of lat. 776 merit a separate study, and will not be discussed further here.

[7] For a table of formulas in mode-5 graduals, see Willi Apel, *Gregorian Chant*, Bloomington, Indiana 1958, pp.346-50. The formulas employed in the respond of *Adiuva sancte* are Fa und f4; in the verse, A13 und A15. It seems likely that the verse ending is F10, but that melisma is not written out at this point in the manuscript, having (presumably) been written earlier.

[8] Schlager, *Thematischer Katalog*, p.30, pp.78-81.

Rich offerings of praise we offer unto you, o Lord, for the honor of your beloved bishop Saturninus, that he who was your priest and altar and sacrifice may take our prayers before the throne of your atonement.

V. We bring magnificent praises and gifts to you, Lord, for your martyr and bishop Saturninus, that he may be for us a constant mediator.

(Refrain: May he take our prayers before the throne of your atonement.)

V. May the gracious martyr Saturninus be our intercessor, he who rather than being the most fierce victim of the bull deserved to be an offering to Christ.

(Refrain:) Before the throne of your atonement.

266

V. Mag-ni-fi-cas lau - des at - que mu - ne - ra
ti - bi de-fe - ri - mus, Do - mi - ne,pro mar - ti-re
tu - o at - que pre - su - le,Sa - tur - ni - no,
ut ip - se sit pro no - bis in-ter - ven - tor
as - si - du - us.

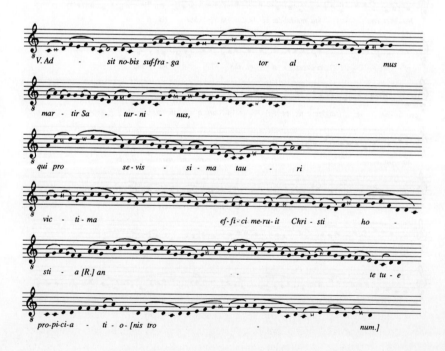

V. Ad - sit no-bis suf-fra - ga - tor al - mus
mar - tir Sa - tur-ni - nus,
qui pro se-vis - si - ma tau - ri
vic - ti - ma ef-fi-ci me-ru-it Chri - sti ho -
sti - a [R.] an - te tu - e
pro-pi-ci-a - ti - o-[nis tro - num.]

For a comparable text serving as an offertory, one need look no further than the Mass for the patron saint in another Aquitanian gradual - the offertory for St. Aredius in Paris, B.n., lat. 903[9]. It reads as follows.

Immaculatas hostiarum preces pro delictis nostris, Christe, tibi offerimus et, ut eas suscipere clementer digneris petimus, qui beatum Aredium tibi elegisti templum et aram, hostiam atque littatorem dignissimum.
V. O inclite atque sublimis Aredi, inter agmina regis celestis, Christum fac nobis placabilem, qui te elegit sibi.
V. Pulcher virtutibus et sanctitate nemorosus, Deo dilectus Aredius protegat nos sub umbraculis pietatis Christi, qui ante secula eum sibi prescivit. (Refrain:) Templum et aram hostiam ...

The spotless prayers of offerings for our transgressions we offer unto you, Christ; and we ask that you, who chose for yourself blessed Aredius as temple and altar, as offering and most worthy teacher, mercifully deign to receive them.
V. O illustrious and exalted Aredius, amongst the hosts of the King of heaven, render Christ, who has chosen you for himself, ready to forgive us.
(Refrain: Temple and altar, offering and most worthy teacher.)
V. May Aredius, beloved of God, beautiful for his virtues, and (like a leafy tree) covered over with sanctity - may he protect us under the shady bower of the goodness of Christ, who knew him and chose him for himself before time began.
(Refrain:) Temple and altar, offering and most worthy teacher.

The imagery in these texts is striking. Some of it is introduced through a play on the meaning of "hostia" as "sacrificial animal" as well as "offering." "Holocausta medullata" means a burnt animal sacrifice rich in marrow. The expression occurs in Psalm 65 and in an offertory based on that psalm, *Jubilate Deo universa terra*, of which the second verse reads as follows (Ps. 65:14b-15a): "Locutum est os meum in tribulatione mea: holocausta medullata offeram tibi" - "My mouth spoke, when I was in trouble: 'I will offer up to Thee holocausts full of marrow.'" Verse 15 of the psalm continues, in the Douay version, "With burnt offerings of rams: I will offer to Thee bullocks with goats." The recollection of a time and a culture in which ritual sacrifice involved living creatures is further evoked in the Saturninus offertory through reference to a human victim -Saturninus- in whose martyrdom an ani-

---

[9] There is a facsimile edition of this manuscript in *Paléographie musicale*, XIII, Solesmes 1925. The offertory is on p.220 of the facsimile edition, fol. 110v of the manuscript.

XIV

268

mal (a bull) was the agent[10]. But Saturninus was worthy to be a "hostia" -an offering- to Christ.

A different theme prevails in the offertory for Aredius, where the saint is described as "sanctitate nemorosus," literally "leafy with sanctity," and he is later asked to offer protection "sub umbraculis pietatis," "under the umbrella of goodness." Both texts are made up of a series of petitions in which there are several references both to the feast day and to the ritual that the offertory chant accompanies. In language, imagery, and sound they bear witness to their authors' poetic gifts[11].

The texts for offertories in the classic repertory are nearly all taken from the book of Psalms, and the various procedures employed in their selection were identified by Helmut Hucke[12]. Recently, Kenneth Levy has investigated the non-psalmic offertories, particularly those on texts of which comparable settings exist in the Mozarabic and Milanese chant repertories. His proposal, that "something like the music jointly transmitted by the MOZ-GREG and MOZ-MED pairs of the tenth to twelfth centuries was already in existence in later seventh-century Gaul," defines a group of offertories as representing one layer in the repertory[13]. The psalmic offertories, in his view, although on texts that are of Roman origin, have music that bears "a Carolingian stylistic overlay in many cases," and which may be, in other cases, "a wholly new 'northern' music."[14] Yet he finds no significant differences in the musical style of psalmic and non-psalmic offertories: the music that appears to date from two different periods is all cut from the same cloth.

Is the music of the offertory *Holocausta medullata* also in this style? Certain of its features are worthy of comment. The antiphon is written in lat. 903 (fol. 115v) in such a way as to indicate that it was regarded as a plagal chant of the protus maneria[15]. One is not surprised, therefore, to find emphasis on F, the reciting tone of the mode, and on D, the final. The verses of the chant do not appear in lat. 903. In lat. 776, their most prominent feature is the melismas which lie fully within the authentic range of the mode, and which emphasize the notes a fifth and an octave above the final. (This type of contrast in range, plagal in the antiphon and authentic

[10] A.-V. Gilles observes that in the mass that begins with the introit *Christe Deus* the only text referring to the martyrdom of Saturninus is this offertory verse. (*Cahiers de Fanjeaux*, XI, p.373.)

[11] Thanks are due to Professor F.A.C. Mantello, of the Department of Greek and Latin at the Catholic University of America, for his kindness in explaining these texts and suggesting translations for them.

[12] Helmut Hucke, *Die Texte der Offertorien*, in: *Speculum Musicae Artis. Festgabe für Heinrich Husmann*, ed. H. Becker und R. Gerlach, München 1970, pp.193-203.

[13] Kenneth Levy, *Toledo, Rome and the Legacy of Gaul*, in: *Early Music History* 4 (1984), pp.49-99, especially p.87.

[14] Levy, p.96.

[15] For an explanation of the conventions governing the notation of lat. 903, see P. Ferretti, *Etude sur la notation aquitaine*, in: *Paléographie musicale*, XIII, pp.54-211, especially p.139.

in the verses, is common among offertories.) There is no monotone reciting in either the antiphon or the verses. The movement of the musical line in the chant as a whole, and especially in the melismas, is purposeful: it progresses in a logical way toward a goal that is anticipated by the listener and which is, most often, the final of the mode.

One would be hard put to describe the style of the traditional chant repertory, for one of its most striking traits is the variety it permits in the formation of individual melodies: in some classes of chant, every profile seems absolutely unique. But it is relatively rare to find chants that conform so closely to 11th-century notions of the modes, particularly their identification with octave species, as does this offertory. There seems every reason to group *Holocausta medullata* with those chants that David Hughes has identified as musically "post-Gregorian"[16] - even though, given the subject matter of its text, this offertory might better be termed "post-Gallican."

This observation suggests two further lines of inquiry. The first is an examination of some of those other chants in lat. 776 that have been identified, on the basis of their liturgical assignment or text, as having a possible origin in the Gallican liturgy (and here the term is intended to refer to the pre-Gregorian repertory of liturgical chant sung in the area around Albi and Gaillac). Is there anything in their musical style that sets them apart from the Gregorian repertory and from later chant as well? Or do these melodies appear to have taken shape under the influence of the modal concepts that seem to govern *Holocausta medullata*? This examination remains to be carried out.

The second line of inquiry extends the study of offertories to the other chants of this genre that are included in lat. 776 but not in the standard early compilations, that is, not in those sources of which the contents were edited by Hesbert in *Antiphonale Missarum Sextuplex*[17]. A list of these non-Sextuplex offertories is presented here as Table 1. In it, the chants are set in order according to type of text, with those on texts from the book of Psalms first, followed by those on other Biblical texts. In some offertories, the subject matter is Biblical, but there is little exact quotation; these are listed next. Slightly over half of the non-Sextuplex offertories in lat. 776 are non-Biblical. Some are based on narratives, as in the case of a brief excerpt from the Life of St. Benedict by Gregory the Great, *Intempesta noctis hora*, of which there are two settings in lat. 776. *Martinus igitur* derives from the account of the death of St. Martin of Tours written by Sulpicius Severus in the form of a

---

[16] Hughes explains this term in *A History of European Music*, New York 1974, pp.16-17 and pp.31-33.

[17] René-Jean Hesbert, *Antiphonale Missarum Sextuplex*, Brussels 1935. Lists of non-Sextuplex Proper chants in five sources are provided by Sr. Antony Marie Herzo in her dissertation. The five manuscripts are Paris, B.n., lat. 780, 903, 776, and 1132, and London, British Library, Harley 4951. Her lists are the basis of Tables 1 and 2 in the present study.

XIV

letter to his mother[18]. And an offertory for the Invention of the Holy Cross,
Veniens vir splendidissimus, has a similar, narrative quality; but - though evidently
non-Biblical - its source has not been identified. The others are prayers.

Among the offertories with prayer texts, several are for use in Masses for the
Dead. These have been studied by Claude Gay, who identified one melody, that of
Erue Domine, as an adaptation, and two others, *Domine Jesu Christe* and *O pie
Deus*, as "original."[19] (*Ego sum resurrectio*, on a text in which several different
passages from John are juxtaposed, is also on an "original" melody.)

Another prayer is *Felix namque es*, a celebrated expression of devotion to the
Blessed Virgin that is familiar as an Office responsory[20]. In lat. 776, two offertories
use this text; they appear on folios 113r and 113v, in the alternate Mass Propers
that are offered for the feast of the Nativity of the Blessed Virgin. The first has as
its verse *"Beata es Virgo Maria quae omnium,"* which is similar to (though not
identical with) the text of another responsory. The music of the offertory antiphon
was published long ago by Dom Pothier, and he judged it to be an "original"
melody[21]. But it has a strong similarity to the melody of the offertory *Factus est
Dominus* for the Saturday of the Fourth Week of Lent, and the resemblance between the two verses, *"Beata es Virgo"* and *"Praecinxisti me,"* (V.2 of *Factus est
Dominus*) is even stronger.

In the second setting of *Felix namque es*, the text of the antiphon is slightly
extended through the addition of the words, *"quem nobis sanctissima placa, alleluia."* This may have been done to render the text more similar in length to that
from which the melody was to be borrowed, the offertory *Stetit angelus*, for the
feast of St. Michael the Archangel. The verse of *Felix namque* in this setting is
"Beata et venerabilis es," also familiar as a responsory text. The beginning of the
melody provided for it is a close copy of *"In conspectu,"* one of the verses for *Stetit
angelus*, but after the first five words the model is abandoned, and recourse is made

---

[18] This is one of the chants studied by Guy Oury in *Formulaires anciens pour la messe de Saint
Martin*, in: *Etudes grégoriennes* 7 (1967), pp.21-40. He identifies twenty manuscripts in which it is
found. The music is analyzed by Martha Fickett in *Chants for the Feast of St. Martin of Tours*,
Ph.D. dissertation, Catholic University of America, 1983 (Ann Arbor, Mich.: University Microfilms, Order number 84-01475), pp.44-54. Dr. Fickett identifies two chants as sources for the melodies employed in verses of *Martinus igitur*, and a third chant from which part of a melisma was
taken.

[19] Claude Gay, *Formulaires anciens pour la messe des défunts*, in: *Etudes grégoriennes* 2 (1957),
pp.83-129, especially pp.96-7 and 126-7. *O pie Deus* is, according to Dom Pothier, similar in many
respects to the offertory *Protege Domine*: "Ce n'est ni un calque, ni à proprement parler une imitation, mais une allure toute pareille, avec plusieurs formules qui, bien qu'identiques ou presque identiques, apparaissent cependant toujours directement inspirées par le sens et la contexture des
paroles." (*L'Offertoire "O pie Deus"*, in: *Revue du chant grégorien* 16 (1908), p.114.

[20] The text is edited by René-Jean Hesbert in: *Corpus Antiphonalium Officii*, IV, Rome 1970, as
6725.

[21] *L'offertoire "Felix namque es"*, in: *Revue du chant grégorien* 15 (1907), pp.105-114.

Holocausta medullata   271

to very routine figuration (there are three stepwise descending passages in close
succession that go through the same interval of a fifth).

For the offertory *Felix namque*, Dom Pothier found four different melodies in the
sources: the two that have just been discussed and two others. One of the others is,
he says, in the same mode as that based on *Stetit angelus*, and in many places similar to it; yet it is "malgré ces imitations passagères ... originale et de bonne facture."[22] The fourth melody is that of *Angelus Domini*, a mode-8 offertory sung on
Easter Monday and on the Sunday following Easter. This adaptation was a very
successful one, so much so that the verse of this chant was put to service as an independent offertory[23]. The exceptional popularity of this melody is a theme that
will return shortly.

Two further texts that are prayers are found in offertories for the Exaltation of the
Holy Cross, *Protege Domine* and *Salve presentem*. The music for the antiphon of
Salve presentem is based largely on musical ideas that are also found in *Stetit angelus* and *Viri Galilaei*, two chants whose similarities have been commented upon
many times[24].

In the discussion thus far, text has been the center of attention. But music has also
come into the discussion, and the reader will have noted that although some of the
non-Sextuplex offertories in lat. 776 are on "original" melodies, many are adaptations. A list of those chants for which the musical models have been identified follows as Table 2.

What strikes the eye immediately is the extent to which certain melodies predom-
inate in the repertory - the melody associated with *Stetit angelus* and *Viri Galilaei*
on the one hand, and that for *Angelus Domini* and *Posuisti* on the other. In addition
to their popularity as models for adaptation, these melodies have certain features in
common. Although adaptation is not at all frequent among offertories[25], each of
these melodies occurs in the classic repertory with two texts, and three of the four
texts are non-psalmic. It is not clear for either pair which of the chants is the origi-

---

22 Ibid., p.108.

23 J. Pothier, *Offertoire "Beata es"*, in: *Revue du chant grégorien* 7 (1898), pp.17-20.

24 Dom Pothier used these similarities as a point of departure for his explanation of what centonization is: see *Offertoire "Viri Galilaei" de l'Ascension*, in: *Revue du chant grégorien* 11 (1903),
pp.149-155. See also G. Björkvall and R. Steiner, *Some Prosulas for Offertory Antiphons*, in: *Journal of the Plainsong and Mediaeval Music Society* 5 (1982), pp.13-35, where reference is made to
additional work on this subject.

25 In *Einführung in die gregorianischen Melodien, III: Gregorianische Formenlehre*, Leipzig 1921,
pp.419-20, P. Wagner gives a list of offertories that are adaptations. Most of them are later additions
to the repertory; they are marked with the symbol (a small cross) that he employs to identify "einen
jüngeren, aber älteren Vorlagen nachgebildeten Gesang im Graduale Vaticanum" (p.377).

272

nal and which the adaptation[26]. For one chant in each pair, Levy has proposed a prominent liturgical role in the old-Gallican Rite: *Angelus Domini* was for Easter, *Viri Galilaei* for Ascension[27]. In both of these texts, angels address mortals in words quoted from the New Testament; in both there is a dramatic representation of events celebrated in the feast of the day. The extent to which the melodies presented in lat. 776 are authentic old-Gallican tunes cannot be determined with certainty, but the matter needs study.

How similar are these two melodies to each other? The differences are more striking than the similarities. The antiphon of *Stetit angelus* includes several shapely melismas, of which that on the word "ascendit" is particularly notable; but in some passages the setting of the text consistents of little more than an embellished reciting tone. In certain of the adaptations, this effect is even more pronounced. *Angelus Domini*, on the other hand, is characterized by a greater variety in melodic formation, so that even though nearly every phrase ends on the final of the mode, one has the sense of a continuously unfolding melody, a melody that develops and amplifies its expression as it proceeds.

Some of the non-Sextuplex offertories of lat. 776 were very widely known. Claude Gay, who searched in 184 manuscripts for offertories for the Mass for the Dead, found *Domine Jesu Christe* in all but ten of them. For *Erue Domine* he found thirty-three sources, for *O pie Deus*, twenty-nine. But for *Ego sum resurrectio* there is only one source other than lat. 776, Madrid, Acad. de la Historia, 18. A study of concordances for the other non-Sextuplex offertories would undoubtedly lead to valuable results.

It is likely that no more than a handful of the offertories in lat. 776 represent a purely local tradition. The compilers of the manuscript seem to have cast their net wide, including many chants that were old and some that were more recent, a few that represented the local use and many that came from the gererally prevailing repertory. This examination of *Holocausta medullata* has focused on an exceptional chant, and provided an opportunity to see it in relation to the repertory as a whole.

---

[26] Wagner (p.419) identifies *Posuisti* as the model, *Angelus Domini* as the adaptation; others seem to see it the other way around. Discussion concerning the relationship of *Stetit angelus* and *Viri Galilaei* is summarized in the article by Björkvall and Steiner cited above.

[27] Levy, pp.90 and 92.

Table 1.

Texts of Non-Sextuplex Offertories

Incipit	Folio	Feast	Source
I. From the Psalms			
Altaria tua	91^r	Mariae, Ded. ecclesiae	Ps. 83:4b-5; 2-3
Lavabo inter innocentes	41^r	Dominica vacat	Ps. 25:6, 11, 7, 2
II. Quoted from Other Books of the Bible			
Spiritus Domini	93^V	Fer. II infra oct. Pent.	Sap. 1:7, Ps. 103:30-31a
Justorum animae	118^V	Omnium Sanctorum	Sap. 3:1, 2a, 3b, 4
Fulgebunt justi	112^r	Felicis et Adaucti	Sap. 3:7, 6
Tu es Petrus	29^V	Petri, Cathedra	Matt. 16:18-19a, 17
Ego sum resurrectio	137^r	Mort., Alia Missa 4	Jo. 11:25b, 5:24b
III. Paraphrases of Biblical Material			
Misit rex spiculatorem	111^V	Joannis, Decollatio	cf. Mk. 6:27-9, 20, Lk. 24:46
Ingressus Paulus	25^V	Pauli, Conversio	
O quam gloriosum	116^r	Cosmae et Damiani	cf. Apoc. 7:9
IV. Based on Non-Biblical Narratives			
Intempesta noctis	30^r	Benedicti, Transitus	
Intempesta noctis 2	30^V	Benedicti, Transitus	
Veniens vir	81^V	Crucis, Inventio	
Martinus igitur	120^r	Martini, Epi	
V. Prayers			
Felix namque	113^r	Mariae Nativitas	
Felix namque 2	113^V	Mariae Nativitas	
Protege Domine	82^r	Crucis, Inventio	
Salve presentem	114^V	Crucis, Exaltatio	
Holocausta medullata	122^V	Saturnini, Alia Missa	
Domine Jesu Christe	136^V	Mort., Alia Missa 3	
Erue Domine animas	137^V	Mort., Alia Missa 5	
O pie Deus	138^r	Mort., Alia Missa 6	
Salvator mundi	146^V		

Table 2

Possibly Original Offertories in Lat. 776

		Harl. 4951	lat. 780	lat. 903	lat. 776	lat, 1132
Intempesta noctis 2	Benedicti, Transitus				30^v	
Veniens vir	Crucis, Inventio	231^r		174	81^v	
Altaria tua	Mariae, Ded. ecclesia		38^v		91^r	
Protege Domine	Crucis, Inventio	284^v	74^r	174	82^r	70^r
Holocausta medullata	Saturnini, Alia Missa	293^v		230	122^v	
Domine Jesu Christe	Mort., Alia Missa 3		120^r	235	136^v	
Ego sum resurrectio	Mort., Alia Missa 4				137^r	
O pie Deus	Mort., Alia Missa 6			237	138^r	
Salvator mundi					146^v	

Adaptations and Reworkings

Modeled on Stetit angelus and Viri Galilaei:

		Harl. 4951	lat. 780	lat. 903	lat. 776	lat, 1132
Tu es Petrus	Petri, Cathedra	155^r	24^v	53	29^v	26^v
Felix namque 2	Mariae, Nativitas				113^v	
Justorum animae	Omnium Sanctorum	289^v	97^v	223	118^v	
Erue Domine animas	Mort., Alia Missa 5			236	137^v	

Much original material, some borrowing from Stetit angelus and Viri Galilaei:

Salve presentem	Crucis, Exaltatio	285^r			114^v	

Much original material, borrowing from Stetit angelus, Viri Galilaei, and Custodi me:

Martinus igitur	Martini, Epi	290^v		225	120^r	

Modeled on Angelus Domini (Fer. II Pasch., Oct. Pasch.):

Misit rex spiculatorem	Joannis, Decollatio	282^r	101^v		111^v	
Fulgebunt justi	Felicis et Adaucti				112^r	
O quam gloriosum	Cosmae et Damiani	286^r			116^r	

Modeled on Memor sit Dominus (In Nat. Pontificis):

Intempesta noctis	Benedicti, Transitus			57	30^r	

Modeled on Laetentur caeli (Nat. Domini I):

Ingressus Paulus	Pauli, Conversio	150^v		45	25^v	

Modeled on Domine exaudi (Fer. IV Maj. Hebd.):

Lavabo inter innocentes	Dominica vacat	172^r		86	41^r	

Modeled on Benedictus qui venit (Sab. Pasch.):

Spiritus Domini	Fer. II infra oct. Pent.			185	93^v	

Modeled on Factus est Dominus (Sab. Hebd. IV Quad.):

Felix namque	Mariae, Nativitas	283^v	102^v		113^r	89^r

XV

The Prosulae of the MS
Paris, Bibliothèque Nationale, f. lat. 1118

Prosulae—words added to melismas in liturgical chant—have been well known to scholars ever since the publication in 1886 of Léon Gautier's *Histoire de la poésie liturgique du moyen âge, I: Les Tropes.* This book was a remarkable accomplishment in its time; it is still being used, as its recent reprinting shows.[1] The information about manuscript sources and many of the facsimiles in it are still useful, as is the comprehensive view it gives of the subject.

Gautier emphasized the prosula technique, the technique of adding only words to pre-existing melodies, at the expense of the troping technique, the adding of new words and music to pre-existing compositions. At one point (p. 153) he went so far as to say, "La théorie des mélodies préexistantes trouve son application non seulement dans les Séquences, mais dans un certain nombre de Tropes [a word used by Gautier to mean both tropes and prosulae] et l'on peut aller jusqu'à dire que c'est un système *presque* général." Since tropes are far more numerous than prosulae in the period Gautier was discussing, this error of emphasis and this confusion of tropes and prosulae have made Gautier the object of recent well-grounded criticism.[2]

Modern musicologists have tended to find the trope, a genre which involves the composition of music along with words, more interesting than the prosula, where only new words are involved. Despite this fact, there have been, along with the excellent recent studies in the field of troping, a number of studies of prosulae. Two important scholars in this field are Joseph Smits van Waesberghe and Bruno Stäblein; both of them have published important studies of Gregorian chant, to which their prosula studies form an appropriate complement.[3]

---

[1] Ridgewood, N. J., 1966. The research for this article was done at the Library of Congress with the aid of microfilms supplied by the Bibliothèque nationale in Paris. I am grateful for the prompt and intelligent assistance I received unfailingly from staff members at both these libraries. Among them Wayne Shirley and Rodney H. Mill of the Music Division of the Library of Congress deserve particular mention.

[2] See especially Richard L. Crocker's article "The Troping Hypothesis," *The Musical Quarterly,* LII (1966), 183-203.

[3] Dr. Smits van Waesberghe discussed a prosula of the early 9th century in his paper "Zur ursprünglichen Vortragsweise der Prosulen, Sequenzen und Organa," *Bericht über den siebenten internationalen musikwissenschaftlichen Kongress: Köln 1958* (Kassel, 1959), pp. 251-54. Prof. Stäblein's article "Tropus" for *Die Musik in*

A number of these texts have been published. There are prosulae for both the Ordinary and the Proper of the Mass; of those for the Proper, most are either for alleluias or for melismas in offertory verses. However, some manuscripts have prosulae for graduals and even tracts.[4] The largest published collections of prosulae for the Mass Proper are those of Clemens Blume and Camille Daux.[5]

In addition to publications of prosula texts, there have been facsimile editions of several manuscripts containing prosulae. Among them are the following:

Paris, B. n., f. lat. 903: 11th century, St. Yrieix (*Paléographie musicale*, XIII)

Benevento, Bibl. cap., VI, 34: 11th-12th century, Benevento (*Paléographie musicale*, XV)

Rome, Bibl. Casanatense, 1741: 11th century, Nonantola (G. Vecchi, *Troparium sequentiarium nonantulanum* [Modena, 1955], part I)

A glance at these volumes shows that prosulae are recorded in them in different ways. In the first two sources the prosulae (called "prosae" at Benevento) are written with musical notation immediately after the chants whose melismas they use. Thus the reader who understands the musical notation can see immediately what the prosula is, if not how and when it is to be performed.

In the manuscript from Nonantola, prosulae are mixed with tropes and sequences, among other things, and then arranged in the order of the liturgical year. The chants from which their melodies come are not

---

Geschichte und Gegenwart, XIII (Kassel, 1966), cols. 797-826, contains a section on prosulae that is an extremely valuable survey of research on the subject, including the most recent and some not reported elsewhere. The analytical study by Karl-Heinz Schlager, "Ein beneventanisches Alleluia und seine Prosula," *Festschrift Bruno Stäblein zum siebzigsten Geburtstag* (Kassel, 1967), pp. 217-25, is one of the latest articles to discuss prosulae.

[4] The first prosula in the Beneventan MS Bibl. cap., VI, 34, on fol. 1, is for the gradual *Universi qui te expectant*. On fol. 75ᵛ of the same source there is a prosula for the tract *Confitemini*.

[5] Blume's collection is in *Analecta hymnica*, XLIX (Leipzig, 1906), 211-265 (in this section many of the texts are not prosulae) and 307-320. Daux's is found in his *Tropaire-Prosier de l'abbaye Saint-Martin de Montauriol* (Paris, 1901), pp. 190-198. Daux's edition is awkward to use because in the manuscript from which he took his texts (Paris, B. n., n. acq. lat. 1871) the section containing prosulae lacks rubrics and capital letters, and there is only occasional musical notation. He was unable to determine the real nature of the texts; as a result, in his edition several prosulae are often printed as one, under a title supplied by Daux which has no relationship to what they are or to the feast for which they are intended. Of the 64 prosulae in this source and published by Daux, 59 also appear in Paris, B. n., f. lat. 1118. (Often an alleluia and its verse are both given prosulae. Because in a few cases another source may have the same alleluia prosula with a substantially different texting for the verse, it has seemed advisable always to count the alleluia prosula and the verse prosula separately.)

XV

given. Generally in this manuscript prosulae are called "prosae"; but
some things called "prosae" here are not prosulae.

There are many other manuscripts that contain prosulae. As yet there
is no complete list of them, but Gautier's book identifies a number of
prosula manuscripts. His references can be checked and updated in
Heinrich Husmann's *Tropen- und Sequenzenhandschriften* (*Répertoire
international des sources musicales*, B V¹; Munich, 1964).

Among the sources of prosulae, one of the most frequently referred
to is Paris, Bibliothèque nationale, fonds latin 1118.[6] The contents of this
source have been summarized by Prof. Husmann; they include tropes,
a tonary, prosulae (fols. 115-31), sequentiae, and prosae.[7] Several scholars
have dated the manuscript as late 10th century, but Prof. Husmann believes that it originated in the 11th century (with some of its contents
copied without change from an earlier source) somewhere in southern
France other than St. Martial.

There are particular reasons for studying the prosula collection of
Paris 1118. It is unusually large, with 91 different prosulae. (There are
also some prosulae for Ordinary chants among the tropes of this manuscript; they will not be considered here.) The texts come in the order
of the liturgical year, with prosulae for 22 offertories and 20 alleluias
mixed. Sometimes more than one melisma in a piece is texted; sometimes
there are several prosulae for a single melisma. There is also a group of
textings for the "fabrice" melismas of the Christmas responsory *Descendit de celis* at the liturgically appropriate point in the collection.[8]

All of the prosulae for offertories, those for the responsory, and
some of those for alleluias are written in Paris 1118 as independent pieces.
In such cases, one sees only the prosula with its melody, not the complete Gregorian chant to which it belongs. There is often an indication
of what offertory a prosula goes with, sometimes not. Thus, the prosula
identified on fol. 120 of the manuscript as "tropus ad finem· de tu
humiliasti" is for the final melisma in the verse beginning "Tu humiliasti"
of the offertory *Tui sunt celi*.[9] Prosulae for alleluias are always ac-

---

[6] For brevity in references to MSS, those in the *fonds latin* of the Bibliothèque
nationale in Paris will be referred to hereafter simply with the name of the city and
their number. Only the name of the library will be omitted from references to MSS
in the *nouvelles acquisitions latines* of the Bibliothèque nationale.

[7] *Op. cit.*, pp. 124-26.

[8] The extensive bibliography on these melismas and the prosulae for them need
not be repeated in full here. Important early studies were made in Gautier, *op. cit.*,
pp. 166-67; and Peter Wagner, *Einführung in die gregorianischen Melodien*, I (3rd
ed.; Leipzig, 1911), 291-92, and III (Leipzig, 1921), 347-48. More recent studies are
those of Jacques Handschin, "Trope, Sequence, and Conductus," *New Oxford History of Music*, II (rev. ed.; London, 1955), 142-45; Hans-Jörgen Holman, "Melismatic
Tropes in the Responsories for Matins," this JOURNAL XVI (1963), 37; and Stäblein,
op. cit., cols. 811-815.

[9] "Prosula" is the term used in Paris 903 to denote the type of text under discussion here. It has been preferred by scholars over the other terms used for such texts

companied by at least a word or two indicating the alleluia verse; sometimes the complete alleluia and verse are written out.[10]

When an offertory prosula is not identified in the manuscript, the chant from which the melisma comes can usually be found. The fact that the texts come in the order of the liturgical year is a help in this. A number of them also appear, clearly identified, in Paris 903. Many of the texts begin or end with the word on which the chant melisma is sung; this can be very useful in identification. At times the subject matter of the prosula suggests what it is. For example, the prosula text "Et ecce angelus apparuitque in monte ubique michael cum drachone fecit bellum omnes angelos ascendit" seems clearly to be for the feast of St. Michael. The offertory for that day, Stetit angelus, has a melisma in its refrain on the words "et ascendit" which matches the melody notated in Paris 1118 for the prosula.[11]

Occasionally there are no such clues in the text. This seems to be the case with the prosula "In deffessa voce" (fol. 130ᵛ). Fortunately, essentially the same text, but with the beginning "In excelsa voce," appears on fol. 264 of Benevento, Bibl. cap., VI, 34. It is notated there after the offertory Recordare mei, containing a melisma from which the prosula melody comes.

What determines whether a particular offertory or alleluia is given a prosula? Not all long melismas are provided with texts. It appears that liturgical considerations are one determining factor. Most collections of prosulae begin with textings for melismas in the offertories for the Sundays of Advent. In Paris 1118, this series is broken between the second and third Sundays by prosulae for the Alleluia Veni sponsa Christi and the offertory Offerentur.[12] These are apparently intended

---

in other MSS. The use of the term "tropus" for prosulae in Paris 1118 may have contributed to the old confusion about the difference between tropes and prosulae.

[10] Sometimes they are written phrase by phrase, with prosula and chant text alternating. This procedure can be seen in the facsimile from Paris 1118 given in Paléographie musicale, XIII, 142.

[11] The next prosula, "Ibique veniet," is for the word "alleluia" in the same offertory.

[12] In four of the MSS that have prosula repertories comparable to that of Paris 1118 (Paris 903, 1240, n. acq. lat. 1235, and n. acq. lat. 1871), the series always includes a prosula for the offertory Exulta satis, sometimes before, sometimes after that for the offertory Ave Maria. Two of these sources also have a prosula for the offertory Offerentur, but that for the Alleluia Veni sponsa Christi appears only in Paris 1118.
   Exulta satis is for the Saturday of Ember Week in Advent. The Alleluia Veni domine and the offertory Ave Maria are now assigned to the following day, the fourth Sunday in Advent. At first it seems fortuitous that Paris 1118 has the Sunday chants before the Saturday chant, but this is not the case. Several other manuscripts give them in the same order, among them Laon 239 (Paléographie musicale, X). When the fourth Sunday of Advent was provided with a Mass, most of its chants were borrowed from the Mass on the Wednesday—Ember Wednesday—of the preceding week. Laon 239 gives for Wednesday a complete Mass with the Alleluia Veni domine and two offertories, one of which is Ave Maria. This is followed by the Masses for Friday and Saturday, and no Mass is given for Sunday. Dom Beyssac

XV

for use on the feast of St. Lucy, Dec. 13. (However, in the troper of
Paris 1118, a different alleluia is specified for this day.)

For the fourth Sunday in Advent there are prosulae for melismas
in both the alleluia *(Veni domine)* and the offertory *(Ave Maria)*. Since
the melismas given prosulae in these two chants are melodically similar,
a comparison of them may be of some interest. Both of these prosulae
will appear in musical examples later in this article.

Table 1 gives a list of all of the offertories provided with prosulae in
Paris 1118, with the feasts on which they are sung.

TABLE 1

*Offertories for Which Prosulae Are Provided in Paris 1118
and Their Feasts*

Ad te domine	Dom. I Adv.
Deus tu convertens	Dom. II Adv.
Offerentur . . . proximae	S. Luciae (13 December)
Benedixisti	Dom. III Adv.
Ave Maria	Dom. IV Adv.
Exulta satis	Sab. Q. T. Adv.
Tollite portas	Vig. Nat. Dni.
Deus enim firmavit	Nat. Dni. 2
Tui sunt	Nat. Dni. 3
Justus ut palma	S. Joannis Ev. 2 (27 December)
Jubilate deo omnis	Dom. I p. Epiph.
Jubilate deo universa	Dom. II p. Epiph.
Veritas mea	S. Marcelli (16 January)
Diffusa est gratia	Purif. S. Mariae (2 February)
Perfice gressus	Dom. Sexag.
Benedictus es	Dom. Quinquag.
Scapulis suis	Dom. Quad.
Benedicam dominum	Fer. II Hebd. II Quad.
Gressus meos	Sab. Hebd. III Quad.
Laudate dominum	Dom. IV Quad.
Stetit angelus	Dedic. S. Michaelis (29 September)
Recordare	Dom. XXII p. Pent.

Striking about this list of days for which offertory prosulae are
provided is that only perhaps a third of these feasts are likely to be
given tropes in medieval manuscripts. Many of them, such as the Sundays
of Advent and those from Sexagesima through Lent, fall during those
times of preparation during which the Gloria is now omitted. Why
should there be prosulae on these days?

(writing in *Paléographie musicale*, X, text, p. 36) expressed the belief that this was
done because it was understood that the Sunday Mass was included in that of the
preceding Wednesday. He thought that it was for the requirements of the Sunday
Mass that this week day fast was supplied with an alleluia and a second offertory;
the introit, one of the graduals, and the communion were to be used on both days.
Other manuscripts giving the Saturday and Sunday chants in this reversed order
are Paris 17436 (9th century); Paris 12050 (9th-10th century); and Paris, n. acq. lat.
1871 (11th century) in its prosula collection.

372

Table 2 lists alleluias given prosulae in Paris 1118. This source does not generally indicate the day for which a prosula is intended, and in this period there is considerable variety among manuscripts in the assigning of alleluias to particular days. The list of feasts in Table 2, like that in Table 1, is based on information drawn from concordances in Paris 903, with modifications suggested by the order in which the prosulae appear in Paris 1118.[13]

TABLE 2

Alleluias for Which Prosulae Are Provided in Paris 1118 and Their Probable Feasts[14]

Veni sponsa Christi (S. 35)	S. Luciae (13 December)
Veni domine (S. 203)	Dom. IV Adv.
Multifarie (S. 389)	Nat. Dni.
Post partum (S. 164)	Purif. S. Mariae (2 February)
Pascha nostrum (S. 346)	Dom. Paschae
Ascendit deus (S. 205)	Ascens. Dni.
Dicite in gentibus (S. 347)	Inv. S. Crucis (3 May)
Dulce lignum (S. 242)	Inv. S. Crucis (3 May)
Mirabilis (S. 128)	S. Nerei et Soc. (12 May)
Vox exultationis (S. 223)	S. Nerei et Soc. (12 May)
Spiritus domini (S. 206)	Dom. Pent.
Fulgebunt justi (S. 41)	SS. Marci et Marcelliani (18 June)
Justus ut palma (S. 38)	S. Joannis Bapt. (24 June)
Ne timeas (S. 395)	S. Joannis Bapt. (24 June)
Justus germinabit (S. 119)	
Justi epulentur (S. 77)	
Hodie Maria virgo (S. 246)	Assumpt. S. Mariae (15 August)
Dilexit Andream (S. 38)	S. Andreae (30 November)
Eripe me (S. 26)	
Qui confidunt (S. 159)	

The last two alleluias in the list are probably for Sundays after Pentecost. *Justus germinabit* is for a day when one saint is honored, perhaps 11 July, the Translation of St. Benedict. *Justi epulentur* is for the feast of two or more saints; again, the particular day is not certain. It seems likely that in the cases where an alleluia was assigned to the liturgy of several different days, its prosula might also be sung on more than one day, so long as it was free of references to one particular saint.

Prosulae are supplied for alleluias in a number of ways. Sometimes a

[13] The troper of Paris 1118 has also been studied, and it should be noted that on occasion its organization of feasts and chants seems less like that of the prosula collection in the same source than does that of the gradual of Paris 903.

[14] The numbers preceded by S. used in this list are those that identify these particular melodies in Karl-Heinz Schlager's *Thematischer Katalog der ältesten Alleluia-Melodien*, Erlanger Arbeiten zur Musikwissenschaft, II (Munich, 1965). They have the advantage of preventing confusion between two different melodies associated with a single text, and of clearly identifying a melody that may be found with a number of different texts.

text is provided only for the alleluia and its jubilus; five of the alleluias given prosulae in Paris 1118 are treated in this way. Sometimes the prosula is made to cover the entire alleluia and the entire verse, incorporating the words of the verse; eight alleluias have prosulae of this type.[15] The other prosulae may be only for the jubilus, only for part of the verse, or for various combinations of all or part of the alleluia and all or part of the verse.

The observation has recently been made that the age of an alleluia may be a factor in determining whether or not the alleluia will be given a prosula.[16] This is a stimulating idea. Were the oldest, most archaic melodies not texted, and were words added only to more recent or even only to the most recent melodies? An investigation of the testimony of accessible early chant manuscripts with regard to the alleluias given prosulae in Paris 1118 suggests that they did not originate at the same time but that some are much older than others.[17] If the late 10th-century dating for Paris 1118 is correct, then it is the earliest source for four of these alleluias, which are not now known to appear in other sources

[15] The technique of incorporating the words of the alleluia verse into the prosula is commented on by several writers, among them Willi Apel (*Gregorian Chant* [Bloomington, Ind., 1958], pp. 433-34) and Dag Norberg (*Introduction à l'étude de la versification latine médiévale* [Stockholm, 1958], pp. 180-81). Paul Evans gives an example of this kind of alleluia prosula on p. 122 of his article "Some Reflections on the Origin of the Trope," this JOURNAL XIV (1961), 119-130. There are additional examples of prosulae in N. de Goede, *The Utrecht Prosarium*, Monumenta Musica Neerlandica, VI (Amsterdam, 1965), pp. xviii and liv-lv.

[16] Crocker, *op. cit.*, pp. 198-99: "The Alleluias involved [*i. e.*, given prosulae] have a way of being those presumably later within Gregorian development . . . , if not actually neo-Gregorian Frankish Alleluias of the 9th or even 10th century." Dr. Crocker finds the alleluia textings of Paris 1118 "a revealing collection in this respect."

[17] Perhaps a word on methodology is appropriate here. There are six MSS from the late 8th to the early 10th century that contain only the words of Mass chants. Their contents were edited and analyzed by Dom René-Jean Hesbert in his *Antiphonale missarum sextuplex* (Brussels, 1935;· hereafter referred to as *Sextuplex*). If one fails to find the words of a particular alleluia in any of these MSS, one may conclude that it came into existence later than the 9th century. If one does find the words of an alleluia in one or more of these sources, this shows that the alleluia was known, with some melody or other, at this time. Whether that melody is the one now most frequently associated with that particular text cannot be determined.

Having looked in *Sextuplex* for evidence about a particular alleluia, one can then turn to MSS of the 10th century. There is a list of them in *Le Graduel romain, II: Les Sources* (Abbaye Saint-Pierre de Solesmes, 1957), p. 172. Four of the six 10th-century MSS listed there are available in facsimile editions; they are Laon 239, Chartres 47, the Mont-Renaud Gradual, and St. Gall 359 (*Paléographie musicale*, X, XI, XVI, and Ser. 2, II, respectively). For information about alleluias in the other two 10th-century MSS one turns to the Schlager *Thematischer Katalog*, but only one of them is reported on there. The Schlager catalogue does record the alleluias in nearly all of the MSS in the next group of *Le Graduel romain*, those assigned to the period around 1000; and so one can move slowly on, checking for the earliest appearance in the sources of a particular alleluia. It should be mentioned that the Schlager catalogue does not distinguish between alleluias which are an integral part of the original MS and those which are later additions.

374

earlier than the 11th century. Of the sixteen remaining alleluias, one is an adaptation of the melody of another to a new text; it seems better to think of these two as one, reducing the number to fifteen. Of them, six do not appear in sources earlier than the tenth century. The remaining nine are mentioned, only by their texts, in one or more of the manuscripts (primarily of the ninth century) whose contents are published in Dom René-Jean Hesbert's *Antiphonale missarum sextuplex* (Brussels, 1935). Two of them appear in all six of the manuscripts, one in five, two in three, two in two, and two in one. In chant, "fixity means antiquity"; one can call perhaps the first three of these alleluias old, but the rest must be later additions to the basic repertoire.

It has been observed that the style of an alleluia is related to its age; but scholars have not been in agreement on criteria to be used in distinguishing older and more recent works. The most important studies are probably those of Peter Wagner, Bruno Stäblein, and Willi Apel.[18] There is general agreement on the antiquity of only a few alleluias. *Dies sanctificatus* (S. 27) is one of them; another is the melody (S. 271) referred to by Stäblein and Apel as *Ostende nobis* and by Wagner as *Dominus dixit*. Here the agreement breaks down, for Wagner and Stäblein see a difference in ending between the alleluia and the verse as an important criterion for antiquity, while Apel finds a relatively narrow range and lack of repetitions in the melismas better.[19]

The three alleluias given prosulae in Paris 1118 that were referred to above as being well enough represented in early manuscripts to be considered "old" are *Pascha nostrum* (S. 346), *Ascendit deus* (S. 205), and *Spiritus domini* (S. 206). Only one of these, *Spiritus domini*, meets all the criteria for an archaic style. *Ascendit deus* has the entire alleluia melody incorporated at the end of its verse. The style of *Pascha nostrum*, the Easter alleluia, presents unusual problems. Prof. Apel has argued that its style is incompatible with the early date assigned to it on liturgical grounds, and he has suggested that the original melody for this text is now lost, and that what is found in even the earliest manuscripts is a later melody that was substituted for it.[20]

Other manuscripts show additional "old" alleluias with prosulae. Even the Alleluia *Dies sanctificatus* (S. 27) is given a prosula on occasion; there are two for it on fol. 53 of the manuscript from Nonantola mentioned earlier. Its melody was a favorite with the creators of adaptations; Dr. Schlager (pp. 30-32) lists 44 different texts found with it. One of the older adaptations is to the text *Video caelos*; in this form it appears in Benevento, Bibl. cap., VI, 34, fol. 21ᵛ with a brief prosula for

18 Wagner, *op. cit.*, III, 397-417; Stäblein, "Alleluia," *Die Musik in Geschichte und Gegenwart*, I (1949-51), cols. 331-350; and Apel, *op. cit.*, pp. 375-392.
19 Wagner, *op. cit.*, III, 398; Stäblein, *MGG* I, cols. 342-43; Apel, *op. cit.*, p. 391.
20 *Ibid.*, pp. 390-91.

XV

the alleluia section of the melody: "Iste martyr glorificatus considerans conditorem seculorum testatus est dicens."[21]

The prosula in Paris 1118 for *Pascha nostrum* covers the alleluia and the entire verse, while that for *Spiritus domini* is for the alleluia alone. The prosula for *Ascendit deus* covers the alleluia jubilus and the re-statement of the alleluia melody at the end of the verse, but not the rest of the verse. Among the more recent alleluias there seems likewise to be no correlation between age and type of prosula; the 10th- or even 11th-century *Dulce lignum* has a modest little prosula which uses only its jubilus, while *Justus ut palma*, which is referred to in three of the manuscripts of *Sextuplex*, has a prosula for most of its verse that exploits its long repetitive melisma to the fullest. *Dilexit Andream* is to the same melody as *Justus ut palma* (S. 38), but its prosula is for the alleluia only.

It appears that the creation of alleluia prosulae was just one aspect of the development of the liturgy that took place between the 9th and 11th centuries. In some cases this development is clearly delineated in the evidence of the manuscripts. The feast of the Finding of the Holy Cross (Inventio Sanctae Crucis, 3 May) is one example. The Compiègne antiphonary is the only 9th-century source to show a Mass proper for it; apparently the observance of this feast in the West was just beginning in the 9th century.[22] It is mentioned in 10th-century sources more frequently. One of the alleluias later associated with it, *Dicite in gentibus* (S. 347), makes its first appearance in the 10th-century manuscript Laon 239 (*Paléographie musicale*, vol. X, facsimile, p. 107) assigned to the Wednesday after Easter. The other alleluia later assigned to this feast and given a prosula in Paris 1118 is *Dulce lignum* (S. 242). It appears in both Laon 239 and St. Gall 359, but only as a later addition; 11th-century sources have it as one of the regular alleluias for this feast. This is not a unique case; many alleluias came into the liturgy during the 10th and 11th centuries, the time of composition also of countless tropes, sequentiae, and prosae. The Gradual of Monza (in *Sextuplex*), of the early

---

[21] This text is for the feast of St. Stephen, Dec. 26. If the prosula is considered purely as a text, it resembles those introit tropes that are narrative and introductory in style. (For a discussion of various kinds of trope texts—narrative, didactic, and devotional—see Paul Evans, "The Early Trope Repertory of Saint Martial de Limoges," Ph.D. dissertation, Princeton University, 1964 [Ann Arbor: University Microfilms, 65-48], I, 70-75. Prosulae are discussed in this dissertation in Vol. I, pp. 12-20; there are examples of them *ibid.*, pp. 155-61.) This style is particularly appropriate here since the verse of the alleluia, which would in performance immediately follow the prosula, consists of words ascribed to St. Stephen in Acts 7:55-56. In the following translation, the prosula comes first, and after it the words of the alleluia verse, which are in italics:

This glorified martyr, regarding the creator of the universe, gave witness, saying: "*I see the heavens opened, and Jesus standing on the right hand of God.*"

[22] *Sextuplex*, pp. lxxxii-lxxxiii, xcii-xciii, 117.

9th century, mentions 33 different alleluias; the St. Yrieix Gradual, of the 11th century (Paris 903), has almost 290.

The variety among the alleluias given prosulae in Paris 1118 can be demonstrated better through a series of examples than through statistics, and *Justus ut palma* (S. 38) is a convenient starting point. Since most of the prosula in Paris 903 for this alleluia was published by Dr. Apel,[23] and since this text is virtually the same as that in Paris 1118, it need not be repeated here. As noted before, this alleluia is in three of the manuscripts of *Sextuplex*. It has a small range (a seventh) and a long inner melisma with repetition of two ideas. The end of the verse restates the entire alleluia and jubilus, but otherwise the music of the verse is independent of that of the alleluia.

The prosula given the Alleluia *Justus ut palma* covers the alleluia and part of the verse. That given the Alleluia *Mirabilis* (S. 128), which was published in full by Dr. Evans, sets the alleluia and the entire verse.[24] This alleluia is found in two of the manuscripts in *Sextuplex*. It has a range of a seventh, but no long inner melisma. Again, the musical references to the alleluia in the verse are limited to a restatement of the entire alleluia melody at the end of the verse.

The Alleluia *Spiritus domini* (S. 206) appears in five of the manuscripts of *Sextuplex*, but not in the modern Gradual. It has a range of a seventh, no repeats in its short inner melisma, and only eight notes in common between the end of its verse and the end of the alleluia. It seems to be a relatively "old" alleluia. The two prosulae provided for it in Paris 1118 are for the alleluia only. (Ex. 1)[25]

Probably the most recent of the alleluias given prosulae in Paris 1118 is the Alleluia *Veni sponsa Christi* (S. 35). It appears with a prosula in Paris 1118 and, without the prosula, in only three other sources, all of them from southern France: Paris 903, Paris 776, and Paris, n. acq. lat.

---

23 *Op. cit.*, pp. 433-34.

24 This JOURNAL XIV (1961), 122.

25 Since the notation of Paris 1118 is usually imprecise with regard to intervals, transcriptions of the melodies of its prosulae have to be made with the help of other sources. Paris 903 is well suited for this purpose. It has nearly all the chants given prosulae in Paris 1118, written in most cases quite clearly. It also has prosulae for 25 offertories and 12 alleluias, but never more than one for a particular melisma. Of the 49 prosulae in Paris 903, 37 also appear in Paris 1118.
The melisma ending the verse of this alleluia is not written out in full in Paris 903. It has been supplied from Montpellier H 159 (*Paléographie musicale*, VIII, 106). The fact that this ending is completely missing from Paris 903 is unusual, but this MS often neglects to write out melismas in one place if they are fully notated elsewhere—for example, earlier or later in the same alleluia, in its prosula, or in a different alleluia with the same melody copied earlier in the MS. Jacques Chailley, seeing in Paris 903 more music in a prosula for the verse of the Alleluia *Post Partum* than was notated immediately before in the verse itself, concluded that there was at the end of the prosula a "cauda sans modèle ajoutée à la prosule." (*L'École musicale de Saint Martial de Limoges jusqu'à la fin du XIe siècle* [Paris, 1960], p. 219.) None of the prosulae in Paris 903 or Paris 1118 have such additions.

Example 1

Alleluia *Spiritus domini* from Paris 903, fol. 91, with prosulae from Paris 1118, fol. 127

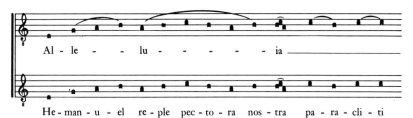

Al - le - - lu - - - - - ia _____

He - man - u - el   re - ple pec - to - ra nos - tra   pa - ra - cli - ti

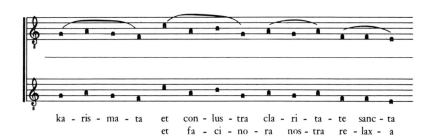

ka - ris - ma - ta   et   con - lus - tra   cla - ri - ta - te sanc - ta
                      et   fa - ci - no - ra nos - tra   re - lax - a

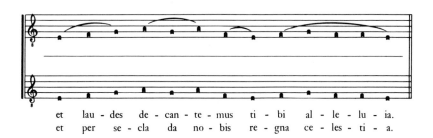

et   lau - des de - can - te - mus   ti - bi   al - le - lu - ia.
et   per se - cla   da   no - bis   re - gna   ce - les - ti - a.

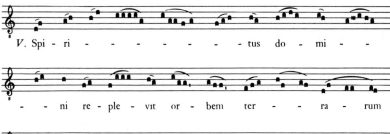

V. Spi - ri - - - - - - - - tus do - mi - -

- - ni re - ple - vit or - bem ter - - - ra - rum

et hoc quod con - ti - net om - - - ni - - - a

378

sci - en - ti - am ⎯ ha - bet vo - - cis. ⎯

1177. Its range is a tenth; it has a long inner melisma with three statements, each slightly different from the others, of one idea. Though the
ending of the verse is not written out in full in Paris 903, it is apparently
intended to include the entire alleluia. (It has been supplied in Example
2 below; the asterisk marks the end of the melody in Paris 903.) The
verse also begins with the melody that opens the alleluia. The jubilus is
quite long; some ideas in it are repeated.

The character of prosula texts can be fully understood only when
the prosulae are viewed in the context of the chants on which they depend. For example, in Gregorian chant texts statements usually involve
third person verbs or pronouns, except in texts taken from the Psalms,
where first person singular may occur. Prosulae, on the other hand,
make frequent use of first person plural in various forms: "laudes
decantemus," "facinora nostra," "da nobis regna celestia." This is the
mode of expression of one who is leading communal worship, not one
engaged in private devotions; and this suggests something about the
purpose of prosulae.

In their style of expression, many prosulae may be regarded as informal prayers that take the liturgical text as a point of departure. Some
include an exhortation to praise. Some are little more than paraphrases
of the liturgical text to which they are added. Allusions to Christ may be
made in prosulae for texts that would otherwise lack them. Prosulae
frequently make references to the specific feast being celebrated, or to
the season.

The prosulae for the Alleluia *Spiritus domini* quoted earlier in Example 1 demonstrate some of these techniques. The verse of this alleluia,
which is for Pentecost, is taken from the Book of Wisdom 1:7: "The
spirit of the Lord has filled the whole world, and that which contains
all things has knowledge of his voice." The first prosula is "Emmanuel,
fill our hearts with the gifts of the Holy Spirit, and enlighten them with
thy holy radiance; and let us sing praises to thee, alleluia." The second
begins the same: "Emmanuel, fill our hearts with the gifts of the Holy
Spirit, forgive our sins, and forever give us the heavenly kingdom." Both
texts are informal prayers; the first also includes the idea of praise.
Except for the reference to the Paraclete, neither of these texts has any
particular relevance to Pentecost. The ideas might easily be used in
prosulae for many other days, as indeed they are.

Among prosulae which give more emphasis to the season than to the particular day for which they are intended are those for the Alleluia *Veni sponsa Christi* given earlier in Example 2. Here the dominant idea is of Christ coming into the world to redeem sinners through his own suffering, a thought appropriate for Advent. Only the brief mention of the Lord as one to whom virgins are betrothed ("virgines sunt desponsate domino") recalls the life of St. Lucy, who preferred to become the bride of the Lord rather than wed the man chosen by her family. The text of the alleluia verse itself, on the other hand, is closely related to the feast of St. Lucy—more closely than are the prosulae.

In Paris 1118, on fol. 117-117ᵛ, there are three prosulae for the melisma "preparavit eum" in the Christmas offertory *Tollite portas*.

Example 2

Alleluia *Veni sponsa Christi* from Paris 903, fol. 104ᵛ, with prosula from Paris 1118, fols. 115ᵛ-116

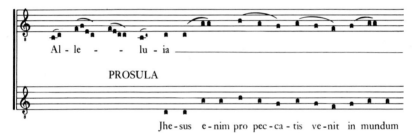

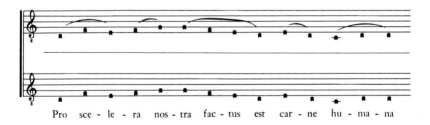

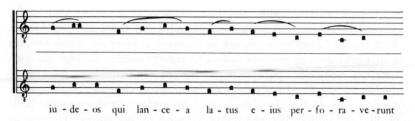

iu - de - os qui lan - ce - a la - tus e - ius per - fo - ra - ve - runt

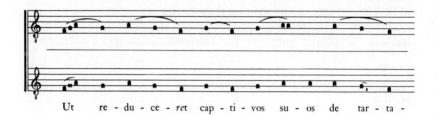

Ut re - du - ce - *re*t cap - ti - vos su - os de tar - ta -

re - a in fo - ros do - mi - nus de - us nos - ter

V. Ve - - - - ni spon - sa Chri - sti ac - ci - pe co - ro

Ihe - sus e - nim est

re - demp - tor om - ni - um de - us Qui *pro* nos pe - pen - dit

XV

382

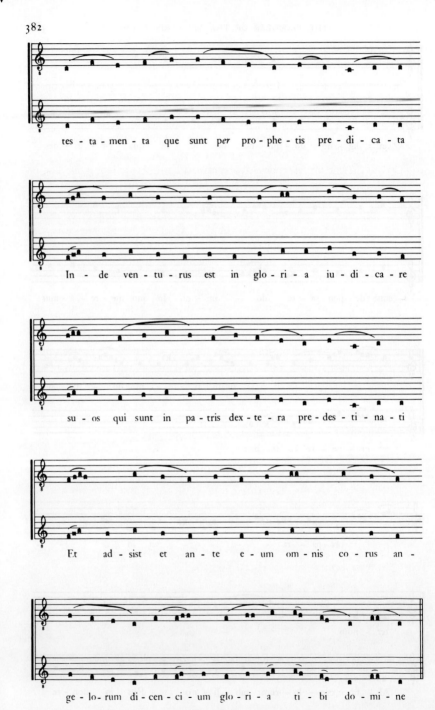

tes - ta - men - ta que sunt *per* pro - phe - tis pre - di - ca - ta

In - de ven - tu - rus est in glo - ri - a iu - di - ca - re

su - os qui sunt in pa - tris dex - te - ra pre - des - ti - na - ti

Et ad - sist et an - te e - um om - nis co - rus an -

ge - lo - rum di - cen - ci - um glo - ri - a ti - bi do - mi - ne

These prosulae stand in various relationships to the text of the offertory, which is taken from Ps. 23.[26]

> Antiphon: (Ps. 23:7) Lift up your heads, o ye gates; and be ye lift up, ye everlasting doors; and the King of glory shall come in. V. 1: (Ps. 23:1) The earth is the Lord's, and the fulness thereof; the world, and they that dwell therein. V. 2: (Ps. 23:2) For he hath founded it upon the seas, and established it upon the floods. ["Preparavit eum" is translated here by "established it."]

Of the three prosulae, perhaps the closest to this text is the one beginning "Preparavit eternus."[27] There is reference in it to the Christmas idea of the coming of the Lord, suggested in the antiphon of the offertory in the phrase "the King of glory shall come in"; and there is also mention of the Creation as evidence of God's power. The ideas of judgement and salvation appear only in the prosula: "The eternal and kind Maker of Creation prepared the earth while darkness and undivided waters had possession of the universe. Coming to judge it severely, may he deign in love and kindness to set it free."

The same ideas occur in another of the prosulae, "Preparavit haec conditor," but to them is added the notion of an enemy.[28] The coming of the Lord is only implied: "The Creator of the sun and moon prepared these things for the redemption of the nations so that he might vanquish their enemy and subject him to himself, and place his redeemed in the citadel of the heavens and give them life for ever."

The third prosula is as follows:

> Redimens nos per intemerato utero puroque virginis
> Sicut sponsus proprie sue procedens de talamo
> De patre suo collocans
> humano filio procreans
> verbo eum.

The meaning of the last three lines is unclear, but the emphasis in this prosula is evidently on the birth of Christ, though his name is not used. The second line of the prosula paraphrases Ps. 18:6.

Among the prosulae that add a mention of Christ to the chants they embellish is "Labia nostra laudent," for the offertory *Jubilate deo universa*, for the second Sunday after Epiphany.

> Antiphon: (Ps. 65:1) Make a joyful noise unto God, all ye lands: (2 a) sing praises to his name: (Ps. 65:16) Come and hear, all ye that fear God, and I will tell you what he hath done for my soul. V. 1: (Ps. 65:13 b) I will pay thee my vows (14 a) which my lips have uttered. V. 2: (Ps. 65:14

---

[26] The numbering used here for the Psalms is that of the Vulgate. The King James translation has been used for Biblical texts except where differences between it and the liturgical Latin text have necessitated slight changes. For another comparison of three prosulae for one melisma, see Chailley, *op. cit.*, p. 219.

[27] The Latin text is published in *Analecta hymnica*, XLIX, as no. 612.

[28] *Ibid.*, no. 614.

384

b) [which] my mouth hath spoken, when I was in trouble. (15 a) I will offer unto thee burnt sacrifices of fatlings.

These words would be suitable for almost any day in the year, as would the prosula for this offertory. In it, however, Christ is mentioned immediately by name and is the focus of attention; and the first person singular of the psalmist is changed to first person plural. The prosula, given below as Example 3, is for "labia mea" (my lips) in verse 1: "Let our lips praise Christ our savior, the eternal king; whom the sun, the moon, the stars, the earth, the sea, the land praise; whom unhappy Hell deplores. Let us all adore him, glorify him, and pray to him that he may deign to save us from our sins; to him, the only Lord, together with the father and the son [be] glory and command, virtue, praise, power now and forevermore."

Just as some prosulae follow more closely than others the text and meaning of the piece on which they depend, so some observe the phrasing of the melisma more carefully. As one studies, for example, a single offertory melisma as it is notated in chant manuscripts, one is likely to find that in the various sources the notes of the melisma are grouped into neumes in the same way. When one then compares these groupings of notes with the prosulae one finds that in some prosulae the beginnings and ends of words regularly fall at points in the melisma where neumes begin and end. In other prosulae this is not the case.

There are two prosulae in Paris 1118 for the melisma "iniusticia" of the offertory *Gressus meos*, for the Saturday in the third week of Lent. They are given below as Example 4.[29]

About half-way through the melisma a series of three-note neumes occurs. The first of the two prosulae, "Iniusticia longe," provides a series of similarly-accented three-syllable words for these neumes: "omnia supera infera media celica terrea infima." The second prosula, "Iniusticia gehenna," does not; beginning at the same point, it has "iustorum gloria solve nostrorum peccamina Ut possimus sumere."

Although the first of these texts observes the phrasing of the melisma more closely than the other, it does not always follow it, particularly in the earlier part of the piece. From the point of view of word accent the first prosula fits the melisma much better than the second. (This melisma is an expanded version of a melody to the same text which ends the antiphon of the offertory. For the same text and melody to be used to conclude both the antiphon and the final verse of an offertory is unusual. One is inclined to believe that this is not the ending of the second verse but rather an elaborated version of the offertory refrain intended to be sung after the verse. This interpretation is suggested also by the

---

[29] The slurs over the notes in this example show the way the notes are grouped into neumes in the notation of this melisma in St. Gall 339 (*Paléographie musicale*, I, 52).

Example 3

Prosula "Labia nostra laudent" for the offertory *Jubilate deo universa* (Paris 1118, fol. 121)

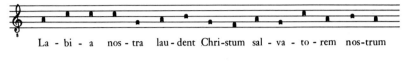

La - bi - a nos - tra lau - dent Chri-stum sal - va - to - rem nos-trum

re - gem e - ter - num quem lau - dat sol lu - na stel - le po - lus

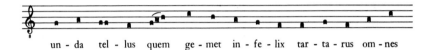

un - da tel - lus quem ge - met in - fe - lix tar - ta - rus om - nes

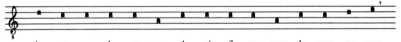

ip - sum a - do - re - mus glo - ri - fi - ce - mus de - pre - ce - mus

ut ip - se di - gne - tur sal - va - re nos a pec - ca - tis que

nos - tris ip - si so - li do - mi - no cum pa - tre et

fi - li - o glo - ri - a et im - pe - ri - um vir - tus

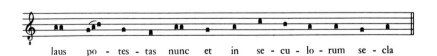

laus po - tes - tas nunc et in se - cu - lo - rum se - cla

386

Example 4

Prosulae for the offertory *Gressus meos* (Paris 1118, fols. 124ᵛ-125)

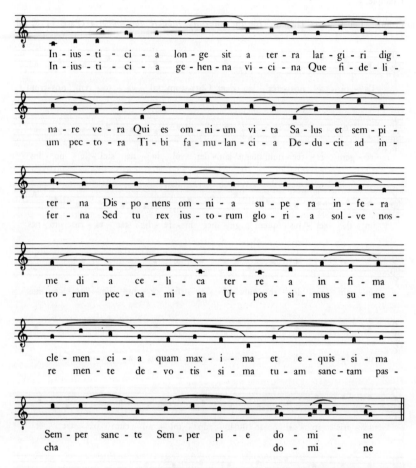

fact that in Laon 239 [*Paléographie musicale*, X, 67] this music comes
after the first verse of the offertory.)

Like other offertory melismas, this melody is recorded in markedly
different versions in various manuscripts. It has not been possible for this
writer to establish a consensus among the diastematic sources which
might be expected to give readings closest to that of Paris 1118. Thus
the melody in the preceding musical example is, regrettably, only an
approximation.[30]

[30] There is an illuminating discussion of problems in establishing readings of
offertories in Hubert Sidler's *Studien zu den alten Offertorien mit ihren Versen*

The text of this offertory is centonized from Ps. 118:

> Antiphon: (Ps. 118:133) Order my steps O Lord in thy word: and let
> not any iniquity have dominion, O Lord. V. 1: (Ps. 188:130) The en-
> trance of thy words giveth light; it giveth understanding unto the simple.
> V. 2: (Ps. 118:75) I know, O Lord, that thy judgments are right, and that
> thou in faithfulness hast afflicted me. [Refrain?:] Let not any iniquity
> have dominion, O Lord.

The first prosula, "Iniusticia longe," is a poetic expanding of some
ideas in the offertory text, expressed as an informal prayer: "May
iniquity be far from earth. Deign to bestow thy truth, thou who art the
life of all and eternal salvation, ordering all things above, below, in the
middle, in heaven, on earth, below the earth, with very great and just
clemency, O Lord, ever holy and ever kind."

In the second prosula, "Iniusticia gehenna," a change is made from
the "I" of the offertory to "we," and there is a reference to preparation
for Easter—an allusion appropriate in a text for Lent. As Clemens Blume
pointed out, the predicate of the first sentence in the prosula has preceded it in the offertory text.[31] "Iniquity allied to Hell, which leads
the hearts of the faithful, thy servants, into Hell. But thou, king, glory
of the just, free us from our sins that we may receive with a most devout
spirit thy holy Paschal gift, O Lord."

Thus, although both of these prosulae begin and end with words
borrowed from the chant melisma, in style (the way the words are
fitted to the melisma) and in content they are quite different. The first
of them observes the phrasing of the melisma more closely and is more
attentive to word accent; the second seeks to broaden the expression of
the offertory by the change from "I" to "we" and to relate its text to
the season of the liturgical year. The first text appears in numerous
sources; the other is less well known.[32]

The prosula texts of Paris 1118 are virtually all in prose; there are
none in quantitative verse meters. Just part of one of them is in an
accentual verse pattern. It is for the "facinora" melisma in the verse of
the Alleluia *Veni domine* (S. 203), for the fourth Sunday in Advent.
A comparison of the prosula and the melisma as it is notated in other
sources shows that some pitches have been repeated to accommodate
extra syllables in the text. The last line of the example is written one

---

(Baden, 1939). See particularly pp. 68-70, where the "veritas" melisma of the offertory *Jubilate deo omnis* is dealt with.

[31] *Analecta hymnica*, XLIX, 319.

[32] There are a number of melismas for which Paris 903 has one prosula which is
among the two or three given in Paris 1118 for the same melody. At such times, the
prosula given in Paris 903 is likely to be more conservative in style—closer in meaning to the chant text, following the phrasing of the melisma more carefully—than at
least one of the others in Paris 1118. Thus, of this pair, it is "Iniusticia longe" that
appears in Paris 903.

tone lower in Paris 903 (fol. 4) than it is in the modern Gradual.
(Ex. 5)

The meter, an accentual version of the classical quantitative trochaic
tetrameter catalectic, is a fairly popular one in medieval Latin poetry. It
is used, for example, by Guido of Arezzo for his *Regulae rhythmicae:*
"Musicorum et cantorum magna est distantia."[33] The reference to ninety
sheep recalls the parable of the Good Shepherd (Matthew 18:12-13; Luke
15:4-7), to which this is the only reference in this particular Mass. There
are in fact ninety and nine sheep in the parable, but the meter of the
prosula appears able to accommodate only ninety of them.

In contrast, tropes are often in quantitative verse. Only one instance
of a trope partly in accentual verse was found by Dr. Evans in Paris
1121. It seems significant that this trope, which begins "Ecce iam
Johannis adest veneranda gloria," is also accentual trochaic tetrameter
catalectic.[34]

Rhyme and assonance appear frequently in prosula texts. Sometimes this seems to be the result of an effort to have the vowels in the
prosula match those of the melisma. In his notes for the prosulae in
Vol. 49 of *Analecta hymnica*, Blume points out frequent instances of
this practice. Paris 1118 has, for example, a prosula for the melisma on the
words "in aeternum" for the verse of the offertory *Recordare mei* in

Example 5

Prosula for the Alleluia *Veni domine* (Paris 1118, fol. 116')

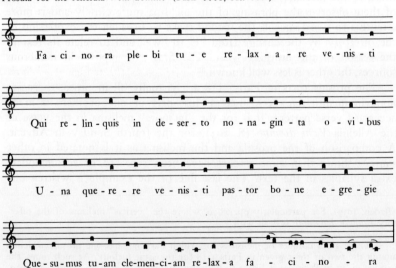

Fa - ci - no - ra ple - bi tu - e re - lax - a - re ve - nis - ti

Qui re - lin - quis in de - ser - to no - na - gin - ta o - vi - bus

U - na que - re - re ve - nis - ti pas - tor bo - ne e - gre - gie

Que - su - mus tu - am cle - men - ci - am re - lax - a fa - ci - no - ra

---

[33] Martin Gerbert, *Scriptores ecclesiastici de musica* (St. Blasien, 1784), II, 25.
[34] Evans, "The Early Trope Repertory . . . ," I, 86.

which this procedure may be seen. The melisma is for the syllable
"-ter-." Note in Example 6 how many of the textual units which rhyme
are set to similar musical figures.

Any discussion of prosulae and the melismas to which they are set
inevitably must touch on rhythm. Prof. Smits van Waesberghe has expressed the belief that prosulae may provide valuable information about
the rhythm of the melismas to which they are set, and also the performance of the ornamental neumes.[35] Because of the differences in style observed earlier among prosulae, it appears that some of them will be better
for this purpose than others.

The prosulae of Paris 1118 are in a very special position with regard
to rhythm. To begin with, this is a fairly large collection of long chant
melismas written not in neumes but in single notes because of the
added texts. The notation, though not perfectly diastematic, is clear
enough in showing the direction of the intervals. What is more, this is
the manuscript regarded by Dom Ferretti as "le document qui, plus
qu'aucun autre, nous a donné la certitude de l'existence d'une notation
rhythmique aquitaine, conforme à celle de Saint-Gall, Metz, Chartres
et Nonantola."[36]

To say that a manuscript proves the existence of a tradition is not, of
course, to say that it is an example of the fullest development of that
tradition. As a matter of fact, the notation of Paris 1118 is often incon-
sistent, and it is frequently difficult to tell dots, which seem to represent
ordinary notes, from dashes, which seem to represent longer ones. When
a melisma is written more than once, as happens when there are two
or more prosulae for a single melisma, the indications of rhythm in it
are almost never exactly the same. There are occasional hints that some
of the conventions of later Aquitanian notation, which lacks rhythmic
significance, are already in effect. One of these is the tendency of Paris
1118 to make every final element in a descending group a dash. One is
tempted to echo the comment of Dr. Evans, made à propos Paris 1121,

Example 6

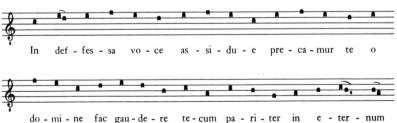

In   def - fes - sa   vo - ce   as - si - du - e   pre - ca - mur   te   o

do - mi - ne   fac gau - de - re   te - cum pa - ri - ter   in   e - ter - num

[35] Smits van Waesberghe, op. cit., p. 251.
[36] Dom Paolo Ferretti, "Étude sur la notation aquitaine," Paléographie musicale,
XIII, 205.

390

that "the precise use of these ['rhythmic'] signs varies so much from manuscript to manuscript, and indeed, the difference between a point and a dash is sometimes so difficult to determine, that the attempt to reproduce them in the transcription would serve no purpose."[37]

Against these negative observations stands the positive one that the rhythmic indications in prosulae in Paris 1118 are often closely in accord with the rhythmic notation of the corresponding melismas in such manuscripts as Einsiedeln 121 and Laon 239.[38]

Example 7 shows two prosulae from fol. 120ᵛ of Paris 1118 for a fragment of the "florebit" melisma in the offertory *Justus ut palma*. Horizontal lines above the notes of the prosulae represent notes lengthened in the manuscript.

Example 7

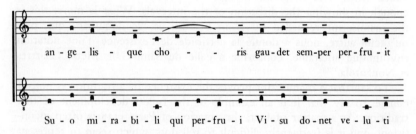

In its notation of the same fragment of the melisma, the manuscript Einsiedeln 121 (p. 41) has a long podatus followed by four descending long puncta, a quilisma connected to a normal porrectus, another long podatus followed by two long and two short puncta, and a long virga. Thus the rhythmic indications in the prosula notation correspond closely if not perfectly with those of Einsiedeln 121. The first three of the four long puncta are long in both prosulae. The two long and two short puncta that appear later are represented in Paris 1118 by two dashes and two dots.

Among the differences between the two prosulae is the setting of the notes surrounding the quilisma as a group in one prosula and as independent notes in the other. (The treatment of the quilisma varies significantly from prosula to prosula, but usually remains constant in one particular work.) The first note of this brief example is long in Einsiedeln and in the first prosula, but short in the second. No reason for this is apparent; such inconsistencies are common and serve as a reminder of the substantial amount of further study that will be needed before the

---

[37] Evans, "The Early Trope Repertory . . . ," II, vi-vii.
[38] These two MSS are reproduced in facsimile in *Paléographie musicale* as Vols. IV and X respectively. There is a useful discussion of the indications of rhythm in them by Dom Amand Ménager in *Paléographie musicale*, X, 177-207.

testimony of Paris 1118 with regard to rhythm can be fully understood.
In a study of supplementary letters used in St. Gall notation, Prof.
Smits van Waesberghe came to the conclusion that the letter x, interpreted
as the abbreviation for "expectare," served as an indication of phrasing,
not of prolongation.[39] This interpretation is often supported by the
prosulae. At points where x's appear in melismas in Einsiedeln 121, the
prosulae frequently have a capital letter suggesting the beginning of a
new phrase. Sometimes these x's and capital letters mark the articulation
between the statement of a phrase and its repetition, as in Example 8,
where Einsiedeln 121 has x's at the points in the melody where the
words "utero," "evo," and the final "angelo" end.[40]

Example 8

Prosula for the offertory *Ave Maria* (Paris 1118, fol. 116')

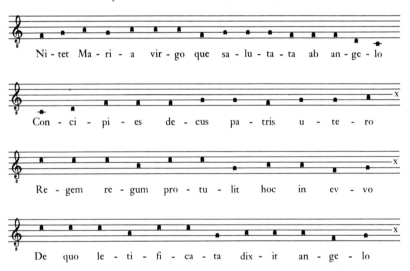

The function of prosulae is an interesting question. When and how
were they performed? Prosulae and motets seemed to Clemens Blume

[39] Joseph Smits van Waesberghe, *Muziekgeschiedenis der Middeleeuwen, Tweede
Deel: Verklaring der Letterteekens (Litterae significativae) in het gregoriaansche
neumenschrift van Sint Gallen* (Tilburg, 1939-42), p. 696.
[40] The neumes in which the "quomodo" melisma is notated on p. 12 of Einsiedeln
121 indicate essentially the same melody as that of Paris 1118. Some notes have been
repeated to accommodate extra syllables in the prosula; this is the case in "salutata"
(an extra g), and in "dixit" (an extra a). In Einsiedeln there is a podatus rather than
a single note at the points corresponding to the beginnings of lines three and four
of the prosula. In Paris 1118 the prosula is followed by the words "quomodo in me
fiet hoc," with neumes, indicating the continuation of the offertory verse.

to be essentially the same thing. The section "Tropi ad Graduale" of *Analecta hymnica*, vol. 49 (pp. 211-265), is a mixture of texts of alleluia prosulae from Paris 1240, 1118, n. acq. lat. 1871, Munich, Bayerische Staatsbibliothek Clm 14322, and many others, with motet texts from sources including Flacius and Florence, Bibl. Laur., Plut. 29.1. Blume believed that in prosulae, as in motets, the new text was sung by some singers while others sang the melisma.[41] Prof. Smits van Waesberghe has shown that not only prosulae but also sequences (that is, prosae) were performed this way.[42] Thus the appearance in manuscripts of prosulae among Proper chants is explained. These texts were sung in the Mass, incorporated into the chants whose melodies they used.

Dr. Stäblein's comments on prosulae in his *MGG* article "Tropus" have recalled another use for offertory prosulae—as introductory pieces for vespers or matins.[43] When used for this purpose, they are sung as individual works. Evidence of this practice is found in the *Office de Pierre de Corbeil*, edited by Henri Villetard in 1907. The prosulae used in this way include "Laetemur gaudiis," set to the "dierum" melisma of the offertory *Deus enim firmavit*, and "Dextera dei cum patre," set to the "dextera" melisma of the offertory *Tui sunt celi*.[44]

"Laetemur gaudiis" is also mentioned in another document, one of great importance in music history for the aid it provides in the dating of works of Leoninus and Perotinus. This is the letter written in 1198 by the Bishop of Paris (Eudes de Sully) spelling out the new regulations for the celebration of the feast of the Circumcision.[45] According to it, "Laetemur gaudiis" is to be sung as an independent piece at the beginning of vespers.

The prosulae of Paris 1118 are varied, both in style and in content. As works of art some far surpass others. Some seem to be no more than a stringing together of slightly paraphrased liturgical formulas; others are quite artistic. Consider, for example, the prosula "Labia nostra laudent" quoted earlier as Example 3. The enumeration of the parts of the universe joined in praise of Christ is striking, and the use of parallel constructions generally through this work has a cumulative effect that is extraordinarily successful. The choice of individual words and their arrangement in the melisma is skillful, particularly in the way in which

---

[41] *Analecta hymnica*, XLIX, p. 212. There are numerous points of similarity between prosulae and early motets: both are texts set to preexisting melismatic melodies, they use a melisma of a Gregorian chant as a point of departure, the device of assonance is used in both, in many examples of both genres the ideas in the text of the parent chant are expanded, commented on, transformed. A detailed examination of these and other similarities might provide valuable insights.

[42] "Zur ursprünglichen Vortragsweise . . . ," p. 251.

[43] *Die Musik in Geschichte und Gegenwart*, XIII, col. 810.

[44] Henri Villetard, *Office de Pierre de Corbeil* (Paris, 1907), pp. 88, 97, 133, 145. Villetard's transcriptions were made from the MS Sens, Bibl. publ., 46.

[45] Quoted *ibid.*, p. 62.

assonance is made to occur quite naturally at the ends of similar musical motifs. Prof. Stäblein has expressed the belief that many prosulae are "feinstdurchdachte kleine Kunstwerke hohen Ranges;"[46] surely this is one of them.

[46] *Die Musik in Geschichte und Gegenwart*, XIII, col. 811.

XVI

NON-PSALM VERSES FOR INTROITS AND COMMUNIONS

Those who have in the course of their work with chant had occasion to look into the manuscript Rome, Bibl. Angelica, 123, a gradual and troper of the 11th century, have found in it much to hold their attention. The neumes (similar in a general way to those in other sources from Bologna) have been called the most striking of all those employed in the notation of chant in Western Europe[1]; the illuminations have been analyzed in detail[2]. The tropes are included among those edited in the series *Corpus Troporum*[3]. Indeed, such is the esteem in which this manuscript is held that it has been reproduced in full in a facsimile edition, and a book-length study has appeared[4]. The main body of chant that is its *raison d'être* has not been discussed quite so much as its other features, perhaps in part because the neumes do not specify the size of intervals – though they are richly varied and often convey valuable information concerning rhythm and phrasing. The present study is intended as a small move toward filling this gap.

In this manuscript (hereinafter LAV) the Introit *Viri Galilaei* is given with two verses, both of which are notated in full[5]. The first, *Omnes gentes plaudite,* is the customary one – the opening of psalm 46, which one might interpret as a cue for the chanting of several verses (if not all) of the psalm. The second reads as follows: «Cumque intuerentur in celum euntem illum ecce duo uiri adstiterunt iusta (= iuxta) illos in uestibus albis qui et dixerunt»[6]. In the Bible this text immediately precedes that selected for the Introit itself; hence in performance one would move seamlessly, as Stäblein says, from this verse into the repeat of the Introit[7]. Here, then, the second verse of the Introit has assumed a function like that of many tropes – that of setting the stage for the action to which the Introit itself refers, identifying the characters, explaining what has taken place up to this point. Different rubrics are used for the two verses; the first is marked «P», the second «V».

---

1   B. Stäblein, *Schriftbild der einstimmigen Musik* (Musikgeschichte in Bildern, III/4), Leipzig 1975, 126: «Jedenfalls ist diese Schrift, wie sie hier in einem besonders umfangreichen und reichhaltigen Dokument vorliegt, die auffallendste in der an eigenständigen Individualitäten keinesfalls armen Geschichte der abendländischen Neumenschrift».
2   E. B. Garrison, «A Gradual of S. Stefano, Bologna: Angelica 123», *Studies in the History of Mediaeval Italian Painting* 4 (1960), 4, 93–110.
3   The siglum assigned to this manuscript there is RoA 123.
4   The facsimile edition is in PM 18; the study is L. Gherardi, «Il Codice Angelica 123: Monumento della Chiesa Bolognese nel sec. XI», *Quadrivium* 3 (1959), 5–114. See also the review of Gherardi's study by J. Froger in *Et. grég.* 9 (1968), 102–9.
5   Stäblein, op. cit., 127, gives a color facsimile of the opening in which this chant appears.
6   In the present study, verses are quoted in the orthography of the manuscript, chant texts in standard spelling. Where readings of the sources differ, that of the first listed is quoted here.
7   Stäblein, op. cit. (Note 1), 126: «Daß der Introitus nicht, wie sonst meist üblich, zu einem Psalmvers, sondern zu zweien gesungen wird, ist besonders in der älteren Zeit nicht allzu selten. Wohl aber verdient die Auswahl dieser zweiten Verse besonderes Interesse. So ist hier beispielsweise beim Fest der Himmelfahrt des Herrn als zweiter Vers die Stelle aus der Apostelgeschichte ausgewählt, die unmittelbar der mit *Viri Galilei* beginnenden Rede des Engels vorausgeht, so daß sich die Wiederholung der Introitusantiphon nahtlos an den zweiten Vers anschließt».

In his study of LAV, L. Gherardi called attention to other unusual verses for Introits and Communions: he spoke of them as *versus ad repetendum* «con clausole dall'andamento tropizzante»[8]. The verses quoted by Gherardi in this connection all seem to be newly composed texts, and they do indeed sound like tropes; but a fuller examination of the non-psalm verses for both Introits and Communions in this manuscript has resulted in the identification of many as being similar in nature to the one to which Stäblein drew attention: they have been selected from the Bible to lead into or to complement the meaning of the text of the chant they accompany. Most often the chants for which such verses are provided are themselves non-psalm (though usually Biblical); and the verse is drawn from the same passage as the main text.

It is not at all unusual for an Introit in LAV to have more than one verse: a quick glance at the «Table Alphabétique» of the facsimile edition will serve to make this clear. In many instances the first verse, but only the first, is from a psalm. The verse or verses that follow may be taken from another book of the Bible (that of the main text); or they may be newly composed devotional texts. The situation with Communions is different, but more in terms of quantity of material than in terms of the procedures that are to be observed. Psalm verses, with the rubric «P», are provided for some Communions in LAV, non-psalm verses (with the rubric «V») for others[9]. Some Communions have both, many have neither. Hence questions arise concerning form, and concerning the function of the Communion (or Introit) antiphon. When there *is* a psalm (that is to say, when several verses from a psalm are included between repetitions of the antiphon), is the antiphon serving to introduce the psalm, is it an accessory to the psalm? When there is *not* a psalm but only a verse, has the verse become an accessory to the antiphon? And what impact does having both a psalm and a verse have on the function of the antiphon?

Here are some examples of non-psalm texts of an introductory character serving as Communion verses in LAV[10]:

- For the Communion *Fili quid fecisti* (fol. 42v; text from Lc. 2:48−49):
  V. Et factum est postriduum inuenerunt iesum in templo sedentem in medio doctorum audientem illos et interrogantes et dixit mater eius ad illum (Lc. 2:46, 48) Fili
- For the Communion *Domine quinque talenta* (45v; Mt. 25:20−21):
  V. Accedens qui quinque talenta acceperat obtulit quinque talenta dicens (Mt. 25:20) Domine quinque
- For the Communion *Venite post me* (146; Mt. 4:19−20):
  V. Ambulans iesus iuxta mare galilee uidit duos fratres petrum et andream et uocauit eos (Mt. 4:18) Venite

---

8 L. Gherardi, «Il Codice Angelica 123» (Note 4), 27. For the term *versus ad repetendum*, see «Introit», NGrove 9, 281−2, and other literature cited there.
9 It perhaps may go without saying that the rubricator is not perfectly consistent in making this distinction; but he does it more often than not.
10 In the course of this article Biblical references are used whenever a passage can be traced with reasonable assurance: they can indicate anything from an exact quotation to only a general similarity in theme. Making a finer distinction along these lines, although not feasible within the limits of the present study, might very well lead to valuable results. The reader is encouraged to check each reference for himself, and to note the extent to which the exact wording of the Vulgate is preserved in a chant or verse. One should keep in mind the possibility that the composer of the chant had at hand a translation into Latin of the Biblical text that was other than (and perhaps earlier than) the Vulgate. Except in a few instances, the references in this study do not specify where all of a Bible verse is used (or drawn upon), and where only a part of one.

Other non-psalm verses for Communions complement the chant text by continuing the narrative implied in it:

- For the Communion *Mitte manum* (116; Jo. 20:27):
  V. Quia uidisti me thomas credidisti beati qui non uiderunt et crediderunt (Jo. 20:29)
- For the Communion *Dicit Dominus implete* (44v; Jo. 2:7−9, 10−11):
  P. Ut supra (i.e., Jubilate deo omnis terra)
  V. Et manifestauit gloriam suam et crediderunt in eum discipuli eius (Jo. 2:11) Hoc signum

A cursory examination of several dozen graduals has led to the identification of five sources other than LAV that include an unusual number of non-psalm verses for Introits and Communions. Each of these will be listed and briefly described below; but first it should be noted that many sources contain a few such verses. The most popular by far is the verse *Cumque intuerentur* for the Ascension Introit that has already been quoted. Nearly as popular is a verse for the Introit *Nunc scio vere* (SS. Peter and Paul, Act. 12:11) that reads as follows:

> Et exeuntes processerunt uicum unum et continuo discessit angelus ab eo et petrus ad se reuersus dixit (Act. 12:10−11)

Also frequently encountered are the following verses:

- For the Introit *Scio cui credidi* (St. Paul; 2 Tim. 1:12):
  De reliquo reposita est mihi corona justitie quam reddet mihi dominus in illum diem justus judex (2 Tim. 4:8)
- For *Gaudete in Domino* (Third Sunday of Advent; Phil. 4:4−5):
  Et pax dei que exuperat omnem sensum custodiat corda uestra et intellegentias uestras (Phil. 4:7)

In addition to these, there are certain Introits for which the standard verse appears to be non-psalm: *Sacerdotes dei* (for which the «psalm» is the Benedicite); *O beatum virum* (for Saint Martin − an Introit based on a non-biblical text which is also the source of the verse); and various chants for the feast of St. Benedict that are similarly based on non-biblical texts. In some sources the Introit *Salve sancta parens,* on a text by Sedulius, has a verse drawn from the same work: these verses vary from one manuscript to another.

Reference was made above to sources in which it is common to find non-psalm Introits and Communions provided with non-psalm verses. In addition to LAV, these include the following[11]:

- Oxford, Bodleian Library, Can. Lit. 366: a gradual from Brescia that is followed by a Breviary; 11th century [BRE]
- Ivrea, Chapter Library, 60: a gradual from Pavia; middle of the 11th century [IVR 1]
- Paris, Bibl. nat., lat. 776: a gradual, including many prosulae, from Saint-Michel-de-Gaillac, followed by a tonary that is now incomplete; 11th century [ALB]
- Paris, Bibl. nat., lat. 903: a gradual, including many prosulae, from Saint-Yrieix, with tropes and sequences at the end; 11th century [YRX]
- Paris, Bibl. nat., lat. 780: a gradual from Narbonne, followed by a tonary; 11th or 12th century [NAR]

---

11 Information concerning provenance and date is as given in *Le Graduel Romain*, II: *Les Sources,* Solesmes 1954. The sigla proposed in that work have been adopted here. Page references to YRX are to the facsimile edition published in PM 13.

444

Working through these sources has involved checking the texts of Introits and Communions against the passages in the Vulgate from which they are said to derive (in such standard works as the *Graduale Triplex*[12]). Those familiar with the problem need no reminder that in the case of some chants, as for example the Introits *Populus Sion* and *Hodie scietis,* the composer of the text worked quite freely with the Biblical material that he had selected for use. Other chants follow the text of the Vulgate closely: no question arises concerning their derivation. Similarly there are many verses, including those previously cited, that are relatively easy to identify. With others the search is inconclusive: the verse has a familiar ring, but even using a concordance does not lead to a positive identification. And in some instances, the verse could come from any one of a number of similar passages. This is the case with such verses as *Dixit hiesus discipulis suis* (LAV, 39).

Often the non-psalm verses stand out in the manuscripts because they are written in full, while psalm verses are given only in incipit. But there are many exceptions to this rule: some manuscripts give all verses in full, some refer to a few of the non-psalm verses by their incipits alone. Thus the verse *Et pax dei* for the Introit *Gaudete in domino* is given in full in five of the sources listed above, while only its first three words are provided in YRX (6). The same manuscript (179) gives only the cue «Cumque intuerentur» for the non-psalm verse of the Ascension Introit. Both YRX and ALB indicate that the verse of the Communion *Factus est repente* begins «Et apparuerunt illis»; it is necessary to consult NAR (84) to learn that what is really intended is «Et apparuerunt illis dispertite lingue tamquam ignis seditque supra singulos eorum», Act. 2:3, a verse that complements perfectly the text of the main part of the chant, which is based on material taken from Act. 2:2 and 4. For the Introit *Ne timeas Maria,* which is based rather freely on Lc. 1:13, 15 and 14, IVR 1 gives the single word «Apparuit» for the verse; it is the beginning of Luke 1:11, «Apparuit autem illi angelus Domini stans a dextris altaris incensi». In the manuscripts that give this Introit verse in full, it has been modified slightly to read as follows: «Apparuit autem angelus domini zacharie stans a dextris altaris incensi et ait illi». Two aspects of this rewording deserve mention. First, the substitution of the proper name «Zacharie» for the pronoun «illi» is the kind of thing that often happens when words are taken out of context to serve as chant texts. Second, the appearance at the end of the verse of an expression that leads smoothly into the main text is a recurring characteristic among these texts. Several examples have been presented above, others are quoted below:

- For the Introit *Terribilis est* (Gen. 28:17, 22):
  Vidit iachob in sompnis scalam erectam et angelos ascendentes et descendentes et ait (Gen. 28:12) (NAR, 82)
- For the Introit *Domine ne longe* (Ps. 21:20, 22):
  Sciens autem hiesus omnia que uentura erat super eum (Jo. 18:4) et cum cepisset orare dixit ad patrem (LAV, 93)

Although it is often the case that the various sources present the same non-psalm verse for a chant, in some instances the verse is different in each manuscript, as in the following examples:

---

12 Solesmes: Abbaye Saint-Pierre 1979.

XVI

- For the Introit *Lux fulgebit* (Cf. Is. 9:2, 6; Lc. 1:33):
  Ante secula natus deo et usque in futurum eius regnum non erit finis (LAV, 28v);
  Habitantibus in regione umbrae mortis lux orta est ei (Is. 9:2b) (BRE, 3v);
  Populus qui ambulabat in tenebris lucem uidit magnam (Is. 9:2a) (NAR, 8)
- For the Communion *Vox in rama* (Mt. 2:18):
  Tunc adimpletum est quod dictum est per ieremiam prophetam dicentem (Mt. 2:17)
  (LAV 36v);
  Iratus herodes iussit occidere omnes pueros qui erant in bethleem iude et in omnibus
  finibus eius (Cf. Mt. 2:16) (ALB, 18)

A corresponding lack of standardization is evident in those cases where a verse is given in a longer form in one manuscript than in another. For the Introit *In medio* (Sir. 15:5), BRE (4v) gives the verse «Iocunditate et exultatione thesaurizauit super eum et nomine eterno ereditauit illum dominus deus noster» (Sir. 15:6). LAV (34v) and NAR (11) give only «Iocunditate et exultatione thesaurizauit super eum». For the Communion *Vidimus stellam* (Mt. 2:2), LAV (41v) gives «Magi ueniunt ab orientem hierosolimam querentes et dicentes ubi est qui natus est rex iudeorum» (Mt. 2:1−2); IVR 1 (28) and ALB (20) end the verse after «dicentes».

In a few instances the non-psalm verse comes from a different biblical context than that of the main text: in BRE (28), IVR 1 (104), YRX (204), and NAR (93v), the verse for the Introit *Scio cui credidi* (2 Tim. 1:12) consists of the first half of 2 Tim 4:8, though the four manuscripts do not agree on how long the excerpt should be. For the Introit *Dicit Dominus Petro* (Jo. 21:18−19), NAR (91) gives the verse «Simon iohannis diligis me plus his tu scis domine quia amo te» (Jo. 21:15), but BRE (28) gives «Ego pro te rogaui petre ut non defitiat fides tua et tu aliquando conuersus confirma fratres tuos» Lc. 22:32). And for the Introit *Modicum et non videbitis* (Jo. 10:14), LAV (117) and ALB (78) give a verse from Jo. 16:22: «Iterum autem uidebo uos et gaudebit cor uestrum».

The manuscripts often place at the end of the verse a cue consisting of the first word or so of the parent chant. Occasionally the cue refers not to the beginning of the chant but to a point about half way through it. That is, the main chant is treated as if it is in two parts, with the latter of them serving as a refrain. One example is the Communion *Amen dico vobis* (Mt. 19:28−29), for which the verse comes from Mt. 19:28, as follows:

Comm. Amen dico vobis: quod vos, qui reliquistis omnia, et secuti estis me, centuplum accipietis, et vitam aeternam possidebitis.
V. In regeneratione cum sederit filius hominis in sede maiestatis suae
[Refrain.] Centuplum accipietis, et vitam aeternam possidebitis. (ALB, 103; YRX, 205)

Two other examples that could be cited in this connection are as follows:

Comm. Video caelos apertos, et Iesum stantem a dextris virtutis Dei: Domine Iesu, accipe spiritum meum, et ne statuas illis hoc peccatum, quia nesciunt quid faciunt.
V. Positis autem genibus beatus stephanus orabat dicens
[Refrain.] Domine Iesu, accipe spiritum meum, et ne statuas illis hoc peccatum, quia nesciunt quid faciunt. (ALB, 16; chant text from Act. 7:56, 59, 60; verse from Act. 7:59)
Comm. Simon Ioannis, diligis me plus his? Domine, tu omnia nosti: tu scis, Domine, quia amo te.
V. Contristatus est petrus quia dixit ei tercio amas me et dixit ei
[Refrain.] Domine, tu omnia nosti: tu scis, Domine, quia amo te. (YRX, 204; chant text from Jo. 21:15, 17; verse from Jo. 21:17)

446

This treatment of the verse and the refrain brings the Communion into a form like that of the Responsories of the Divine Office[13]. What other similarities are there between the two genres? Considered simply as texts, many of the verses to which attention has been called in the course of this study resemble verses for Responsories; and their musical settings, like those of responsories, consist of modal formulas. Although there are a few rare instances of overlapping between the two repertories – Communions and Responsories – it appears that in the present instance what we have been observing is not direct borrowing but the adaptation in a rather casual way for use in Communions of a way of handling text that originated in Responsories.

There is also a connection with troping, particularly when the non-psalm verse serves textually as an introduction to the repeat of the main text. Since tropes are occasionally themselves quotations from the Bible, one can imagine the same text being put to use in both roles – as an introductory trope, and also as a non-psalm verse. Only one example of this was identified in the six sources examined for the present study. It is a text associated with the Introit *De ventre matris meae* (Is. 49:1–2), «Audite insule et adtendite populi de longe dominus ab utero uocauit me» (Is. 49:1), which is treated musically in ALB (98v) and YRX (196) as an Introit verse, but in IVR 1 (99v) as a trope. The texts edited as tropes in *Corpus Troporum* I and III include several that have here been identified as verses.

Clearly an edition of all these verses would be useful. There follows an assortment of them collected from the six manuscripts; it may serve to demonstrate the richness of the genre.

A Selection of Non-Psalm Verses for Introits and Communions

Intr. *Puer natus est* (Nat. Domini III; Is. 9:6):
Multiplicabitur eius imperium et pacis non erit finis (Is. 9:7) (LAV, 31v; BRE, 4; ALB, 13v)

Comm. *Quinque prudentes virgines* (S. Agnetis I; Mt. 25:4, 6):
Moram autem faciente sponso dormitauerunt omnes et dormierunt (Mt. 25:5) (IVR 1, 33v)
Et quae parate erant intrauerunt cum eo ad nuptias (Mt. 25:10) (ALB, 24v)

Comm. *Qui vult venire* (S. Vincentii; Mt. 16:24):
Qui enim uoluerit animam suam saluam facere perdet eam (Mt. 16:25) Et tollat (ALB, 25v)

Intr. *Missus est Gabriel* (Annuntiatio S. Mariae; Lc. 1:26–28):
Que cum audisset turbata est in sermone eius et cogitabat qualis esset ista salutacio (Lc. 1:29; NAR, 25v)

Intr. *In nomine Domini* (Fer. IV Maj. Hebd.; Phil. 2:10, 8, 11):
Propter quod et deus illum exaltauit et donauit illi nomen quod est super omne nomen (Phil. 2:9) (IVR 1, 64)

Comm. *Pascha nostrum* (Dom. Paschae; 1 Cor. 5:7–8):
Expurgate uetus fermentum ut sitis noua consparsio noua etenim (1 Cor. 5:7) Pascha (IVR 1, 74v)

---

13 The similarity is even greater when the Doxology is added to such Communions, with the refrain coming between the Verse and the Doxology, and the full Communion at the end. This happens rather often in ALB; and it merits further study.

Comm. *Surrexit Dominus* (Fer. II Pasch.; Lc. 24:34):
Cito euntes dicite discipulis quia surrexit dominus (Mt. 28:7) Et apparuit (ALB, 73)

Comm. *Si consurrexistis* (Fer. III Pasch.; Col. 3:1−2):
Cum enim xpistus apparuerit uita uestra tunc et uos apparebitis cum ipso in gloria (Col. 3:4) Si consu<rrexistis> (ALB, 73v)

Intr. *Venite benedicti Patris mei* (Fer. IV Pasch.; Mt. 25:34):
Esuriui enim et dedistis mihi manducare sitiui et dedistis mihi potum (Mt. 25:35) (ALB, 73v; NAR, 66v)

Intr. *Victricem manum* (Fer. V Pasch.; Sap. 10:20−21):
Tulerunt spolia impiorum et decantauerunt domine nomen sanctum tuum (Sap. 10:19−20) et victricem (NAR, 67v)

Comm. *Populus adquisitionis* (Fer. V Pasch.; 1 Petr. 2:9):
Vos autem genus electum regale sacerdot<i>um gens sancta (1 Petr. 2:9) (ALB, 74v; NAR, 67v; see also LAV, 113)

Comm. *Data est mihi* (Fer. VI Pasch.; Mt. 28:18−19):
Ego autem uobiscum sum omnibus diebus usque ad consumationem seculi (Mt. 28:20) Data est (ALB, 75)

Comm. *Omnes qui in Christo* (Sabb. Pasch.; Gal. 3:27):
Omnes enim uos filii dei estis per fidem in xpisto iesu domino nostro (Gal. 3:26) (LAV, 115)

Intr. *Quasi modo geniti* (Oct. Pasch.; 1 Petr. 2:2):
Vos autem genus electum regale sacerdocium populus adquisitionis (1 Petr. 2:9) Quasimodo (LAV, 115v; see also BRE, 23v and ALB, 76)
Deponentes igitur omnem maliciam et omnem dolum et simulationes et inuidias et omnes detractiones (1 Petr. 2:1) (NAR, 69v)

Comm. *Ego sum pastor bonus* (Dom. II p. Pasch.; Jo. 10:14):
Sicut nouit me pater et ego agnosco patrem et animam meam pono pro ouibus meis (Jo. 10:15) Ego sum (LAV, 116v; see also NAR, 70)
Bonus pastor animam suam ponit pro ouibus suis (Jo. 10:11) Ego sum (ALB, 77)

Comm. *Dum venerit paraclitus* (Dom. IV p. Pasch.; Jo. 16:8):
Non enim loquetur a semetipso sed quecumque audiet loquetur et que uentura sunt annunciabit uobis (Jo. 16:13) Ille ar<guet> (LAV, 117v)
Si enim non [h]abiero paraclitus non ueniet ad uos si autem [h]abiero mittam eum ad uos (Jo. 16:7) Dum uenerit (ALB, 78v)

Intr. *Spiritus Domini replevit* (Dom. Pent.; Sap. 1:7):
Quoniam renum illius testis est deus et cordis eius scrutator est uerus et lingue illius auditor (Sap. 1:6) (BRE, 26)

Intr. *In voluntate tua* (Dom. XXI p. Pent.; Esth. 13:9−11):
Et nunc domine rex regum deus habraham miserere populo tuo quia uolunt nos inimici nostri perdere et hereditatem tuam delere (Esth. 13:15) (IVR 1, 137)

LISTE DES ABRÉVIATIONS

AH *Analecta hymnica medii aevi*, éd. G.M. Dreves, C. Blume, H.M. Bannister, 55 vol., Leipzig 1886−1922

AMS *Antiphonale missarum sextuplex*, éd. R.-J. Hesbert, Bruxelles 1935

Bull. Bulletin

CAO *Corpus antiphonalium officii* (Rerum ecclesiasticarum documenta, series maior, fontes 7−12), éd. R.-J. Hesbert, 6 vol., Rome 1963−1979

CCL *Corpus christianorum, Series latina*, Turnhout etc. 1954−

CT *Corpus Troporum* (Acta universitatis Stockholmiensis, Studia Latina Stockholmiensia [= SLS])

XVI

CT I	*Corpus Troporum I, Tropes du propre de la messe. 1 Cycle de Noël*, éd. R. Jonsson et alii (SLS 21), Stockholm 1975
CT II	*Corpus Troporum II, Prosules de la messe. 1 Tropes de l'alleluia*, éd. O. Marcusson (SLS 22), Stockholm 1976
CT III	*Corpus Troporum III, Tropes du propre de la messe. 2 Cycle de Pâques*, éd. G. Björkvall, G. Iversen, R. Jacobsson (SLS 26), Stockholm 1982
CT IV	*Corpus Troporum IV, Tropes de l'Agnus Dei. Edition critique suivie d'une étude analytique* par G. Iversen (SLS 26), Stockholm 1980
CT V	*Corpus Troporum V, Les deux tropaires d'Apt, mss 17 et 18. Inventaire analytique des mss et édition des textes uniques* par G. Björkvall (SLS 32), Stockholm 1986
CT VI	*Corpus Troporum VI, Prosules de la messe. 2 Les prosules limousines de Wolfenbüttel, Herzog August Bibliothek Cod. Guelf. 79 Gud. lat.* par E. Odelman (SLS 31), Stockholm 1986
CT VII	*Corpus Troporum VII, Tropes de l'ordinaire de la messe. Tropes du Sanctus. Introduction et édition critique* par G. Iversen (SLS 34), Stockholm 1990
Ephem. liturg.	Ephemerides liturgicae
Et.	Etudes
Et. grég.	Etudes grégoriennes
Fs.	Festschrift
JAMS	Journal of the American Musicological Society
Jb.	Jahrbuch
MGG	*Die Musik in Geschichte und Gegenwart, Allgemeine Enzyklopädie der Musik*, éd. F. Blume, 17 vol., Kassel 1949–1985
MGH	Monumenta Germaniae Historica ..., Hannover etc. 1826–
MMMAe I	*Monumenta monodica medii aevi I, Hymnen (1). Die mittelalterlichen Hymnenmelodien des Abendlandes*, éd. B. Stäblein, Kassel etc. 1956
MMMAe II	*Monumenta monodica medii aevi II, Die Gesänge des altrömischen Graduale Vat. lat. 5319*, éd. M. Landwehr-Melnicki (introd. B. Stäblein), Kassel etc. 1970
MMMAe III	*Monumenta monodica medii aevi III, Introitus-Tropen 1. Das Repertoire der südfranzösischen Tropare des 10. und 11. Jahrhunderts*, éd. G. Weiss, Kassel etc. 1970
MMMAe VII	*Monumenta monodica medii aevi VII, Alleluia-Melodien I. bis 1100*, éd. K. Schlager, Kassel 1968
NGrove	*The New Grove Dictionary of Music and Musicians*, éd. S. Sadie, 20 vol., London 1980
PL	*Patrologiae cursus completus, Series latina*, éd. J.-P. Migne, 221 vol., Paris 1844–64
PM	*Paléographie musicale. Les principaux manuscrits de chant grégorien, ambrosien, mozarabe, gallican.* Publ. par les Bénédictins de Solesmes, 21 vol., Solesmes etc. 1889–
Rev.	Revue
Rev. bén.	Revue bénédictine
Rev. grég.	Revue grégorienne
RISM	Répertoire International des Sources Musicales

XVII

The Canticle of the Three Children as a Chant of the Roman Mass

It is to Wulf Arlt that we are indebted for the most detailed examination of the work of those medieval liturgists who on occasion flaunted the general rule that the form and style of a chant are determined by liturgical function.[1] As Professor Arlt has shown, what they did was to substitute chants in incongruous styles for the «official» chants of a service. It is days between Christmas and Epiphany that are affected – days reserved for special celebration by the clergy – and the sources in which such substitutions are most abundant are relatively late and come from northern France: Sens, Beauvais, Laon. A key principle is that the text of the substitute chant is either the same as, or a paraphrase of, that of the regular chant. The sense of the words must coincide with that of the original; everything else – including the words themselves – can be changed.

These substitutions have long been recognized as manifestations of ecclesiastical exuberance that could be tolerated because the time when they occurred was one in which all Christians had good reason to rejoice. By providing texts with melodies that were more elaborate than their usual ones, they enhanced the richness of a service.

What appears to be another instance of substitution occurs in a very different context. It is the settings of the Canticle of the Three Children as the chant following the fifth lesson in Masses of Ember Saturdays. Four different musical settings are involved, and at least four different texts. All have the same liturgical function, and the meanings of the texts overlap, when they do not coincide precisely. Yet they are musically quite different. Where did these chants originate, which of them is the oldest, why do the sources differ so much in the way they present them?

The Canticle of the Three Children is part of a long interpolation into chapter 3 of the book of Daniel.[2] The first part of the interpolation (Daniel 3:24–45 in the Vulgate numbering) is known as the Prayer of Azariah; it is followed by a brief prose narrative (Vss. 46–51). Next comes the first section of the Canticle of

---

1 *Ein Festoffizium des Mittelalters aus Beauvais* (2 vols.; Köln, Arno Volk Verlag, 1970). See also H. Villetard, *L'Office de Pierre de Corbeil* (Paris: Librairie Alphonse Picard & Fils, 1907), D. Hughes, «Music for St. Stephen at Laon,» *Words and Music: The Scholar's View*, ed. L. Berman (Cambridge, Mass.: Harvard University Press, 1972), 137; and «Compline,» *The New Grove Dictionary of Music and Musicians* 4:598–9.
2 The best introduction to the book of Daniel is that of Louis F. Hartman and Alexander A. Di Lella, in *The Anchor Bible*, vol. 23 (Garden City, N. Y.: Doubleday, 1978). See also M. Delcor, *Le Livre de Daniel* (Paris, 1971). For the Latin text of the Canticle see *Biblia sacra iuxta vulgatam versionem*, ed. R. Weber (2nd ed., rev.; Stuttgart: Württembergische Bibelanstalt, 1975), Vol. II, pp. 1348–1351. Concerning the interpolation see Carey A. Moore, *Daniel, Esther, and Jeremiah: the Additions* (*The Anchor Bible*, vol. 44; Garden City, N. Y.: Doubleday, 1977), pp. 39–76. Moore presents a detailed review of the scholarly literature, one that the reader of the present study will undoubtedly find enlightening. For his bibliography, see pp. 35–8.

the Three Children (Vss. 52–56), which begins «Benedictus es Domine Deus patrum nostrorum», exactly as does the Prayer of Azariah. It has a refrain in which the wording is varied in each use. The second section (Vss. 57–90) is known as the «Benedicite», and has an almost completely regular refrain.

Although no ancient Semitic version of these texts has been preserved, there is a modern translation of the «Benedictus es» and the «Benedicite» into Hebrew verse. The translation works so well that it permits «the presumption of a Hebrew original.»[3] According to Moore, it is difficult to date the texts on internal evidence, and to guess just when they were incorporated into the Daniel narrative; but the effect of the interpolation is to shift attention from Nebuchadnezzar to the three young men, and from what they did to what they believed. Setting the prayer at the head of the series of interpolations came later, and it led to some inconsistencies in the telling of the story.

The «Benedicite» is a long and beautiful song of praise to God, one that seems originally to have been composed for use in public worship. Here it represents the response of the children of Israel to yet another miracle, their preservation in the face of certain doom. The whole story of the fiery furnace, especially the response of the three men to the king's threat, is an expression of religious pacifism, an ideology that was strong among Hasidim even at the time of the horrifying persecution of the Jews by Antiochus IV Epiphanes, which reached its climax between 167 and 164 B. C., and came to an end only with the revolt of the Maccabees. Thus the editing of the first six chapters of Daniel is thought by many to have occurred during this period.[4] And for the early Christians, too, suffering persecution, parallels between their plight and that of the Three Young Men must have been evident; the motif appears again and again in wall paintings in the Catacombs.[5]

Our understanding of the liturgical practices of early Christian communities is still imperfect; we do not know every one of the stages by which the development proceded, from «psalms, canticles, and spiritual songs» to the official public worship according to established formulas of later times. But references to the Canticle of the Three Children are so numerous in accounts of the customs of widely separated religious groups that it must have been used almost as often as the psalms, and known at least as well as they.

In a series of lectures published under the title *Comparative Liturgy,* Anton Baumstark called attention to the wide use of the «Benedicite»: he spoke of its appearance on a fragment of papyrus representing «an ancient Egyptian office book,» in the night office of the Copts and that of the Maronites, in the Sunday Matins of the Nestorians, and in the Matins of the Armenians.[6]

---

3 Moore, p. 48.
4 Hartman and Di Lella, pp. 43–5.
5 The classic study is that of H. Leclercq, «Hebreux (les trois jeunes),» in *Dictionnaire d'Archéologie Chrétienne et de Liturgie,* VI.2 (Paris, 1925), cols. 2107–2126. See also Carlo Carletti, *I tre giovani Ebrei di Babilonia nell'arte cristiana antica* (Brescia, 1975), and the review of that work by Marguerite Rassart-Debergh in *Byzantion,* 48 (1978), 430–455.
6 Anton Baumstark, *Comparative Liturgy,* trans. by F. L. Cross from the 3rd French edition, rev. by B. Botte (Westminster, Md., 1958), pp. 35–6.

Indeed, it would be very interesting and, no doubt, highly rewarding to study all of the liturgical uses of the «Benedicite»: in the East and in the West, in the Mass and in the Office. But for the purpose of this discussion it is necessary to focus on a single topic; the one I have chosen is the use of the «Benedicite» as a chant of the Mass of the Roman rite – specifically, as the chant following the fifth of the six lessons on Ember Saturdays.

These Ember Saturday services are well represented in the Mass antiphonals studied by Hesbert in *Antiphonale Missarum Sextuplex,* as they are in the earlier lectionaries and sacramentaries.[7] The sources agree in indicating that the fifth lesson on all four days is drawn from the third chapter of the book of Daniel, leading directly into the chant. The one exception is the Würzburg lectionary, the earliest source of the distinctively Roman lectionary; its omission of the Daniel lesson indicates – according to Hesbert – that neither it nor the Canticle was included in the Mass for Ember Saturdays as originally formulated in Rome.[8] Their introduction into these services in manuscripts prepared for use in France reveals an influence of the Gallican liturgy. In the Mozarabic sources, where the Canticle was regularly sung in the Mass on Sundays and feast days, its text is presented in a number of different arrangements, which have been surveyed by Brou.[9]

Only one of the antiphonals of the Roman Mass surveyed by Hesbert in *Antiphonale Missarum Sextuplex* gives the text of the «Benedicite» in full, preceded by the verse, «Benedictus es in firmamento caeli et laudabilis et gloriosus in saecula» – that is, in essentially the same form as that in which it appears in the earliest sources with musical notation.[10] One of the other sources gives the incipit of the chant, preceding it with the rubric «Lectio Danihel Prophetae», and the beginning of that lesson, «In diebus illis Angelus Domini». One manuscript never refers to the chant at all; the other three refer to it by the title «Benedictiones», using this term in a context which bears description.

It is to be remembered that among the other chants for these Ember Saturdays are four graduals. These are written in full (or given in incipit, according to the procedure generally followed in the source) in the Ember Week of Advent – the first time they appear in the liturgical year. Thereafter (in the later Ember Weeks), references to them take the form, «RESP. GRAD. IIII». There is no mention of any form of the Canticle of the Three Children in the Ember Week

7 R.-J. Hesbert, *Antiphonale Missarum Sextuplex* (Brussels, 1935; reprint ed., Rome: Herder, 1967), pp. XXXIX–XLIV.
8 Hesbert, p. XLIII, fn. 2. The early history of the Ember Weeks is examined by G. G. Willis, in *Early Christian Liturgy* (London: S. P. C. K., 1964), pp. 51–75. Until the end of the 5th century at Rome there were ordinations only in the December Embertide, making it the most important one. It is evident from early references to the Embertides, and also from the texts employed in the liturgy – particularly Gospels and Communions – that the Lenten Embertide (the fast of the first month) was a later addition (Willis, pp. 53–57). The manner in which the Embertides are presented in the Gelasian Sacramentary (of *ca.* 560) makes it appear that the Lenten Embertide «was coming in about that time» (Willis, p. 57). Nonetheless, the manner in which Ember Weeks are presented in the Mass antiphonals (none of which is earlier than perhaps the end of the eighth century) often makes the Lenten Embertide seem more important than the others.
9 L. Brou, «Les 'Benedictiones' ou cantique des trois enfants dans l'ancienne messe espagnole,» *Hispania sacra,* 1 (1948), 21–33.
10 The manuscript in question is the Compiègne Antiphonal, Paris, Bibl. nat., lat. 17436; see Hesbert, pp. XLI and 61.

of Advent in any of these MSS; this is particularly striking in view of the fact that – as I said – the graduals are written in full.

The three manuscripts that use the term «Benedictiones» without providing a text incipit (in Ember Weeks other than that of Advent) do so by simply adding it to the rubric that I have just given, so that it takes the form «RESP. GRAD. IIII ET BENEDICTIONES.» One infers that, just as the singer is expected to know what the graduals are (because he has seen them earlier in the book), he is also expected to know the «Benedictiones.» But where is that chant given?

What the reference to the Canticle of the Three Children, in one form or another, under the title «Benedictiones,» suggested to Hesbert is that it was not a chant in the usual sense of the word – not something to be included in a book intended for the use of cantors. The reason is that what is involved in the lesson and the Canticle is a single passage from Daniel, of which the first part is read – to the customary lesson tone – while the second, of which the text is in the style of a lyric, is given a somewhat more elaborate musical setting. References in some other manuscripts indicate that here and in other passages of similar dual character a single lector performed both sections, chanting the first, singing the second.[11]

The manuscripts surveyed in *Antiphonale Missarum Sextuplex* thus may give evidence of two different phases in the development of this chant – one, in which the Canticle was performed by the lector, to a formula only slightly more elaborate than that he had used for the lesson preceding it; and another, in which the Canticle had been given a more fully developed musical setting, and entrusted to the cantors for performance. (In the first phase, where the lector executed the Canticle, I see no reason not to imagine the congregation participating in its performance, chanting the fixed refrain, «Laudate et superexaltate eum in saecula.»)

I should like to propose to my colleagues in the round table yet a third explanation of the term «Benedictiones» as employed in these manuscripts. If, as Hesbert has suggested, the inclusion in the service of the Daniel lesson (and a chant to accompany it) was made out of deference to local custom in the Frankish Empire, in an effort to find a place for materials that were traditional there, then Gallican settings (or adaptations) of the Benedictiones may have been employed. Now one of the things that characterizes the treatment of the Benedictiones in the Mozarabic rite (and very possibly also the Gallican, though here the evidence is less abundant) is a multiplicity of settings of the Canticle, texts selected and arranged in many different ways: there are 26 different Benedictiones in the Leon Antiphoner. In an act intended to show deference to local custom, making a choice of one or another (of the Benedictiones) would have struck exactly the wrong note: the general term «Benedictiones» may indicate that here some choice is possible, the choice to be made from a local repertory which had no place in a book of official, «Roman» chant.

Let me pass on now to a consideration of what we find in manuscripts that present the Proper chants of the Mass with musical notation. The form of the Can-

---

11 Hesbert, p. XLII, including fn. 1.

ticle that one finds in the early chant manuscripts is a setting of the whole of the
«Benedicite» preceded by the verse, «Benedictus es in firmamento caeli.» The
setting is elaborate and formulaic; analyses by Wagner and Ferretti have identified the structure of the tone and the points at which it is enriched by melismas.[12] The refrain, which begins in this setting with the words, «Hymnum dicite,» is set after every third blessing, rather than every single one, as in the Bible.
There is a good deal of detail in the rhythmic notation of it in such manuscripts
as Laon 239 and Einsiedeln 121: it is clear that it is a chant for the cantor, and
an occasion for particularly brilliant vocal display. It is this form of the «Benedicite» that one is most likely to find in the early Gregorian Mass manuscripts:
it is the only one in Laon 239 and Chartres 47; and when there is reference to
others in St. Gall 359, that comes in a later hand.
Another chant used to follow the Daniel lesson in Masses for Ember Saturdays
begins «Benedictus es Domine Deus patrum nostrorum,» that is, with verse 52
of what we have called the «Benedictus es.» It continues with a series of blessings,
«Benedictus es in templo sancto gloriae tuae,» «Benedictus es super thronum
sanctum regni tui,» and so on, that are not, at least in part, exact Biblical quotations, and which vary both in their number and in their order from one source
to another. In numbering the verses of this chant as it appears in Einsiedeln 121,
I have set aside the opening, and I am not taking into account the ending, which
varies too much from one source to another to be dealt with effectively here.

Table 1
The chant «Benedictus es Domine Deus patrum nostrorum»
ORDER OF INNER VERSES

1 2 3 4 5 6 7:   Einsiedeln 121
    (St. Gall? beginning of 11th c.)
    Graz, Universitätsbibliothek, 807
    (Klosterneuburg, 12th c.)
    Leipzig, Univ., St. Thomas, 391
    (Leipzig, end of 13th)
    Leningrad, O v I 6
    (use of Bec, 12th c.)
    London, B. L., Add. 12194
    (Sarum, ca. 1275)

1 2 4 5 3 6 7:   Ediger/Mosel, Pfarrarchiv
    (Rheinland, end of 12th c.)

1 2 3 5 4 7 6:   Durham, Univ., Cosin V V 6
    (Canterbury, Durham, ca. 1080)

1 2 4 3 5 6 7:   Paris, B. n., lat. 1087
    (Cluny, 11th c.)
    Brussels, Bibl. roy., II 3823
    (Souvigny [Cluniac], beg. of 12th c.)
    Paris, B. n., lat. 1107
    (St. Denis, 13th c., 2/2)

12 P. Ferretti, *Esthétique grégorienne* (Solesmes, 1938), pp. 203–212; P. Wagner, *Gregorianische
Formenlehre* (*Einführung in die gregorianischen Melodien,* III; Leipzig, 1921), pp. 361–366.

1 x 2 3 4 5 6 7:	Rome, Bibl. Angelica, 123
	(Bologna, beg. of 11th c.)
1 2 x 3 4 6 5 7:	Paris, B. n., lat. 776
	(St. Michel de Gaillac, 11th c.)
1 2 3 x 5 4 6 7:	Monza, Bibl. cap., 12/75
	(Monza, beg. of 11th c.)
1 2 5 3 y 4 6 7:	Modena, Bibl. cap., O 1 7
	(Forlimpopoli [Ravenna], 11th or 12th.)
1 2 x 3 4 3 6 5 7:	London, B. L., Harl. 4951
	(Toulouse, 11th c.)

If the order of the inner verses in Einsiedeln 121 is taken as the standard (this is not to imply that it is necessarily the earliest or best) and that of the other sources is compared with it, the lack of consistency is immediately apparent. (See Table 1.) Some later sources from German-speaking regions, such as one from Klosterneuburg, agree with Einsiedeln; but the gradual of Ediger – an Augustinian source from the end of the 12th century, the earliest gradual from the Rheinland that has come down to us – gives the verses in a very different order. A Leningrad manuscript that represents the use of Bec agrees with Einsiedeln, as does the Sarum Gradual; but a source copied at Canterbury and sent to Durham around 1080 gives the verses in an order that did not occur elsewhere among the sources consulted for this study. Two Cluniac sources and a St. Denis missal agree.

An additional verse, «Benedictus es super sedem sanctam divinitatis tuae» (or «Benedictus qui sedes super sedem,» etc.) is sometimes added to the chant; it is designated as x on the chart. You will note that it may come second in the series (in Rome, Angelica 123), third (in lat. 776), or fourth (Monza 12/75). There is a different additional verse – designated y on the chart – in a manuscript from Forlimpopoli. Can we infer that «Benedictus es Domine Deus» did not originate as a chant with a fixed text and a definite length, but as an open-ended series of benedictions – a well-known kind of prayer, one that might be developed differently on different occasions, in response to circumstances and the sense of the congregation, though its central theme would always remain «Blessed art thou, O Lord God of our fathers»? The musical setting is a variant of the 7th-mode psalm tone.

If the inference is correct, that this was once an open-ended text, it was the only one in the chants used in this liturgical role. The other forms of the «Benedicite» used after the Daniel lesson on Ember Saturdays follow the «Benedicite» closely, either in exact quotation or in paraphrase. But this is not to say that there are no differences between the Vulgate edition of the «Benedicite» and the form in which it appears in its chant settings. There are differences, here and there, and particularly in what might be called the second stanza of the text, Daniel 3:64–73. This organization into stanzas is roughly regular in terms of number of lines, and follows content. As Moore expresses it,[13] in the first stanza it is said

13 Moore, pp. 42–3.

that creations in the highest heavens should praise God, in the second, that elements coming from heaven should praise God, in the third, earthly creations, and in the fourth, all mankind.

Table 2

Vulgate	Chant	Theodotion B
64 imber et ros	64 imber et ros	
65 omnis spiritus	65 omnis spiritus	
66 ignis et aestus	66 ignis et aestus	66
67 frigus et aestus	71 noctes et dies	71
68 rores et pruina	72 tenebrae et lumen	72
69 gelu et frigus	69 frigus et cauma	69
70 glacies et nives	70 pruina et nives	70
71 noctes et dies	73 fulgura et nubes	73
72 lux et tenebrae		
73 fulgura et nubes		

In Table 2, I have contrasted the order of elements in the second stanza with their order in the chant. I have used the third column to show the order in which they are given in one early Greek version of the text, the one referred to in scholarship in this field as Theodotion B.[14] The point is clear: the chant text follows an ancient edition of the Canticle in which things are arranged differently than in the Vulgate. There is no need to blame the composer of the chant for rearranging the text, or to credit him with doing so. And there is evidently a parallel in this to the borrowing of texts from the earlier, Roman psalter, rather than the later Gallican psalter, for musical settings in the classic repertory of Mass chants. The word «cauma» in verse 69 comes straight from the Greek.[15] The word is not unknown in Latin; but (according to Fischer) it occurs just once in the Vulgate, not in the «Benedicite» but in the book of Job.[16]

The most familiar substitute for the «Benedicite» in the Mass is the Alleluia that stands in its place in those Mass formularies for the Ember Saturday after Pentecost that have as their lesson chants five Alleluias and a tract. To trace this development adequately would be impossible here. I should like to go on directly to another substitute for the «Benedicite,» a paraphrase of it in verse – in accentual Adonics – that is attributed to Walafrid Strabo (809–*ca.* 849), Abbot of Reichenau and advisor to Louis the Pious.[17] It begins, «Omnipotentem semper adorant,» and, as I have suggested, follows the «Benedicite» very closely. In what corresponds to the second section, there is inevitably some rearrangement of the elements, for the sake of the meter, but the use of «cauma» indicates that the model is the chant of the Benedicite, rather than the Vulgate text:

14 Moore, pp. 71, 30–33.
15 Moore, p. 71, in the note concerning v. 45. For a reconciliation of Moore's numbering of the verses with that of the Vulgate (employed here), see pp. 66–9.
16 Bonifatius Fischer OSB, *Novae concordantiae Bibliorum sacrorum* (Stuttgart: Frommann-Holzboog, 1977), 1:735.
17 The poetry of Walafrid Strabo is discussed by F. J. E. Raby in *A History of Christian-Latin Poetry* (2nd ed.; London, 1953), pp. 183–9.

Sic quoque limphe queque superna ros pluvieque spiritus omnis
Ignis et estus cauma geluque frigus et ardor atque pruina
Nix glaciesque noxque diesque lux tenebreque fulgura nubes

The opening section is repeated, in full or in part, as a refrain after each of the verses, which are all sung to the same melody.

The work appears in a number of manuscripts, not always with the same music. Bruno Stäblein gives two melodies for it in his collection of medieval hymns.[18] The oldest source to present this text with musical notation has recently been identified by Peter Jeffery as the front flyleaf of the manuscript Laon, Bibl. municipale, 266, which dates from the last quarter of the ninth century; it is also the oldest source that assigns this text a role in the liturgy.[19] The melody there is neumatic, and more or less matches that given in the Einsiedeln manuscript, where it is in an appendix – not in place in the liturgical year. London, B. L., Harley 4951 also gives essentially the same melody; but lat. 1121 has a different setting, one that is in almost entirely syllabic style, in which the refrain is called for after every half-verse.

The presentation in lat. 1121 of the «Benedicite» and its alternates follows an organization of the liturgical year that ends in Advent, rather than beginning there.[20] «Benedictus es in firmamento» is given first, then «Benedictus es Domine Deus,» for «Secunda Sabbato, in Iunio»; then «Omnia opera Domini Deum benedicite,» «In autumno»; and finally, «In hieme» (in winter, that is, Advent), «Omnipotentem semper adorant.»

The same organization of the year underlies the way in which «Benedictus es in firmamento» and the «Benedicite» are divided up among the four Ember Saturdays in some Beneventan manuscripts: the beginning of the text is sung on the Ember Saturday of Lent, the next section on that after Pentecost, the next in the fall, and the last, in Advent, with the full antiphon beginning the chant each time.[21] (The four sections into which the «Benedicite» is divided do not coincide with what we have called the stanzas: Lent has rather more than its share, and Advent the smallest part. But grouping the blessings in threes makes following that scheme exactly impossible in any case.)

In lat. 1121, the chant for the fall, «Omnia opera Domini,» is an antiphon that introduces the «Benedicite» chanted to a formula that is practically a psalm tone. (It is shown in Plate 1.) But «Omnia opera Domini» is not one of the hundreds of antiphons collected and edited by Hesbert in *Corpus Antiphonalium Officii;* and Randel's index of Mozarabic chant leads us to an antiphon with almost the

---

18 *Monumenta monodica medii aevi, I.: Hymnen (1)* (Kassel: Bärenreiter, 1956), pp. 489–90, with commentary on p. 620.

19 Peter Jeffery, «An Early Cantatorium Fragment Related to MS Laon 239,» *Scriptorium.* 36 (1982), 245–252.

20 This may reflect a system of arranging the Ember Weeks according to the civil (rather than the liturgical) year, setting them in the first, fourth, seventh and tenth months. For the connection between the Ember Weeks and the Roman seasonal fasts observed at the time of sowing and of harvesting corn, and of harvesting grapes, see Willis, pp. 53–4.

21 [R.-J. Hesbert], «La tradition bénéventaine dans la tradition manuscrite,» *Paléographie musicale.* XIV (Solesmes: Abbaye Saint-Pierre, 1931), pp. 223–4.

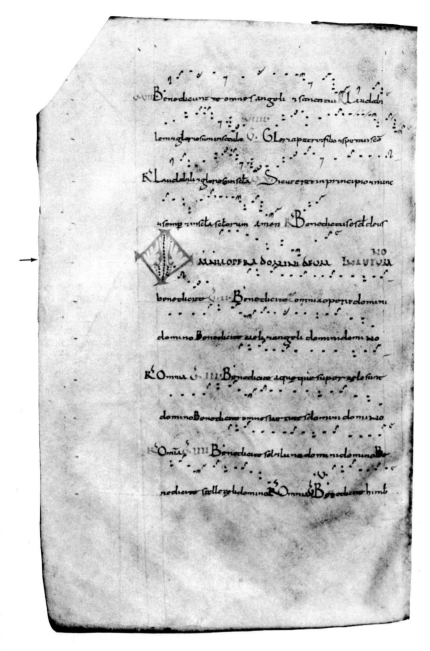

Plate 1: Paris, Bibliothèque nationale, ms. latin 1121, fol. 88ᵛ

same text but a different melody.[22] The only other source that has yet come to light for this antiphon is an 11th-century Aquitanian antiphonal – Toledo, Bibl. cap. 44.1 – in which it lacks notation.

To sum up, what lat. 1121 shows is three chants based on the «Benedicite» (Daniel 3:57–90). One presents the text in paraphrase; each of the other two provides an introduction and refrain for it, and states it completely. It also has one chant that takes «Benedictus es» (Daniel 3:52–56) as its point of departure. The texts are not identical in character, and the differences between them are significant. «Benedictus es» is a prayer of the type known as «berakah,» or benediction, in which God is blessed; there are many examples of this type of prayer in the Old Testament.[23] The form is flexible, and may be developed in a number of different ways. The «Benedicite,» on the other hand, is like a poem (Moore refers to it as a hymn); in it a systematic organization rules the length of sections and their development. In light of that, it is not surprising that in the Gregorian manuscripts the «Benedicite» is given complete rather than reduced to a series of excerpts. But how can the diversity of musical styles be explained, and the fact that one finds sometimes one of these texts, sometimes the other?

Perhaps the explanation lies in the relatively late date at which the Daniel lesson became part of the service for Ember Saturdays. But there may be another reason, one having to do with the meaning of the text. The effect of the interpolation in chapter 3 of the book of Daniel, as has been said earlier, is to shift attention from what the three young men did to what they believed. It was a miracle of faith that enabled them to live to sing the praise of God in the fiery furnace. Can the diversity of forms for their prayer, and of musical settings for their hymn, have been the product of reluctance to establish one set way of representing in the liturgy a turn of events that is as astonishing and dramatic as any in sacred literature?

---

22 R.-J. Hesbert, *Corpus Antiphonalium Officii*, III (Rome: Herder, 1968); Don Michael Randel, *An Index to the Chant of the Mozarabic Rite* (Princeton, N. J.: Princeton University Press, 1973), p. 305.
23 Paul F. Bradshaw, *Daily Prayer in the Early Church* (London: Alcuin Club, 1981), pp. 11–18.

XVIII

The Liturgical and Musical Tradition of Bec

In the National Library of Russia in St Petersburg is a manuscript of Gregorian chant dating from the end of the 12th century. It is a gradual that was prepared for a priory (a dependent house) of the celebrated Norman monastery of Bec.[1] The manuscript has special importance for our understanding of the transmission of chant during the 11th and 12th centuries because of the distinctive role played by monks from Normandy and especially from Bec in major political and cultural developments.

Bec was founded around the year 1039 by an individual—Herluin—who had been brought up for a career in the military and who turned to religious life as a man of mature years.[2] It grew rapidly from poor beginnings, in great part as a result of the arrival in the community about the year 1042 of one particular man—Lanfranc. He was Italian by birth, and a lawyer by training; and he had come to Normandy in order to advance his career as a teacher and a man of learning.[3] When he felt the call to the monastic life he turned to the most humble community he could find. Life at Bonneville, the first site of the community, in the early years is described by David Knowles as follows:

---

[1]   Marie Pascal Dickson, OSB, *Consuetudines Beccenses* (Corpus Consuetudinum Monasticarum, IV; Siegburg: Apud Franciscum Schmitt, 1967), XII, note 19. The manuscript was at Saint-Germain-des-Prés in Paris at the time of the French Revolution, having been brought there for study by the Maurists from the Bec priory of Bonne-nouvelle. During the turmoil of the Revolution it disappeared, coming to light subsequently in the remarkable group of manuscripts belonging to Prince Pierre Dubrowski that was incorporated into the collection at St Petersburg. A complete facsimile edition was published in 1912 by J.-B. Thibaut in *Monuments de la notation ekphonétique et neumatique de l'église latine* (St Petersburg: Imprimerie Kügelgen, Glitsch & Cie). The priory for which the book was intended is Meulan, an identification made by Dickson on the basis of feasts in the sanctorale. But she observes, 'l'ensemble de ce manuscrit nous livre bien la liturgie du Bec', and it will be referred to throughout the present study as 'the Bec gradual'.
[2]   Dickson writes (XXXV-XXXVI), 'La naissance du Bec, *e nihilo* peut-on dire, demeure un fait absolument original. . . . Toutes les conditions manquèrent qui, á l'époque, étaient regardées comme nécessaires à l'établissement viable d'un monastère, à savoir la protection d'un seigneur puissant pour doter la nouvelle institution, un lieu bien choisi quant à la salubrité et aux ressources, enfin une colonie de moines déjà formés venant d'un autre monastère'.
[3]   Margaret Gibson, *Lanfranc of Bec* (Oxford: Clarendon Press, 1978), says that Lanfranc left Pavia 'at a time of acute tension between the emperor and the Italian cities' but refrains pointedly from asserting that this was the reason for his departure (16).

The little group worked all day clearing land, farming, gardening and building; as yet they had little in common with the tradition of Cluny or Dijon. . . . Recruits came, but the community remained simple, poor and laborious; the mother of the founder lived nearby and washed the garments of her son's followers. Herluin himself felt deeply his inability to guide the growing family. . . . He had no definite programme of the monastic life to oppose to that current in France at the time, and . . . the simplicity of the early life was in a sense accidental.[4]

Lanfranc was the thirty-fifth man to join the community. On the day he arrived he found the abbot repairing the oven.[5]

For the first three years, acquiring a monastic formation was Lanfranc's principal concern: he studied Scripture and learned the Divine Office.[6] His biographer, Miles Crispin, who was himself a cantor, reports that when it fell to Lanfranc to serve as lector, he had the cantor listen to him perform the lesson beforehand (presumably to advise him on the traditional ways of matching phrase endings with musical formulas).[7] At the end of this period, Lanfranc resolved to leave the community secretly in order to live as a hermit. Herluin found out about this plan and was able to head it off by naming Lanfranc as prior. Thus Lanfranc may have had some role in an early

---

[4]   David Knowles, *The Monastic Order in England* (Cambridge: Cambridge University Press, 1963), 90.
[5]   [Miles Crispin], *Vita B. Lanfranci*, in J. P. Migne, *Patrologiae . . . series latina*, 150 (Paris, 1880), col. 31.
[6]   *Vita B. Lanfranci*, col. 32: 'Postquam factus est monachus, in discendis officiis diurnis et nocturnis curam maximam impendere voluit, ut sciret Deo laudis sacrificium persolvere, sicut noverat. Sic per tres annos vixit solitarius'. How full an observance of the Divine Office was there at Bonneville in those days? Miles Crispin's work dates from perhaps around the year 1130 (Knowles, 107, note 2), and his own experience as a cantor during this later period may have caused him to have undue expectations with respect to the amounts of time and attention devoted to formal worship in the years just after the founding. A tendency in this direction may be evident in the stress on official liturgical prayer in his account of Lanfranc's experiences during the night before he arrived at the monastery (col. 31). Having been attacked by thieves and tied to a tree, Lanfranc found himself helpless. 'Nescius quid ageret, suum infortunium lamentabatur. Tandem nocturno silentio in se reversus, voluit Domino laudes debitas persolvere, et non potuit, quia ad hoc antea non vacaverat. Et conversus ad Dominum: "Domine Deus, ait, tantum tempus in discendo expendi, et corpus et animum in studiis litterarum attrivi; et adhuc quomodo te debeam orare, atque laudis officia tibi persolvere non didici. Libera me de hac tribulatione; et ego, te auxiliante, sic vitam meam corrigere, et instituere curabo, ut tibi servire valeam et sciam."'
[7]   *Vita B. Lanfranci*, col. 32: 'Denique, ut fertur, lectionem non volebat legere in ecclesia nisi prius eam cantor audisset'. For an anecdote concerning reading at table (quite a different matter), see ibid. and Gibson, 45.

codification of the customs of the community;[8] and it was he who planned and oversaw the relocation to Bec.

Students began flocking to Bec to study with Lanfranc: among them were several who were to become the most important churchmen of the next generation; one of them was the future Pope Alexander II. The sixty-eighth recruit was another Italian, Anselm, who was drawn there—perhaps in 1057—by Lanfranc's reputation and by the fact that Bec had by then become 'the intellectual centre of Europe north of the Alps'.[9]

Bec's influence was further enhanced through a personal relationship that developed between Lanfranc and that William, Duke of Normandy, who is known in history as William the Conqueror. Lanfranc had served as the duke's adviser for some years but angered him by expressing disapproval of William's plan to marry Matilda of Flanders, a union that had been forbidden by Pope Leo IX. William was not deterred by this opposition, and went ahead with the marriage (the year is uncertain, but it was perhaps 1052). The two men were soon reconciled; Miles Crispin tells a charming anecdote concerning the occasion on which they resolved their differences.

> The duke sent an order that he was at once to leave his dominions. Lanfranc left Bec with one servant, and on a lame horse, the best which the house could give him. On his way he met William, and said pleasantly that he was obeying his command as well as he could, and would obey it better if the duke would give him a better horse. William was pleased with his spirit, entered into conversation, and was reconciled to him, Lanfranc promising to advocate the duke's cause with the Pope.[10]

From that time forth the relationship between William and Lanfranc was close and mutually beneficial.

After the Conquest, bringing the monasteries under the king's control was a matter of pressing importance. Their wealth and particularly the amount of land they possessed made them powerful both economically and politically; they were also centers of intellectual life, places in which opinion was shaped. William had seen the benefits of monastic reform in Normandy and wished to

---

[8]   Dickson, XXXIX: 'Il est donc tout à fait plausible que Lanfranc, dès sa nomination comme prieur se soit efforcé d'ordonner la vie religieuse au Bec et d'y établir de coutumes durables. . . . Il ne s'ensuit pas nécessairement que Lanfranc ait rédigé lui-même le premier coutumier du Bec'.
[9]   Knowles, 90.
[10]   William Hunt, 'Lanfranc', in *Dictionary of National Biography*, ed. L. Stephen and S. Lee (London: Oxford University Press, 1892-93; reprint ed., 1949-50), XI, 525. The Latin on which this is based is in *Vita B. Lanfranci*, col. 35.

XVIII

promote it in Britain. His first choice of an individual to oversee this work was Hugh of Cluny; when Hugh refused, he turned to Lanfranc. The principal means by which William and Lanfranc worked was appointing Norman bishops and abbots whenever openings occurred in the British church. Their goal was 'a strong hierarchy under a powerful primate and powerful king'.[11]

To what extent did the placing of Normans in positions of ecclesiastical authority result in the introduction into Britain of distinctively Norman liturgical practices—particularly chant? How did the organization of chant in Normandy differ from that of Britain, and how significant were the differences in the actual melodies? It should be remembered that neither in Normandy nor in Britain was there uniformity either in liturgy or in chant; hence comparisons must focus on specific documents. K. D. Hartzell has shown that a manuscript copied at Christ Church, Canterbury, after the Conquest presents the chant repertory in an organization like that of Bec, while giving the melodies of individual chants in distinctively British forms.[12] At present St Albans seems to have been almost the only British monastery that adopted the melodic tradition of Bec.[13] In demonstrating the musical dependence of St Albans on Bec, David Hiley made use of a technique devised by the monks of Solesmes. It begins by selecting, from all the variants among the sources, a certain number for which there is a clear division; and then the number of times any two of the manuscripts agree on those particular points is taken as an indication of the extent of their agreement overall. For the comparison to be valid the passages in which these variants appear must be in chants that occur in all the sources being compared, and the chants must be given in nearly identical readings from one source to the next. The variants that are tabulated

---

[11]   Knowles, 90.

[12]   K. D. Hartzell, 'An Unknown English Benedictine Gradual of the Eleventh Century', *Anglo-Saxon England* 4 (1975): 131-44. Hartzell's evaluation of the manuscript Durham, University Library, Cosin V.V.6 as 'one of the most important sources for the history of music in England in the Middle Ages' (133) seems entirely correct, and his article is a major contribution.

[13]   David Hiley, 'The Norman Chant Traditions - Normandy, Britain, Sicily', *Proceedings of the Royal Musical Association* 107 (1980-81): 1-33, identifies St Albans as 'the most assiduous follower of Bec practice' (9). In 'Thurston of Caen and Plainchant at Glastonbury: Musicological Reflexions on the Norman Conquest', *Proceedings of the British Academy* 72 (1986): 57-90, Prof. Hiley describes the comparisons of variants in gradual verses in the St Albans book Oxford, Bodleian Library, Laud misc. 358, and in sources representing the uses of Bec, Winchester, Worcester, and Corbie that make evident 'a clear correspondence between St Albans and the Bec tradition'. Since St Albans was founded in 1077, this correspondence provides indirect evidence of the stability of the Bec musical tradition, and provides additional support for Hartzell's judgement that the Cosin Gradual preserves 'the type of chant used in the pre-Conquest church', rather than the readings of a gradual of Bec earlier in date than the St Petersburg manuscript (Hartzell, 138-9).

are minor, rather than important, differences in the melodies.

This method of comparison is enormously useful in grouping manuscripts. It is less useful in identifying salient features of a chant tradition—the features by which it would be remembered as distinctive. For this, more conspicuous musical features need to be focused upon—unusual melodies, or melodies in which unexpected turns of phrase appear. Identifying such features systematically would require going through the whole of each source comparing each melody with its equivalent in a traditional reading; and even then it would be difficult to express precisely the extent and significance of such departures from tradition. But for the question, 'How different would the chant of Bec have seemed to a monk from Jumièges?' a few examples of such divergences—to be shown later—can serve to suggest an answer.

Yet another point on which chant manuscripts can be compared is the style of the neumes that make up their musical notation. For the Bec manuscript such study is particularly fruitful. Facsimile 1 shows the Alleluia *Salva nos christe* as it appears on fol. 156v. In the verse, at the end of the melisma for the first syllable of the word 'nobis', one finds a climacus, representing three notes that descend, written as a virga, punctum, and apostropha. Earlier in the melisma, one finds four descending notes written this way, and even five—with the first written as a virga, the last as an apostropha, and those in between as puncta. These symbols are arranged along an imaginary line that crosses the staff lines at an angle of approximately 45 degrees.

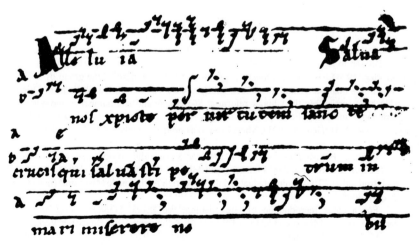

Facsimile 1: The All. *Salva nos Christe* (St Petersburg, National Library of Russia, O.v.I.6, fol. 156v)

6

This manner of writing groups of notes that descend is common to many manuscripts. It is found in the Mass tonary from St-Bénigne, Dijon, written around the beginning of the 11th century,[14] and as late as the Sarum gradual, of the 13th century.[15] (See Facsimile 2.) It is not, however, standard in two manuscripts which come from Norman monasteries and date from about the same period as the Bec gradual: a troper from St-Evroult (Paris, Bibl. nat., 10508)[16] and a missal from Jumièges (Rouen, Bibl. mun. A 401). (See Facsimile 3.) In both of them this form typically has its last note written as a punctum; St-Evroult occasionally uses the comma form. But otherwise the form is similar, and the angle at which the notes descend is the same.

In the Bec gradual, however, there is another way of writing descending groups, one that is used far more often than the one just described. It can be observed in Facsimile 1 in the jubilus of the Alleluia, which is identical musically to the melisma that was examined earlier in this study. This method involves using a series of broad strokes that are tilted slightly upwards (like the punctum of this manuscript) and aligned vertically in a column that crosses the staff lines at a right angle. The broad strokes are linked by slender diagonal strokes. Each of these groups begins with a form representing the first two notes that is identical with that employed for the clivis in this source. It consists of a horizontal line with a distinctive dip joined to a broad vertical stroke that ends in a thin line curving up to the right as the pen leaves the paper.

This is the only form employed for the clivis in the Bec gradual. It is not

---

[14]   There is a facsimile edition of this manuscript, Montpellier, Bibliothèque Interuniversitaire - Médecine [formerly Bibl. de l'École de Médecine], H 159, in *Paléographie musicale* VIII (Tournai: Descl, Lefebvre & Cie, 1901-5). The contents were transcribed by Finn E. Hansen in *H 159 Montpellier: Tonary of St Bénigne of Dijon* (Cophnhagen: Dan Fog Musikforlag, 1974). Hansen cautiously suggests (21*) that the head of the group of scribes who wrote this manuscript may have been Guillaume de Volpiano (=Bd. William of Dijon, d. 1031), who carried out the Cluniac reform at St-Bénigne and at a number of monasteries in Normandy, including Fécamp and Jumièges. In *Les Tonaires: Inventaire, Analyse, Comparaison* (Paris: Heugel, 1971), Michel Huglo examines the relation of this book to other tonaries.

[15]   London, British Library, Add. 12194; for a facsimile edition, see W. H. Frere, *Graduale Sarisburiense* (London: Plainsong and Mediaeval Music Society, 1894). Part I of Frere's introduction, 'The Sarum Gradual and the Gregorian Antiphonale Missarum' (ix-xxxiv) is still quite useful.

[16]   For a color reproduction of one opening, see Bruno Stäblein, *Schriftbild der einstimmigen Musik* (Musikgeschichte in Bildern, III, 4; Leipzig: VEB Deutscher Verlag für Musik, 1975), 119. Dickson (XLIII) speaks of 'le tropaire du Bec' as 'emprunté dans sa quasi totalité à Saint-Evroult', but that statement stands in need of clarification. Lanfranc spent some time at St-Evroult, having been sent there by Herluin to reform the monastery; but this attempt met with little success, and Lanfranc returned to Bec.

Facsimile 2: The Intr. *Nunc scio vere* (London, British Library, Add. 12194, 189; Montpellier, Bibliothèque Interuniversitaire - Médecine [formerly Bibl. de l'École de Médecine], H 159, 40; St Petersburg, National Library of Russia, O.v.I.6, fol. 142v)

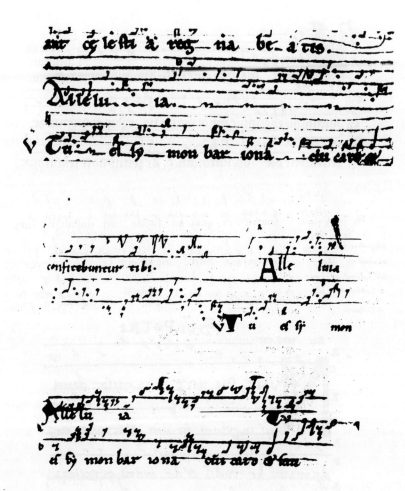

Facsimile 3: The All. *Tu es Simon bar Jona* (Rouen, Bibl. mun. A 401, fol. 74v; Paris, lat. 10508, fol. 77r; St Petersburg, O.v.I.6, fol. 143)

unique to this source, however. It is found in many manuscripts and even in the two Norman sources to which reference was made above. In the latter sources it is treated as having special significance with regard to pitch: it is employed only for a group of which the first note repeats the pitch that came immediately before. The neume plays this role in both lat. 10508 and Rouen A 401 near the beginning of the verse of the Alleluia *Tu es Symon Bar Jona*, as is shown in Facsimile 3. The clivis on the word 'es' is the normal one; the clivis just before it is the special form. In Bec, which employs only the special form, it is used in both places.[17]

One of the other notations in which this form of the clivis appears is that of Brittany.[18] The most complete source in which this notation is employed is a late ninth-century gradual from Brittany that was MS 47 in the Bibliothèque municipale of Chartres until it was destroyed in a bombardment in 1944. Fortunately the manuscript is available for study in a facsimile edition published in *Paléographie musicale* in 1912.[19] In a manner similar to that of the Bec manuscript, Breton notation writes the notes of descending passages in a vertical column, though without joining them. This can be observed in Facsimile 4 in the melisma on the words 'et eripe me' which ends the antiphon of the Offertory *Domine Deus meus in te speravi*. There are too many differences between Breton neumes and the forms of the Bec manuscript to warrant drawing a close connection between the two.[20] For example, the

---

[17] The total number of different neume forms in this gradual is rather small in comparison to those in the Jumièges and St-Evroult manuscripts. Whether this can be taken as evidence of archaism is open to question. The transition from notation *in campo aperto* to notation on the staff seems often to have entailed a standardization of forms and a reduction in their number. Of the 'special' neumes retained after the transition to staff notation at Bec the most striking is the *pes stratus*, which appears in Facs. 2 on the first syllable of the word 'dominus'. It is noteworthy that this neume is also found in the Sarum Gradual on the same word. The use of the *pes stratus* in these sources contrasts to its use in sources from St Gall, where it occurs only in chants that have been imported into the Gregorian repertory from other chant traditions. See E. Cardine, *Sémiologie grégorienne* (Solesmes: Abbaye Saint-Pierre, 1970), 131-2.

[18] See Michel Huglo, 'Le domaine de la notation bretonne', *Acta musicologica* 35 (1963): 54-84. Solange Corbin discusses Breton neumes in *Die Neumen* (Palaeographie der Musik, I, 3: Cologne: Arno Volk-Verlag, 1977), 81-7.

[19] The discussion of the notation of the Chartres manuscript that appears in the introduction to *Paléographie musicale* XI (Solesmes: Abbaye Saint-Pierre, 1912) gives particular emphasis to the rhythmic connotations of the various neumes.

[20] In *Le Graduel Romain, II: Les Sources* (Solesmes: Abbaye Saint-Pierre, 1957), 58-9, the notation of the Bec gradual is said to be 'à points liés français avec certains neumes rappelant la notation messine'. Later in that same work (185), the space reserved for a list of manuscripts with Breton notation on a musical staff is left empty. Corbin speaks of Breton neumes as 'eine sehr alte Neumenschrift, die früh verschwand, ohne sich weiter entwickelt zu

Facsimile 4: Excerpt from a melisma in the Off. *Domine Deus meus in te* (Chartres 47, 33; St Petersburg O.v.I.6, fol. 40)

Breton oriscus (just before the final punctum of this melisma) has no counterpart at Bec; and generally there is a far greater variety in the neumes of the earlier source.

In other respects, however, there are important similarities—both liturgical and musical—between the Bec gradual and Chartres 47. The musical similarities were identified by the monks of Solesmes in the course of their examination and comparison of the musical readings of the chants of the gradual in many manuscripts, employing the method described above.[21] This made it possible to draw up for each manuscript a list of the other sources whose readings were the most similar to the ones it contained. As a result of a careful selection, what was studied in this process was the kind of musical events that can be expressed just as clearly in neumes as in staff notation. Thus it led to the identification, for each major source in neumes, of the sources in staff notation that come closest to presenting the same musical tradition.

For Chartres 47, the most similar manuscripts are two that are also notated in Breton neumes.[22] Next on the list are the Bec gradual and a missal from Bec that is in the Bibliothèque nationale in Paris.[23] These are the sources in staff notation, of all the hundreds of manuscripts taken into account in this comparison, that contain musical readings that are most similar to those of the Chartres gradual, which is itself the most complete source of the Breton chant

---

haben'.

[21]   *Le Graduel Romain, IV, 1: Le Groupement des Manuscrits* (Solesmes: Abbaye Saint-Pierre, 1960).

[22]   Ibid., 209. These manuscripts are Paris, Bibl. nat., lat. 9439 (from Rennes, first half of the 12th century) and Angers, Bibliothèque municipale, 91 (from Brittany, 10th century).

[23]   Lat. 1105. For an edition of the texts but not the music, see Anselm Hughes, *The Bec Missal* (Henry Bradshaw Society, 94; London, 1963).

tradition. The tradition is particularly important because Breton notation is taken to be one of the oldest forms of chant notation known today.[24] In a list drawn up by Jacques Froger of sources representing the nine 'unities'—'versions of the neumatic text which may provisionally be considered as more or less independent'—the graduals of Chartres and Bec are paired as representing one of the 'unities'.[25] Thus it is planned that the readings of the Bec gradual will be given particular weight in the preparation of a critical edition of the chants of the Roman gradual.

How did it happen that a chant tradition from Brittany came to be perpetuated in a monastery in Normandy? The history of Brittany in the ninth and centuries was punctuated by Viking raids. On several different occasions monks had to abandon their monasteries near the sea and seek refuge inland. Huglo finds remarkable parallels between the areas in which additions in Breton neumes are made to manuscripts, or in which Breton forms are mixed into notations of other types, and the areas that received colonies of monks from Brittany and even relics of Breton saints.[26] Herluin's initiation into religious life was at the hands of the bishop of Lisieux, who also consecrated him as abbot. It seems possible that the liturgical and musical tradition adopted at the new monastery may have come from Lisieux, which itself may have inherited a Breton, rather than a Norman, tradition as a result of this kind of cultural exchange.

What was the form in which that tradition was received? I think we must assume it came in two forms—as oral instruction (a teacher sent from a cathedral or from another monastery), and in books. And it is in those books—all of them now utterly lost to us—that the antecedents of the musical notation used in the Bec manuscript must lie. What can we know of their other characteristics?

Of the liturgical similarities between the graduals of Chartres and Bec, the most striking is the series of Proper chants to which the Offertory *Domine Deus meus in te speravi* belongs—those for the Second Sunday of Lent. In

---

[24]   Huglo, 'Le domaine', 84.

[25]   Jacques Froger, 'The Critical Edition of the Roman Gradual by the Monks of Solesmes', *Journal of the Plainsong and Mediaeval Music Society* 1 (1978): 84-5.

[26]   One of the places in which Breton notation is found is the monastery of Crowland. The offices for Saints Cuthbert, Benedict, and Guthlac in London, British Library, Harl. 1117 are beautifully notated in Breton neumes (Huglo, 'Le domaine', 71). In the Leofric Missal (Oxford Bodleian Library, Bod. 579), the neumes for the common preface are Breton. Huglo thinks it possible 'que cette addition soit de la main de Léofric lui-même qui, selon certains, était originaire de Cornouailles' (ibid.). Breton neumes are also found in northern Italy. The most important source is a gradual now in Ivrea (Biblioteca capitolare, LX) which appears to come from Pavia. Evidently there was traffic in both directions along the route that joined northern Italy and northwest France; Lanfranc himself came from Pavia, Anselm from Aosta.

XVIII

12

the earliest sources, there are no Proper chants for this day; in most later sources, those of the preceding Wednesday are repeated. But in Brittany, a few centers in northern Italy, at Bec, and later in Britain, this special series of chants appears.[27] It includes the Introit *Sperent in te, Domine*; the Gradual *Justus es, Domine*; the Tract *Dixit Dominus mulieri Chananeae*; a second Tract, *Benedicam Dominum in omni tempore*; the Offertory to which reference has already been made; and the Communion *Custodi me, Domine*. The same series of chants is included in the Bec missal edited by Hughes, where the first of the tracts is said to be *Ad missam matutinalem,* the second *Ad majorem missam.*[28] The series was later dropped from use at Bec; Hughes describes a marginal notation that indicates this. Although none of the chants were included in the *Graduale Romanum* of 1908, the Offertory appears in Karl Ott's edition *Offertoriale sive versus offertoriorum.*[29]

The 11th-century Mass tonary of St-Bénigne, Dijon, includes the Introit, Gradual, Offertory, and Communion of this Mass with musical notation, and the text of the first of the Tracts, but without notation. Only a few manuscripts include the verses for this Offertory; but in both the Bec gradual and a 14th-century gradual from Jumièges (Rouen, Bibl. mun., A 233) they are given in full.[30] As at Bec, the series was later dropped from use at St-Bénigne; in a 13th-century gradual (Brussels, Bibl. royale, II, 3824), the Proper chants for the second Sunday of Lent are those of the preceding Wednesday.

In a preliminary survey of the music of the Bec gradual, certain melodies stand out as worthy of comment. One of them is associated with the Communion *Oportet te.* This is one of the five Lenten Communions that have a text derived from the Gospel of the day rather than from the expected psalm.

---

[27]   There is a remarkable correspondence between the areas in which this series of chants was sung and the areas in which Breton notation was at one time or another employed; Huglo ('Le domaine', 61) speaks of the Mass *Sperent in te* as 'propre aux manuscrits bretons et à quelques graduels de l'Italie du Nord'. He observes that since the earliest of the sources in which it appears dates from the 10th century, it must have been composed no later than the beginning of that century (83). But there is yet another group of sources in which this Mass appears—at Westminster, Abingdon, and St Augustine's, Canterbury, it is given for the 24th Sunday after Pentecost. (Hughes, *The Bec Missal,* ix-x.) Presumably this series of chants reached Britain through Bec.

[28]   Ibid.

[29]   Paris: Descleé, 1935.

[30]   The Offertory has been the focus of some undeserved attention. In both of its modern editions it is transcribed from the Montpellier manuscript, where the trimming of the outer edge of the leaf caused some notes to be deleted from a melisma. The leap of a seventh that results from that accidental deletion has on occasion been used as an example to demonstrate the unusual musical formations found in Offertory verses.

THE LITURGICAL AND MUSICAL TRADITION OF BEC

All five appear in the sources with several different melodies; but *Oportet te* is particularly remarkable in that eleven different melodies for it have been found.[31] The Bec melody for *Oportet te* is shown below. It would be highly instructive to have a list of the other manuscripts that use this melody (at present I know of none).[32]

O - por - tet te fi - li gau - de - re.

qui - a- fra - ter tu - us mor - tu - us fu - e - rat, et re - vi - - xit:

pe - ri - - e - rat, et in - ven - - - - tus est.

Another distinctive melody is that given for the Offertory *Felix namque es*. Long ago Dom Pothier observed that for this text there are four different Offertory melodies, two of them borrowed from older chants, and two newly composed, though to a certain extent dependent on one of the others.[33] *Felix namque es* does not appear as an Offertory until the eleventh century; and Pothier's explanation for the multiplicity of melodies is that when a new text entered the liturgy in this later period and was transmitted from one church to

---

[31]   Michel Huglo, 'Communion Antiphon', *The New Catholic Encyclopedia* (New York: McGraw, Hill, Inc., 1967), 4:40.

[32]   S. Marosszéki wrote in *Les Origines du Chant cistercien* (Analecta Sacri Ordinis Cisterciensis, viii; 1952) 104, that Gabriel Beyssac had worked for over forty years tracing the various melodies for the five Communions in 710 manuscripts. His finding were never published, and it is not known whether the card file he assembled still exists. In the spring of 1987, Michael O'Brien, a graduate student in musicology at the Catholic University of America, compared several of the melodies for *Oportet te*. He found that the melody in the Bec gradual 'bears the loosest structural attachment of any single melody to the aggregate as a whole'.

[33]   Joseph Pothier, 'L'Offertoire "Felix namque"', *Revue du chant grégorien* 15 (1907): 105-114. The adaptations Pothier identified are on melodies borrowed from the Offertories *Angelus Domini* and *Stetit angelus*, both of which are employed for other texts in addition to this, and neither of which is, in significant ways, a 'typical' Gregorian Offertory. See K. Levy, 'Toledo, Rome and the Legacy of Gaul', *Early Music History* 4 (1984): 49-100, especially 74-77, 87, 90. One of the melodies Pothier called 'original' has been identified as an adaptation of the Offertory *Factus est Dominus*, for the Saturday of the fourth week of Lent; see '*Holocausta medullata*: An Offertory for St Saturninus', *Festschrift für Helmut Hucke*, ed. M. Heisler and P. Cahn (Hildesheim: Olms, 1993).

another, sometimes it travelled with its music, sometimes alone.[34] If, as it seems, the text was originally a responsory, and only later acquired a second role, this explanation seems acceptable. The melody for it in the Bec gradual is essentially the same as that in the *Liber Usualis*,[35] one that reworks some material borrowed from the mode-1 Offertory *Stetit angelus*. Rather surprisingly, at Bec this melody is transposed up a fourth to G and provided with a B-flat (at least at the beginning; the tight binding of the book prevents it from being fully opened, and the left edges of the lines of music cannot be seen.)

The verse in the Bec gradual is not the expected one, *Beata es virgo Maria*, but instead *Beata et venerabilis es*, which is set to a verse melody borrowed from a different Offertory, *Posuisti Domine*. This is a chant of the eighth mode; and it serves as the musical model for all of *Felix namque es* in some other sources. Evidently in the Bec gradual the antiphon was transposed in order to have it connect smoothly with a verse of a different mode. (This degree of musical eclecticism seems unusual.) At Jumièges, by contrast, the melody for the Offertory antiphon *Felix namque es* was a fairly close adaptation of that for *Stetit angelus*; Rouen A 401 does not include a verse for it (fol. 78v). A monk from Jumièges who tried to join in the singing of this chant at Bec would have had a hard time of it.

Another chant for which different melodies were employed at Bec and St-Evroult is the Alleluia *Nos autem gloriari*.[36] It seems likely that additional examples of this kind will be found as more extensive comparisons of the musical readings of the two manuscripts are carried out.

The principal goal of this study has been to identify distinctive features in

---

[34]   Marosszéki reports that this theory is also used to explain the fact that for some Communions several different melodies are found. But, he continues, 'nous avons vu, en effet, un bon nombre de paléographes et d'historiens respectables pour qui l'idée même d'une pareille supposition est "monstreuse." Selon eux, un text liturgique ne se peut concevoir sans l'accompagnement obligé de sa mélodie' (102, note 3). Huglo adheres to this belief: he writes, in relation to these Communions, that 'in the Middle Ages, the text of a chant was never set down without its being clothed at the same time with its melody'. The reason he gives for the multiple Communion melodies is that the original settings for these texts were like those of antiphons, and 'in various churches it was thought desirable to replace this simple melody by a more elaborate one that would conform to the style of the other Communions' (*New Catholic Encyclopedia*, 4:40).

[35]   In *The Liber Usualis, with Introduction and Rubrics in English* (Tournai: Desclée, 1950), 1271, it is prescribed for Saturday Masses in honor of the Blessed Virgin from Christmas to the Purification. The Offertory for such Masses in Paschal time (1272) is *Beata es virgo Maria*, formerly a verse, but here put to service as an independent chant.

[36]   The St-Evroult melody for the Alleluia *Nos autem gloriari* has been published by Karlheinz Schlager in *Alleluia-Melodien I: bis 1100* (Monumenta Monodica Medii Aevi, VII; Kassel: Bärenreiter, 1968), 339-40.

one particular manuscript, and to indicate areas in which further study might be profitable. The most striking single characteristic of the manuscript is its individuality, the extent to which it stands apart from those sources it might be expected to resemble most. In this respect, there is a parallel between the Bec gradual and the customary of the same house. In her magisterial introduction to the edition of the latter, Marie Pascal Dickson compared liturgical practices of Bec with those of other houses, and found, once again, a striking independence.[37] Her conclusion was that Bec 'lived its own life', even as it did not shrink from putting to good use practices observed elsewhere.[38]

---

[37]   Dickson, XXXVII-XLII.
[38]   'Ces coutumes, le Bec ne les a donc reçues de nulle autorité ne emprise extérieure quelconque, il a vécu sa vie propre' (XLII).

ADDENDA AND CORRIGENDA

The CANTUS database contains complete indexes of the chants in many of the sources to which reference is made in this book. Work on the database began at the Catholic University of America in 1987, but after only a few years it had become a broadly collaborative undertaking, with contributors in several different countries in North America and Europe. All the index files created or edited at Catholic University are included on the TML/CANTUS CD-ROM, which may be obtained from the Center for the History of Music Theory and Literature at Indiana University.

About ten years after its founding, the CANTUS database moved to the University of Western Ontario, where it is available on an Internet Website at http://publish.uwo.ca/~cantus/. Some index files have been published in book form by The Institute of Mediaeval Music, Ottawa; among them are those of Paris, lat. 12601; Utrecht, Bibliotheek der Rijksuniversiteit, 406 (3.J.7); Toledo, 44.2; and Karlsruhe, Aug. LX.

I   In his doctoral dissertation 'Music at Cluny' (Princeton University, 1997; University Microfilms 98-09172) Manuel Pedro Ferreira questioned the attribution of Paris, B. n., lat. 12601 to Cluny itself. His opinion is that the manuscript 'was written at a Cluniac priory in the southeast of the Amiens diocese (or just possibly in the northwest area of the Noyon diocese) on the basis of an exemplar borrowed from Cluny', (Chapter 2, p. 50) and he suggests that the priory in question was Lihons-en-Sangterre. Ferreira's evidence is of two kinds. First, the original notation of the manuscript, although consisting mostly of French neumes, also includes some neumes of the Lorraine type. (In a few instances, the notation of a chant begins in Lorraine neumes and continues in French neumes.) Second, the lessons of the manuscript differ in some respects from those in sources that unquestionably originated at Cluny.

The extent to which this knowledge must affect the way one thinks about lat. 12601 is for others to determine; the habit of thinking of it as a Cluny breviary has become very deeply ingrained in the author of these studies. Using it to study the liturgy and chant of Cluny is perhaps as defensible as is using the Meulan gradual described in article XVIII to study the liturgy and chant of Bec.

VI   For an analysis of Josquin's polyphonic arrangements of these chants, see Richard Sherr, 'Conflicting Levels of Meaning and Understanding in Josquin's *O admirabile commercium* Motet Cycle', in Dolores Pesce, ed. *Hearing the Motet. Essays on the Motet of the Middle Ages and Renaissance* (New York: Oxford University Press, 1997), 193-212.

            P. 307, fn. 2. For a facsimile edition of the manuscript with an introduction by Ike de Loos and an index by Charles T. Downey, see *Utrecht, Bibliotheek der Rijksuniversiteit, 406 (3.J.7)* (Publications of Medieval Musical Manuscripts, No. 21, Ottawa: The Institute of Mediaeval Music, 1997).

            A more detailed version of Downey's index of the source was published under the title *An Utrecht Antiphoner: Utrecht, Bibliotheek der Rijksuniversiteit, 406 (3.J.7). Printouts from an Index in Machine-Readable Form* (Ottawa: The Institute of Mediaeval Music, 1997).

VII   Chants that serve both as Responsories and Communions are discussed in Willibrord Heckenbach, 'Responsoriale Communio-Antiphonen', *Ars Musica Scientia: Festschrift Heinrich Hüschen*, ed. Detlef Altenburg, Beiträge zur Rheinischen Musikgeschichte 126 (1980):224-32; and James McKinnon, 'The Eighth-Century Frankish-Roman Communion Cycle,' *Journal of the American Musicological Society* 45 (1992):179-227.

X   See also Thomas Kelly, 'Neuma Triplex', *Acta musicologica* 60 (1988):1-30.

XI   See also Thomas Kelly, 'Melodic Elaboration in Responsory Melismas', *Journal of the American Musicological Society* 27 (1974):461-74.

XVIII   In the retyping of this article the names of the libraries in St. Petersburg and Montpellier were revised to conform to current usage, and a few other superficial changes were made. The offertory to which reference is made on p. 12, footnote 30, is discussed more fully in article XIII, pp. 171-2.

INDEX OF MANUSCRIPTS

All references in **bold** type indicate musical examples (either transcriptions or facsimile reproductions) or illustrations.

INDEX OF CHANTS BY GENRE

GENERAL INDEX

Omnipotentem semper adorant: XVII 87-
88, **89**
Ott, Carl: XIII 163-66, 168-71

Paula, Roman widow: XI 129-31
polyphony: I 91
processions: XII 178-80
    psalms as chant texts: I 95-99;
    XVI 441-42

Regino of Prüm: I 99-100; XIII 177
repetenda (communions): XVI 445-46
responsory: I 84-85; XII 163-67
responsory verse melodies: XII 164-65
rhythm in chant: XV 389-91

Sarum Antiphoner (Frere): III 133;
    XI 120; XII 163-65
Saturninus, Bishop of Toulouse: XIV
    263-65
Schlager, Karlheinz: XI 121
Sens, Cathedral of: XI 130-31
Sherr, Richard: VI 311, 314
Smits van Waesberghe, Joseph: XV 367

Stäblein, Bruno: XI 113; XV 367, 374,
392
Strabo, Walafrid (Abbot of Reichenau):
    XVII 8 /
substitution of chants: XVII 81
Sundays after Pentecost (offertories):
    XIII 179-80

Theodotion B: XVII 87
Thesaurus Musicarum Latinarum
    (Thomas Mathiesen): VI 308
tonaries: I 99-109, **101, 103-105, 108**;
    XIII 177
tonus peregrinus: I 112; VIII 7-10, **9**
tropes: XVI 442, 446
transposition: XIII 164, 166-171
Trisagion: VIII 7

uniformity in Mass chants: XII 162

versus ad repetendum (introits): XVI 442

William the Conqueror: XVIII 5-10
Würzburg *Capitulare evangeliorum*:
    VII 3-4